DATE DUE

MY 22'00		
MY 26 05		
AP 17		
MY 26 07		

The Stolen Legacy of Anne Frank

THE STOLEN
LEGACY OF
ANNE FRANK

Meyer Levin, Lillian Hellman,
and the Staging of the *Diary*

Ralph Melnick

Yale University Press
New Haven & London

Published with assistance from the Charles A. Coffin Fund.

Designed by James J. Johnson and set in Goudy type by The Composing Room of Michigan, Inc. Printed in the United States of America by Thomson-Shore, Dexter, Michigan.

Library of Congress Cataloging-in-Publication Data

Melnick, Ralph.
    The stolen legacy of Anne Frank : Meyer Levin, Lillian Hellman, and the staging of the diary / Ralph Melnick.
        p.   cm.
    Includes bibliographical references (p.   ) and index.
    ISBN 0-300-06907-3 (cloth : alk. paper)

    1. Levin, Meyer, 1905–1981—Knowledge—Holocaust, Jewish (1939–1945).   2. Holocaust, Jewish (1939–1945), in literature.   3. Frank, Anne, 1929–1945—In literature.   4. Hellman, Lillian, 1906–   —Influence.   5. Jews in literature.   I. Title.
    PS3523.E7994Z76   1997
    812'.5409358—DC21   96-46853

A catalogue record for this book is available from the British Library.

The paper in this book meets the guidelines for permanence and durability of the Committee on Production Guidelines for Book Longevity of the Council on Library Resources.

10 9 8 7 6 5 4 3 2 1

For Rachel,
with whom I share Anne's world,

and for

Joshua and Ross,
that they might never experience it

It would be terrible if my diary were lost.
ANNE FRANK

I would probably never know how the manipulation was carried out.
MEYER LEVIN

The truth as I saw it, of course, doesn't have much to do with the truth.
LILLIAN HELLMAN

Contents

Preface

The Lillian Hellman crowd is vindictive in the extreme, and should you be connected with me, they could go as far as to make trouble for you. I don't want to lead you into possible difficulties . . . so you might want to consider this," Meyer Levin had cautioned me in May 1979.

We had been corresponding for several weeks concerning his failed attempt in 1952 to win approval for the dramatization of Anne Frank's *Diary* that her father, Otto, had encouraged him to write, when he asked whether I would be willing to pursue the "documentation of the origin of his troubles" by gaining access to Otto's papers in Basel, as he could not.[1] He was convinced that I would find evidence there of ideological censorship, that the suppression of his more accurate adaptation of the *Diary*, parts of which, he believed, had been incorporated into the Broadway production, was "the clearest textual example of the campaign . . . to reduce the psychological barrier against further attacks upon Jews . . . [by] blurring the uniqueness of the Final Solution."[2]

Meyer had long feared that an examination of "the entire entourage on Broadway" responsible for the Pulitzer Prize–winning play could be used to support McCarthyism. Nonetheless, he was convinced that he and Anne's *Diary* had been victims of "Stalinization" and that the story of what had happened to them both needed to be told. Meyer had himself published an account of this matter a few years earlier, but lacking corroboration, he had been dismissed as paranoid or accused of Red-baiting.

Meyer, in fact, cared little about the politics of those involved in denying the truth of the Holocaust. The threat to Jewish survival appeared to him to be universal, stretching from one end of the political spectrum to the other. That Hellman was a Stalinist, as others in her group may or may not have been, was of concern to him only as the immediate cause for the silencing of Anne's voice. And so, as the years had passed, and millions had applauded the Broadway play's distorted vision of the Jews' fate, Meyer had grown ever more adamant that his own treatment of the *Diary*, with its clear delineation of the Holocaust's victims as Jews, victimized because of their Jewishness, had to be staged in response.

I had first written to Meyer in the early spring of 1979, seeking permission to use his correspondence with the American Jewish writer Ludwig Lewisohn about whom I was then writing a biography. Along with his approval, he had included "an item I am sending out at present which is part of a long trouble you may have heard about." I had, in fact, read a few articles about the matter, as well as Meyer's own account of his involvement with Anne's *Diary*, and I was intrigued by his query whether I or someone I knew might further research the story. Meyer's first cautionary note to me, that his "interest has to be unmentioned," was far too enticing to leave without some encouraging response.[3] Yet neither of us could then finance my trip to Europe, and so we continued to correspond about what he further characterized as "the Stalinist engineered omission of Anne's most impressive Jewish avowal from the Broadway play."[4]

I knew of this omission, but it seemed to me and to those with whom I spoke that there were perhaps other, equally egregious reasons for this decision, both commercial and assimilationist. Our society was still reeling from the Vietnam War and its shadows of Red-baiting, against which I had fought. I wondered whether Meyer might not be as wrong in his assessment as so many had claimed. "My intent, if such correspondence is found," he wrote, "is in proving by it that a conspiracy existed very early on to suppress my work for ideological motives akin to Stalinism."[5] I could not simply accept his judgment. But nor could I abandon the search for proof, wherever it might lead. For I, too, as a part of the antiwar movement, had witnessed acts of censorship by those who had themselves been censorship's victims. In June, I agreed to do what I could for Meyer's cause. "I'm indeed pleased that you have decided to go ahead in the project," he responded, not just for his own sake, but because of the larger "importance" of the questions he had been raising.[6]

Meyer was then dividing his year between Europe, Israel, and New York, and I was working as a librarian in Charleston, South Carolina, so we put the research on hold until we could meet in New York late that fall. In mid-December we took a taxi across Central Park from the West Side's Olcott Hotel to a townhouse just off Fifth Avenue in the mid-70s, where, in the basement, behind three locked doors, were several locked file cabinets containing Meyer's papers.[7] Gerald Green's television series *Holocaust* had appeared the year before, and as we rode across the park, Meyer told me that his warning to Green—that the theme of the series would endanger his critical and financial prospects—had already been confirmed by the writer himself. As Meyer now unlocked one door and then another and another, only to reveal the locked file cabinets, and as he informed me that I was about to be locked into the basement room while I spent the afternoon examining his papers, I wondered how exaggerated the claims of his paranoia had been.

Yet however accurate those claims may have appeared that day, the files I saw suggested that Meyer's claims of conspiracy might indeed have some basis in fact. Two letters from Otto to Meyer surprised me more than anything else I found, for here was evidence of how easily Otto could have been manipulated into becoming an unwitting coconspirator. "I am sure that it is necessary to have sensitiveness for the Jewish sphere, but in the whole play it must not prevail,"[8] he had written shortly after consulting with others, Hellman among them, about Meyer's script. A check of the letter's date, January 8, 1953, revealed that this rejection of Meyer's adaptation coincided with Stalin's last great anti-Semitic purge, the infamous Doctors' Plot, then unfolding in Moscow. Otto had followed this letter by writing Meyer the next day, "There is, to my mind, little doubt that the play would be much more readily accepted on its merits if it were written by a non-Jew."[9] Was it all just coincidence, I left the basement wondering that day.

Three weeks after copying out little more than two letters from Meyer's files, I received a photocopy of another that he had earlier pulled from his papers and which he was convinced stood as proof of this conspiracy. Here was Otto's directive to Meyer, written six months earlier in June 1952, that he should "not make a Jewish play of it!" because "it is not a Jewish book." This same letter made reference to "reports" and "beautiful letters" that Otto had been receiving from a Doubleday editor whom Meyer believed had been a crucial part of the conspiracy. This was evidence enough for Meyer that others had encouraged this predisposition in Otto so that they could ultimately gain access to the *Diary* for their own purposes.[10]

Although I realized that this was but one reading of the limited evidence I had thus far seen, I also knew that it was in the nature of a conspiracy to leave little hard evidence behind, and that at times individuals are used for ends to which they are not conscious parties. Had Hellman so manipulated the situation as to recut the *Diary* to fit her own ideology? Or was this appearance of conspiracy nothing more than a product of Meyer's own faulty understanding of events that had worked against him artistically and financially, without the intrusion of more sinister motives? Was he a victim of nothing more than Broadway business as usual, as even his wife would later assert?[11] And although Hellman's veracity had long come into question by serious literary figures who had witnessed its erosion in favor of political and personal preferences, her dishonesty was no proof that Meyer was right.

And yet I sensed that he was more than a casualty of the theatrical process.

For all of my skepticism, there seemed to be enough evidence in what I had already examined to indicate the need to go further, to try to see Otto's files if I could. But there was something more that needed to be considered before proceeding, a problem of even greater moment. By the late 1970s, revisionists were already actively pressing their case that the Holocaust was all a Zionist hoax. There had been a long-standing attempt, beginning in 1957, to discredit the Diary as a forgery and thereby to deny the truth of the Jews' Holocaust experience. I feared that any public examination of Meyer's claim could lend aid and comfort to this growing movement. Meyer and I continued to correspond in the months that followed my visit to the locked files, but our discussion of these developing efforts at Holocaust revisionism only served to make the pursuit of his case more problematic for me.[12] Ironically, as I would learn ten years later, these efforts were grounded in Meyer's own intimate involvement with the Diary. Through several permutations, his role as the document's reviewer in the New York Times had quickly become twisted into that of its forger, as his relation to the Diary became further distorted with each subsequent turn of the story within the Nazi press, from Denmark to Norway to Germany.[13]

Otto died in August 1980, and Meyer passed away the following July without ever having his assertions verified or his name vindicated—or his claims shown to be unfounded. During these same months, the Netherlands State Institute for War Documentation, responding to growing pressure from an assortment of revisionist groups, had submitted the Diary to analysis by the State Forensic Science Laboratory of the Ministry of Justice, which conclusively demonstrated its authenticity in 1981. In time, the ministry's report became part of a larger effort to publish a critical edition of the Diary designed to further demonstrate its historicity. A number of introductory essays were added to this scholarly volume, including one that refuted Meyer's accusations, calling them a series of "distorted accounts of events that had never taken place."[14] When the edition appeared in English in 1989, the New York Times reviewer responded to this summary dismissal by writing that its author was "either disingenuous or uncharacteristically uninformed."[15] With the authenticity of the Diary now confirmed, and the questions Meyer had raised once again before the public, I could no longer leave the matter unresolved.

It is now more than a half century since Anne Frank left her Diary behind for us. Otto's files were opened a few years ago in Amsterdam, and the papers of the other players in this drama are available in archives scattered around the United States. A part of me had hoped that they might prove Meyer wrong, though I was nearly certain of what had happened—of how and why and by whose hands. But there are no winners here, as Meyer would have been the first to acknowledge. Only a cautionary tale emerges. And if the Holocaust has diminished us all, so, too, has this theft of Anne's legacy.

Acknowledgments

As with all historical investigations, this study has been a collaborative effort. There are many more to whom thanks are due than I can name here. I hope they know who they are, including the many librarians and archivists at Boston University, the Ransom Humanities Center at the University of Texas at Austin, the Wisconsin State Historical Society, the Manuscript Division of the Library of Congress, and Columbia University. I am deeply indebted to Yt Stoker, archivist at the Anne Frank Center in Amsterdam, for her many kindnesses over the years. To the family of Meyer Levin belongs a special note of appreciation—his wife, Tereska, who opened her home to me at the beginning of my quest for the truth; Gabriel and Mikael, his sons, who met with me at the beginning and end of the process, respectively; and in particular his son Jo (Eli), who has read the manuscript, shared his perspective in depth, and befriended a pilgrim in the Southwest. I can only guess at how trying the events detailed in this book were for those who lived through them. Thanks also to Meira Penchina, a cousin of the Levins who put me in contact with Tereska and her sons.

To those who granted permission to quote from unpublished materials, I want to express my awareness of their feelings of trust in my ability to handle their part in the story with fairness. Among these are Robert and Richard Rifkind, Garson Kanin, Eli Levin (Jo Basiste), Edward Costikyan, Samuel Fredman, and Buddy Elias of the Anne Frank–Fonds in Basel, who deserves special mention and thanks for access to the papers of Otto Frank.

Rick Teller, typist, critical reader, and friend, posed questions that helped to clarify a number of issues. As always, Deborah Tomasi lent her expert hand and spirit. Ruth Wisse of Harvard University offered a generous and positive assessment of my work, as did David Bellow, whom I thank for suggesting that I show it to Yale University Press. Dan Heaton, my manuscript editor at Yale, has done a wonderful job of smoothing the text and saving me from errors that have inevitably crept into the notes. And Chuck Grench, editor in chief, has earned the thanks of a writer who was heartened by his enthusiasm and ongoing faith in the project. Stephen Whitfield of Brandeis University deserves to be mentioned here, as well, for he expressed an interest in my efforts early on, as he has done before. To see his joyful smile over scholarship is reward in itself.

But of all those who merit special thanks, none outshine the family I love. My siblings, Mike, Bill, Don, and Barbara, have had to listen to this tale for years, and have shown the patience and interest that belong with families. Indeed, my sister accompanied me on one of my visits with Meyer Levin when she was only sixteen and remembers it vividly still, though more years than that have since passed. As always, my parents, Evelyn and Lester, have unfailingly supported me and demonstrated their unqualified love. No one could have been blessed better than I have been since they gave me life a half century ago. Nor could I have had sons whose presence in my life has been more joyful and fulfilling than Joshua's and Ross's. They have encouraged me throughout the years to pursue my goals and to seek more. And finally, my deepest sense of gratitude belongs to my wife and life's partner, Rachel, always understanding, always supportive, always sharing the needs that have driven me to explore. The life we have built is evident on every page.

Chronology

1942

June 12 Anne Frank receives diary and writes first entry

July 6 Frank family goes into hiding in the annex (Achterhuis)

1944

Spring Meyer Levin goes to Europe as war correspondent

August 1 Anne's last entry in the *Diary*

August 4 Frank family arrested

1945

March After imprisonment in Amsterdam, Westerbork, and Auschwitz, Anne is murdered at Bergen-Belsen

June 3 Otto Frank, the lone survivor in his family, returns to Amsterdam

August With Anne's death confirmed, Miep Gies returns *Diary* to Otto

1947

June 25 *Het Achterhuis*, edited by Otto, is published in Holland; Otto subsequently contracts with New York agent to sell *Diary* for publication, theater, and film

1950

French edition of *Le Journal de Anne Frank* appears; *Diary* continues to be rejected by English and American publishers; Meyer publishes *In Search*, describing his exposure to death camps and need for a Holocaust voice

September   Otto and Meyer correspond regarding a possible English or American edition of the *Diary*, as well as Meyer's hope to adapt Anne's book for the stage and his willingness to seek a producer

September 29   Otto accepts Meyer's offer to seek an English-language publisher and encourages him to work on *Diary* adaptation

October   Meyer contacts the publisher Valentine Mitchell, and negotiations for English publication of the *Diary* begin, with contract concluded the following month

1951

April 9   After negotiating for some months with Little, Brown, Otto accepts Doubleday contract offer for an American edition and authorizes the publisher to act as film agent, making no mention of Meyer's involvement

1952

February 20   Otto pleased that Eleanor Roosevelt's *Diary* introduction emphasizes Anne's "ideals" of "human spirit—peace"

March 31   Otto issues written authorization for Meyer to act as his agent for a period of one year, with Otto retaining the right of final approval

April 14   Lillian Hellman appears before HUAC

June 18   Otto tells Doubleday editor Barbara Zimmerman that he wants the publisher to be stage and film agent, with Meyer as consultant

June 23   Doubleday proposes that Maxwell Anderson adapt *Diary*

July 8   After stormy meetings with Meyer, Doubleday withdraws as agent, and Meyer submits long list of interested producers, with recommendation of producer Cheryl Crawford

July 30   Crawford accepts Otto's offer to produce Broadway play, promises contract for Meyer, and advises that a "top" playwright (Hellman) is studying the *Diary* for possible collaboration or sole authorship

August 1   Kermit Bloomgarden cables Otto of his interest as producer

August 23   Meyer sends Otto radio script

October 7   Crawford, who had earlier expressed enthusiasm about Meyer's treatment, rejects his script with unspecified objections, advises he show it to other producers

October 29   Peter Capell, whom Meyer had secured to produce the play, is rejected by Otto

October 30   Meyer presents Otto with revised script

November 11   Zimmerman and Crawford suggest to Otto that Carson McCullers might agree to adapt the *Diary*

November–December   Meyer fails to find interest among a prescribed list of producers, while Herman Shumlin is rejected by Otto's attorney

1953

April 22   Crawford withdraws as producer

June   McCullers withdraws from project

September 9   Otto approves Bloomgarden as producer

October 1   Otto signs contract with Bloomgarden indemnifying him against any future claims by Meyer

November 19   Leah Salisbury tells her clients Frances Goodrich and Albert Hackett, longtime friends of Hellman, that Bloomgarden wants them to adapt *Diary*

1954

January 21   Hacketts complete first draft

February 9   Meyer raises issue of "political factors" influencing Bloomgarden's decision against his script

May 20   Hacketts' fourth draft finished, to be sent to Salisbury, Otto, Bloomgarden, and Hellman for "help"

June 14   Otto rejects Hacketts' play, sends suggestions

August 23   Hacketts send fifth draft to Salisbury, Bloomgarden, and Hellman

September 5   Hacketts receive "brilliant advice on construction" from Hellman

October 8   Bloomgarden approves sixth draft, will produce

October 18   Script sent to Garson Kanin as possible director

October 25   Otto approves latest Hackett script, and follows with suggestions

November 16   Hacketts arrive in London to work with Kanin on changes

December 5   Seventh draft completed

December 19   After trip to Amsterdam, eighth draft completed

December 30   Meyer files suit against Otto and Crawford, claiming breach of contract and fraud

1955

January 14   Eighth draft rewrite completed

March 30   Court grants Otto's motion to vacate service of suit, leaving Crawford alone to defend herself

May 2   Ohel Theatre in Israel interested in Meyer's play

June 3   Meyer hospitalized because of emotional and physical distress, but vows to fight until permitted a hearing for his play

June 17   Otto approves Meyer's Israeli production if public appeals stop, but Otto's attorney objects

August 16   Further revisions made to Hackett script following meeting with Hellman

August 22   First rehearsal of The Diary of Anne Frank

September 9   "Because we are Jews" removed from climactic speech

September 10   Hellman adds new scene to script

October 6   Play opens in New York to good reviews by general press, though soon severely criticized in Jewish and Dutch journals

October 14   Meyer informs Otto of intent to sue for plagiarism and continues to send negative reviews of play

1956

January 6   Meyer prevented from staging Israeli production of his play

February 14   Meyer files suit against Otto and Bloomgarden on issues of fraudulent representation of facts to induce Otto to reject him as writer, and for plagiarism

April 23   Meyer's earlier suit against Otto and Crawford amended to eliminate Otto from causes of action, focusing instead upon Crawford

September 30   Hacketts' "Diary of the Diary" published in New York Times, giving details of script's many drafts and of Hellman's involvement, angering Otto and Bloomgarden's attorneys, supporting Meyer's case

October 25   Otto signs film contract, will rely on judgment of Hacketts and Kanin, though still concerned it be "worth the play and the book"

1957

May 20   Otto signs film contract with Fox

1958

January 9   Meyer wins plagiarism finding in court, Hacketts and others in "shock"

January 11   Judge sets aside damage award, claiming jury not professionally competent to decide amount

February 27   Judge grants new trial, but Meyer's lawyer appeals ruling

March 19   Meyer files motion to reinstate jury verdict

September 5   Meyer states Hellman's opposition to *Diary*'s Jewish content is motivated by her Stalinist ideology

1959

February 24   Judge denies Meyer's appeal

July 10   Rather than return to court, Meyer agrees to allow a committee of three, selected by him, negotiate a "fair and reasonable settlement"

October 20   Final settlement reached, assigning copyright to Otto, a minimal monetary award to Meyer, and a joint statement exonerating all parties, though statement not made public

1960

February 5   In violation of settlement, Meyer reopens public debate

1961

November   Otto's attorneys respond to Meyer's public accusation of a Communist "grab" of *Diary* for ideological use; Bloomgarden and Hellman formulating separate responses

1970

Meyer receives World Federation of Bergen-Belsen Association's award for struggle over *Diary*

1972

April 16   Meyer's play is produced at Brandeis University without Meyer's involvement

1973

Meyer publishes *The Obsession*, an account of his struggle to produce his play

1976

Hellman publishes *Scoundrel Time* as answer to *The Obsession*; Varon publishes "The Haunting of Meyer Levin" in response

1980

August 21   Otto dies

1981

May 27   Meyer issues "My Ethical Will as to Authorship" declaring need to seek truth and fight censorship
July 9   Meyer dies

1983

First professional production in America of Meyer's *Diary* adaptation, at Boston's Lyric Stage

1989

"Critical Edition" of *Diary* publishes passages, many previously cut by Otto

1995

"Definitive Edition" of *Diary* restores passages for more general readership

1997

Hackett play scheduled for fall Broadway opening

CHAPTER ONE

With My Own Eyes

eyer Levin's search for an authentic Holocaust voice began shortly after he entered the first of the many Nazi death camps to which he would bear witness as a war correspondent in the final days of the killing. Among them was Bergen-Belsen, the camp in which Anne Frank had been murdered. The mere hint of the camps' existence had left him "haunted by the need to go forward, to learn the whole truth" of those horror-filled days.[1] Five years later, in 1950 he wrote in his "book about being a Jew," *In Search*, that "of all the commandments, I feel this to be the only one that was eternally applicable in the same form in which it had been issued . . . the commandment of truth, the commandment against bearing false witness."

It was a revelation that had first come to him while returning a Torah to a decimated Jewish community in Germany in the early days after the killing had stopped. "For me, this was the essence of our fate. . . . This then was my inmost behest." And though he knew that "the practice of absolute truth must be crippling in an imperfect world," he had persisted, writing not the falsely "hopeful story . . . of the indestructibility of the Jewish community" that others would insist upon in the decades ahead, but "of the Jews of Europe as they were: broken, finished."[2]

Thomas Mann later praised Meyer's memoir *In Search* as "a human document of high order, written by a witness of our fantastic epoch whose gaze remained both clear and steady, notwithstanding the shocking turmoil about him." It would serve the future, Mann added, "as a source of enlightenment and as a living image of all that we had to experience," for here was a book "bent on preserving what humanity is only too ready to forget."[3]

"It was not for me to bear false witness," Meyer would affirm again and again, for the visions had remained as sharply drawn as when he had first brought them to his readers in America, Jew and non-Jew alike:[4]

> Buchenwald, May 2 [1945]—All week I have been talking to Jews who survived the greatest mass murder in the history of mankind. Each one owes his continued existence to a succession of miracles, accidents, oversights. My mind has become in the faintest way like their minds; I am beginning to understand how they feel. No one who has not been through their experience can ever understand them, for these people have gone through a sieve of death four years, five years, six years continuously. Tons of ashes, the ashes of seven million of their people have gone through the sieve, and these few are the last bits of cinder and stone somehow adhering to the mesh. My mind, after this week, faintly reflects their minds. It is a composite image of trains running three-tracked into smoking crematoriums, of remote Polish villages whose mud ruts were filled with human bodies, of a German officer, playfully lining up a group of Jewish children until they were precisely one head behind the other and then putting a single bullet through the line, of a woman holding her baby aloft over her head while savage police dogs ripped her apart, and through every image I see the brown, earnest undeniable eyes of a survivor who tells me this, and over each image is stamped the ever-recurring line, "I saw it, I saw it with my own eyes."[5]

It was Meyer's wife, Tereska Torres, who passed along the recent French translation of Anne Frank's *Diary* to her husband in the late summer of 1950. Tereska, a member of the Free French Army whose first husband had died in combat while she carried their child, had grown increasingly aware of the survivor's guilt afflicting Meyer, in part because of the marginal role he had played in the struggle to stop the slaughter. "This is the guilt of the living," he would write after returning home from the war, "a guilt that has invaded all humanity." Yet for all the Holocaust's universality of meaning, it was the Jews who had "sense[d] this guilt more painfully because they were closer to the center . . . yes, even . . . the Jews of America . . . who escaped because their forebears made the journey from Europe in steerage." And if Jews everywhere questioned why they had survived, few did so with greater intensity than Meyer. "Isn't there something we must do to pay for being alive?"[6]

The answer came for Meyer in the words of an adolescent, clearly and powerfully spoken, thoughts that he could not adequately express himself. "How could he know, how could anyone here know, what was real?" he had written three years earlier in a novel of Holocaust victimization and survival.[7] Here, at last, was "the voice from the mass grave" for which he had long been searching, and the means by which he could repay the debt owed for his own survival. Perhaps the *Diary* could provide some release from a part of his own suffering, if only he could share Anne's book with those whose lives had remained largely untouched by the revelatory event out of which it had come. At work on a film adaptation of an earlier novel based on his life as a young Zionist on a kibbutz in the 1920s, Meyer at once put the script aside and finished reading the *Diary*. "From the first page the seizure was complete," he wrote in his 1973 account of *The Obsession* that had captured his soul. "As I read on, I became certain—this was the needed document. For here, instead of a remote story-book journey, was an urban family with which every American reader could feel empathy."[8]

On September 8, 1950, Levin wrote the *Diary*'s French publisher, Calmann-Levy, asking for the agent handling the work in France and for the address of Anne's father, Otto.[9] Meyer was determined to see that an English-language edition appeared as soon as possible. "So I began a campaign to find a publisher," he later wrote of the events that were to lead him "into a trouble that was to grip, occupy, haunt, and all but devour me, these twenty years."[10] On the nineteenth, Otto politely thanked Meyer for his interest, explaining that his "Paris agent Maison D. Clairouin are busy at present to place the English and American rights of Anne's Diary, so that I cannot give you an option at present."[11]

Meyer was pleased to have established contact with Otto and sent him a copy of *In Search* two days later, "so that you may have some notion of my work." He wished to assure Otto that his interest in the *Diary* was not commercial but "one of sympathy" with the experiences and ideas expressed throughout. It was his wish to translate the work and to "suggest . . . to my contacts in these fields" that it contained "the material for a very touching play or film." While he believed that the likelihood of finding a commercial producer for such a project was "remote," he hoped that with Otto's consent, he could "feel free" to approach those whom he knew.[12]

Otto had not yet begun to read *In Search* when he sent a long, detailed answer to Meyer's several requests. Had Otto read his book, he might have responded with less enthusiasm, given its emphasis on Jewish themes and identity. He had, however, seen Meyer's film on the *Yishuv*, the Jewish settlement in Palestine, and had been favorably impressed. Otto said that his friend of several decades, Nathan Straus, the president of New York's WMCA Radio and scion of the influential Straus family, was at the moment discussing with Random House the possibility of British copublication. But he wanted Meyer to know that "in case you should have some ideas on the direction of the film, you are absolutely free." And though he gladly placed himself at Meyer's "disposal" should he need "any assistance," he found it difficult to see how Anne's book, whose "value . . . is laying in her thoughts," could be transferred to the screen.[13]

Perhaps Otto's disavowal was sincere, but he had nonetheless included

dramatic, radio, film, and television rights in his 1947 contract with Ernest
Kuhn, a New York attorney who continued to represent him in any negotiations with American and Canadian publishers.[14] Otto could hardly have been
as surprised by the idea of dramatization for screen or other medium as he must
have appeared to Meyer. Although nothing had come of a Twentieth Century
Fox reading of the *Diary* a few years earlier, Otto had some hope that it could
be sold now that he had witnessed the interest of a major film company.
Without offering a firm commitment, Otto encouraged Meyer to do all that he
could to secure a producer, aware not only of the role of an agent, but of the
difference between one under contract and another who worked without a
binding agreement. If dramatized, the film would in all likelihood be the first of
its kind, Otto noted six days after his first letter to Meyer, "the situation of a
hiding family . . . not yet worked out in a film as far as I know." He hoped to
hear from Meyer again, even if a film of Anne's work would ultimately "be
rather different from the real contents of her book," a prospect seemingly of
less concern to him than one might otherwise have expected.[15]

Meyer assured Otto that no such compromise was necessary, that given "a
sensitive and daring producer, a very wonderful film could be made, staying
very close to the book," even filming in the house to give it "the fidelity of a
record . . . if the thought does not shock you." Meyer must have wondered at
Otto's willingness to compromise his daughter's work for the sake of a cinematic treatment, and assured him that "such a film could do a great deal toward
bettering human understanding" without "the thoughts and ideas of the book
. . . [being] changed or lost." He would soon be going to New York for several
months and, with Otto's permission, would raise the possibilities of publication and a film, "if after reading my book you feel I am the right person." Meyer
believed that his ideas resonated in Anne's and that Otto's consent to this
search would be acknowledgment of this fact. It was a reasonable expectation,
given Meyer's repeated request that Otto consider his thoughts on Jewish
identity and Zionism before agreeing to such an arrangement. So convinced
was Meyer of this spiritual bond between himself and Anne that he further
offered to undertake, as a "mitzvah" (a morally sanctioned religious act), the
translation of the *Diary*. Together with his help in securing a publisher and a
producer, he was offering Otto "a combination in which I may be of use . . .
with no commitment on your part."[16]

"I want to answer your kind letter of Sept. 26 immediately and thank you
for it," began Otto's encouraging response. Although an English translation
was already under way (ultimately to be replaced by another), he encouraged
Meyer to "find the right connection or person," as long as it was not "an
unknown house." Otto confided to Meyer: "I rather prefer to wait" than give
the book to an obscure publisher, though he was soon to receive a rejection
from Random House, the book's sixteenth from an English or American press.

Victor Gollancz, Albert Heinemann, Allen and Unwin, Macmillan, Scribner's, Sedgewick and Jackson, Doubleday Doran, Viking, Vanguard, Warendorf, Simon and Schuster, Appleton Century, Knopf, Schocken, and Hutchinson had all previously rejected the *Diary*. Otto was far more encouraging to Meyer concerning the prospect of a film, for no other agent in Europe or America was now actively at work on this possibility. Thanking Meyer again for his interest "in Anne's book and my person," he supported the suggestion of using the actual hiding place ("I would try my best to overwin my inner feelings") and expressed new confidence that "a good solution to bring out the thoughts and ideas" of the *Diary* might be found, rather than seeing "the exciting and thrilling actions . . . prevail to please the public." Otto's favorable impression of Meyer's Zionist film, *My Father's House*, had convinced him of the seriousness with which Meyer was likely to undertake the project and promised that "if you see it in another way you just go on and I shall not interfere."[17]

Even before receiving Meyer's response, Otto essentially granted him the role of American agent. Clairouin had been told that no decision regarding English-language publication would be taken "before I heard from this gentleman." Meyer was to meet in New York with Random House and "to let me know your opinion about the chances as soon as possible." Should they decline or offer an unacceptable arrangement, he was to send Otto his further "suggestions."[18]

Without a contract, and acting solely on good faith, Meyer had already made preliminary inquiries with the British Jewish publisher Valentine Mitchell, which, as Meyer immediately wrote Otto, was "eager to have Anne's Diary." Meyer, however, was reluctant to assume the position offered by Otto, having learned from him that others were already engaged in this role on both sides of the Atlantic. "I feel a little like an unnecessary intermediary," he commented to Otto, though he promised to do what he could with the publishers. More important, he was pleased to report that his conversation with a film producer had resulted in "at least a preliminary interest in the project."[19]

Otto wrote again on October 9 concerning Random House and thanked Meyer "for all you are doing!"[20] But Meyer thought it best for Otto to deal directly with the publisher and to allow his Paris agent to pursue the progress already made with Valentine Mitchell. Meyer would, of course, be willing to help with publication of the *Diary* if a problem developed.[21] Two weeks later, Meyer wrote Otto from New York of the interest shown by two film producers, for whom Otto then sent copies of the French translation. With Random House awaiting "further word" concerning publication arrangements with Valentine Mitchell, Meyer advised Otto to sign with the British house so that an American contract could at last be negotiated.[22]

On November 13, Meyer published a brief summary of the *Diary* in the

American Jewish publication *Congress Weekly* as a part of the larger discussion of "the restricted market" for "too special" Jewish material. He wrote of the ease with which the prominent non-Jewish writer John Hersey had found a publisher for *The Wall*, a fictionalized account of the Warsaw Ghetto with a universal message of human triumph over evil, and compared it with the difficulty in placing Anne's *Diary*, "a real document" of specifically Jewish suffering. To date it had been rejected by many of the same publishers who had recently declined to bring out *In Search* (as they had other Jewish works he had proposed over the previous two decades). Was Anne's book, like his, "too Jewish"? Was it merely a commercial decision, as some insisted, pointing to *The Wall*'s marketable author? Or was there an overriding reluctance to speak to the particularity of the Jewish condition, to its uniqueness and to the moral questions and imperatives evoked and imposed by that uniqueness? "I bring this out to emphasize that work in our field continues to suffer a handicap, based upon obscure and sometimes not-so-obscure desires to be relieved of the continuous confrontation of the conscious problems evoked by the Jew." Whatever the personal cost, he had no intention of removing himself from this struggle. "For myself, I believe that we must keep up the fight for attention, even if it sometimes makes us appear to be disagreeable characters."[23]

Otto's search for an American or British publication arrangement continued to involve Meyer in the weeks that followed. Otto sought Meyer's opinions regarding the best house, the proper tone of translation, and the intricacies of negotiating simultaneous contracts separated by three thousand miles. "What do you think?" and "Thanks for everything" became repeated refrains in his correspondence with Meyer.[24] The high level of assistance rendered by Meyer was acknowledged by Otto in a letter to Nathan Straus, with whom Otto continued to discuss the possibility of Random House, though he had himself begun to encourage Little, Brown. "I am writing to another man too," he told Straus, "Mr. Meyer Levin, an American writer who is very interested in Anne's book. It was he who advised [me] to take up the matter with Valentine Mitchell. He spoke to Random House about it [a] short time ago."[25]

Otto similarly credited Meyer's ongoing efforts in letters to him on November 23 and 24, though by now Little, Brown had made a solid offer, which Otto was inclined to accept. (The publisher may have been influenced by Janet Flanner's "Letter from Paris" in the *New Yorker* of November 11, praising it as the work of "a precocious, talented little Frankfurt Jewess . . . [who] rightly aimed to be a writer when she grew up."[26]) "I hope that I do not bother you too much with my affairs," Otto wrote Meyer, "but I know how interested you are in this book. I want you to know all steps taken." Meyer responded immediately, unaware that Otto had already cabled Little, Brown with an acceptance of its offer, together with his suggestion that "details regarding translation" be discussed with Valentine Mitchell, whom he had decided upon as the *Diary*'s British publisher.[27] Meyer spoke of Little, Brown as a "first class" house but advised going with whomever demonstrated the greater "enthusiasm and decisiveness." He further urged Otto to retain all rights beyond simple publication, "particularly drama and film," and to offer only a small percentage to whichever house he went with. "As the book is already known, anything you allow would be generous," he wrote. "Convinced that the journal has stage and film possibilities," he concluded with his "hope that in these matters you will refer to me, should any offers arise."[28]

Meyer continued to offer his assistance with the translation to assure its "literary flow" and to prevent the incursion of "Americanisms . . . providing the publishers and translator consent." He was hesitant to tread on another's territory but wanted the *Diary* to retain its authentic voice and not sound as if it had been written by an adolescent from the States. Meyer added news of his ongoing search for a producer, that he was "continually trying to interest friends of mine in the theater here, and also film people." Certain that "the appearance of the book [would] undoubtedly stimulate interest in these fields," he was concerned that the right person be found, not merely the best commercial arrangement. "It is here that it would be necessary for true sympathy in order that the material can be transferred from one medium to another without loss of fidelity." Having witnessed Otto's quick turnarounds regarding publishers and translators, Meyer worried that a compromise might be reached that would sacrifice Anne's thoughts and vision.[29] (Otto had already consented to two English translations, both of which he was now willing to reject for a third in order to sign with Little, Brown. Neither translator would ever receive compensation, though Otto thought the work of one "a good base for another translation."[30])

From the start, Meyer's emphasis on the critical importance of "fidelity" to the text was tied to his belief in the consonance between his own ideas and Anne's. It was for this reason that he had sent Otto a copy of *In Search*, which Otto had begun to read by mid-November ("It will take some time to get through," he commented), and why he was now forwarding a copy of his *Congress Weekly* article concerning the fate of publications considered to be "too Jewish."[31]

Otto responded twice to Meyer's latest appeal, informing him of the arrangements with the two publishers and of his having "warned Little, Brown to have it translated by someone who is not in school in [the] USA as the charm of the book could be spoiled." He then reassured Meyer that he would not grant film or theater rights to either house but that "if I get inquiries . . . I shall let you know and do nothing."[32]

When a dispute arose with Little, Brown, Otto wrote Meyer detailing his concern that a contract with them might force him to concede these rights. To protect himself, he asked Meyer to inform the translator and publisher that he was "busy in this matter already and . . . that the American publishers (or the English and others) had no [dramatic] rights as the book is known already." Whether sincere or merely following his business sense, Otto assured Meyer that "it is self-understood that I refer to you in case someone else would write me about these rights." Although Meyer would not participate in this questionable scheme ("I didn't feel that I should further interject myself," he wrote Otto upon his return to Paris on December 29), he was pleased to receive Otto's confirmation that he would indeed play a prominent role as a writer in any future dramatization of the *Diary*.[33]

Having heard from Meyer that efforts "to interest people in the film and stage possibilities" were continuing, Otto again promised that "about film and stage rights we will stay in contact."[34] It is curious that Otto made no comment on Meyer's "Restricted Market" *Congress Weekly* other than to thank him for the "fine article." He continued to read *In Search*, but being "pretty nervous" and unable to "find yet rest," he still had not finished the book. (When Meyer later raised the issue of Otto's emotional state at this time, Otto denied ever having experienced such agitation.) Negotiations between Little, Brown and Valentine Mitchell over Canadian rights were in the meantime delaying publication. "It is their fault," Otto told Meyer, as Little, Brown had initially asked only for "U.S. rights"; Canada was a Commonwealth nation and rightly Valentine Mitchell's.[35]

While Meyer independently continued his search for a producer over the next two months, little occurred beyond negotiations with Little, Brown concerning film and theater rights. Then, on March 14, 1951, Francis Price, Doubleday's European agent, wrote Otto for the second time of their interest in the *Diary*. Having failed to receive a response to his first inquiry some months earlier, he repeated Doubleday's firm offer of terms financially similar to Little, Brown's.[36]

More than twenty years later, Price responded to the claim of a former Doubleday editor, Barbara Zimmerman, of a central role in the book's publication and success, by sketching the sequence of events that had led to the publisher's offer:

> The facts of the matter are this: In September of 1949 I was sent to Paris to open Doubleday's first editorial and sales office in Europe, and the very first book for which I contracted for American publication was Manes Sperber's "The Burned Bramble." Manes was then (and still is) an editorial consultant for the Paris publishing house of Calmann-Levy, and in this capacity he had come across "The

Diary of Anne Frank," which at that time had been published only in Amsterdam. He immediately recognized the unique quality of the diary and arranged for its translation and publication in France. And as soon as the French translation was completed, he brought it to me. I sent it on to Donald Elder, the senior editor at Doubleday who was in charge of liaison with the Paris office, with the strongest possible recommendation for its acceptance. A month later I was authorized to offer an advance and a contract to Anne's father, Otto Frank.

Although Zimmerman was "present at the creation," Price denied any legitimacy to her "truthfully claiming to be the mother." Rather, the Diary's "success came about primarily as a result of something over which they had no control—Meyer Levin's memorable front-page review . . . in the New York Times Book Review."[37] Zimmerman's otherwise crucial role in the Diary's postpublication history, however, remained forever unknown to Price.

The arrival of Price's letter even as Little, Brown continued to demand a significantly larger percentage of the sale of the book for film, radio, television, and theater settled the matter for Otto. Little, Brown maintained that its offer had been based on this assumption of "special rights." No matter how lucrative the book might prove, the publisher insisted that such additional revenues were necessary to offset the "high operating costs in publishing now" and it had taken the liberty of restoring this "special rights" clause, which Otto had crossed out when signing the contract several days earlier.[38]

On March 21, Otto informed Price that he was willing to discuss the Doubleday offer now that negotiations with Little, Brown had foundered, though "the question of moving picture and dramatic rights" was "more a matter of sentiment on my side than a financial one." Perhaps a film or play might never be made, but if one were, it had to be done from a particular perspective. "I do not want a film to be made based on terror, bombardment and Nazis spoiling the ideal base of the diary and therefore want to keep these rights under control," including the "right to interfere" so that Anne would be seen as he wished to portray her according to these ideals. The "decision depends on it to a great extent," he carefully stated, promising to discuss contract possibilities "as soon as I know your standpoint about the film question."[39]

Having edited the Diary, Otto insisted upon the right to determine Anne's theatrical portrait as well. It is clear, however, that in selecting material from her original text, he had altered not only her growing sense of terror and the seriousness with which she regarded her situation, but, more significantly, her search for peace both in a comforting God and in a deepening awareness of herself as a Jew. Although she disdainfully recorded her mother's efforts to make her read prayers during their opening weeks in hiding, Anne wrote after a year in the Annex, "My fear vanished, I looked up in the sky and trusted in God." Two months later she added: "I know that I have God . . . and that's what keeps me going. Without the voice that keeps holding out comfort and goodness to me I should have lost all hope long ago, without God I should long ago have collapsed. I know I am not safe, I am afraid of prison cells and concentration camps, but I feel I've grown more courageous and that I am in God's hands!"[40] Otto chose to delete all of this, together with numerous other entries expressing similar thoughts, thereby offering a distorted portrait of Anne. Thirty years later, he still insisted that "she didn't show any feeling for religion," though privately, to the second Mrs. Frank, he had admitted as early as 1945 to being profoundly astonished at discovering her deep faith. Fritzi Frank related after his death that it had taken Otto a long time to read the *Diary*, "as he found it such an overwhelming emotional experience. When he finished it he told us that he had discovered that he had not really known his daughter. Although, of course, he was on good terms with her, he had never known anything about her innermost thoughts, her high ideals, her belief in God and her progressive ideas which had surprised him greatly."[41]

Otto similarly removed many of the passages that reflected Anne's deepening awareness of herself as a Jew. "This morning Miep told us that last night they were dragging Jews from house after house again," Anne had recorded during their early weeks in hiding. "If I just think of how we live here, I usually come to the conclusion that it is a paradise compared with how other Jews who are not hiding must be living," she noted some time later. After only three months in the Annex, Anne wrote, "Yesterday it was Yom Kippur, and there can't be many people who will have kept it as quietly as we did." More than a year later, she further noted the passage of Jewish time by recording how the group had "skipped Chanuka" in their second year of hiding, an event unparalleled in the life of her family. Each of these references, and others, Otto would delete, denying Anne her own voice as she grew. In "the second half of 1943," she noted in a similarly excised passage, "I became a young woman, an adult in body and my mind underwent a very great change, I came to know God!"[42] Having so carefully molded the Anne he wished the world to see, an Anne reflective of his own background—secular, uneducated in Judaism, and anti-Zionist—Otto could not allow others to reshape his daughter's portrait in her own image.[43]

Price, of course, was excited by the possibility of acquiring the *Diary* for Doubleday, and he responded immediately upon receipt of Otto's answer, feeling "quite sure there would be no difficulty with Doubleday about leaving all of the motion picture, dramatic, and television rights in your control." All of this would be in a letter from Clairouin. He asked only that Otto inform him of his decision so that he and Clairouin might settle the details of their contract.[44] On March 27, Otto notified Little, Brown that because of its insistence upon unfavorable terms concerning dramatization rights, "it would not serve any useful purpose to continue our correspondence."[45]

Before leaving for Amsterdam, Otto fulfilled a long-standing promise to visit with Meyer and his family.[46] The contents of their conversation on March 30 were later the subject of much dispute. For the moment, it was a chance for all to meet. Meyer and Tereska repeated their interest and thoughts concerning Anne's *Diary* and the young woman they had come to know through it, while Otto thanked them for the kindnesses they had shown over the past half year toward him and his efforts to bring Anne's work to an ever-greater audience. Just how much discussion took place at this time regarding Meyer's efforts to secure a film or theater producer ultimately became the basis for an extended legal battle.

From Amsterdam, Otto wrote Clairouin on April 3 that he had begun to negotiate with Doubleday on his own and that despite the agency's having made initial contact with Price, it was no longer needed. He promised, however, to keep the agency informed of developments.[47] Clairouin's Madame Tschebeko responded three days later and wrote again after another three weeks, arguing that the agency was entitled to a standard commission for all its work over the last year or more and for a continuing role in the negotiations.[48] But by that time, Otto's contract with Doubleday had been signed.

Price had sailed to New York immediately after his meeting with Otto in Paris and had secured a contract for him with the unusual stipulation that "the ultimate decision" concerning all nonprint use of the *Diary* would "remain entirely in your hands."[49] Receipt of this contract had allowed Otto to send his final note of refusal to Little, Brown on April 18. "I suppose that it is useless to go further into the matter," he wrote, without mentioning that he had reached an agreement with another publisher.[50]

Otto's signing with Doubleday on April 27 brought him great relief. Within days, word of the *Diary*'s future publication in English prompted the first request to reprint portions of it. Otto was pleased to refer the leading American Jewish journal *Commentary* to Doubleday as proof to himself that the search begun four years earlier had been happily concluded.[51] There were, however, significant costs to others that Otto felt free to disregard. Clairouin had opened several doors for him, including Doubleday's, and was entitled to a full commission by all standards of fairness. Otto's direct negotiation with Price had not been an amateur's oversight. In a letter to Nathan Straus the previous August 11, Otto had already discussed the possibility of bypassing Clairouin in his negotiations with Random House. "If I would have asked Clairouin to write . . . I would have to pay agents fees for something they did not work for," he wrote Straus with self-justification. On the other hand, "if they bring a firm [offer], this is without discussion."[52] (Little wonder that he had been so eager to have Meyer, who asked for no compensation, negotiate with Random while in New York.) Yet, when the contract with Doubleday was signed, following Clairouin's initial contact and several conversations with Price, Otto saw himself as free of all monetary obligations toward the agency. (Had Otto neglected to encourage Price's first approach in order to avoid this fee?) Price, unaware of Clairouin's extensive work on the project in the years before his involvement, agreed with Otto when he sought advice on the matter.[53] Only after a rancorous exchange of letters did Otto agree to pay a third of the customary agents' fee "pour les efforts que vous avez fait en générale."[54]

Equally questionable, in light of Otto's encouragement of Meyer's efforts on his behalf, were the actual terms of the media clause with Doubleday. Promising to make no decision without Meyer's involvement, he had negotiated terms with Doubleday that clearly could jeopardize Meyer's interests. There is no evidence that Otto had ever mentioned Meyer to Price, whose understanding "after our discussion" in Paris was that Otto would want Doubleday "to handle any approach . . . from a film or radio concern, should there be interest in the dramatization in one form or another."[55] As yet unaware that Otto had signed a contract, Meyer wrote him three weeks later of new interest in the *Diary* by an American film producer. "And what finally came of the American negotiations?" Meyer asked, still believing himself to be an important part of the process of bringing Anne's message to the world. "Is Doubleday going to do it?"[56]

Meyer requested a copy of the *Diary*'s English translation to give to this potential producer for consideration. Otto advised Meyer that although Valentine Mitchell's retranslation was only partially completed, the earlier English version was available and would be sent. It was the translation whose rendering he had encouraged but for which, because it would not be published, he had refused to make payment. Still not mentioning his Doubleday contract, Otto asked Meyer what he knew of the Italian film producers who had shown some interest (a question he also had recently put to Price).[57]

Meyer advised Otto on May 12 that the best Italian producers had focused exclusively on "Italian life" and that with finances being an essential question everywhere, it would be best to continue looking in England and America, where "one would [not] have to 'sell' one of the producers on doing the film."[58] Otto again thanked Meyer and, without mentioning the Doubleday contract, continued to encourage representation in these matters. "I have enough confidence in you and your wife [whose ongoing interests had begun with her letter to Otto a day before Meyer's first] to leave the film question to your judgment, knowing that you will not start any binding arrangements and keep things in hand." By spring 1951, Otto had managed to secure the services of two agents in his search for wider exposure for Anne's *Diary*.[59] But to one, he had made no binding commitment of his own.

CHAPTER TWO

A Real Story of Jews Under Nazism

It is quite some time that we heard from each other," Otto wrote Meyer on September 21, following a four-month break in their correspondence. Yet there was little new to report. The *Diary* had appeared in Germany, but sales, not surprisingly, were light. Only a few newspapers had reviewed it. Assuming that Meyer had learned of Doubleday's plans to publish the newly translated *Diary* in America, Otto wrote of its probable appearance by Christmas of that year. For now, they would all have to wait. "It always takes a long time," he reminded Meyer, wishing him well for the Jewish New Year. Yet he ended the letter by asking Meyer if he still had the "bad translation" he had sent that summer, as if he suspected it might be used without his permission.[1]

Several days later Otto was pleased to learn from Doubleday's Donald Elder that serialization of the *Diary* in *Commentary* had become a firm possibility. Given their mutual interest, Otto assured him that he had "all the confidence in your firm and in you personally to do what you judge best." Elder had been engaged in negotiations with *Commentary* and was now seeking Otto's approval to finalize the arrangement. "I trust that you will inform me in case you succeed," Otto responded, assuring Elder that he would wait patiently "until I get further news on this matter" and on "the rest" concerning the *Diary*.[2]

On October 2, Price wrote Otto from Paris that the probable serialization had led Doubleday to delay the book's publication until spring, with the hope that this added exposure would increase sales.[3] Three days later, Otto was in Paris to discuss these developments with Price. That afternoon he made an unannounced visit to Meyer's house but found only Tereska and the children there to greet him.[4] Concerned with controlling every aspect of his daughter's work, Otto may have decided to take this opportunity to retrieve the "bad translation," perhaps no longer trusting Meyer's judgment in sharing the *Diary* with potential producers.

Still worried three weeks later, Otto wrote to Barbara Zimmerman, who had been chosen to assist Otto during Elder's leave of absence. He suggested to Zimmerman that it would "be wise to deposit a synopsis of the book to a certain authority in order to prevent others [from using] it for film or theater purposes."[5] Zimmerman was to play an increasingly "influential [role] in this whole affair," as Price wrote Meyer in 1973.[6] Noting Otto's deep concern, she reminded him that the book's copyright was already in his name. He was "legally protected automatically" from all possibilities of the *Diary*'s "being used for such purposes outside [his] control." Before closing, Zimmerman further noted that although negotiations concerning serialization had not yet been concluded, Doubleday had initiated a discussion with Eleanor Roosevelt's editor on the possibility of her writing a brief introduction for the *Diary*.[7]

"After receiving your last letter I have the feeling that the matter of Anne's book is not only a commercial question for you but also a personal one," Otto wrote with appreciation to Zimmerman, who acknowledged that "everyone who has read it here has taken a great interest in it."[8] In time, Otto came to see in Zimmerman, a young contemporary of Anne, the daughter he had lost. Zimmerman even resembled Anne physically, as another wrote some twenty-two years later. How "perfectly at ease" Otto felt with her "in the question of film," promising that "in case something might turn up we'll handle it together."[9] Otto had cherished being a father more than any other role he had played in life. Bereft at the loss of his family, he had earlier insisted that a young fellow inmate at Auschwitz call him Papa Frank. "I have this need to be a Papa to someone," he had confessed in the camp. How profoundly tragic Anne's death had been for him. Zimmerman appears to have been willing to accept this surrogate role, if only out of compassion for Otto's inconsolable loss. In time, he would affectionately present her with an antique gold pin, as he would have Anne, had she survived.[10]

Late in the year Meyer's request for a copy of the new translation to show potential producers interrupted two months of silence, prompting Otto to write Zimmerman on January 1, 1952, "concerning the matter of the dramatic rights."[11] "We shall send him a set of proofs as soon as they are ready," she assured Otto in February. And while there was still no sale of the book to *Commentary*, she could report that Doubleday was continuing to discuss serialization as a part of its marketing strategy, as they were Mrs. Roosevelt's introduction. The book's publication was, in fact, being postponed an additional month, to June 12, in order to "ensure wide review space and early publicity about the book—all of which is extremely important in presenting the book to the public." Doubleday was now convinced that the *Diary* would "have a very wide and very profound appeal here in America." Once galleys were ready, she would send a copy "so that you will be able to tell how our edition will be."[12]

The following week, Zimmerman sent Otto a copy of the introduction provided by the "very enthusiastic" Mrs. Roosevelt. "I know that you must be anxious to see it," Zimmerman wrote. "We are enormously pleased, a fine tribute to the book."[13] (Meyer later asserted that Zimmerman herself had either written or significantly edited Roosevelt's text, a view to which Zimmerman herself lent credence some years after.[14]) Yet if Otto was pleased that the introduction would "make propaganda easier" and work toward financial success, he was equally concerned that commercial interests might be gaining an upper hand. "For me it is still more the human spirit that counts," he thought to remind Zimmerman and her colleagues.[15] And when Zimmerman's next letter, announcing that galleys were being sent, included additional promotional ideas for what "well might become a minor classic," Otto quickly repeated his thoughts on the importance of Anne's ideas. Mrs. Roosevelt's introduction, "a splendid piece, not too long and very impressive," had cheered his heart. "I felt that she understood Anne and she picked out her ideals in many of the letters Anne was writing. Human spirit—peace! Let us hope that her introduction will inspire many people," as he hoped Anne's Diary would.[16]

But nowhere in Mrs. Roosevelt's introduction or in Otto's letter praising it was there any mention of Anne's growing awareness that her persecution was a function of the fact that Jews had been singled out for total extermination— and that such a phenomenon had been the culmination of a long history of attack against her people, whose fate and vision she had come to share. This was clearly not Otto's focus. He wished instead to see Anne as Mrs. Roosevelt had, as a symbol of their fight against the world's suffering.

Otto had repeatedly emphasized this image of Anne to Meyer and to Price in the past; now he hoped to share it with Zimmerman as well. Zimmerman soon fulfilled his wish. When she wrote a month later about the serialization of the Diary, she carefully explained that "although [Commentary] deals with Jewish affairs, it is primarily a magazine of general interest" with "an excellent reputation in this country among the general and not strictly Jewish market."[17] It was now clear to Otto that Meyer's emphasis on the Holocaust's victims as Jews, among them Anne, need no longer be a concern.

Whatever Otto's fear that Anne's thoughts might be overlooked, his interest in the commercialization of her work prompted him on March 6 to ask Meyer whether he had received a copy of the galleys.[18] They had just arrived, Meyer wrote back from New York, where he had relocated with his family. He assured Otto that "a very enthusiastic review" would appear in the New York Times now that he had been asked to write it. More important, Stanley

Kramer was now reading the copy of the *Diary* he had sent to him in Hollywood. Knocking on doors everywhere, Meyer was about to submit the *Diary* to one of television's best directors with a suggestion for a one-hour treatment. He promised to involve Otto immediately in any response he received, and similarly asked to learn of any possibilities that Otto might be discussing. Repeating his desire to attempt the adaptation, Meyer promised Otto to retain Anne's voice in whatever medium might be employed. "I hope that if you receive any film or stage inquiries, you may direct them to me as I would very much want the opportunity to work on such an adaptation, for I am sure that it will come, and must be done tenderly, and with utmost fidelity."[19]

Meyer wrote again four days later, detailing his various efforts on the *Diary*'s behalf. Having reread the translation, he was more enthusiastic than ever and had begun to pressure the *New York Times* into allowing a far lengthier review than had been planned so that a "groundswell of prepublication interest" would be generated. Yet in spite of this deepening commitment to the *Diary*, he needed to know whom Otto preferred as his agent in matters beyond the book's publication. "I will try to do the things an agent would normally do, but without obligating you in any way. . . . I say this again to make sure there is no embarrassment between us or between myself and Doubleday." Keenly aware of the dangers that might lie ahead, Meyer was prepared to step aside in their favor or to recommend an agent, should that be Otto's decision. "This book should have every chance, and I want to help out." His only real desire was "to adapt it should an opportunity arise."[20]

Otto was pleased that Meyer was willing to assume this responsibility. Without sufficient confidence in Doubleday, "not on financial reason, but because I did not want them to be able to do anything in a line unsuitable," he would rely on Meyer, "as you know more about these matters than I do." Nor did Otto wish to sign with another agent, preferring "to leave things in your hands, and to pay agents taxes to you. Why should another earn it when we know best what is in the line of Anne's book and that the ideas prevail?" He was, however, willing to offer Doubleday the same percentage he would have paid Little, Brown had they not insisted on controlling more than "a moral right by publishing and doing advertising." The exact amount he would leave to Meyer's discretion. "You can judge better what would be fair."[21]

Authorized by Otto to negotiate with publishers and producers, Meyer approached Doubleday several times over the next week, "transmit[ting] to them your feeling that you would not be averse to having them share film and play rights, should any arise." After extended discussions concerning the financial commitment that a dramatic production would involve, it had been agreed to "leave the matter open." Meyer advised Otto that "if there is a possible film and play offer," all sides would be able to negotiate without prior obligations of any kind.[22] "I think this is fair," Otto told Meyer, without relating how, through Zimmerman, the role of agent had already been promised to Doubleday.[23]

Meyer's repeated promise to search for a producer without seeking a commission for his efforts had simply been too good an offer for Otto to disregard. Once copies of the printed book were in his hands, Meyer said, he would "put on a real campaign." He had contacted Darryl Zanuck at Twentieth Century Fox five days earlier, outlining the Diary's story and mentioning his own wish "to work on the production." Meyer merely asked Otto for "what is normal . . . should I do the adaptation." He assumed, once again, that Otto would not "distort or misuse the book, for no version could be presented without your consent." Convinced "that an almost literal adaptation can be made, and that it will be effective provided it preserves the spirit of the book," Meyer had even suggested to Zanuck that it be shot in Amsterdam to guarantee greater authenticity.[24]

To further assist him with potential producers, Meyer asked for a written statement acknowledging his role as Otto's agent, suggesting that it read, "Meyer Levin is authorized to negotiate for motion picture, television, radio, and dramatic adaptation of Anne Frank: The Diary of a Young Girl, for a period of one year from this date, with the stipulation that I, as sole owner of these rights, shall require to approve any such agreements, and my adaptations of the material in this book, before public presentation."[25] Thanking Meyer for "all the explications," Otto immediately forwarded the authorization without altering Meyer's wording.[26]

Otto went on to ask Meyer whether portions of the Diary might be read aloud by Mrs. Roosevelt "for purposes of propaganda," as they previously had in Holland and Germany. But Meyer assured him that the book's promotion was in good hands. Such readings were unnecessary. Zimmerman, "who identifies herself with the book because Anne would be her age," was hard at work, doing all that she could to ensure the Diary "the attention it deserves." As for his own efforts, the New York Times was allowing him to double the length of his review, "an important presentation and I hope . . . a good augur." Similarly, "all those to whom I have presented the book have had a very warm reaction to it. We have not been turned down by anyone." Radio, television, film, and theater were each "seriously considering" its possibilities.[27]

In the meantime, Meyer planned to return to the novel he had begun in Paris. His growing family needed the money. He would find a place for the summer and spend his time more profitably than in "running around New York" seeking support for the many other projects he contemplated. Life as an artist was "too insecure," he confessed to Otto. He only hoped that his oldest child, Eli, though recently accepted at New York's High School of Music and Art, would find a more stable and lucrative career.[28]

In preparation for his absence from New York, Meyer contracted with

Howard Phillips "to act as my representative in disposal of the film rights, being myself authorized to Mr. Otto Frank, owner of these rights, to act as his agent for the sale." All proposals would, of course, continue to need the approval of both Otto and Meyer. Having forwarded a copy of this agreement to Otto on April 28,[29] Meyer actively continued his efforts as Otto's agent throughout the remaining weeks of spring, contacting both United Artists and Columbia Pictures after they responded positively to his initial approach. On June 9, the *Reader's Digest* film division thanked Meyer for the opportunity to consider the project, pleased to learn "about really good stories from friends who, like you, know what they are talking about."[30] And days after the *Diary*'s publication, *Variety* reported that Meyer was "agenting the tome for possible filmization or legit treatment."[31]

Yet if Otto welcomed Meyer's participation, he nonetheless had serious reservations. Choosing to leave them unspoken for the moment, he instead thanked Meyer for pursuing these possibilities and noted with particular pleasure the concession he had won from the *New York Times*. With the review's appearance on the front page of the *Book Review* only three days away, Otto urged Meyer to "keep contact," in expectation of the attention the book would receive once it reached the public.[32]

Of the "great many exciting things that have been happening this week," Zimmerman chose to begin her letter of June 12, the day of publication, with a discussion of Meyer's review. "This is one of the most important things to happen to any book, especially since the *Times* is the most influential paper in the country. The review itself is a beautiful one, both because the review is so wonderful and because of the great amount of space which has been allotted to it." With reviews appearing in other newspapers and magazines as well, all they "had been hoping for has happened. . . . I feel sure the sales will be extremely good. *Anne Frank* will receive a wonderful reception in America!" Sharing with Otto the excitement felt throughout Doubleday, she emphasized her own strong belief in the book's significance: "As a psychological, historical and a literary document . . . [it is] one of the very important Diaries of all time."[33]

Meyer could not have agreed more with Zimmerman's assessment. "It is so wondrously alive, so near, that one feels overwhelmingly the universalities of human nature," he wrote in the opening to his review in the *Times*, a point to which he returned at its conclusion. "Surely she will be widely loved, for this wise and wonderful young girl brings back a poignant delight in the infinite human spirit." But Anne had brought more than this to the world, Meyer pointedly reminded his readers, for "hers was perhaps one of the bodies seen in the mass grave at Bergen-Belsen." It was imperative, then, that her wish "to go on living after my death" be honored by allowing her to express "all that is in me," both the "unfolding psychosocial drama of a girl's growth" and the tragedy "of six million vanished Jewish souls." Both were intertwined "as an intimate whole."

"The double significance of this document . . . frees Anne's book from the horizontal effect of most diaries," Meyer argued impressively out of his "anguish in the thought of how much creative power, how much sheer beauty of living, was cut off through genocide." In Anne, the notion of universal suffering had assumed its human face in the specificity of Jewish victimization.[34]

Meyer stressed this idea of the particularization of the Holocaust in his *Congress Weekly* review the following day: "There has not been a single work which made the victims understandable as simple human beings. At last, the voice of the six million may be heard in America," not in an abstract or fictionalized account of the tragedy, but with the authenticity and consciousness of who and why the victims were made to suffer the unspeakable.

"In the flow of Anne Frank's intimate and tender book, there is the very pulse, the frightened but courageous pulse of the six million Jews who kept their faith in life to the very last moment, while waiting for the executioner," Meyer wrote. Emphasizing Anne's portrait of her family as more "conscious of their faith" than observant of "the essential traditions," he chose to quote at length what he saw as Anne's crucial affirmation of herself as a Jew (what Ludwig Lewisohn would identify in the *Saturday Review* as "her culminating insight"), written as her time in hiding was drawing to its fateful end:

> Who has inflicted this upon us? Who has made us Jews differently from all other people? Who has allowed us to suffer so terribly up till now? It is God who has made us as we are, but it will be God, too, who will raise us up again. If we bear all this suffering and if there are still Jews left, when it is over, then Jews, instead of being doomed, will be held up as an example. Who knows, it might even be our religion from which the world and all peoples learn good, and for that reason and that reason only do we have to suffer now. We can never become just Netherlanders, or just English, or representatives of any country for that matter, we will always remain Jews, but we want to, too.[35]

The overwhelmingly positive critical and commercial response to the *Diary* suddenly altered forever the positions previously held by Meyer and Doubleday concerning theatrical and film production. The morning after the *New York Times* review appeared, Zimmerman and Meyer cabled Otto. "May Doubleday have authority to handle these rights for you at usual agent's fee of 10% of proceeds? We feel strongly we could handle these rights in a way suitable to the book."[36]

But why had Meyer so quickly surrendered the independent role he had so carefully nurtured for nearly two years? Early the next morning Meyer's own cable to Otto arrived. "Please await my letter before answering Doubleday's request for agency power." As Meyer had explained in his letter to Otto the previous afternoon, "all [had been] attended to in [the] meantime."[37] Edmund Goulding, a director at Fox, would soon ask his studio "to buy the film rights for him." Added Meyer, "He agrees that the film should be made very faithfully, in Europe, and I am confident he is the kind of man who would handle it well."[38]

Meyer, of course, saw this advocacy as a part of his larger effort to secure his own position as the *Diary*'s playwright. "It is my hope to do the adaptation of this book," he had written Goulding the day after the *New York Times* review appeared, adding that he had received "two calls on it this morning," as further enticement for Goulding to move ahead quickly.[39] If Meyer had acquiesced to the pressure of Doubleday's sudden commercial interest, it had been solely to enhance Otto's position. As he explained to Otto in a second letter that morning, and would again in a deposition five years later,

> when Doubleday received the inquiries they found out that I was the person in control of this aspect, and Mr. Ken McCormick, the editor in chief of Doubleday, telephoned me, telling me that my review had made the book an overnight success, that they were out of copies, that they expected great things for it now, that there were inquiries about the dramatic rights, and that he had a request to make of me. The request was that I permit, or that I recommend to Mr. Frank that Doubleday should become the agents for the film and dramatic rights, because Doubleday could do as he put it a better job of negotiation than I, a writer unaccustomed to such negotiations on a highly commercial level, could do. I told him that I had never been interested in handling these business negotiations. That I was sure they could do better.[40]

"I did not want in any way to stand between you and Doubleday at this time, as their full enthusiasm should continue, in order to take advantage of the wonderful start the book has received," he had written Otto on June 16, sincerely believing that the publisher could better represent his financial interests. But there was more at stake here, about which Meyer had asked Otto not to respond to Doubleday before receiving his explanation and advice:

> As you know, I have from the beginning, even before there was an American publisher, had my heart in making a play and a film from this material. If I had the money, I would have offered to buy the rights from you. I have tried to be the agent for the book until now in the hope that I could secure an arrangement whereby I would do the writing for the play or film. I think that I can honestly say that I am as well qualified as any other writer for this particular task; indeed I feel I would do the best job, or I wouldn't be writing to you now to ask you to keep this task for me, as far as possible. I would therefore like you to stipulate to Doubleday, if you care to do so, that they have the agency rights and the rights to ten percent of the value of

any sale, but that no sale shall be made unless the conditions of the agreement are approved by me, and by yourself. It would then be possible for either one of us to stipulate that I should be the writer, or at least one of the writers, in any play or film treatment. Of course, should the situation arise where a production by a famous playwright is possible only if I step aside, I would step aside. However, I should be heartbroken if the material were sold to some producer who would simply appoint any friend of his to write the play or film. Also, from your own point of view of safeguarding the artistic content of the material, I think it wise to keep control through a consultant, and I hope you are satisfied that I am the right one. Even in our previous agreement making me the agent, I wrote you that I would not take an agency fee, but would hope to do the writing, and that is still what I want. And as you had previously said that you thought it fair for Doubleday to have a share in any such sales, giving them a 10% agency commission will take care of the two matters at one time.

As before, Meyer proposed a cable for Otto to send that would allow Double-day its role as broker and his as scriptwriter: "Consent to Doubleday as film and play agent providing conditions of any sale of such right be approved by Meyer Levin and myself. Desire Meyer Levin as writer or collaborator in any treat-ment."[41]

Though torn by several interests—the propagation of Anne's ideas as he saw them, the desire to see this accomplished through other media beyond publication, and the need to be fair to Meyer—Otto agreed to the proposed cable, but with a modification designed to limit Meyer's influence over any future developments. Doubleday was not merely to act as agents in some general way but, more specifically, with "authority to handle film and play rights with [the] usual agent fee." Final approval would rest with Otto alone, while Meyer's role would be limited to the Diary's adaptation, as long as his work remained faithful to the "idea of [the] book."[42] As worded, the cable would now afford Otto the escape he would exercise in the months ahead, using against Meyer his own less guardedly worded offer to step aside should a "famous playwright" wish to write the adaptation. Worried that his cable would upset Meyer, Otto immediately expressed his thanks for all he had done to promote the book, including a recent radio appearance. Promising to do "all I can" to support Meyer's interests, he hoped that Meyer, in return, would agree with his decision. "If you have any remarks, kindly make them frankly," he added disarmingly.[43]

By this time, Zimmerman's own letter of explanation concerning her joint cable with Meyer had arrived in Holland. Doubleday was protecting not only Otto's own interests, she stressed, but Meyer's as well: "It has been difficult for Mr. Levin, I believe, to deal with these people [producers] without an active organization behind him and it seemed to us likely that the situation could get out of hand." To help Meyer avoid this difficulty, she proposed that Doubleday's "successful and competent department" work with him "closely" so that the *Diary* would be handled "suitably and with taste." Doubleday, she promised, would "insist" upon this "to the best of our ability."[44]

But in truth Doubleday's concern was far less altruistic. As Zimmerman wrote Price that same day, "Although Levin himself was *not* after selling the rights for base financial reasons, he seemed to be screwing up the whole deal and I think, as Ken [McCormick] does very strongly, that it would be best if we handled the rights and worked closely with Levin."[45] Meyer's role was to be redefined from that of adapter, as Otto had promised, to "advisor and collaboratory agent," entitled to share half of Doubleday's agent's fee.[46]

Otto was clearly uneasy with this change. Yet however troubled he was at seeing Meyer's role becoming little more than that of a consultant working alongside another writer, he still wished to believe "that everything can be settled in the sense of close understanding," regardless of all that Meyer was about to lose:

> Mr. Levin did a lot for the book and is entirely filled with it. I know that he understands Anne perfectly and therefore I have all confidence in him. On the other hand I imagine that no one who buys the rights wants to have a prescription what he has to do. How do we get over this point? I do not want to handicap your endeavors and on the other hand want to be fair to Mr. Levin and want to keep the style and the ideas of the book and a certain influence in the matter. Of course I know that a film producer has his own ways and knows how to attract the public. It is his affair and I have to compromise. The film will probably not be quite what the book is, but the main thing is to keep the general idea. Any suggestions you propose in this sense are alright. The ideal solution would be if Mr. Levin would be convenient to the person interested. Then everything would be easy.[47]

Further discussions between Doubleday and Meyer only demonstrated how compromised his position had become. "Trying to be [as] objective as I can," he wrote Otto in self-defense, "I should say that my outstanding qualification for this book is the fact that I have specialized in this kind of material, since the war, so that my feeling for it is very high." Few others could make such a claim, and certainly none of the "famous dramatists, such as Maxwell Anderson, who may become interested in doing this dramatization." Doubleday had already been approached by a number of "highly successful people," several previously secured by Meyer himself. "It is here that my problem arises," he naïvely alerted Otto. Having worked out the best possible arrangement he could negotiate, given his now weakened position, it was still "suggested . . . that if definite offers were received from theatrical producers, naming dramatists of the first rank for the task . . . I [should] collaborate on the adaptation. That we would give preference to whichever dramatist accepted me as collaborator. That if no first rank 'name' dramatist offered to adapt the play, I should have preference over other writers. That if the situation should come down to the point where only one producer wanted to do the show, and where he would accept only a dramatist who refused to have a collaborator, the decision as to whether I should step aside would have to be made by someone other than myself."

With Doubleday's insistence, Meyer had agreed to accept half of the agent's commission. Yet his real concern remained the *Diary*'s adaptation. He continued to press his case, diplomatically reminding Otto that he and not Doubleday should be the final arbiter in this matter. Fearful for himself and the *Diary*, Meyer warned Otto that he would "undoubtedly be approached by many people who will try to influence you for one person or another" now "that the possibilities can involve several hundred thousand dollars." "There is also the possibility that an 'important' playwright might try to inject too much of himself," he further cautioned, before adding, "that even the most important of them have had many failures, and that some of them are no longer at the height of their powers."[48]

Throughout these many months, Tereska had maintained her own purely personal relationship with Otto. As someone who deeply admired his daughter's writing, she cared for him both as Anne's father and as a man forced to go on after his family had been so brutally destroyed. They had corresponded, met, and telephoned, enjoying their contact and expressing interest and concern for each other and their respective families. But the nature of this relationship had now changed. Guardedly, she reminded Otto that Meyer had worked tirelessly on his behalf, accounting in part for the great success the *Diary* enjoyed. Surely he could see how important Meyer's continuing efforts were in "find[ing] people who really understand it."[49]

By June 23, Meyer and his family had moved to Fire Island. Two hours from New York, he hoped to escape the summer heat and to block out as much uninterrupted time as possible for the novel he had begun—and, perhaps, to work on the *Diary*'s theatrical adaptation. His previously empty field was now crowded and there was little time left before whatever small advantage he might still possess would be lost forever. When Meyer went to New York for the day to see "two top-class producers," Tereska took the opportunity to again remind Otto of her husband's well-deserved role in the process. Including news of the day's meetings, she spoke of Meyer's preference for one producer in particular "because he has produced really good and intelligent plays. . . . He could be right for Anne's book, as he understands it well."[50]

But Zimmerman continued her own efforts, writing that same day of the great commercial success that the *Diary* was enjoying as "one of the biggest books that has been published in America in a long time." And while she did not wish to speak about "dramatic rights," she felt compelled to mention the many offers Doubleday had received "from the most important playwrights in America today!" Knowing that Otto would soon be in contact with Price, she further emphasized how as Doubleday's European representative, he had been "an enthusiastic advocate of Anne's *Diary* from the very beginning."[51]

Following his talks in New York, Meyer had yet another frustrating meeting with Doubleday, after which he had telephoned Otto seeking information for an assignment with the *New York Post* on those hiding with the Franks or assisting in their survival. It had been a tiring and upsetting day, and before setting out for home, he cabled a cautionary note to Otto, apparently in somewhat of a panic—"Await my letter regarding dramatic offers."[52] Had he read Zimmerman's letter to Otto, with its attempt to counter any feelings of loyalty toward Meyer, he would have found the journey home that afternoon even more painful. For Zimmerman was slowly helping Otto to abandon Meyer, instilling growing confidence that she, Price, and the others at Doubleday were as equally committed to Anne as was Meyer, and better able to conduct the business that lay ahead.

Later that evening, aware that Price was in Amsterdam and that Doubleday would be contacting Otto the next day, Meyer wrote as promised. "I must present my point of view to you as forcibly as I can," he insisted, before reviewing the "seven offers of production from highly placed producers" now under serious consideration by him. Three had stated no prior preference of a playwright, while three others "are quite willing to let me do the play." Only one had specifically stipulated the playwright. But "Doubleday, as a big firm, leans to the big operator." This was a mistake, Meyer advised Otto. In "a matter of creative works, no one could guarantee whose would be better."[53]

It was Meyer's hope that in reaching a final decision, Otto would "keep this Anne's book by choosing [him] to adapt." Minimally, he should insist upon Meyer's collaboration should someone like Anderson, Doubleday's present choice, be given the nod. In a meeting called by Jospeh Marks, a Doubleday vice president, Anderson had told Meyer that he could not accept him as his collaborator. It had all proven terribly painful for Meyer, leaving him to wonder whether Marks had arranged the meeting merely "to so embarrass me that I would back down in the face of this important playwright."[54]

Instead, Meyer urged Otto not to allow Anderson "to take the whole thing for himself," for above all else there remained the far larger issue of the play's faithfulness to the *Diary* itself. "Here I think I am the right person." Anderson's recent work had been "heavy-handed" and a critical failure. More important, Anderson was unfamiliar with the total experience that cried out to be portrayed. He was certain to distort the *Diary* and overshadow Anne's thoughts with his own. "If he writes the play it will undoubtedly be known as Maxwell Anderson's play about the little girl, what was her name? It seems to me that the play should be identifiable as Anne's work."

To further ensure the script's fidelity, he insisted that only a Jewish writer be allowed to tackle the task ahead. "You may not think this is a point— Anderson is not a Jew." As with John Hersey's story of the Warsaw Ghetto, *The Wall*, Anderson's play would be doomed to a level of inauthenticity that could be avoided. At the risk of appearing too "nationalistic," he stressed the need for "writing honestly about Jews" and the difficulties one encounters as a Jewish writer in attempting to do just that. "Naturally, I would like in this case to have the opportunity myself."[55] Such "prestige" as Anderson might bring to the project, Meyer wrote Otto again the next morning, would be offset by the damage his style would cause. "Several more people" with whom he had consulted that day had agreed. Nor was it needed. "Anne was able to write the book without such aid, and I think I can dramatize it just as well."[56]

Otto was cordial when Meyer telephoned on the twenty-third. Pleased to hear from him and Tereska, Otto repeated his belief that all could be settled amicably, even if Meyer's role had been redefined. A letter from Otto followed, outlining the information that Meyer had again requested that day. Thanking Meyer for his "elaborate letter" detailing the various production offers, Otto once again promised "not [to] decide anything or give any authorization without first having been in touch with you and Doubleday. . . . Let us hope the results will be gotten and of course I want you to have a share, both financially and as a writer."[57]

In acknowledging Otto's letter, Meyer excused himself for continuing to be "not in the best condition to think clearly" because of a "poison ivy infection" that was slow to heal. Still, he was able to send another densely written description of several new producers who had spoken with him in the last three days. Among them was Cheryl Crawford, "the outstanding woman in the theatrical field," with a record of twenty-five years of success with the Theatre Guild, the Group Theatre, and as an independent.[58] Crawford's press agent, Wolf Kaufman, had first approached Meyer about her role as the play's producer, while Crawford, recalling her interest in one of Meyer's plays in the 1930s, was agreeable to his adapting the *Diary* for her.[59] (Crawford's friend Leah Salisbury, an agent soon to be involved with the *Diary*, had written her in 1943, after reading Meyer's play *Dupont Circle*, that "he writes like nobody's business."[60]) "Her idea is to have me make a dramatization while working closely with her and the director, and if the dramatization is not right, another writer would be called in for extra work," as was "often done and seems reasonable to me."

Otto needed to be patient and "to hold back" from signing any contracts "until everything is really clear and sure," Meyer advised. "A few more days makes no difference, as the work is going ahead full steam" now that he himself had begun to write the script.[61] Though thankful for Otto's assurance that he wanted him "to work on the material as a writer," Meyer was deeply concerned and angered that Doubleday was "exerting all sorts of pressure upon you to eliminate this condition," including the accusation that Meyer was an "opportunist." Reminding Otto that his loyalty to the Diary had persisted "longer and more fervidly than the Doubledays and the Markses," he once again cautioned Otto not to accept Doubleday's choice but to allow him to present "the first sketch" which could then be used in a collaborative effort, if necessary, "as Cheryl Crawford suggests."[62]

Tereska had spoken with Otto the day Meyer had again telephoned him and had found something in the tenor of his response that prompted her to send him a seven-page, strongly worded defense of her husband's stake in the play or film that was now all but a certainty: "From what I know [of] the situation . . . for the moment," it had become obvious that in blatant violation of the agreement reached between the three parties only days before, "Doubleday wants a famous name to write the play and tries to push away all other producers willing to take Meyer as a writer."

So minimal had Doubleday's prepublication faith in the Diary been that a mere three thousand copies had been printed. Only after Meyer's review had caused this first printing to be sold out within the first hours of business the next morning, while one producer after another telephoned about rights to the property, was Doubleday's interest piqued. "Harassing him to take them as agents for theatrical and movie rights," Meyer had capitulated, convincing himself that it was in the book's best interest. This, Tereska stressed, was Meyer's fatal mistake. "As soon as Doubleday had Meyer accept for them to send you their first telegram about them becoming agents, they tried to get rid of Meyer. It's been an incredible and (in a detached way) fascinating thing to watch—the big company against the writer who was not their writer!" Where once they lacked faith in the Diary, now they lacked faith in Meyer, preferring "a big American name for the big public," someone who could not write "for Anne, as she would have liked it, and as near to her diary as possible."

Though uncertain that Meyer's own treatment would prove successful, she was convinced that no one else would bring as much "heart, comprehension, and talent" as he. "He loves sincerely and truly the book of Anne." Had he not demonstrated this repeatedly over the past two years? Now that producers, smelling success and profit, were reversing their earlier decisions and approaching Meyer about rights to the Diary, "with Meyer as writer," he was experiencing Doubleday's subversiveness. Each time Meyer would refer them to Marks, in accordance with their agreement, "Doubleday's people . . . [would] try to dissuade them and to propose . . . their own writers," causing great confusion for the would-be producers. With whom, they wondered, were they to negotiate?

To move forward, Tereska advised Otto to decide upon a producer. Until that choice had been made, nothing else could be accomplished. But in doing so, Otto had to make the commitment to Meyer that was his due, or at least be forthright with him. *"Do you want Meyer to try to write that play for her?"* Tereska insisted upon knowing, underlining the question to emphasize her demand. "Your decision at this point is 'indispensable.'"[63]

Tereska's appeal arrived too late to influence Otto's thinking. While she sat composing her carefully reasoned argument, he was in the process of mailing Meyer the decision he had reached after "long talks" with Price, that "in the question of playwright," Meyer would at best collaborate. "You can imagine how exciting all the news are for me and how difficult to judge," he tried to explain on June 28, as much for his own benefit as for Meyer's. Although Otto, too, was conflicted, it was clear that any dispute between Meyer and Doubleday would be decided in the latter's favor. "I have faith in you but I also have in Doubleday after all they did, knowing Mr. Price and reading the beautiful letters of Miss Zimmerman."

"I do not know what to say and hope that we shall get to an understanding on all sides," Otto continued. "I hate the idea of misunderstanding between you and Doubleday." Surely, "all we are working for is to do things in the sense of Anne." Absolving himself of any involvement in whatever disputes might soon arise, Otto noted that he would himself ultimately be powerless, that even if he retained a "veto right," he would no longer control the product once a contract with a producer was signed. "Even if you have the right and a powerful man wants to do differently, he will. What can you do—Start a lawsuit?" Otto concluded, believing this an impossibility.

Most shocking of all for Meyer, however, was Otto's position concerning the Jewish element of his daughter's story. "As to the Jewish side you are right that I do not feel the same way you do. I always said that . . . it is not a Jewish book . . . though Jewish sphere, sentiment and surrounding is the background. . . . So do not make a Jewish play of it!" Otto admitted, "I never wanted a Jew writing an introduction for it"; he saw it as a book "read and understood more by gentiles. In some way of course it must be Jewish, even so that it works against antisemitism." But this, too, he placed in a context that could render Anderson an acceptable choice. "If Anderson did not work on Jewish problems he certainly worked on discrimination." Otto had read Anderson's *Lost in the Stars*, a work that had left him "strongly impressed. It is on a high level and I could imagine that he would bring Anne to a high level, too, even if it is not as a whole identifying."[64]

Could Otto have so missed the point of Anne's *Diary*? Did her experience and ideas need to be brought to "a high level," Meyer must have wondered in amazement and concern? Fearing that his letter "sounds harsher than I mean it," Otto wrote Meyer again two days later with the "hope that you understand my feeling towards you and how split I am." He insisted that "we all did our best to give the book the right start. We all want to keep the high level."[65]

Otto need not have worried that Meyer had misunderstood. He had heard it all before when the same "series of respectable (and largely Jewish) American publishers," possessed of assimilationist doubts and fears not unlike Otto's, had at first refused to publish his own *In Search*. Much of postwar Jewry still clung to the notion that Jewish cultural self-identification was a disability and that greater acceptance by the larger society would be found the further one traveled down the road of religious and ethnic denial. But here and now, with Anne's *Diary*, was to be found "at long, long last the book that makes us live with all the Jews who disappeared in Europe."

Meyer could no longer countenance the self-deprecation that had failed to shield so many from Hitler's wrath. In answer to all who would silence a Jewish voice far more important than his, he wrote in a third review published that same day that Anne "records what she thinks about being a Jew." Under the title, "At Long Last We Have a Real Story of Jews Under Nazism," he urged the Jewish community and its leading organizations to use "their public relations funds . . . to disseminate this book and its contents, in every possible form." They "could do nothing more useful" than to employ Anne's *Diary* in the service of her people. While Otto hoped to raise his daughter's experience to what he and others believed to be "a high level," Meyer wanted Jew and non-Jew alike to hear only her voice, "for this little girl's day-to-day story explains [the Holocaust] to us better than a thousand treatises, sermons, and surveys. Anne Frank, one little girl, at last leads us back into contact with six million souls whose fate was like her own."[66]

CHAPTER THREE

A Particularly Powerful Force
Against Bigotry

long list of producers interested in the *Diary* appeared in the July 2 issue of *Variety*. In a story almost certainly placed by Marks, Doubleday was said to have "received [these] queries."[1] Nowhere was Meyer mentioned, either as Otto's representative or as a possible playwright for the adaptation.

Meyer had inadvertently learned as well that Otto had been invited to New York by Doubleday to discuss the entire matter of theatrical agency and production. Frustrated with what he saw as Marks's duplicity, Meyer wrote Otto that Marks had "made everyone feel . . . that the rights will go to someone who doesn't want me" as the script's writer. Even those producers whom he had referred to Marks were suddenly considering others. "My dismay over the situation is not because other names are being mentioned, but because Mr. Marks has been dishonest in the way he handled it with me. I have absolute proof of this from four producers who are ready to put it in writing." In his first venture into the theater, Marks appeared willing to do whatever was needed to secure the "big deal." For the well-being of the *Diary*, it was imperative that Otto know what was happening, as much as it was for Meyer himself to be able to plead his case. Until Marks had intervened, "you seemed to have no doubts about me as a writer, even a few weeks ago, as you were willing to specify in your cable that I should adapt or collaborate in the adaptation. . . . You have been persuaded since then that it would be better to have someone else."

Doubleday's motive was purely commercial. But why had Otto so readily acquiesced when, as he had so often told Meyer, financial considerations were not paramount? It had now become clear to Meyer that if they shared a concern for Anne's "ideas" and how best to disseminate them, then only a differing understanding of her *Diary* could have caused this abandonment. "As to the Jewish question," Meyer wrote cautiously, "I should explain a little better what I meant." Sensitive to the assimilationist argument against expressing a strong Jewish identity in a dominantly Christian society, he steered the discussion away from the ideological issue and onto the question of fidelity to the text. While John Hersey "had made a very earnest effort" with his description of the Warsaw Ghetto uprising in The Wall, it seemed evident to many "that he had somehow not been able to feel with the people of Warsaw and to bring alive the Jewish characters." Not that it was impossible to make the imaginative leap required, but the odds of doing so were too narrow to risk. "I don't mean to say it is a rule that no artist can successfully create people of another group than his own, this would be absurd. But nevertheless the chances are better with an artist from the same group, and the very simple proof of this is that most writers describe their own people. That is why I feel that a non-Jew would be handicapped with this material. As a collaborator, it wouldn't matter, but alone, I think it does."[2]

That same day, unaware of Meyer's growing concern and frustration, Otto sent word that he might soon be in the States. Zimmerman had written of the need for him to deal with the issues of adaptation and production firsthand, now that so much interest had been generated. Doubleday was anxious to finalize arrangements with one or another producer, and with a writer other than Meyer. "So I went to the Consulate right away," Otto told Meyer, while hoping that the several weeks' wait for a visa might make the trip unnecessary. "Perhaps you decided already in the meantime?" Otto asked, appearing as unaware as Meyer of Doubleday's surreptitiousness.[3]

The following day, having heard from Doubleday that Otto was indeed planning to come to New York, Meyer once again presented his case to him, blaming Marks for the delay in signing a producer, which in turn had slowed the writing process itself. "You could have come here to see a good first draft of a script," he argued, "confident of my ability in the techniques of play-writing. The rest . . . is the material to be dealt with, and that is Anne's, and the general quality and sensitivity of the adaptor, of which in this case I think you are convinced," as, he believed, were the various producers who had approached him, including Cheryl Crawford. Yet Meyer had come to recognize how sharply he and Otto differed concerning "the Jewish point." To allay Otto's growing concern that he might somehow interject the same degree of Jewishness found in his film and memoir, Meyer offered a lengthy explanation of his position:

> I did not mean to suggest that I would write a "Jewish" play. I wrote you my point of
> view knowing you might disagree, but out of the sense that I should not withhold
> what is to me important. The emphasis was on the lack of opportunities open to

Jewish writers to deal with their own material, not on any undue emphasis they might give to the Jewish quality of the material. In my view, an adaptor should simply try to put the book on the stage with the very best of dramatic technique, but without in any way changing the emphasis of what is in the book. It should be as Anne would have written it, were she the playwright. My function, as I see it, or any adaptor's function, would be to do this, and not to inject his own ideas, his own art, his own personality.[4]

Meyer experienced a temporary stay when Doubleday unexpectedly withdrew as Otto's agent on July 7. The publisher's decision, Meyer wrote, had come "as a climax of my difficulties with Mr. Marks," including a stormy meeting at which Marks refused to talk with Sheppard Taube, a producer whom Meyer had invited. But for Doubleday, the withdrawal would prove to be a wise tactical move, perhaps predicated on a belief that Meyer's inability to finalize arrangements with a producer would drive Otto back into the publisher's camp. Confident that Doubleday was now permanently out of the picture, Meyer hastened to remind Otto of his continuing "wish to be the writer" and offered him an analysis of each of the ten producers he had found interested in the *Diary*—Cheryl Crawford, Max Gordon, Leland Hayward, Joshua Logan, Sheppard Taube, Kermit Bloomgarden, Maxwell Anderson, Norman Rose, Robert Whitehead, and Harold Clurman. Of these, Meyer's first choice was Crawford, who in lengthy conversation had evinced "a sensitivity and understanding which I think would be desirable for this play."[5]

Crawford appeared to be equally positive about Meyer's role in the *Diary*'s adaptation. He would write the script, and a collaborator would be brought in only if Crawford found one necessary after reading his draft. She had specifically mentioned two close friends: Elia Kazan, her codirector at the Group Theatre, whose film *Gentleman's Agreement* had so powerfully portrayed anti-Semitism in America three years earlier, and Lillian Hellman, one of America's leading playwrights, who had cleverly indicated her interest in working with Meyer. Crawford's mix of Meyer, Kazan, and Hellman proved a goad to Hellman's efforts to gain control of the *Diary*, though she never understood what had happened. Twenty-five years later she spoke of it as an example of the many theatrical "abortions" experienced by all producers—"those sperm that find the egg but don't produce a bouncing child"—and blamed Meyer for being "unable to accept the arrangements he had agreed to."[6]

Lillian Hellman had recently defended herself before the House Un-American Activities Committee, using the evasively worded statement written by her attorney, Joseph Rauh, to preclude all need to deny her Communist Party membership and support of Communist Front organizations beginning in the 1930s.[7] Hellman capitalized on this appearance as a part of the heroic myth she constructed for herself in later years, but Rauh acknowledged after her death, "There was never the slightest danger of her going to jail . . . and Hellman knew it." Nonetheless, she had emerged from the hearing with her future in Hollywood and on Broadway uncertain and with the single-minded desire for vengeance. "Don't touch me. You're dirty!" she told Budd Schulberg some time after he had offered HUAC his testimony, though they had been friends since their earliest days together as Hollywood writers.[8] So vivid was her memory of the anger and vindictiveness she had felt that she recorded a quarter of a century later in her memoirs of the period, *Scoundrel Time*, how "punished by what I thought was a group of political villains, I was evidently driven to find another kind of villain and another kind of punishment."[9]

Norman Podhoretz, a witness to the vindictiveness of both sides, later noted that "each engaged in secret name-calling and gleefully unearthed the most sordid motives to explain the other's views. Once again friendships were made and broken on the basis of political views alone, and self-righteousness reigned supreme, as it always does, on both sides of the sectarian fence."[10] So powerful were these emotions that Hellman's attack in *Scoundrel Time* upon Diana and Lionel Trilling, erroneously intimating that they had been supporters of Joseph McCarthy, still drew a response from Diana Trilling nearly twenty years later. "Lillian was one of the most charming and entertaining people I ever knew," she told a reporter. "She made everything lively. But she could also have a very ugly, ugly spirit. That book 'Scoundrel Time' was a disgrace. It was a total distortion of history."[11] Trilling's assessment was not without merit. Privately, Hellman attempted to justify tampering with the facts, telling Zimmerman four years after the book appeared, "Nobody can ever say they told the complete truth."[12]

Kazan's decision to testify before the committee later qualified him for Hellman's contempt. (Crawford, despite her sympathies for the Soviet peoples' struggle against their former oppressors, was able to overlook his decision, perhaps because of her own experience with an attempted takeover of the Group Theatre by avowed Communist members some years earlier.[13]) Kazan's attack upon anti-Semitism made him doubly offensive to Hellman, who had long held negative feelings concerning her own Jewish identity. Meyer's Jewish ethnicity and Zionism similarly made him a target of her wrath. Both positions were antithetical to the Stalinist ideology to which she adhered ever more fervently in the face of HUAC's challenge. "I think there are more of us who have a positive reaction to our development as Jews," Meyer had written in the *New York Herald Tribune* four years earlier. "We enjoy being Jews. We come out with a plus instead of a minus." And although "there have always been Jews who felt better as non-Jews, we hold no rancor toward them."[14] As he added two years later, assimilationists appeared to be suffering from "psychic cancers, ugly secret growths that our people have so long buried in their souls."[15] Hellman would confirm this, stating with pride as late as 1981, "I myself make very anti-Semitic remarks. . . . I wasn't brought up as a Jew. I know almost nothing about being one—I'm sorry to say—though not sorry enough to go to the trouble of learning." There seemed to Hellman no real point to the effort. "I don't want it to alter my point of view about things."[16]

Hellman had, in fact, repeatedly ignored the anti-Semitic attacks of the Soviets, the frequency of which had steadily increased since the 1930s, becoming more organized with Stalin's campaign for "the purity of Russian art" in 1942.[17] Festering for the next several years, Stalin's anti-Semitic designs would prominently surface again in late January 1949, when a *Pravda* editorial, "On an Unpatriotic Group of Theater Critics," declared that "the disengagement of [Jewish] writers from the life and struggle of the Soviet people leads to sorrowful and fateful results." Their "shameless cosmopolitanism," the editorial continued in a manner reminiscent of the Nazi characterization of Jews as vermin in need of extermination, was "as harmful as the parasites that gnaw at the roots of useful grain." Here were "people contaminated with the remnants of bourgeois ideology who still try to poison the healthy, creative atmosphere of Soviet art with their noxious breath." Only those engaged "in the struggle for communism" were "on the right path."[18] Three weeks later, *Izvestiya* provided a solution for those not properly rooted in this struggle. "Wipe Out the Unpatriotic Group of Drama Critics," it demanded, condemning "these rootless cosmopolitans [who] have disseminated deleterious bourgeois ideas." And to this previously identified "Group" were added those "cosmopolitans who had found refuge in film making" as well.[19] By April the campaign's swift effectiveness had virtually destroyed Jewish culture throughout the Soviet empire, with important Jewish writers and artists imprisoned, many soon to be executed.[20]

So acceptably thoroughgoing had this purge of Jews from the arts become that the following year the Bolshoi Theatre canceled its long-scheduled production of Camille Saint-Saens's *Samson and Delilah* on the grounds that the opera "undoubtedly possesses messianic, biblical, and Zionist features." Even after a rewriting of the libretto, the government's Agitation and Propaganda Department would allege that "the main theme of persecuted and baited Jews who seek revenge for their destiny is sometimes brought to the fore." As such, it was likely to "play a negative role . . . as a stimulus for kindling Zionist sentiments among the Jewish portion of the population, especially if we take into account certain well-known facts of recent years." In February 1952, the Soviets would extend this effort to deemphasize the Jewish particularism of the Holocaust by suppressing the *Black Book* collection of Holocaust documents on the grounds that it was a product of "bourgeois Jewish nationalism." As such, it contained "serious political errors" and could not be published.[21]

This silencing of the Jewish artistic voice found its parallel in Hellman's treatment of Meyer and the *Diary* at the very time when Stalin's most notorious and potentially dangerous anti-Semitic attack was beginning to unfold, in the guise of what came to be known as the Doctors' Plot of 1953. Falsely accusing Jews of treason against the Soviet people as a part of an international scheme to destroy their just society (as Jews had already been convicted of in a Czech show trial the previous November), *Izvestiya* claimed on January 12 that "the disgusting face of this foul Zionist espionage organization has now been fully exposed." The paper accused "corrupt Jewish bourgeois nationalists" of conducting "extensive spying, terrorist, and other subversive activities."[22] Stalin's ultimate intent was to commit genocide against the entire Jewish population through a series of purges, pogroms, and, ultimately, deportation to camps in the East to "get rid of the rest." Only Stalin's death six weeks later stopped the readied transports.[23]

"I am not only not a well-known Zionist, but Zionists have accused me of being an anti-Zionist," Hellman wrote to the Jordanian Tourist Information Center in 1964, when attempting to gain a visa for a *Ladies Home Journal* assignment.[24] Zionists in America, she wrote in the article, "were angry that I wasn't."[25] In fact, those who knew Hellman—even those who agreed with her politics—had winced at the vehemence of her anti-Zionist and anti-Semitic sentiments.[26] She opposed Jewish immigration to the United States in 1940, accepted Stalin's anti-Semitic rejection of Benjamin Gitlow in favor of Earl Browder for leadership of the American Communist Party, and remained silent when Jewish writers were murdered by Stalin and again when news of the Doctors' Plot executions reached her, only to speak of the "Jewish vulgarity" she found a month later in Miami Beach. She expressed such feelings time and again, most shockingly one evening some three decades later, when she exclaimed that her Park Avenue apartment building was home to "an awful lot of kikes."[27]

As a thoroughly self-hating Jew and a Stalinist, Hellman found her Jewish ethnicity particularly troublesome, endangering both her carefully created persona and her claim of loyalty to what the Party considered to be the more worthy cause of universalism. Stalinist anti-Zionism was a convenient mask behind which she could hide her anti-Semitic feelings while directing them against those whose presence so sharply reminded her of what she wished to deny about herself. "Zionism is an atavism," she proclaimed, a part of her primitive ancestry that she had consciously worked to leave behind.[28]

In this she echoed Karl Marx himself. "The incapacity of Marxism in later years to cope with nationalism and ethnicity doubtless has many sources, but one of them is the rootless, godless Karl," the intellectual historian Frank Manuel has written in his *Requiem for Karl Marx*. Equally relevant is the "unbroken continuum between the émigré cannibalism of the 1850s in London and the triumphant Muscovite revolution devouring its children seventy years later," to which can be added the decades in America that led to Hellman's involvement with the *Diary*.[29]

Following Marx, Lenin had characterized Zionism as the work of "Jewish reactionary philistines" who "clamor against 'assimilation.' . . . Jews in the civilized world are not a nation, they have in the main become assimilated. . . . Jewish national culture is the slogan of the rabbis and the bourgeoisie, the slogan of our enemies." Zionists were "an enemy of the proletariat, a supporter of all that is *outmoded*." The true struggle of humanity was, ultimately, a struggle between this "bourgeois nationalism" and "proletarian internationalism."[30] Stalin had further prepared the foundation for the last of his Jewish purges by repeating and acting upon this charge throughout the period of his rule. His efforts culminated in the issuance of a new "Agitator's Handbook" to the Party membership days before the first Doctors' Plot arrests were made. Here, Zionism was again defined as the "reactionary nationalist trend of the Jewish bourgeoisie." Having lost his bid for a sphere of influence in the new Jewish state, Stalin angrily claimed that the "Zionists who seized power there were transforming the country into . . . a stronghold of reaction in the Near East"—unlike the ideal nationalist-free Jewish culture being pursued within his own borders. "While it is equally opposed to any manifestation of 'Jewish Nationalism,' the Soviet position is that its aim is a multi-national State in which Jews, like any other group, have a correct and proper place."[31]

The New York edition of the *Daily Worker*, the Party's official organ, had repeatedly opposed anti-Semitism and applauded Israel's earliest efforts as a sign of victory over Fascism. Yet many on its largely Jewish staff remained blind to Soviet anti-Semitism. Arguments articulated in Moscow against the Zionist leadership of the new Jewish state, and against Zionism itself as an international conspiracy to destroy the "Socialist" efforts of all peoples, were supported in New York. In a series of essays and editorials, the *Daily Worker* characterized the forced confessions and show trials central to the Doctors' Plot as positive acts in support of oppressed peoples everywhere. "What we here wish to emphasize," Louis Harap would write in the first part of a three week–long series, "is that the target was not Jews, but adherents of an ideology which is only one of a number held by Jews."[32] A month after Harap's series ended, the American Communist monthly *Masses and Mainstream* proclaimed "Leninist-Stalinist policy . . . a policy of struggle against bourgeois nationalism . . . the opposite of proletarian internationalism." Zionism, it declared, was "a major form of that bourgeois nationalism which is specifically Jewish."[33]

"In one form or another, the artist's work expresses a definite attitude toward this struggle," a writer in the *Daily Worker* had noted in 1946 with regard to the more general struggle against all bourgeois nationalist oppression. "And since the artist reaches people and has an impact on their ideas, emotions, and behavior, his work is a 'weapon' in the struggle."[34] Pablo Picasso, on the occasion of his seventieth birthday, echoed this imperative in a statement given to the Communist *Les Lettres Françaises* in 1950. The artist was to be "a political being, constantly alert," and his art "an instrument of offensive and defensive war against the enemy."[35] "Our specific intention is to fight on the cultural front, in the battle of ideas," and nowhere more importantly than in Hollywood, the editors of *Masses and Mainstream* wrote in their first issue.[36] Broadway, where "the theory that human nature is corrupt spreads its fumes like smog," was to be cleansed as well by the proper interpretation of the work of writers like Chekhov. (It may not be insignificant that Hellman would edit Chekhov's letters following her HUAC appearance.[37]) This purification would, in fact, take place "wherever people proclaim their love of humanity, their belief in art as an instrument of progress."[38] The task of the "greatest writers" was to act as "mirrors in which every man could test his conscience and know whether he stood with oppressor or oppressed."[39] According to Stalin's dictum, the writer was an "engineer of human souls helping to remold the consciousness of the people."[40]

At times this would force audiences to abandon reason and imagination, as it did the evening that James Earl Jones played the short, pale, Jewish son in Howard Fast's play *The Hammer*, performed before a left-leaning Jewish audience who sat in disbelief.[41] In the name of ideological purity, material written out of a specific ethnic consciousness had, in the same period as the *Diary*, been denied the reality its authors had intended to portray.

Meyer had years earlier voiced his objection to this misuse of the creative process, cautioning his fellow playwrights in a 1931 essay to remember that while "the artist impulse is generally to the left," as was his own, he must not violate "the distinction between art and propaganda" by making "heroes of people instead of seeking, as an artist, for deeper implications within them." The artist "must avoid externally imposed themes," Meyer had argued vigorously in "Playwriting and Protest." "To set out with the mere purpose of protest, to select one outrage or another . . . and then to write a play, cannot be a natural procedure. But if among the characters that grow within an author's mind there are people who have suffered any of these outrages, if among them he finds one who is expressive of a typical rent strike or of a case of racial discrimination, he has a work to write that may become a proletarian work, or a work otherwise of social significance. But the writer must keep himself from joining a race to a popularly cried goal, even if that goal be the creation of 'proletarian' literature. He must keep his own pace, go his own way." Above all, "writers are artists" whose "cry for justice in times of widespread horror . . . must arise from within . . . and not in trivial obedience to some leader's trumpet."[42]

Among the many tributes to Stalin following his death, Masses and Mainstream declared him "the liberator of peoples to whom turn not only the surviving Jewish ghetto fighters, but the whole of humanity." Yet nowhere in this article commemorating the Warsaw Ghetto Uprising was the Holocaust mentioned. Instead, the uprising was portrayed as a "turning point" in the "final battle . . . of the international working class."[43] And when the same journal published a poem entitled "The Six Million," their identity and the role of this identity in their being selected for murder would be left unspoken as a part of the mythology of a common fate for all humanity.[44]

"Lillian Hellman Defies Un-Americans' Witchhunt" was the headline on a lead article in the Daily Worker the morning after her appearance before HUAC, and in a Masses and Mainstream listing of authors whose work had been "Banned, Branded, Burned," she would take a center position in August 1953.[45] Hellman often claimed not to be political, yet she was drawn to this arena, her views purely black and white, sides drawn, conflict engaged, opposing all who disagreed.[46] By the mid-1930s, she had read and committed herself to Lenin and Stalin; later she fiercely defended Stalin's butchery as "the watchdog of Party orthodoxy," even after it had been revealed by Nikita Khrushchev.[47] Realizing the depth of this commitment in his client, and her unwillingness to be critical of Communist Party activities, Rauh had in 1952 advised Hellman before her forthcoming appearance before HUAC to "seriously consider whether a forthright declaration that you had been wrong in joining . . . is not the only road to follow here," lest "you just confirm what the House Committee is setting out to prove."[48] For Hellman, after first defending the Hitler-Stalin Pact, had now willingly accepted Stalin's notion that the war against Germany was the ultimate struggle by which a "free world for all men" would be secured, as she had written in her 1943 play The North Star, apparently untroubled, then as earlier, by the hypocrisy of the 1939 Hitler-Stalin Pact. The Holocaust thus became for her a mere extension of the peoples' struggle against Nazism. As a leading Jewish character in her play proclaimed before his fellow Russians, "We are a people." Even the murdered children of the Lodz Ghetto were never identified by Hellman as Jews.[49]

Theater was meant to be propaganda, Hellman asserted in 1939 in accord with Stalin, and the means by which a moral message was to be brought to the people, however great the distortion of fact and thought. "Unless you are a pathological escapist, there must be some sort of propaganda in everything you write," she insisted, a belief she extended to the writing of film reviews for the nascent newspaper *PM* some months afterward.[50] Yet she disingenuously claimed thirty years later not to have "deliberately set out to write propaganda," though she had consciously made the characters in her plays the tools whereby these ideas could be expressed.[51] As she argued when reviving *The Children's Hour* in a 1952 Kermit Bloomgarden production, "It's not about the liar, it's about the lie!"[52]

She herself recorded near the end of her life that "in the three memoir books I wrote, I tried very hard for the truth . . . but the truth as I saw it, of course, doesn't have much to do with the truth."[53] "What a word is truth," she wrote in the preface to her novelistic memoir, *Maybe*. "Slippery, tricky, unreliable. I tried in these books to tell the truth, I did not fool with facts."[54] Her biographers would confirm that much of her autobiography was fabrication, citing dozens of indisputable instances.[55] The zenith of the attacks on Hellman's credibility was Mary McCarthy's televised accusation on the Dick Cavett Show that Hellman was a "dishonest writer" whose "every word . . . is a lie including 'and' and 'the.'" When Hellman filed a lawsuit against McCarthy, Diana Trilling added her understated corroboration, calling Hellman "a gifted writer of fictions."[56] "Hellman constantly rearranged unpleasant truths," Gore Vidal wrote of her many attempts "to appear other than" she was.[57]

"Everybody lies all the time," Hellman had written in her 1934 play *The Children's Hour*. "The bigger the lie, the better, as always," she would add when analyzing the play's theme during its 1952 revival (which she refused to allow Kazan to direct). At one point she claimed to have no recollection of how the play's story had come to her, only to admit, when pressed further, that her lover, Dashiell Hammett, had suggested it to her from an eighteenth-century British news account he had read.[58] "We all steal," Hellman told an interviewer in 1958. The real skill, she emphasized in teaching the art of playwriting at Harvard University, was in knowing "how to steal and yet make something your own."[59] She claimed to have "deliberately avoided rereading [Bernard Shaw's] 'Saint Joan'" while adapting Jean Anouilh's *L'Alouette* as *The Lark* in 1955, but similarities abounded in the "mish mash" that resulted. "I can't tell which is Anouilh's Joan and which is mine," she claimed, forever denying her theft from Shaw.[60] Anouilh, of course, recognized the interpolation of these and other ideas, objecting most strenuously to the injection of Hellman's own political beliefs into his play.[61]

Not until 1976 did Hellman grant a qualified acknowledgment to "the sins of Stalin Communism." There had been, she casually remarked in her fanciful memoir of the period, *Scoundrel Time*, "plenty that for a long time I mistakenly denied." But even then, she justified her poor moral judgment by citing, in a voice modified from that of an earlier draft, what she held to be the far more egregious acts of the "children of timid immigrants" who had failed to support her struggle against HUAC.[62] When subsequently called upon to defend this anti-Semitic reference to East European Jews, she simply replied, "Perhaps I worded it badly. I don't know."[63] Even this indefensible act found her evasive, fearing that her carefully tailored cover would unravel and she would have no choice but to face the truth of the moral charges laid against her.

By considering Meyer and Kazan (who was now directing Crawford's latest production, Tennessee Williams's *Camino Real*), Crawford had sealed the enmity between Hellman and herself.[64] Hellman would do all that she could to engineer the removal of Crawford from the project while making it a tool for her own propaganda—particularly now that the *Diary*, through its wide appeal, could become a useful instrument in the ideological struggle to which she was committed. Poor judgment had placed Crawford within the enemy camp of a congressional collaborator and an avowed Zionist, and Hellman could no longer trust her. Hellman, despite having been effectively censored by HUAC, was willing to censor and censure those who dissented from her millenarian's vision, and from what she had deemed necessary to achieve it.

After years of reflection, Budd Schulberg, a former member of Hellman's political circle in Hollywood, concluded that if she "ever got into power I think no one would ever have any freedom."[65] Others had perceived this danger from the American Communist Party many years before. As early as 1940, the editor of *The Nation* informed her staff that the Party had instructed her not to publish the work of those who appeared on a "blacklist" as violators of Party orthodoxy, either as Trotskyites or non-Marxist leftists.[66] That same year Benjamin Gitlow, who had by now broken with the group, acknowledged, "We in America sank so low in our ethical standards that we resorted to gangster tactics against fellow-Communists because they disagreed with us. That confronts us with the horrible speculation: had we Communists attained power in America, myself included, would we hesitate to go through with blood purges?"[67]

Neither Crawford nor Meyer had yet experienced the effects of Hellman's efforts by July 1952. Rather, having secured a producer, Meyer had advised Otto to allow him to go forward with the writing of the script while "the success of the book is still at its height." Now that "the feverish part of this matter" had passed, "it would . . . seem the simplest thing for me to go to work so as to lose no further time." All Meyer required was a "tentative agreement" with Crawford (or another producer, should Otto disagree with his choice) based upon a contract between her and Otto "as the owner of the rights." The right of adaptation would revert to Otto within "a few years" should a play not be produced, though Meyer believed this unlikely. "Something good will result," he promised.[68]

The arrival on July 8 of Meyer's cable and of another from Doubleday notifying Otto of their withdrawal as agents prompted Otto to reverse his earlier decision and to reaffirm his prior commitment to Meyer as his agent. "I never lost confidence in your person!!!! I won't do anything without your advice." In fact, Otto planned to do nothing until he came to New York, where he hoped "to get matters straight" with Doubleday. He advised Meyer that they need not rush into any arrangements, particularly because he was a "terribly nervous man near to a breakdown and *must* be careful not to hasten matters." Nowhere in his letter, however, did Otto discuss Meyer's role as the writer, preferring instead to remain silent on this issue.[69]

But arrangements were already being made, as Crawford wrote Otto the next day. Knowing that Meyer "has talent," she had granted him "the first opportunity" to write the script. Kazan, as the director, would then assist in dramatizing the material. Meyer would be given eight weeks. If he failed, another playwright would be engaged. "He is willing to take the chance I have suggested," she assured Otto.[70]

Everything seemed primed for success, with the promise of fidelity to the *Diary* assured. As Meyer wrote three years later, in a letter addressed to Anne Frank, entitled "Another Way to Kill a Writer," that "Miss Crawford and I seemed to be in accord that a truly faithful adaptation was required, rather than a free adaptation of your diary. She even pointed out, as I had already noted, that many scenes contained dialogue that could be transferred intact to the stage, if the scenes could be woven into the dramatic structure. So as to lose no time, I went to work, with a general verbal understanding as our agreement. We hoped to present the play in the fall season while your book was, as they say here, still 'hot.' I was to write the first draft in seven or eight weeks, in time for your father's arrival."[71]

Yet on the tenth Meyer wrote Otto that although Doubleday had formally withdrawn from its role as agent, the publisher had clearly retained too deep an interest in the project. At his final meeting with Meyer, Marks had read "the summaries of his talks with various producers, he several times paused, skipped passages, and said 'this was confidential.'" Meyer remained baffled by his actions, and somewhat suspicious of them. "I could not understand how there could be anything confidential in his discussions with producers on this matter." A few days later, Meyer warned Otto against listening to "any factual doubts" that Doubleday might raise. "I hope you will communicate them to me for my explanation."[72]

There was in Meyer's view, however, a still more serious "political" concern, which he hastened to raise so "that we should by every means avoid it. As you may have read, there has been very unpleasant activity in America against some people in the film industry who were said to be communists. This same kind of thing happened with the radio industry, and it could happen in the theatre. Now, among the producers who applied for the play are one or two who could be involved in such an enquiry, and I think it best to avoid them, as there is absolutely no reason for exposing this material to the possibility of such a controversy." However much he deplored the government's action and the response of the studios, he wanted nothing to interfere with bringing Anne to the stage and screen.[73] His own exposure in years past to the ideology of some now under attack by HUAC, either while actively engaged in labor activities or in the trenches of Civil War Spain, left him unwilling to endanger the Diary's future for the benefit of their struggle.

"I wrote to Meyer today," Otto began his note to Tereska on July 12, "very disturbed by the situation." As Meyer had suspected, Doubleday had not truly withdrawn. "My nerves are so down. . . . I feel it would simplify matters if I come."[74] With "letters piling from all sides!" Otto insisted upon Doubleday's involvement, claiming it would be impossible to "continue with one partner alone." He had already made an appointment to see Price, a "neutral agent" who could offer "neutral advice." "It is only fair to await him before further steps," he told Meyer that day in a separate letter. Even then, he would wait until he could meet "the whole crowd of them" (Crawford, Bloomgarden, and the others) in New York before signing any contracts. Price was to help him sort through the various possibilities without angering any of the parties. "I have to keep in good terms with them." Besides, "there are special reasons for me not to sign anything here in Holland."[75]

Otto and Price met on July 16 and decided to allow Crawford and Meyer to proceed, despite Otto's apprehension over his handling of Anne's image and thoughts. "Agree in principle to your ideas," they cabled Crawford. "Please await letter."[76] Otto hoped to rely upon Crawford's many years of experience and "never need to make use of my right of veto," he wrote her five days later. Meyer was a "fine novelist" who had "judged right from the beginning with sensitiveness the value of the Diary for dramatization," and so he, too, was willing to take a chance, though he remained uncertain whether Meyer was "the right dramatist." There was more to the enterprise than "sentiment," he reminded Crawford. "A play is a commercial matter." It would have to be of "the high level of the book" to guarantee that its investors would do well, while still "help[ing] to bring Anne's ideas and ideals in all circles to the best of mankind."[77]

Otto had as yet barely responded to Meyer's several letters. In more than a week, the only communication from Otto to reach Meyer was a brief request that he not issue a statement concerning the choice of Crawford as the play's producer.[78] Of Meyer's unanswered letters, the latest spoke of his progress "working quite hard at the play, since I think it is the best way for you to see what is what." The general outline of the scenes was now completed, "not in fullest detail, but well enough to make me feel the structure is in hand. . . . I think it is very sound, and truly faithful to the material." It had come easily, "forming itself in my mind for so long."

Encouraged by Otto's cable, Meyer had invited him to stay with his family when he came to the States, but Otto, in a terse reply, declined with thanks, relating how Zimmerman, in "writing the most charming letters, insist[s] that I be [Doubleday's] guest."[79] Three days earlier he had written her of the decision reached with Price, and of his desire "not [to] interfere" with Crawford's judgment on the acceptability of Meyer's script. "Crawford shall certainly not accept a draft she does not like." Once the draft was completed, he would come to the States, probably in September.[80]

Meyer wrote Otto on July 22 that Kazan had now read the *Diary* and was "very much interested in doing it." According to Crawford, Kazan "would be available for consultations this summer during the writing." A firm contract with her had now become necessary, Meyer advised. In the meantime, he had received a request from the American Jewish Committee for Otto's permission to produce a half-hour dramatization of the *Diary* during the Rosh Hashanah– Yom Kippur period. There would be little if any payment, Meyer assured him, but "it would be very good for publicity." It was, to date, the sole offer for a public airing of Anne's work.[81]

News of Otto's acceptance of Crawford's offer reached Meyer at the end of July, though he was again asked not to make it public for fear that it would complicate Otto's decision to rejoin his family in Switzerland by creating a "disadvantage to him vis-à-vis the Dutch authorities." As Otto's Basel representative, Erich Elias, had revealed, even writing from Holland would place a tax liability (nearly 20 percent) upon Otto that he wished to avoid. But the silence was troublesome for Meyer, who several days later asked Otto to allow Crawford's office to "make a *small* announcement now, so as to clear the air."[82] On July 31, Otto agreed to the notice, "if you think it necessary," providing it was short enough to miss the attention of the Dutch.[83]

Otto agreed, as well, to the request for a radio script, as long as Crawford was in agreement, "and if you think they [AJC] won't spoil anything." His only other provision was that either Meyer or Crawford see the text, the author of which had not yet been chosen, before it aired. "The ideas have to prevail!"

All else, Otto told Meyer, was in order. He foresaw "no trouble about the contracts" and hoped that Kazan would agree to help with the script and direct the play. "He has a big name here too." Otto planned to vacation before coming to New York in September, his nerves still quite unsettled, and would await news from Meyer and Crawford before arranging ocean passage and a New York hotel. "After we had the chance to talk everything over," he would move to the home of Nathan Straus, just north of the city in White Plains.[84]

Crawford was pleased to receive Otto's confirmation on July 30, and promised to "make every effort to fulfill your confidence." She further reported that "Meyer has been working on the script even though we have no contract." (Meyer's lawyer had been on vacation, and a meeting was scheduled for August 5.) Like Otto, Crawford had "promised . . . he could work on it and submit it for our approval. . . . If he cannot write a satisfactory script I would be at liberty to give it to another writer or call in a collaborator." For the moment, then, she was "studying the book carefully" and making notes for an upcoming meeting with Meyer "to see how he is progressing." Yet, without seeing his work, she had already "asked one of our very top playwrights to study the diary with the idea of a collaboration or [of] taking over completely."[85]

Hellman, an old hand in the ways of Broadway and the commercial interests that ruled it, knew that by raising the spectre of an unstageworthy script, she could discredit Meyer, remove Kazan from the scene, and then recommend individuals to fill these vacated roles. Her own acquisition of the film rights to Norman Mailer's novel *The Naked and the Dead* five years earlier, though her work had ended in failure, had taught her much that she could now apply.[86] She would prove so successful at manipulating the players that while Crawford involved herself in the process of developing a play from the *Diary*, Hellman could work with her friend, producer, and sometime lover, Kermit Bloomgarden, to usurp the play for their own use.

It was Bloomgarden who had first alerted Hellman to Kazan's plan to testify before HUAC and "name names." While having drinks with Kazan in a bar at New York's Plaza Hotel some weeks before her own scheduled appearance in Washington, Hellman had excused herself and had telephoned Bloomgarden to ask why Kazan seemed so "odd." "I thought you knew," Bloomgarden responded, telling her of Kazan's offer to the Committee.[87] Afterward, Bloomgarden produced Hellman's revival of *The Children's Hour*, with its tale of lives ruined by slanderous accusations, as a counterattack against HUAC. He also mounted her next production in 1955, *The Lark*, a play with striking thematic parallels to the *Diary*, also produced that year. [88] Bloomgarden's ties to Hellman had originated nearly two decades earlier, when, as an accountant, he had managed the finances for her producer and lover, Herman Shumlin. After leaving him, Bloomgarden had reproduced a number of Shumlin's treatments of Hellman's plays, beginning in 1946.[89]

First agreeing to consult and possibly work as collaborator or writer on Crawford's project, Hellman encouraged Bloomgarden to declare his interest in the *Diary*. Aware that Otto had a previous arrangement, Hellman moved with Bloomgarden to sow seeds of doubt and to suggest a successor to Crawford and her playwright, should problems develop. Hellman did all that she could in the coming weeks to see that her plans bore fruit. She had little to lose. She was already a part of the project and could remain so, no matter how the script developed. Crawford herself had ensured that. But Hellman hoped to settle outstanding scores against Meyer and Kazan, and against Crawford for her unforgivable misjudgment in seeking to work with them. Their failure to produce an acceptable script might then allow her to treat the *Diary* as she wished.

Within days of Hellman's agreement to assist Crawford and of Crawford's letter to Otto regarding this promise, Bloomgarden cabled Otto of his interest and dedication to Anne's "fine sensitive diary which you have considerately and generously given to all of us to enrich our understanding and experience by sharing hers." Among his qualifications as "the right producer" was his work with Hellman. It was "at the suggestion of Meyer Levin," he claimed, that he was now making this formal request, though Meyer had last spoken with him several months earlier.[90]

The day before cabling Otto, Bloomgarden had arranged for a mutual friend to contact one of Otto's American relatives, Rosalie Davies, and to ask that her husband, Val Davies, a player in Hollywood, cable Otto with word that Bloomgarden was "a completely responsible, sensitive and sincere individual and a major figure on the Broadway scene."[91] Davies cabled Otto several days later, describing Bloomgarden as a "conscientious, sensitive producer who fully appreciates [the] quality [of the] beautiful book."[92] But by then, Otto had already responded to Bloomgarden's offer, sending his regrets that he was bound by a prior commitment to Crawford, though he was certain that Bloomgarden had "the right feeling for the book." Should "serious differences . . . arise in making the contracts," Otto promised to write him. "Even if we do not get to business," he hoped they could meet in New York.[93] Might it "have been better to give the rights to him," Otto wondered?[94]

Bloomgarden could hardly have been disappointed with Otto's response, having known through Hellman of the agreement with Crawford. News from Rosalie Davies the following week, that Otto had placed Bloomgarden next in line as the *Diary*'s producer, surely brought an added moment of satisfaction to both Bloomgarden and his mentor, seeing all they had secured in so short a time.[95] Otto's erroneous crediting of Bloomgarden with the Dutch production of Arthur Miller's *Death of a Salesman*, which he had produced only in New York, seemed added assurance that he would be offered the *Diary* should Crawford step aside.[96] Only this obstacle remained.

Meyer, of course, knew only a small part of this latest exchange. He continued to work on his script in preparation for the meeting with Crawford that was "to make things definite," after which they would make a statement to the press, with Otto's permission. "The reason [for delaying the news] hadn't occurred to me until we received your explanation," Meyer told Otto after hearing from Elias. Following his meeting with Crawford that first week of

August, he returned to the play. "I am working ahead and feel that the form is coming very well. I hope I will not have any distractions in the coming month, so I can stay here and keep at it." He had found a neighbor's shed useful as a studio, a quiet place where he "finally fled from the children."[97]

Otto responded to news of an imminent contract by notifying Meyer that he was not ready to sign anything. It was a good business decision. Should either Meyer or Crawford prove unsuitable, he could then deal with the situation without this added burden. Still, Otto sent Meyer his hope "that something fine will turn out . . . with the draft you are working on." He did, however, express concern at not hearing anything further regarding Kazan as the play's director. Had Meyer any news from Crawford? "Or was the name only given without serious consideration?" Otto asked with obvious suspicion. "It is certainly very essential," he added, as if to hint at the possibility of withdrawing from his still-unsigned agreement with Crawford. Nor would he sign it while Zimmerman was on vacation, he told Meyer, leaving Meyer to wonder what role she might still be playing despite Doubleday's withdrawal as Otto's agent.[98]

In early August, Meyer wrote Otto that his draft was progressing. Each scene had either been sketched or fleshed out with dialogue, though for the moment he was putting it aside to work on the radio play Crawford had agreed to produce for the American Jewish Committee. The shorter format would allow him to try several dramatic ideas for the Diary. As for Otto's inquiry concerning Bloomgarden's suitability as the play's producer, Meyer repeated his belief that while he was "very top-knotch . . . political considerations might creep in as he is generally thought to be in the communist group."[99]

Meyer's concern was not without substance. By the summer of 1952 there was fear that HUAC, following its success in Hollywood, would soon move its witch-hunt to Broadway. Meyer had already expressed his concern to Wolf Kaufman that none of this must touch "the Anne Frank situation, if it is avoidable." Yet although Meyer feared governmental interference and the subsequent loss of an audience, his concern that the Diary's Jewish content might be distorted in favor of ideas contrary to Anne's remained far greater. When Bloomgarden suggested that Arthur Miller be asked to adapt the play, Meyer grew even more troubled. "I immediately shrunk from this proposition" and from the prospect of Bloomgarden's involvement as its producer, Meyer later testified. He doubted that Miller "could write a play that would be detached from political implications." Whatever relation Miller might have had to his own Jewish past, other considerations had taken precedence. "In my own view, from what I knew of the work of Mr. Miller, he was not related to Jewish material . . . in the way that would make it possible for him to interpret the Jewish material in the Diary in the way that Anne Frank wrote it."[100]

Otto's only response to Meyer at the time, however, was that Bloomgarden, though he "tries his best," had simply been "too late." Viewing the situation from a purely business perspective, Otto was certain that Bloomgarden's interest "will help in the contracts with Cheryl Crawford."[101] Meyer's news of Crawford's continuing interest in the project—her contact with Kazan and Kazan's desire to see Meyer's script, and her insistence upon a share of the film rights (supported by Meyer's description of the natural progression of such a property)—further confirmed Otto's sense that he had proceeded wisely with the *Diary*.[102]

With Crawford's encouragement, Meyer was now hoping to have a "readable draft" for Otto when he arrived in New York. Crawford had placed announcements in the *New York Times* and elsewhere of this "tentative" arrangement, the final decision being dependent upon the *Diary*'s "translation into dramatic form."[103] Meyer advised Otto that such notices in the New York press had been issued to protect his interests. He himself now felt more secure in his role as playwright, recommending to Otto that he delay his trip until the draft had been completed and could be discussed in greater detail.[104]

"It is time enough to come a little later," Otto agreed, noting that it might be easier for him to arrive in early October. He would soon be moving from Amsterdam to Basel and anticipated the exhausting effort it would require. With the *Diary*'s great success in the United States, and with personal matters occupying his attention in the coming weeks, there was every reason to proceed slowly and cautiously, particularly in following Meyer's suggestion that including film rights in any play contract might not be in his best interest. A poorly written play might discourage the production of a film or require payment for rights that should have remained exclusively his own. Appreciating the uncertainty of the moment, Otto decided not to tie one to the other but rather to "wait and see!" so as not to jeopardize "the chance of higher rewards."[105]

"From my part I do not want to press you at all," Otto repeated in a letter to Meyer on August 15. The move to Switzerland had caused "a certain tension" in both countries. "As a bringer of hard currency (royalties) . . . there is still a danger of difficulties," and, therefore, the greater need to settle these matters judiciously and without further complication before leaving for the States. Although Crawford "wanted to have the play as soon as possible, *I* can wait!"[106]

Meyer, of course, continued to advise Otto on how best to handle his negotiations with Crawford "so that if the play doesn't go, and there is still an eventual sale from the book, you won't lose by it."[107] Meyer had similarly begun to work with his own attorney, Floria Lasky, on a "proposed agreement" with Otto. Lasky was reluctant to grant Otto as thoroughgoing a right of script approval as Meyer had suggested and told him that she would be happier to "amplify the agreement in many other broad legal respects . . . if you think his personality can stand a stiffer agreement." Nor was Lasky comfortable with the unusual situation of leaving so many specifics untouched in the contract. Whether out of concern for Otto's emotional state or from his own sense of dealing cautiously with a businessman of differing Jewish identity, Meyer told Lasky that to treat these negotiations in a "normally speaking" manner "would be unwise with this man," and therefore, only a fifteen hundred dollar advance from Crawford, in three installments, had thus far been agreed upon.[108]

In the meantime, Otto had grown curious about the reception of Meyer's adaption for the American Jewish Committee. "I can imagine that Miss Crawford will not have liked it," he interjected without explanation. "I cannot blame her," he added, though he had neither received a copy from Meyer nor heard from Crawford.[109] Had Zimmerman, to whom he was "writing again regularly," reported on the radio script's decidedly Jewish focus? By the time Meyer's suggestion of an October 15 arrival in the States reached Otto five days later, he had already booked passage for a September 29 docking in New York, further suggesting his growing concern over the direction of the play.[110]

Because of the play's function as a holiday presentation, Meyer had "concentrated on those parts of the Diary which deal with Jewish matters." Anticipating Otto's objection, he tried to reassure him, albeit with a touch of irony, that the script was "not an example of what the play will be like, since the Jewish question recedes in the general proportion of the play, whereas here it is emphasized . . . particularly for the non-Jews, to familiarize them with things Jewish . . . sympathetically prepared." He sent Otto a draft and instructed him, "If you have any extensive revisions to suggest, please let me have them at the earliest possible moment."[111]

Later the same day, Meyer sent Otto a second letter to which he attached a draft of the contract "we will have to make." The Dramatists Guild required such an agreement with the copyright holder, not the play's producer. Only then could the producer contract with the playwright. Crawford, Meyer added, was "in turn ready to make the standard agreement" with him, as evidenced by the advance she had offered, which Meyer was prepared to "share equally" with Otto. In good faith, Meyer was offering a shorter than usual period in which to produce his play, reduced from the standard two years to one. "I am sure that if we are on the right road you will make an extension of time possible." Anticipating that he would complete the play within a month, Meyer again suggested that Otto postpone his coming to America. He would send the "first draft" and "if there is not too much to discuss, you might want to wait until the actual rehearsals are under way."[112]

But Otto was determined to come to New York as soon as possible. "To-day I got my papers in order!" he wrote Meyer from Amsterdam the following day.

"So I am leaving for Zwitserland [*sic*]," where he would remain until September 15, before going on to England and then America. He was troubled, however, that his arrival would be on Yom Kippur, although he believed that it was "of less importance for me" than for others. Not "want[ing] any Jew to come and fetch me," he would make his own way once the boat docked. In fact, he had wanted to tell no one "except Miss Zimmerman" of his arrival date.[113] Meyer, however, assured Otto that he "really need not be disturbed about arriving on Yom Kippur," as the "vast majority" of American Jews were of "the more 'modern' viewpoint" and, at best, "marginally observant."[114]

Otto's surprisingly few "suggestions" for the radio script arrived a week later on September 4, leaving Meyer rather puzzled to find him suddenly asserting that in general, "the Jewish parts have to prevail."[115] He appeared to agree with Meyer's ending, in which Anne's affirmation of Jewish identity and her consciousness of the uniqueness of Jewish suffering were highlighted by her confrontation with Peter, the object of her budding affection. In response to Peter's bitter objections to remaining identified as a Jew should he survive the war, Anne is permitted to voice what she had written in the *Diary*. Peter is emotionally exhausted and decries having this condition of being a Jew "inflicted . . . on us. Who has made us Jews any different from all other people!" he demands, the anger bursting forth. But Anne is certain in her faith that "it is God who has made us as we are, and it will be God, too, who will raise us up again," lending redemptive meaning to their suffering. Affirming her identity as the cause of her strength and faith, she declares, moments before being discovered and sent to her death, that, "We will always remain Jews. We want to, too. Who knows, it might even be our religion from which the world and all peoples learn good, and for that reason and that reason alone we have to suffer now. God has never deserted our people. Right through the ages there have been Jews, through all the ages they have had to suffer, and it has made them strong." Nor did Otto object to emphasizing Anne's credo as he is made to declare, "That was what our Anne said. . . . She lives forever in her words. Perhaps that is why I was spared. So that I might come back to this house, to give my little daughter to the world."[116]

Meyer had exercised dramatic license and out of concern for Otto's disapproval had explained that all such "invention" of scenes and dialogue were in "consonance" with Anne's *Diary*. Otto wrote Meyer that he fully understood the need to work with her text in this manner. "Don't think that I would like to have everything as it *was*. Take the liberty of the writer and make it as good as possible to make an impression on the public, as long as it is not sensational. But this I am not afraid it will occur."[117] Otto's confidence in Meyer's handling of the material had won for the script his unconditional approval.[118]

Following discussions with the American Jewish Committee on September 9, Meyer added a brief Sabbath Eve service and several additional passages from the *Diary* to emphasize Anne's spiritual side.[119] With these final changes in place, rehearsals began the next day in preparation for a September 18 broadcast. Meyer had by now returned to New York with his family, intending to resume his work on the larger script. But life quickly proved too disruptive. "The interruptions are constant and the expectancy of being interrupted brings a terrible tension." With the hope of finishing "a readable draft" by the time of Otto's arrival, he fled back to Fire Island alone.[120]

Meyer's concern for the script's completion had become so all-consuming that he was now willing to set aside all further discussion of contract differences until then. He had already attempted to explain to Otto the Dramatists Guild's standard agreement between producer and playwright involving previously copyrighted materials, and only after believing that a "general understanding" with both Crawford and Otto had been reached had he sent a draft of the contract which Otto had found "not in accordance with the correspondence I had with Miss Crawford," particularly the sense that "I am bound to you." Consumed by work on the script, Meyer decided to wait until the day following Otto's arrival in New York to resume their contract discussion.[121]

But Meyer had not suspected that Otto would send a copy of his letter to Crawford, along with a promise "not [to] sign anything before I know your judgment about the play." Otto hoped somehow to circumvent the explicit terms of the Dramatists Guild's policy, to which she, too, was professionally bound. "My impression was that I had to make a contract with you," he wrote after learning from her that she had made "special agreements with Mr. Levin about his work."[122]

Crawford's immediate response was to claim to have "discovered that the first contract would have to be between you and Meyer," though she, too, promised Otto to "discuss the contract face to face" when he arrived. "As you are coming here so soon, perhaps it was wise to wait." She was, however, pleased to report that Meyer had completed more than half of the script, and though she wished not to see any of it until it was finished, she "liked his approach and the way he planned to break it into scenes." If the "first draft seems satisfactory," she would obtain the services of one of the previously mentioned directors "to work further with him," as she had promised earlier.[123]

Crawford had every reason to feel certain that Otto would continue to favor her role in the process. With his eye on the business aspect of the *Diary*'s publication and theatrical production, he had already benefited by deferring to those more practiced in these matters. Doubleday's judgment had brought sales of the *Diary* "to the second place!" according to Zimmerman, who "is always writing the nice and clever way," while the radio script's approval by the American Jewish Committee had been seconded by the critics. When Meyer's news of the script's completion arrived, Otto quickly reminded him that "the main thing is the reaction of Miss Crawford and later the audience."[124]

Meyer, too, had good reason to believe that his efforts on behalf of Anne's *Diary* would be well rewarded. The full script was an expansion of what he had written for the radio, and all who were involved with it and with the larger project for Broadway seemed as pleased. The *Billboard* review of the radio production had been singularly positive and encouraging, finding Meyer's dramatization "a particularly powerful force against bigotry . . . its impact as entertainment alone . . . as shattering to the emotions as its sociological message." The script, *Billboard* continued, "retained all of the sensitivity and moving qualities of the original, which is a high tribute to his delicacy of selection, since the most sincere diary scribblings are apt to take on maudlin overtones when translated into the spoken word."[125] *Variety* echoed this praise, noting that Meyer had "achieved a blend of dramatic and narrative segments" and that "those segments which were acted out, as the coming of the Gestapo, the air raids, the flight into hiding, Anne's discussion with young Peter came over with more impact. . . . The diary soliloquies, so different from radio's usual superficial handling of emotions (and particularly those of teenagers), made good listening."[126] Shortly before Otto's arrival Crawford telephoned Meyer to say that she had read his stage play, "that it was good," and that they would "move ahead."[127]

CHAPTER FOUR

Judgments About His Script

Otto arrived in New York as scheduled on Yom Kippur, Monday, September 29, and was met by Zimmerman, whom he would see daily throughout his stay.[1] As promised, Otto saw Meyer the following afternoon, received a copy of the playscript, and began contract negotiations.[2] That evening he read the play. When Otto joined Meyer the next day for a 3 P.M. meeting with Crawford at her office, he told his producer and playwright that "he could not imagine how any writer might have better grasped and written" about the people and their years in hiding.[3] Crawford agreed. "She liked it," Otto commented in a recapitulation of his New York stay based upon "note-books" kept during those weeks.[4] Meyer himself later recounted in his "Dear Anne" letter that "I took him to see Cheryl Crawford, and he was delighted that everything was working out well. We discussed various directors. We arranged to go earnestly to work at Miss Crawford's place in the country [on Sunday]. Your father wrote to your grandmother, in Switzerland, telling her of all these plans, and she wrote to my wife, who had been corresponding with her, of how good it was that your diary would be on the stage."[5] That evening, Otto dined at the Levins' home, where they were joined by William Zinneman, an executive with the Loews film company, whose praise for Meyer's script was met by Otto's tacit agreement.[6]

But by Thursday the script's progress toward the stage was in question. Crawford unexpectedly summoned Meyer to her office and related how, after completing yet another reading at 4 A.M. (the exact number of readings varied in Crawford's differing accounts), she had "found that emotionally and dramatically it did not touch me sufficiently, that the characters were stated but not explored." Crawford, in fact, had found the script "too faithful" to the *Diary*. What she had wanted was more of the story of Anne and Peter, of "their antipathy, their gradual coming together in loneliness, their tentative approach to love and Anne's mature realization that Peter is not for her." Although Meyer had done "a good construction job of putting together the material," and had clearly "made [a] contribution in form and in time," Crawford had not found his script moving.

"This news was a great shock to Meyer," Crawford acknowledged to Otto. Levin returned home "dazed" and without fully understanding how her thinking had changed so precipitously. By her own admission, Crawford's reaction to the script was "necessarily suggestive . . . and hard to communicate in terms of criticism," based rather on "my own taste and experience." She would give Meyer the weekend to rewrite it, though not at all certain that he could "clarify the issue." They would then meet again on Monday to "see if he had been able to understand and agree with my criticism," as she explained to Otto. "He is a man of great integrity who must naturally write as he feels, and although he will try to do what I suggest, it is not easy." Anticipating Meyer's inability to alter his vision of Anne and the play, she planned to see Otto shortly after speaking with Meyer that day. "Convinced that there is a good play in the *Diary*," she promised Otto that she would "help realize it as I see it," even if another writer became necessary.[7]

Meyer was unaware that arrangements for another writer were already being made. Nor did Crawford perceive that she, too, would soon become a victim of this general atmosphere of duplicity. Yet it is clear that Crawford's deceptiveness toward Meyer contributed to her own removal from the project, though she never suspected that Hellman's decision not to collaborate with Meyer and to recommend Bloomgarden as an outside reader of his script were tied together in an effort to seize control of the *Diary*. Instead she remained blinded by her own concern that the script must reflect her vision of Anne, whatever the price others might have to pay. Otto, too, became an unsuspecting part of this larger scheme, kept as he was from much of the discussion concerning his daughter's work. Although he hoped to honor Crawford's agreement with Meyer, even to the point of paying for the help of a second dramatist, Crawford was already planning to replace Meyer with Hellman or another playwright whom she and Hellman could agree upon. Exactly when they decided to offer the *Diary* to Carson McCullers is uncertain, but with Otto continuing to defer to the judgment of others, Crawford knew that Meyer could easily be removed. Nor could Otto have been surprised by Meyer's sudden ouster by week's end, for Crawford had repeatedly alluded to the possibility of replacing Meyer with another playwright of greater stature. "As I always said, I am not the best person to judge a dramatization," Otto told Tereska a month later in an attempt to excuse his abandonment of her husband.[8]

Hellman, of course, remained intimately involved throughout this process.

The change in Crawford's attitude toward Meyer's script came not only after a series of conversations with Marks ("a pivot guy . . . very much anti-Levin," who "wanted a 'name' playwright," according to Crawford's assistant at the time, Wolf Kaufman), but, more significantly, following her discussions with Hellman, with whom she had shared the script. (Banned by Hollywood but not by Broadway following her HUAC appearance, Hellman was now in New York preparing to begin rehearsals for the revival of *The Children's Hour*.[9]) Kaufman recalled Crawford's having thought Meyer's first draft to be "pretty good," and had, therefore, been surprised enough by Marks's continuing conversation with her to have mentioned it to Tereska at the time.[10] Although Kaufman had found Crawford "a strange woman who mistreated me rather shabbily after many years of close and good association," he continued to think of her as a person of "basic integrity," insisting that "the line to Bloomgarden" had come through Hellman. It was she who had been the underlying cause of all that had happened to Meyer's script and to Anne's *Diary*.[11]

With advice from all quarters militating against Meyer, it was only a matter of days before Otto conceded, setting the stage for Bloomgarden's triumphant entrance. "After I received the judgements about his script from Miss Crawford, Mr. Bloomgarden, Mr. Whitehead, and others [Hellman?], I was convinced that his dramatization is not what I want to have for Anne," Otto later recalled. "From this moment on my confidence in Levin's script was vanishing."[12]

On Monday, October 6, Crawford greeted Meyer in her office, took his revised script, and promised a quick response. "I still do not feel emotionally involved," she began her rejection the following day, repeating that her problem with the script was not one of construction. "My criticism is harder to pin down, to convey or discuss." Perhaps the fault was her own. "Perfectly aware that my judgment is very personal," she suggested that he have another producer read the script, and recommended Bloomgarden, "as I know he was greatly interested."[13] Meyer, of course, remained unaware of these maneuvers and was still in shock from this sudden reversal. Soon after his meeting with Crawford, he saw Otto and explained that "he had discussed his approach with her and that she had approved of it and that he therefore could not understand her negative reaction," as Otto later acknowledged under oath.[14]

With Meyer now seemingly out of the picture, a series of meetings was arranged for Otto. Within hours after informing Meyer of the rejection, Crawford and Otto were discussing their next step in the project. On Friday, October 10, Otto met with John Wharton of Paul, Weiss, Rifkind, Wharton & Garrison, the prestigious New York law firm that was to manage his legal affairs for the duration.[15] Paul, Weiss had long handled Bloomgarden's and Hellman's theatrical affairs and those of their friends, most notably Dalton

Trumbo, a member of the Hollywood Ten blacklisted after his HUAC hearing. Their willingness to represent Trumbo was apparently proof enough for Hellman of their reliability.[16] It was Wharton's partner, Lloyd Garrison, a friend of Nathan Straus, who had introduced Wharton to Otto.[17] Emerging from his meeting that morning, Otto would note the conclusion that Wharton had helped him reach: "first need help of Bloomgarden." After an intervening weekend, the two met with Bloomgarden in his office.[18]

Throughout the week, Meyer had continued his attempt to persuade Otto to drop Crawford and allow him to seek another producer. Between his other discussions, Otto would telephone or meet with Meyer, "more often than noted . . . in my note-book." Presumably, they spoke not only of the play's structure, but of Otto's continuing concern over its "too Jewish" focus. Price later told Meyer that Otto had given this as his reason for personally rejecting the script.[19] On Friday evening, October 17, Meyer brought Otto to his synagogue and then home for a Sabbath dinner, hoping to stir some greater consciousness of the Jewish issues involved.[20]

Meyer may have had some success in renewing Otto's interest in his script, for after again talking with Crawford the following Monday, Otto met the next evening with Peter Capell, a producer whom Meyer had recommended the previous summer after Crawford and Bloomgarden. But word of his discussion with someone outside of Hellman's circle created deep concern within it. By the following afternoon, Otto was again meeting with Wharton, who added one of his more able theatrical lawyers, Myer Mermin, to the conversation.[21]

Following Crawford's suggestion, Meyer had in the meantime given the script to Bloomgarden, whose reaction proved "so negative as to appear to me irresponsible." "No producer would want [his] play," Bloomgarden had told Otto. "I think he was so extreme as to disqualify himself as a calm judge," Meyer wrote Crawford, reporting how Bloomgarden had stressed that he "had 'not dramatized the book' which I felt was in variance with your own feeling that the dramatic structure was satisfactory."[22]

Meyer had by now approached several directors and producers with the assistance of Miriam Howell, a well-regarded agent who "had enough faith in the play to devote herself to it." Capell had been among these. Two days after Otto's visit with Capell and his partner, Norman Rose, Meyer delivered a copy of his script to their office. Encouraged by what they had read, they quickly offered Otto "an advance on royalties . . . as an indication of our seriousness" and asked to meet again with him and his "representative" as soon as possible. Although it was not yet in its final form, they believed that Meyer's efforts had already yielded the basis of a strong play. "We think that Mr. Levin has very successfully captured the flavor of the book and has preserved its atmosphere and characters in such a manner as will be most appealing to American audiences." With minor changes, already agreed to by Meyer, the script could be ready for production that year.[23]

Two of Broadway's leading figures, Harold Clurman and Herman Shumlin, had also expressed interest. Where Crawford had thought the play "cold," Clurman believed that "many of the scenes will play beautifully just as they are." Shumlin had similarly found the first draft "very promising." "What you have done is remarkable," he noted, adding that the play appeared to be nearing its final form.[24]

Encouraged by these positive reactions, Meyer told Crawford that he no longer felt bound by their agreement. As he understood it, her rejection could be predicated only on "the question of dramatic technique," about which she had expressed no objections. "Your judgment in the intangible matter of emotional content . . . in the light of further opinions" could no longer prevent him from making his play "available to producers acceptable to Mr. Frank." Having "suffered through several hallucinating weeks while awaiting other opinions," he was now asking Crawford to release Otto from his "present sense of obligation to you. . . . I believe that I have the right to contend now that this book will not lose in any respect through being represented by my play." If, however, his play "did not find a suitable producer, I am sure Mr. Frank would still turn to you." It was Meyer's naïve hope that all this could be worked out between himself and Crawford, "as I particularly would like to avoid further distress to Mr. Frank."[25]

But Mermin was already moving quickly to end all further discussion of Meyer's script. "At the request of Mr. Otto Frank," he notified Capell the day after Meyer's letter to Crawford that she, indeed, continued to be Otto's only choice for producer. He, therefore, did not wish "to enter into any discussions or negotiations on this subject."[26] Mermin sent a much stronger response to Meyer, accusing him of violating the understanding reached in July between the three parties. While Otto held the right to veto "any script in order to be sure that it did not violate the spirit of the book," he had agreed to allow Crawford to "judge the dramatic values of a script," as had Meyer, "in accordance with your original understanding with her." To do otherwise would only further distress Otto, who "feels indebted to you for all you have done for the book." Mermin stressed that Otto did "not want to be in the position of rejecting any of your requests," nor "be called upon to over-ride Miss Crawford's judgment." Persistence would lead only to the project's collapse. "Mr. Frank, being the kind of person he is, will prefer to withdraw the book entirely from dramatization rather than prolong a painful controversy."[27]

But Meyer would not be deterred, sending Otto a second draft containing "a number of changes." Others would have been made, he confessed, "but now I just haven't the heart to keep on working." And though "dreadfully sorry" for "all this trouble," he was nonetheless making this final appeal out of fear that Crawford's "subjective" decision "might prove unfair to Anne's book." "It does not take a technical knowledge of the stage to respond to emotion in writing," he tried to convince Otto, hoping to instill in him the confidence to override Crawford. On this level, "your own judgment may be counted as well as anyone else's." Was it not true, he argued further, that an objective evaluation of the script clearly demonstrated how he had "simply tried to retain Anne's view, throughout? . . . I have from the very beginning felt that any play or film derived from this book would have to have the same quality as the book: the sense that this was what really happened. The great effect of Anne's book comes from its being a diary, and therefore having a guarantee of truthful revelation. I wrote my play very close to the book because I believe that is the only way in which audiences will feel the same truth. To change the characters, to trick it up with dramatic effects, to invent new actions when it is not necessary, would in my opinion detract from this most important quality, and be dangerous for the entire enterprise."

Yet Meyer was certain that Otto would not easily take it upon himself to make such judgments and asked instead for "recourse to another opinion." He would submit his script to "the normal list of producers," though many were "already prejudiced by [Crawford's] opinion." To do otherwise would be to allow her to "kill my play." Meyer advised Otto not to feel reluctant in shedding Crawford for another producer, reminding him of his having earlier rejected Little, Brown after discovering that preliminary agreements with them "could not be harmoniously carried out."[28]

Meyer immediately sent a copy of this letter to Otto's lawyer, explaining that he could no longer "advise Mr. Frank to regard [Crawford] as an infallible judge, in whatever treatment is made of his daughter's diary. . . . I do not know what whim moves her, but I cannot submit my fate and my reputation to her unsteady opinion." Given his involvement with the book over the past two years, and "inasmuch as I carried out my work without waiting for an agreement to save time for Mr. Frank," Meyer believed himself to "have every moral right to ask for further submission opportunity." Surely his claim was greater than Crawford's "rather harsh" wielding of a "sole veto" over "the fate of that work." The ultimate choice, of course, should be Otto's, and "out of personal regard for Mr. Frank," he "would make no claims upon him, whatever his decision." But there was clearly ample reason for Otto to reconsider. "An impersonal regard for the best chances for the book would seem to me to dictate that the widest range of opinions should be the guide in this matter, rather than the opinion of one sole person whose opinion does not remain consistent."[29]

Meyer sent a third letter that day, to his own attorney, Floria Lasky, to which he attached copies of those to Otto and Mermin. In it, he raised the possibility of resorting to a "public statement" regarding the matter. Lasky, whose clients included Crawford and McCullers, strenuously objected, characterizing such a move as "most unfair to all parties and damaging to the whole project." Mermin, she added, had "never been 'irresponsible, cynical, or insulting' in his talks with me about you." Even his disparaging comment about "people who accept for production plays without reading them" should not have been taken personally. Moreover, she was now convinced that she could no longer represent Meyer's interests. "Under ordinary circumstances a difference of opinion between you and me need not be serious, but under these circumstances and your attitude, I think it best that you have someone else advise you." Ethically, she could not condone nor be a part of Meyer's plan to go public, given "the basis on which you had originally assumed the task of writing the adaptation." Nor did she wish to play a part in causing Otto to "abandon the project because of your request of him that he alter his commitment to Cheryl Crawford."[30] Lasky's withdrawal would be the first by several attorneys in the years ahead, all of which would add to Meyer's difficulty in seeking redress.

"I can only plead excessive strain and fatigue—my doctor tells me the heart-warnings are not to be dismissed, and I must find myself some minimum of security," Meyer wrote Lasky two days later, apologizing for the "outburst" during his subsequent visit to her office. "Please forgive me for having sort of lost control of myself the last time I made an oration about art," a reference to his strident defense of his right to artistic integrity. "It is not unimportant to me that you seem to feel I am in the wrong on this whole matter." Still, having reexamined his position several more times, he could not concede the right of final judgment to Crawford. Nor had his appeal to Otto met with complete refusal. "It appears that I may now have an opportunity to make some other submissions." If these also failed, then only he would suffer. Aware of Mermin's displeasure, Meyer felt too encouraged to consider its possible long-term effect. "As to the import of Mr. Mermin's remarks," Meyer naïvely commented, "I think I made it clear to him how I understood them, and he offered no correction."[31]

Two weeks passed before Otto formally responded to Meyer's request of October 30, though he had in conversation explained his inability to answer sooner. "It is a difficult position for me altogether as I understand your feelings," he finally wrote Meyer, asking him to realize that he had no choice but "to rely on others . . . as I feel that I cannot judge in this matter being too involved in it as a subject." Crawford's promise to compensate Meyer "for his work" should it "not seem satisfactory," and her equal willingness to immediately "engage another playwright" had further enhanced her position with

Otto, particularly after she asserted that Meyer was "willing to take the chance I have suggested." Refusing "to decide on any adaptation," he would defer to Crawford, whose recent offer to Meyer of "eight weeks to make a draft" and to produce it "if it turns out well" appeared "fair." It had all grown "so complicated emotionally that I may prefer to drop the whole idea," he wrote Meyer that November 6, perhaps hoping that he would withdraw rather than endanger the project.[32]

"I am sorry you did not send me the text of Miss Crawford's letter," Meyer began his agitated reply, his "nerves . . . all shot out by this affair." "It is clear to me . . . that she never had any serious intention of accepting a play I wrote . . . [as] the tone of her letter to you does not correspond at all with the tone of her discussions with me." He was certain that Lasky would confirm the contents of his negotiations with Crawford, who had, in fact, agreed to "all sorts of provisions besides a simple 'having a try.'" But apparently "she received your adherence through me on the basis of different representations to each of us," having first "draw[n] me into this arrangement" despite her "weak faith in me," and without any intention of ever honoring what had been "clearly understood" between them, "that there would be chances for revision, and the alternative of a collaborator, and that rejection was a very small possibility."[33]

In light of this latest disclosure, Meyer felt justified in offering Otto several new options in addition to his previous assertion of the right to seek another Broadway producer. Among them were a trial reading by a "basic cast" assembled merely to "find out something about the play," a nonprofessional production of the script outside of New York, and one by an Israeli theater company. "Perhaps we can arrive at something tomorrow," Meyer concluded, hoping that they could now resolve their differences, having discovered Crawford's duplicity as their source. "Naturally, all this you could not know," he offered sharply. The next afternoon, they met in Mermin's office to discuss these options and to consider a formal agreement that would allow Meyer to pursue a new producer after Mermin had selected several possibilities from a list of twenty-eight names that Meyer would present.[34]

Before leaving that Friday evening for a weekend in Chicago, Otto sent Tereska a response to her "sweet and moving letter" of the previous Monday. "You know that I do not want to do injustice to anybody and surely not to Meyer." He was "disturbed altogether . . . [and] feeling very sad about the whole situation," particularly because "you and Meyer and myself are very much the same in understanding the characters, etc. . . . But if well known producers, known for their taste, reject Meyer's script, I have to be worried." Emotionally and professionally unable to judge the quality of the dramatization, he had sought the counsel of "different people who instructed me about the difficulties." Surely she agreed that "just because this thing is so important, we have to do the *best* we can."[35]

Otto had by now booked passage home, lending a sense of urgency to these last days.[36] Early in the afternoon of November 11, only hours after his return from Chicago, Zimmerman and Crawford met with Otto to discuss the possibility of having Carson McCullers write the script.[37] In fact, Price had already met in Paris with McCullers several weeks earlier at Crawford's request in order to gauge her interest in the project.[38] Crawford's ten-year friendship with McCullers, fifteen years her junior, had earlier brought the younger writer her first exposure to the inner workings of the theater and the opportunity to imagine a new relationship following the death of her lover, Annemarie Clarac-Schwarzenbach. When McCullers adapted her own novel, *The Member of the Wedding*, for theatrical production in 1950, it was Crawford to whom she first showed it, hoping that the producer might bring it to Broadway. Although Crawford declined, her careful reading of the script had enabled her to advise McCullers on whom to approach for dramatic and technical assistance, and on a possible cast. The immense success of the play a year later brought McCullers new friends, among them Hellman, who became a frequent dinner guest with Crawford at McCullers' New York home, or a host to McCullers at her own farm north of the City.[39]

In time, Meyer would come to believe that he had been used by Crawford to help win Otto's confidence so that she might apply her own design to the *Diary*. But had it all been so neatly prearranged? Is there evidence to suggest that Hellman had recommended McCullers knowing that McCullers, physically frail, emotionally unsteady, and growing more so with time and alcohol, could not long withstand the pressure that Meyer was certain to put upon her? Although we may never know with absolute certainty, it is clear that once Hellman had destroyed Crawford's limited confidence in Meyer and had suggested McCullers as his replacement, he could not have competed against the emotional ties that existed between Crawford and McCullers. So strongly bound were they that it was Crawford who, several months after offering her the *Diary*, raised the funds needed to return McCullers' deceased husband's body to the States following his suicide in Europe.[40]

Otto himself appears to have agreed with the choice of McCullers, backed as it was by Crawford's theatrical expertise, Hellman's imprimatur, and Zimmerman's repeated assurances that success meant a "big name" writer. Two days after meeting with Otto, Crawford offered McCullers the *Diary* with Otto's blessing, claiming that she had "won the right to dramatize it against stiff competition from other producers and movie companies," all of which was untrue. Crawford again promised Kazan's assistance with the play's "construction," though she had known for some time that Kazan was fully committed elsewhere for a year or more. "I'd like to know if you would be interested in dramatizing it," Crawford wrote McCullers in Paris, encouraging her to meet with Otto to discuss the play. To sweeten the offer, she added the possibility of writing an introduction to a volume of Anne's short stories that Zimmerman was now editing for Doubleday.[41]

Although Otto knew of these developments, he accepted the Levins' invitation to dine at their home, on the condition "that we did not want to discuss matters but mainly wanted a private talk."[42] He and Meyer agreed to meet the following noon to discuss the play. "Pressed into the position of one who had brought all this strain" upon a "nerve-torn and weary" Otto, Meyer nevertheless "pleaded with him," as he later recorded. It was the last opportunity he would have to make this appeal face to face. Their conversation centered around the possibility of a test production in Israel, but ultimately nothing was decided, leaving Meyer deeply troubled as he, together with Tereska, Marks, Zimmerman, and several others, accompanied Otto to his ship the following day, November 15.[43]

As expected, McCullers was pleased with the opportunity to consider writing the *Diary*'s script. "I am very much interested," she immediately cabled Crawford as she carefully weighed the promise of "invaluable" advice from Kazan.[44] McCullers, of course, did not know that he was unavailable, though Crawford had already told Otto before he left New York.[45] Crawford's receipt of McCullers' positive response prompted Zimmerman to telegraph Otto with the news while he was midway across the Atlantic. She sent him McCullers' Paris telephone number to facilitate their immediate contact, closing her cable, "All my love, Barbara."[46] Meyer would later be surprised to learn of Zimmerman's involvement in these matters, having found her to be "so mousey and silent as to her views all through the discussions" the previous month.[47]

Otto appears to have been waiting for this response from McCullers, for three days later, with the added security of a well-known writer's interest, he offered Meyer the one-month extension he had begged for. Whatever their respective motives in offering Meyer this additional month to find a producer willing to work with his script, the nature of the agreement clearly demonstrated the lack of candor of those who had presented it to him. Having first eliminated Herman Shumlin, one of the American theater's leading producers and the one person who had shown the strongest interest, and having then cut the remaining list in half during the busiest part of the theatrical season, a time when it was least likely to find a producer willing to commit to yet another project, they had made Meyer's task all but impossible. Without "a letter signed by one of the above producers," delivered to the offices of Paul, Weiss by December 21, 1952, his script would be considered "withdrawn." In that instance, the agreement continued, "you shall not use or exploit your script in any manner whatever, and [Otto] shall have the right, free of any claims by you, to engage any other dramatist or dramatists to dramatize the Book and any producer or producers to produce such dramatization."

In signing, Meyer forfeited not only the ability to have his play produced independently of Otto's authorization (except, as agreed upon four days later, in Israel, in "a Hebrew version . . . subsequent to the New York opening" of the authorized play), but his right to the radio script as well. The only provision favorable to Meyer was his protection against other "dramatists willfully mak[ing] use of any new character created by you or new situation or plot created by you and not found in the Book," but only if he signed the full agreement as presented. Without acceptance of this "understanding," it further read, "you will not have the right to claim an infringement of the dramatization written by you, nor will you institute any legal proceedings or seek in any way to recover any damages or compensation for any such alleged infringement."[48] This provision was later violated, but with neither foresight nor recourse, Meyer signed the document and its supplement. Although he had "stormed and screamed" as the list was pared down, there had been little choice but to consent to what he would later acknowledge to have been only "a short reprieve." With "a list approved by Mr. Mermin and Miss Crawford . . . [and] under protest, I signed this miserably unfair agreement."[49]

Still, Meyer believed that perhaps there was reason to hope that a last chance actually existed. According to their signed agreement, the "right of approval" of the final script would "be based solely on the question of truthfulness . . . to the characters in the book and to the spirit of the book." Had not Otto's attorney noted in the agreement that there were "no objections of this nature to Meyer Levin's script in its present form"?[50]

There was now little time to waste as Meyer and Howell contacted everyone on the list within the first ten days, explaining the situation, its background, and the need for an immediate decision.[51] But even this phantom hope faded quickly once it became evident that those whose names had been so carefully retained by Crawford and Mermin wished to have no part of this already controversial project. Growing desperate, Meyer approached several well-known producers and directors not on the official list, hoping that Otto might accept one as a "big name."

Of these, Herman Shumlin, the most qualified of those contacted, already had been declared by Mermin to be a director rather than a producer, despite having produced Hellman's greatest successes, including *The Little Foxes, Watch on the Rhine, The Searching Wind,* and *The Children's Hour.* Otto later claimed not to have been a party to Shumlin's ouster from the list, admitting only that he "did not intervene when [he] heard that Shumlin's name was barred," having been told that "he had not produced successful plays for several years." Mermin, he maintained, had drawn up the agreement only after mediating between Crawford's and Meyer's interests, "Levin [having] exerted moral pressure on me to give him this chance."[52]

The reason for Shumlin's removal is clear. Before the list was finalized, Shumlin's attorney had spoken to Mermin of his client's interest in Levin's script, only to be told, lawyer to lawyer, that it was the intention of the parties involved "to get rid of the Levin adaptation." Mermin had confirmed this himself while discussing the matter with Meyer's agent early that November.[53]

Zimmerman further corroborated this objective in a conversation with Shumlin in 1955. Without explaining that she was gathering information for Mermin, she telephoned Shumlin and introduced herself as "a friend of Otto Frank . . . [who] wished to know if he had in fact made an offer to produce Meyer Levin's adaptation. . . . He said, Yes he had," she reported. "He was all set to direct it. I asked, Had he offered to *produce* it. Yes, he intended to co-produce with Norman Rose and Peter Capell." Mermin's decision had angered Shumlin, who knew that the list, despite Zimmerman's continuing assertion that it had been Meyer's, had in fact not been drawn up by him and therefore should not have been binding. "This was a bona fide offer from a bona fide producer so what difference is a list," Shumlin argued. "I don't care any more but I just want to get facts straight." (Crawford had apparently agreed with Shumlin's assessment of Capell's ability, having invested in his play at the very time she was cutting him from the list.)[54]

Otto had told Meyer that Mermin's role had been that of an "intermediare," who, after negotiating between Crawford and Howell, had "submitted 14 of the best." Otto further asserted that "if your agent would have protested, perhaps she would have had success."[55] Yet Howell and Meyer had done precisely that. "Both I and my agent *protested* most vigorously to his exclusion from the list," Meyer angrily responded, bitter that Otto had allowed Crawford's involvement in the list's preparation. "Since Mr. Shumlin did make an offer for the play, and since this exclusion therefore makes all the difference between a yes and a no, between a production and zero, I cannot take it lightly, and I have to assume that Miss Crawford was adamant about excluding him for the very reason that she understood he would want to produce the play." Given the "tangled circumstance," she should have been eliminated from all future consideration.[56]

But Otto would not consider removing Crawford, particularly after receiving such "good reports" about her friend McCullers. Having earlier praised Meyer for fully understanding Anne's ideals, Otto soon repeated precisely the same praise to McCullers. After she had written him of the "love and wonder and grief" she felt for his daughter from reading the *Diary*, he expressed his belief, once again, that she understood Anne "in every respect"; and though she had yet to give any thought to the *Dairy*'s dramatization, she immediately expressed her hope that they would soon meet.[57] Struck by his certainty and the responsibility it seemed to impose upon her after his visit to her cottage outside Paris, McCullers grew more nervous than usual, developing a severe rash; for as she soon told a friend, Otto had already made his choice clear to her, that she was the writer he most wanted for the play.[58]

Otto immediately contacted Crawford and related his conversation with McCullers. The next day Crawford wrote McCullers, "delighted [that] you are interested in Anne's story." Meyer, of course, was still somewhat in the picture, she cautioned, though she was confident that he would soon make his final exit. "I think we should wait out the month. I doubt if anyone will buy the Levin version, but I wouldn't want you to start before we know. . . . Keep your fingers crossed."[59]

Meyer's desperation had naturally deepened as the last days of his month's reprieve approached. On December 9, responding to Kazan's letter declining the opportunity to direct his script because of prior commitments, Meyer asked only that Kazan authorize the use of his name. "If he knew you felt I had done a good job so far," Otto might give him more time "to extend the list." He merely wanted the same advantage exercised by Crawford. Meyer assured Kazan that there was "no moral obligation on your part" but hoped that he could read through the script.[60]

Unable to await a decision from either Kazan or Otto, Meyer wrote to Brooks Atkinson, the drama editor of the *New York Times*, seeking to correct reports emanating from Crawford's office "that she may produce my dramatization of *Anne Frank*. . . . The fact is that Miss Crawford for several months has had no such intention. I have been fighting for the life of my play, and have only a few days left before Miss Crawford is free to kill it."[61]

Otto, too, was growing impatient, and several days after first discussing the *Diary* with McCullers he visited with her again, only to learn that other responsibilities and an assortment of emotional strains would not allow her to undertake the project.[62] Having had no contact with Meyer for three weeks, Otto wrote him soon after returning to Basel from this second meeting with McCullers. "I had a lot of work waiting for me in Amsterdam," he gave as the reason for his silence. "Whereas in New York everything concentrated on the book, I had to turn around to business matters, the book and all the questions attached to it working subconsciously." With McCullers' talk of withdrawal, Otto once again held out some hope to Meyer. Acknowledging that his search for a new producer had been "a big strain," he counseled Meyer to become "master of your nerves" and "wait patiently the results. . . . Have confidence that the final result will be the best for Anne's ideas."

Otto's advice had arrived with a check for a portion of the payment he had received for a second production of Meyer's radio play, Meyer having earlier forwarded it to him as contracted. "I think one can change an agreement if it does not come out, in mutual understanding," Otto noted. With the year drawing to an end, Otto wished Meyer and his family "a good, healthy and successful 1953," adding that he planned to remarry. His future wife would arrive in Basel "before Xmas."[63]

Two days later, Kazan sent Meyer his final refusal. "I just literally have not time right now to read your play on account of I have not two heads!" While he liked the *Diary*, knew that Meyer was "a good writer," and was "still interested in seeing a play from the book and certainly one that you have written . . . it will have to be after this Spring's work is over." To do otherwise would be to give Meyer's script "one or two flip readings" which "will be making some kind of a liar out of me." Kazan simply refused to "go through the motions" at a time when "I could not take on your play if it were Hamlet." Nor had he ever promised anyone he would. "I did not speak to Mr. Otto Frank and I did not give Cheryl Crawford permission to speak to Mr. Frank." He had merely expressed a "casual" interest in seeing a play based on the *Diary*, "and did not mean it except casually."[64]

Meyer's last hope disappeared with the arrival of a letter from Richard Myers, a producer from Mermin's list, two days before the deadline. Myers's partner, Richard Aldrich, had just returned from Europe and, having read the play, was unable to agree upon joining him in a coproduction. "We of course do not go into anything on which there is not complete agreement," Myers wrote, adding that he was truly sorry "that things didn't work out." "I feel you've done an excellent job of writing," he wanted Meyer to know. He was certain "that with the obvious merit of your dramatization, you will be able to find another producer." Should Meyer write something more for the theater, they would be "only too glad to have a look."[65]

With the passing of the deadline, Meyer's ability to restrain his anger weakened. A recent television play based upon the *Diary*, which Otto had contracted for while in New York,[66] elicited Meyer's first full attack in a three-page letter on December 22. "The script, to my mind, was presumptuous in attempting to improve on Anne's words," he began, noting further, and with prescience, that it was "filled with stereotyped phrases and clichés . . . the sort of thing I am afraid will happen in a play." One of his greatest fears for the *Diary* had been realized, as it would be again on the stage.

But Meyer expressed even greater concern that Otto, too, had been the victim of those who had sought to remove him as playwright. Having no further illusions, and being "pretty worn out by the whole thing," Meyer wanted only to report "frankly on my own side of the matter, since perhaps your distance from America will give you a clearer view of what happened here. I couldn't speak to you, here, of certain elements of bluff and deception which are abhorrent to me, for you might have thought I was trying to run down other people who were in opposition to me in this matter. But since my play has not been sold, and there is no question of my having anything to gain by what I tell you, I believe I can speak to you quite frankly in the hope that what I say may still be of value to you." Meyer pointed to Crawford's deceptive use of Kazan's name to win Otto's support for her bid. Once her position as producer had been secured, she had then manipulated events to engineer his ouster. "As to her actions here, you know them as well as I do. I am convinced that she never intended to use a play of mine, and that she used me only to get at you." (Crawford herself later boasted that "in spite of some formidable competition, I was able to induce him to give me the rights.")

Unaware that Crawford had, in fact, largely determined the list of producers presented by Mermin, Meyer condemned Mermin's "assumption of the role of literary arbiter." What "incredible nerve" he had displayed "in taking it upon himself to decide who could and who could not produce a play." How could he be "anything but enraged," Meyer asked Otto, after seeing Shumlin and four other producers "who had originally, like Cheryl Crawford, expressed an interest in the material . . . ruled off the list?" The setup seemed obvious to Meyer, for "this meant that we were forced to try to interest people who did not want the material in any case, and our results showed it."

Still, it was Meyer's hope "that a good play [might be] created and produced . . . for your sake and the book." Should this happen, he told Otto, "I doubt if the play will be essentially different from mine. It will just be by someone who is 'in' with the crowd that runs the theatre in this city." His fear, however, was that the *Diary* would be tampered with by those "who use deception and manipulation," and by "lawyers who pretend they know more about art than artists." They alone were the objects of his anger, not Otto, whom Meyer believed innocent of all complicity. "You were absolutely straight and generous. . . . There were simply professional things in the background which you could not understand." He regretted only "that you did not have more faith in what I wrote. . . . In my book, *In Search*, I said that none of us could tell what happened to the Jews of Europe, but that some day from amongst them a teller would arise. I took Anne's book for the answer to my prediction. In adapting it, I was true to it." He could say no more than to wish Otto "every happiness" in his "new life," and to promise that he would "try to forget it."[67]

But Meyer could not reconcile himself to his fate, and the very next day he sent Otto a detailed accounting of the fourteen listed producers' reactions. Among these, only two had expressed wholly negative views of the script, the others having a broad variety of constraints or questions that would not allow them to readily make an offer.[68] The Jewish Theological Seminary, however, preferred his radio script to their own recently produced television adaptation.

Within the next several days, Mermin cabled Otto seeking his permission for the Seminary to use it at a dinner to be held on January 7.[69]

Meyer's promise to withdraw would be forever nullified once he learned of the plan to engage McCullers to write the adaptation. With fortuitously symbolic timing, Meyer wrote Otto on Christmas, arguing that he could not remain silent in the face of such an affront not only to himself and to all those with legitimate rights to the *Diary* but to Anne and to all victims of the Holocaust. "I am disgusted and enraged at the thought that a non-Jew has been selected to write the play. I should think Miss Crawford would have had more tact. You may say it does not matter and all the rest of it, but after the way my work was treated, to bring it to a gentile writer over the dozens of excellent Jewish writers that are here, to have it produced by a gentile when important Jewish producers who were eager to do it were ruled off the list, is scandalous beyond measure." He simply could not remain silent any longer. "I will write about it wherever I can. It is adding insult to injury. I will tell the whole story of Cheryl Crawford's double-dealing, in the press, and I will protest the way in which Mr. Mermin saw to it that my play would be killed."[70]

Moments after mailing the letter he had "written in an excess of nervous rage," Meyer rushed to control the damage he had caused to his relationship with Otto, and to what little hope might yet have remained for his script. In a hurriedly posted note, he attempted to defend his "tantrums" as the product of "a situation which, even in my cooler moments, I cannot accept as entirely fair." Had Crawford been "dropped" along with himself, he could have withdrawn with some grace, but "as long as she is connected with the matter I shall feel that emotional factors based on subterranean impulses had too much to do with the decision"—most of which he had yet to enumerate, or fully understand.[71]

Meyer then contacted McCullers directly, rehearsing the history of his involvement with the *Diary* and the deception by which he had been victimized. Crawford's "verbal agreements" had been purposefully "ambiguous," he argued. "No contracts were drawn," nor had it ever been her intent to do so, yet something more fundamental upset Meyer, and at the risk of being "offensive," he felt it was his duty to speak. "As a Jewish writer, I feel a certain sense of wrong in this material being interpreted by others."[72]

It was this same issue that drove Meyer on New Year's Eve to offer Otto what he hoped would be his "last words on the matter." For however "deceptive" and "ignoble" Crawford had been, the possibility of a non-Jew adapting the *Diary*, in violation of the profoundest element of artistic integrity, was far more troubling. "All literature, all art, is an expression of the soul: no stranger can as well express the soul of a people as someone from that people." Crawford's latest "gesture" of recommending the project to McCullers had shown such enormous "insensitivity" to "our own people who welcomed and made Anne's book," as they would the play, if not alienated from it by her misdeeds.

Yet, however much Meyer tried to force Otto to face the issue and not dismiss it as merely "a chauvinistic reaction,"[73] Otto nevertheless continued to sidestep it, concentrating instead on "the idea that Miss Crawford intended to put you aside," unable to "think such a thing in my character." Nor would he acknowledge having any awareness "that someone will write the play now, a non-Jew." He merely expressed his thanks "for the nice Xmas card" (a cynical touch on Meyer's part) and promised to "keep contact" in the new year.[74]

CHAPTER FIVE

The Most Suitable Producer

t is of the nature of a conspiracy that it leaves little hard evidence to prove its existence. By legal definition, a conspiracy requires only that individuals undertake actions to further a common goal. Nor need there be knowledge of the intended goal by all parties, some of whose own purposes may have been different. Such unwitting coconspirators may even be victims themselves. This was certainly the case in the scripting of Anne's *Diary*.

Fortunately, much of the "paper trail" has survived to demonstrate how Lillian Hellman, in the ongoing struggle to wrest control of the story, contrived to have the thoughts of others spoken in Anne's name and thereby given authority and a wider audience than might otherwise have gathered to hear them. Hellman, acting almost exclusively for ideological purposes, took advantage of each fortuitous turn and, when possible, engineered the next. There can be little doubt that Cheryl Crawford and Carson McCullers were unaware of Hellman's designs and were involuntary participants in them. So, ironically, was Meyer Levin, who soon served to eliminate both Crawford and McCullers, thereby helping to clear the way for the producer, director, and playwrights of Hellman's choosing.

"The Anne Frank book is free now," Crawford wrote McCullers on January 3, 1953. "Have you thought any more about it Carson? I want to have a play from it ready by June or July."[1] But Meyer was doing all that he could to stop this from occurring. Three days later, after Otto Frank's evasive response to the issue of a non-Jewish writer, Meyer related his "dismay" at finding an announcement of McCullers' involvement with the script in the *New York Times*. "Mrs. McCullers' proposed entrance into the project has been precipitated by a major disagreement between Producer Cheryl Crawford and Meyer Levin, originally designated to adapt the current best-seller," the article reported.[2] Friends and strangers alike had begun asking Meyer "whether there was anything that could be done." As a result, he could no longer "keep silent on the whole matter" and had informed Mermin "that as long as there are people who want to express their opinion about the choice of playwright . . . I will join them, for it would be irresponsible of me toward the book and toward the public to remain silent." Nor could he remain silent while Crawford, "a person who could be so insensitive as to suggest such a choice," continued as its producer. "The offense which I felt in Miss Crawford's announcement is one which goes quite deep."[3]

So deep, indeed, that having violated every basis upon which they had entered into their agreement the previous summer, she could no longer expect Meyer to remove his script from contention. "Such a tactless and inappropriate choice of an adaptor," coupled with Crawford's receiving "preference as a producer . . . through a ruse" involving Kazan's name, "makes me feel that I have no moral right to consent to any arrangement which leaves her as producer," Meyer told Mermin. "I therefore want you to know that in my more moral judgment my dramatization is not withdrawn." Crawford's actions were so reprehensible that he would do all he could "to see that the original work, which I had some responsibility in making popular, is not given into the hands of Miss Crawford to do with as she will."[4]

Chosen to counter Meyer's charges, Zimmerman wrote Otto the following day, speaking of "what Mr. Mermin has told me, as well as . . . what I myself gather." Nothing improper had occurred, Zimmerman assured Otto. Crawford had been "more than fair" with Meyer, whose "bitterness has no basis in fact." She was happy to report, as well, that Crawford "was absolutely delighted now that everything was clear and she could go ahead." McCullers, according to "everyone I've mentioned this to," appeared to be an excellent choice. "I am absolutely sure that what has happened is in the best interests of you and of Anne's book!"

Although Otto continued to ignore Meyer's insistence on a Jewish writer, Zimmerman and the others, knowing that Meyer would continue to press the issue, counseled Otto that Anne's message would be better served by a non-Jew. Were not her experience and reflections more "universal" than Jewish? Would not a Jewish writer improperly cast them with too narrow a focus, limiting the audience they all hoped to reach? As Zimmerman reminded Otto, "We once talked about the question of whether a Jew or a non-Jew should write the play. Naturally a Jew will feel in certain ways stronger about the book, but in other ways this might be a disadvantage. I don't believe that a non-Jew will not feel as strongly in other ways about Anne's book, and at the same time they will not have the danger (which a Jew might have) of limiting the play to simply Jewish experience. The wonderful thing about Anne's book is that it is really universal, that it is a book, an experience, for everyone. And I think that just a little objectivity would, on the part of the writer, ensure this very broad appeal." So well had the *Diary* sold that first half-year, particularly during Christmas, that Otto's royalties were already approaching twenty thousand dollars. By framing the more substantive issue of appropriate authorship within a discussion of finances, Zimmerman all but guaranteed that he would agree with the choice of McCullers, no matter how well others had received Meyer's script, no matter what revisions he might propose.

Zimmerman went on to deny any knowledge of "the Kazan business," though she was certain that Crawford would not have "approach[ed] anyone to do the play while the rights were up in the air." Kazan's name had been raised, but "only as a future possibility, once everything was settled and negotiations were under way!" she insisted. There was no need to worry about such matters, nor about Meyer, who, she was pleased to say, had "not behave[d] badly at the end." She even admitted feeling somewhat "charitable" toward him, "*understand[ing]* how he must have felt," though she "could never agree with him." She promised to write Otto "a less involved letter soon," and "very much . . . look[ed] forward to having another note" from him. Sending her "very, very best," and closing "With all my love," she noted in a handwritten postscript that "the royalty statement and check will officially arrive in a few weeks."[5]

As Zimmerman's letter made its way across the Atlantic, Otto rushed to answer Meyer's. Admitting that he had discussed the possibility of McCullers with three individuals ("one not-Jewish") while still in New York, he claimed to have "refused to talk to her about the play as long as things were not decided." But in truth, Otto's first conversation with McCullers had taken place during Meyer's month-long extension, before he could realize how compromising it might become if the chronology were ever established. "Never we shall know if your script was better or not," Otto lamented disingenuously. "Nobody ever will be able to tell. And that is what makes me feel sorry, this and the idea that I cannot do much about the whole question."

If Otto felt some sympathy for Meyer, about whom he had "no question that you acted fairly and frank always and tried to do the best," on January 8 he was far more certain than ever of his response to the issue of Jewish authorship. "The greater part of the readers are non-Jews," as were those who had written to him, he told Meyer. Here was the audience to whom the play should be directed, as he himself had tried to do with the *Diary*. "I am sure that it is necessary to have sensitiveness for the Jewish sphere, but in the whole play it must not prevail." Perhaps a Jewish director "can do much to preserve the Jewish sphere," he offered, though here, too, his hands would be tied "if Miss Crawford took the option," to which he added with feigned dismay, "even I cannot interfere about the writer." In fact, although he soon learned that a contract with Crawford had not yet been signed and that he was therefore free to allow a test reading of Meyer's script, Otto refused to do so and backed away from his declaration in the letter that "from my part there is no objection as you can imagine." Should all of this grow too troublesome, he threatened to simply "let [it] all go, as I am not capable to handle the matter."[6]

McCullers had by now overcome her earlier reluctance to deal with the project and had developed a body of "impromptu ideas" concerning "structure and dramatic material." As she wrote Crawford in response to her inquiry of January 3, it had become clear to her that she would need absolute freedom in bringing this understanding of Anne to the stage. "I think we should have the freest liberty in drawing the essence from the Diary and we should be free to delete and develop so that the purity and drama of the Diary will come through as a play."[7]

Anxious to secure her role as playwright, McCullers telephoned Janet Flanner, whose *New Yorker* column had praised Anne's *Diary* two years earlier, asking that she send Otto what Flanner herself described as "a long redundant telegram" repeating Crawford's news of Meyer's removal and of McCullers' acceptance of the assignment. "When I kept reading her book and saw her po' li'l face and then Ah looked at Cheryl's photo then Ah jus' thought mah heart would never forgive me ef Ah did'n do that play," she had told Flanner in declaring her commitment.[8] McCullers then sent Otto her own cable indicating her continuing interest, to which Otto answered supportively with his best wishes for success.[9]

But Otto, once again removed from the immediacy of New York, was growing increasingly concerned that developments were occurring without his knowledge or involvement. On January 9, he wrote Zimmerman about the play "from my side," including his decision not to return to Paris but to await word of the contract from Crawford or Mermin. "You can imagine that there is again a certain tension until we know how everything will turn out," he offered as he anxiously awaited news from Zimmerman "that Miss Crawford took the option."

Otto also wanted Zimmerman to know that he had received several letters from Meyer, including a copy of Kazan's note regarding his lack of involvement as a director, portions of which Otto was forwarding to her "confidentially." More important, he wanted to explain his own position concerning the issue of a Jewish author. Equivocating now where he had not before, he advised Zimmerman that his own "meaning [was] not so definite in this direction." Perhaps "it might be advisable to have a Jewish director in case of a non-Jewish writer." Without this "Jewish sphere," he feared that the play might alienate those "big Jewish circles who helped to propagate the book."[10]

Responding as well to Meyer's repeated objection to Mermin's involvement in an artistic decision, Otto insisted that the lawyer's function had remained a purely "legal one."[11] But Meyer retorted on January 12 that Mermin's refusal to consider a number of willing producers, including "a man like Herman Shumlin who in my opinion is worth ten Cheryl Crawfords," was, in fact, an "artistic judgment, the net effect of which is to suppress my play." Under these circumstances, he refused to withdraw his script from contention and, having signed the extension agreement under protest, would "reserve the right to sue Miss Crawford. I don't believe Mermin's contract will stand up in court because he forced unjustifiable restrictions upon me." Furthermore, he warned Otto, "I will not have my work throttled by the Mermins and the Crawfords"; instead, he suggested that Otto "instruct Mermin to accept the offer of one of those who is ready to do my version."[12]

To prove he could not be silenced, Meyer sent a detailed history of the project to Hobe Morrison, the editor of *Variety*, hoping that its publication would dissuade others who might consider adapting the *Diary*. "I think that any writer who may be asked by Cheryl Crawford . . . should want to know the history of my adaptation of the book . . . [and] consider also my side—the writer's side—of this matter," he wrote. "That Miss Crawford, who rejected *A Member of the Wedding* [sic], now ironically enough suggests that she wants to have Carson McCullers supplant me as adaptor," was clear evidence that the month's extension had been "a set up." No writer, he warned, should expect to see his play get "a fair trial."[13]

Meyer's public campaign, which would soon include an appeal to *Variety*,[14] was at first of minimal concern to Mermin. Both of these efforts failed to reach the public. Mermin meanwhile continued to focus on Otto's rights to the *Diary* as a commercial property. After weeks of negotiation with the BBC for a televised adaptation, he advised Otto against granting such permission, believing "that the small fee did not warrant the creation of a cloud on the radio, television, and other dramatic rights." Mermin was particularly fearful that "any similarity" between the BBC adaptation and those that might come after would raise the "question of fact as to whether it was inadvertent or deliberate." Otto, Mermin concluded in his letter to the *Diary*'s British publisher, "is entitled to protect a valuable property from the jeopardy of possible legal complications."[15]

It was with this same attitude that he now responded to Meyer. "Your letter challenges Mr. Frank's right to make his own decision about the producer or adaptor for 'Anne Frank' and seems to threaten interference with his arrangements if you disapprove of them." Did he fully understand the implications of this challenge "both in relation to Mr. Frank, and in relation to the property?" Setting aside all "legal claims against Miss Crawford," which were not his to judge, Mermin argued that there were no legal bases "of any kind which justify you in interfering with any honest and sincere decision by Mr. Frank." Mermin cautioned Meyer, "It is high time that you recognized your obligations to Mr. Frank in this situation." He emphasized the seriousness of the matter by informing Meyer that copies of their correspondence were being sent to Otto, Crawford, and Howell.[16]

There was good reason for Mermin's letter to Meyer, and for its timing. In the week since Meyer had written, Crawford had agreed to Otto's terms. A contract would soon be drawn up and sent, Zimmerman had notified Otto the very day that Mermin had written Meyer.[17] The next day, with all arrangements seemingly secure and in order, Otto composed what he believed would be his final response to Meyer on the matter. "You know that I wished nothing more than that your script would have been accepted, not as a Jewish writer but as I appreciate you personally and knowing how deeply you are impressed by Anne's book." He regretted that all had not worked out to Meyer's benefit, but he could not "enforce the playwright to the producer, . . . hav[ing] come to the conclusion not to interfere any longer." Instead, he conveyed his "hope that our personal relations will not be troubled," remembering "all you did for Anne."[18]

Faithful to the promise he had made to Otto, and not yet aware of these contractual developments, Meyer responded to Mermin that the extension agreement had been anything but "equitable," having been drawn up under circumstances "that can be classified only as extraordinarily hostile toward me." Nor had Otto been allowed to exercise the "fundamental task" of a "fair assessment" of his script, given the many "devices to get rid of me and my work." Thus, while Harold Clurman (McCullers' director for *The Member of the Wedding*) and others continued to express their interest in his script, he would "use everything at my disposal to carry through my convictions,"[19] including yet another appeal to Otto. "If there had been a spirit of trying to find out truly the value of my play . . . rather than of arranging how most quickly to destroy it, we would all be in a much better position now," he told Otto. "Instead of wasting time these months in argument, work could have been done." And certainly, another producer could have been found. "Anyone with enough money, and the sense to get the right director, can be a producer." But with lawyers and businessmen dominating the process, it had become impossible. "That is the situation in which I find myself," however much it remained "not customary to execute someone when new evidence proves the conviction based on false assumptions."[20]

Zimmerman, hoping to counteract Meyer's possible influence, wrote Otto that "Meyer has done everything in his power to ruin everything." Apologizing for her bitterness, she attempted to discredit his claims by questioning his sanity: "Meyer must stop this needless destruction. He is behaving more rashly than one could ever imagine." By his continuing threat of intervention, "he seems bent upon destroying both himself and Anne's play," she asserted. Crawford, "understandably upset and frightened," and uncertain of McCullers' participation, had suddenly put her contract signing on hold until she could consult with her lawyer. "She told Mermin that she was afraid less for herself than for Carson McCullers who is her very old, good friend," Zimmerman reported. Crawford feared that the contract could force McCullers "into a situation which might involve her in legal difficulty, even though Levin has no legal case whatsoever." Zimmerman admonished Otto to "realize that Crawford wants this very much, that she was so very pleased when the negotiations seemed to be going well. Yet now, understandably, she is simply afraid."

Still, the more serious issue, if measurable by the length of Zimmerman's discussion, remained Meyer's insistence that a Jewish writer was essential. "You know as well as I" that more Christians than Jews had purchased the *Diary*, she began. The *Diary* was not "simply a book for Jews. Its greatness lies in the fact that it is for everyone, everyone can identify with it, everyone can find in it so much! All this I needn't tell you." It meant nothing, then, that McCullers was not a Jew. "One does not have to have statistical details of what life was like in 1944," she argued, as if Anne's Jewish experience of the Holocaust were not at the center of her *Diary*. Instead, Zimmerman located the *Diary*'s importance in its ability to capture the more universal story of adolescent development. "One simply needs a warm heart, understanding, sympathy and the kind of talent which [McCullers] has shown. One couldn't make of this play anything alien to the material," she assured Otto, though several lines later she would accuse Meyer's radio script of being a "Religious Adaptation" and "false to the book." Although "the Jewish material is there . . . so much else is there too!"

Zimmerman felt compelled to emphasize this aspect in the face of what appeared to be a weakening of Otto's resolve. "I am a Jew and I've thought about it deeply and I do feel honestly that the problems of whether a Jew writes this or not makes no difference at all." Nor should he be concerned about not finding a Jewish director, she asserted, "since all of them are," though "that too makes no difference." And though she listed Kazan, an Anatolian Greek, among them, she asked Otto to trust her objectivity in these matters "since I have no literary reputation to gain or lose, simply your very valuable to me friendship and my very deep affection for you."[21]

Had Zimmerman extended herself merely out of affection for Otto? Or was she, too, invested ideologically in seeing that the "universal" was emphasized over the Jewish? Whose interests might she have been protecting when she again wrote Otto the next day of the "heartbreaking trouble" Meyer had caused both Crawford and McCullers with his threat of a lawsuit, should they accept Otto's offer? "Levin simply refuses to give up. It would be absurd if it were not so upsetting," for clearly, Meyer "is simply making things up." The one producer he had stressed most, Zimmerman told Otto, was on the list. If Shumlin had thought so well of it, why had he not offered to produce it? Otto, however, knew that Shumlin had been eliminated by Crawford and Mermin.

Zimmerman further asserted that Meyer was "totally crazy" regarding Crawford's use of Kazan's name to lure Otto, though this, too, had been established independently. Using the stereotypically negative imagery of East European Jews long held by their German coreligionists, she then warned Otto that Meyer would be encouraged to "start peddling" his script among "inadequate producers," should Crawford withdraw. "I do think that somehow pressure must be born upon Meyer to make sure he does not show his script to anyone else. . . . He ought to be out of it definitely since even if another producer of some standing takes it . . . [Meyer] will only cause trouble later. . . . I am afraid to think of it!" she cautioned. "I can't think that we can trust Meyer any longer to behave himself." Having expressed some understanding of Meyer's frustration the previous day, she had now reversed herself. Offering this wholly negative picture, she promised to cable Otto with any news of Crawford's and McCullers' decisions.[22]

Deeply angered, Otto wrote Meyer accusing him of violating Anne's spirit to satisfy his own ego by attacking Crawford rather than settling their differences in a less belligerent manner, as Anne would have done. "I told you that it is against the ideas and ideals of Anne to have disputes and quarrels, disagreements and sueing. . . . I start to see you as a different person," someone who "enjoy[s] hurting me and others and even yourself." Otto judged Meyer's actions to be disrespectful, his play not an adaptation but his "own creation," and advised him to reexamine his position. "I hope you will understand my very straight letter and I would be very much pleased if you would stop with every kind of troublemaking as this is unjust and below your standing. Get awake, use your good and common sense."[23]

He had been in a "very, very angry mood," Otto wrote Meyer the next day, apparently somewhat embarrassed. Still, he asserted that this uncharacteristic display of emotion had been justified by Meyer's own attempt to force his hand against Crawford. "Every agreement verbally or in written form is sacred to me, even if the result turns out to my disadvantage," he assured Meyer. "You are a bad loser." How could he ever trust Meyer to enter into a contract that would not find him "making trouble and trying to get out of it if some items don't please you afterwards?"[24]

Yet, however forthright Otto had been, he was nonetheless disturbed by Meyer's claims that Mermin was acting as if he were Crawford's attorney and not Otto's by blocking Clurman's desire to produce Meyer's script. And so

Otto asked Mermin whether Meyer had, in fact, signed the extension agreement "under protest," despite Zimmerman's assurance that this had not been the case. Although Meyer had exhibited "crazy behavior" in going public with the story and admittedly had no legal standing, Otto needed to know whether there was any truth to his repeated assertion. If so, he was now willing to consider Clurman provided Whitehead, who had been on the list but had never responded, was interested in collaborating with Clurman on Meyer's script—but only if Crawford approved this "prolongation of the agreement." There seemed to be a "moral right" involved in Meyer's latest request, though not a legal one, Otto stressed. Still, Otto feared that even this acceptance of Meyer's script could no longer bring peace. "I am become afraid of the personality of Levin. . . . I still do not see how we can get out of this mess, but I hope that you will find a fair solution."[25] Otto then cabled Crawford "to postpone all decisions" and wrote McCullers, detailing the various messages he had received from Crawford, Zimmerman, and Meyer, and his own "strong letter" to Meyer. "Now we have to await the result of my letter. So nothing can be done in the meantime."[26]

"Dearest Darling Barbara," Otto began his letter to Zimmerman the next morning. While declaring it "indiscreet" to send her a copy of a letter he had received from Tereska, he nonetheless quoted her as saying that she was "very strong against the idea of sueing" Crawford. So, too, had he learned that Crawford had not told McCullers of the "difficulties" that had arisen regarding her contract with him. He asked Zimmerman to keep both confidential, adding that if Crawford "had only . . . taken the option after December 20, when she had a right to do so, we would not have to worry any longer. . . . Now again everything is in trouble and actions press one another."

Otto admitted having earlier felt more positive about rejecting Meyer's script. "I was so glad that so very few good reactions were known of his script." But he was "in doubt again" after McCullers had spoken so well of Clurman and Whitehead. Their "willingness" to produce Meyer's play, if firm, could be used by Meyer as proof "that his play was a good one" and that he had not been given enough time to find a "first class producer." Claiming "a moral right . . . he could make trouble in the public." Otto told Zimmerman: "I hate to think of the idea." At least they were in agreement on the "Jewish question." She need not concern herself with it any further. Instead, he advised her to plan a fall visit to Basel ("I shall have to miss you longer. But we will make up for the loss of time, won't we?") before closing with "All my love to you, dear little one."[27]

Crawford, after receiving a telegram from Otto that day, wrote McCullers to encourage her to continue to work on a first draft ("as too much conferring at the start might chain [your] creativity"), though there was no contract. She finally conceded. "Things still muddied because this man Levin is a psychotic in my opinion and is making all sorts of wild claims and threats which I don't wish to expose to you."[28] McCullers, in a far less delicate state than feared, responded with a strong telegram of her own, "demand[ing] action on the Anne Frank Project now" if she were to continue her involvement. "I say to the devil with threatened suits and commercial hazards of subject matter and also Levin. Otto Frank and I believe in it and want it. I think it is a good workable idea for a powerful play."[29]

In a final attempt to end all contention between them, Meyer wrote Otto that while he and "many Jewish writers" held "views very deeply felt" that differed from his, he would "respect the fact" of their difference. "It is saddening to have provoked such an angry letter from you." He would, of course, make no claim against Otto or interfere with his plans for the *Diary*'s dramatization. But against Crawford, who "seems to have expressed herself in different terms to you and me," he might possibly seek justice if calmer minds agreed with his perception of events. If shown to be wrong, he would "let the matter drop," though he felt a continuing obligation to make his feelings known to "any writer who undertakes the assignment . . . as I would want to know if I were on the other side of the situation."[30]

But the receipt of Otto's next letter, charging him with being a "bad loser" and of violating the "sacred" nature of agreements, forced "another effort on my part to explain my morality." For Meyer, the issue was not one of competition but "of the right thing and the best creative thing being done." He had gone public only after the volume of response to the announcement of McCullers' selection as scriptwriter had "demonstrated" that it was a "matter of public interest." Yet this issue, along with Crawford's deceptive use of Kazan's name and other related matters, was secondary. "The whole matter boils itself down to a judgment of the play." In this, "intrigue and personal jealousies" had influenced Crawford's decision, as they had "the angry Kermit Bloomgarden." He vowed that had he "the energy and the money, I would seek some kind of objective judgment" against her. Otto, he still felt, was himself innocent of all wrongdoing and a victim of her deception as well. "It is about her motives and actions that I have personal doubts."[31]

"That his reactions are bitter, I can understand, but I do not see any danger," Otto told Zimmerman after receiving Meyer's indemnifying reassurance on January 26. Perhaps it would be better to replace Crawford with Whitehead, while retaining McCullers as the preferred writer. "I always feel that Levin would be satisfied with another adaptation if only Miss Crawford would not be the producer." If she would agree to step aside, "further troubles" could be avoided.[32]

Two days later Meyer excitedly wrote Otto that Crawford was pulling out.

"I should now like the opportunity which I have asked for since the difficulty with Miss Crawford began—that is to secure a good producer for this play on the open market." To proceed, Meyer asked Otto for permission to conduct test readings and a possible tryout and "to reapproach producers who have expressed interest in my play." It was Meyer's hope that "we can all view this situation without rancour," for had Crawford "felt fully justified in her actions, she would go ahead." Surely, he could not be blamed for her decision.[33]

Certain that Meyer would attempt to reenter the picture, Zimmerman stepped up her attack against both his character and his sanity. Two weeks earlier, she had characterized him as "impossible to deal with in any terms, officially, legally, morally, personally . . . [and] a compulsive neurotic who was destroying both himself and Anne's play."[34] Now she again wrote Otto that Meyer's letter to *Variety* had been "most confused, and vicious," the work of a man "so out of touch with reality that I can't see how we can trust anything he says!" His attack upon Crawford was not motivated by "any real grudge against her," Zimmerman argued, "but because she is the most convenient person to attack." It was her judgment that Crawford had a moral claim to the production, while Shumlin, "a director [who] rarely produces plays," was clearly an "unwise" choice.[35]

Late the next afternoon, at Mermin's request, Zimmerman reported to Otto that Crawford, having calmed herself after being "at first so upset by Levin's senseless and vicious attack that she just couldn't think," had asked for a few extra days to make a decision. She still wished to produce the play, but only if it could be done "without trouble." Her lawyer would contact Mermin, who, in the interim, had already contacted Clurman and Whitehead to assess their interest. "How much harm Levin has done!" Zimmerman exclaimed, before "incidentally" mentioning that Shumlin, "a second-rate producer," had been taken off the list of potential producers "because he has been going downhill and his reputation has suffered."[36] Denied access to the *Diary*, Shumlin turned his efforts toward producing the critically acclaimed and financially successful *Inherit the Wind*, which appeared on Broadway before the *Diary*. In 1963 he added the controversial Holocaust play *The Deputy* to his credits.

Otto could no longer maintain his attempt at civility when Meyer's news that Crawford had withdrawn reached him on February 2, 1953, together with his denial of all responsibility and a request to again pursue possible producers. "I want to tell you that I know positively that if Miss Crawford is retiring it would be on account of your actions, which I consider being intrigues of the sort you warned me [of] so often from others. You simply do not realize that you did not hurt [only] Miss Crawford, but also Anne's book and myself." There was "no reason to be proud of your actions," he assured Meyer. Otto promised that he would "never . . . agree to offer the script in the open market," thereby effectively ending all possibility of Meyer's ever seeing his adaptation performed. Where only the day before he had closed with "Love to all of you . . . Otto," a cautious and angry businesslike tone had descended upon their relationship. He now signed the letter with his full name, preceded by "Sincerely yours."[37]

To shore up the collapsing structure that he had tried to put in place for the Diary, Otto explained to Crawford that he had written Meyer so "energetically . . . that Levin finally will be impressed and quiet down so that we can get to a satisfactory solution." Impressed with McCullers and her work, he hoped that Crawford would not allow Meyer to force her from the project. "As all the rights are on your side in case you want to go ahead, I suppose that you can easily reject unjust attacks."[38] But Crawford took little comfort or support from Otto. "With poor Meyer's psychosis, I just don't know what he is likely to do or say next." As concerned as she was for herself, she was again more worried about the impact of this "messy situation" upon McCullers. "Carson is so fragile and I have always been her protector so I must be very wise and certain about the right thing to do." She would await clarification from Mermin concerning the Clurman/Whitehead interest before deciding whether to "proceed and face the attacks which I am sure will continue to come."[39]

Zimmerman still hoped to maintain Otto's support for Crawford in the face of other possible producers. "Crawford does very much want to do it," she wrote, citing Mermin's "weekly report" on the situation. (Zimmerman and Mermin had offices in the same building, facilitating their coordinated effort—"We are thinking very much about the situation.") A "definite negative" from Clurman and Whitehead was now expected. With "something definitive to go on," there was "a strong likelihood that Miss Crawford will see her way clear to go ahead . . . if Levin quiets down considerably." It was Zimmerman's recommendation that Otto work on Meyer's "feelings of guilt . . . since he is totally responsible for the entire situation." There was, of course, no certainty that this tactic would succeed with someone who "works in such peculiar and upsetting ways." Still, it was worth the try.[40]

But Otto's scathing attack merely intensified Meyer's defensiveness, allowing him to concede only that like everyone else involved, he, too, had "acted badly." He refused to assume any guilt for having stood by his work, which Anne herself had asserted was an author's right. Crawford's accusation that he was the reason for her contemplated withdrawal was merely a sign of her "insincerity" and troubled conscience. Had she herself not told him of the theater's cruelty? "Certainly it is not the writers who have brought this about," he assured Otto. If there was intrigue, it had not been pursued by him. "I have always told you everything openly, and referred everyone to you." Could Otto say the same of himself, Meyer asked by implication? He had expected so much more of Otto, believing that he understood writers, anticipating that he "would not permit [him]self to hurt anyone's feelings." Deeply troubled to discover otherwise, Meyer hoped to find some personal solace in remembering that "in my short time of work this summer, there were times when I felt pure creative excitement, felt myself truly within the work." But how he "would have liked to see it on the stage."[41]

By mid-February, it seemed that Meyer was indeed "quieting down." With McCullers seemingly out of danger, it was time for Crawford "to show her sincerity." "Our patience was the right way to act," Otto told Zimmerman with newfound confidence in the situation, and with some sympathy for Meyer. "I am still not as angry as you are about him, always trying to see his situation and his love for the book." Tereska had written Otto of Meyer's eased tensions, and Otto had passed the letter to Zimmerman as proof that if "his actions were wrong and ugly . . . in his innermost he is not a bad man." Using characterizations first drawn by Zimmerman and Crawford, he spoke of Meyer as merely "difficult, not 100% normal, oversensitive," adding with mixed feelings, "I pity him, but we have to go our way."[42]

However confident Otto may have felt or wished to appear, he could no longer wait for Crawford's decision. On February 16 he told Zimmerman of his need for a "definite" word from Crawford before Meyer's "better spirits" faded. Meyer was certain to accept it "*now* without further attacks," as he would have had Crawford signed the contract immediately after the month's extension had lapsed. A second such moment could easily be lost. "I know that it still hurts him deeply that nothing could be done with the play." Why chance his change of mind now that he appeared to want to put it all behind him?[43]

Zimmerman, aware of Otto's impatience with Crawford, blamed Meyer for the earlier delay, claiming that Mermin had "wanted to give Levin a few weeks' extra chance in case something was to happen." There was, of course, no evidence of this, only proof to the contrary, as McCullers had been involved long before the month had run its course. Only Meyer's attacks had prevented Crawford from signing the contract with Otto, Zimmerman declared, and her continuing fear now prolonged her hesitation. "Crawford wants this still very much," Zimmerman reassured Otto. "So you see, it was not her fault." Had she signed then, "it would have made him even angrier," though given Meyer's nature, "he would have made trouble in any event whether a contract had been signed or not."[44]

By the eighteenth, Otto had yet to hear from Crawford and had begun to lose all hope. Worse still was the potential loss of McCullers' script, which any number of producers could have staged. McCullers had meanwhile prepared a draft introduction to Anne's collected short stories and had sent it to Otto.

Using its receipt as the pretext for writing McCullers, he told her how Crawford's last letter had given him the "impression that everything will develop satisfactorily," while neglecting to mention that two weeks had passed since the letter had been sent.[45]

Ten days later, on February 28, Mermin wrote Otto that while he could not provide "a final and definitive report," certain issues had "become clarified to a certain extent." He first wanted to ease Otto's conscience, knowing that he was "troubled by the possibility that there may be some truth in Levin's claims with respect to Clurman." Having now received Clurman's response, it was clear that he had "no more than a willingness to read the next version of a script." But Mermin's characterization was itself a distortion; he neglected to tell Otto that Clurman had, in his own words, "considered the first draft of the play promising" and had been "interested in reading it again if [Meyer] did further work." Instead, Mermin continued at some length about Crawford's continuing interest and McCullers' enthusiasm, the future of which was dependent upon "whether Miss Crawford will feel sufficiently satisfied that Levin won't make life difficult" should she sign to do the play. "Perhaps we will learn at that time whether the volcano is still active," he advised Otto.[46] (Clurman's interest in the Diary was, of course, completely unacceptable to Hellman, for he had played a central role in keeping the Group Theatre out of the control of its Communist Party members in the mid-1930s.[47])

A week later Zimmerman sent Otto the most encouraging news to date. Clurman's response had "substantially cleared the situation." Crawford was now prepared to sign the contract. "SO! Thus far everything looks very good indeed." She would cable Otto as soon as Crawford had returned the signed documents, after which "we'll feel just a bit safer."[48]

But three and a half more weeks passed without the contract's return, as Crawford struggled on the road with tryouts for Camino Real. When it opened on Broadway to mixed reviews, Crawford worried that substantial money might be lost. This, in turn, threw her involvement with the Diary into question. Without an existing script, it promised to be an even more expensive undertaking. Crawford was seeking firm commitments from backers before signing. "I have no doubt that this will be taken care of early this week, that the contracts will be signed and all will be settled at last," Zimmerman tried to reassure Otto.[49]

But Otto had grown increasingly concerned as each letter from Zimmerman and Mermin lacked the certainty he sought. "I hope we are finally on the way to a constructive program," Mermin had concluded in his report of February 28.[50] When Zimmerman's promise to "definitely have word by the first of next week!" did not materialize and another month passed, Otto, as an astute businessman, sensed that it was time to move on.

On Monday, April 5, Otto wrote Mermin that "in case things do not turn out the way we wished, I want to remind you that it was Kermit Bloomgarden who did all possible to get the play. But he was too late," Otto added, as if it had merely been a matter of timing, all other factors having been of no consequence. When they had met in New York in October, Otto had promised to let Bloomgarden know "if by any chance the agreement with Cheryl Crawford would not be fulfilled." It seemed now that he was "the most suitable producer" available.

Still, the question of a playwright remained. Meyer, of course, was not to be considered. His last letter to Otto, now two months old, had been left unanswered. Otto continued to view McCullers as a viable possibility even if Crawford ultimately withdrew. He planned to visit McCullers in Paris the following week "in order to discuss matters with her."[51] But here, too, there was need to look beyond the moment. What of George Tabori, whom Mermin himself had mentioned in his February 28 letter?[52] "Is he a well known writer? Would we not risk again that a play would be written and we had to look out for a producer afterwards?"[53] Had Otto known of Tabori's association with Bloomgarden, he would certainly have rested more easily.[54]

These questions would take on greater importance when the New York Times reported on April 19 that Crawford had bowed out. Though McCullers remained "willing" to work on the adaptation, the notice continued, "Crawford's enthusiasm has waned."[55] Dropping the evasive posture of the past several months, Crawford wrote Otto three days later of her decision "not to go ahead with the book, much to my regret." A few weeks after writing McCullers that she was abandoning the project for financial reasons, she now told Otto of the need to meet the "popular demand . . . for lighter entertainment" so as not to be "out of business" after her recent failure. Her lawyer's warning that Meyer was almost certain to drag her through a lawsuit should she proceed with the Diary had further persuaded her to abandon the project, though she had made no mention of this to McCullers. Four years later she offered Meyer's failure to honor his agreement with her as her sole reason for withdrawing, and she cited the same reason in her theatrical memoir.

Having often used McCullers' "fragile" constitution as reason for her own reluctance to sign with Otto, Crawford now advised Otto that "Carson may still wish to dramatize the book." In thanking him for the opportunity to consider producing Anne's Diary, she promised to be available to help with the play in "any way I can."[56] But a new set of characters was already mounting the stage for the next act, in which Crawford was destined to play the one role she feared most.

CHAPTER SIX

Things You Should Never Tell Anybody

lthough McCullers had not yet abandoned the project, Meyer lost little time in asking Otto to offer his script another chance. "I am sorry that things seem to have turned out pretty much as I had predicted they would," he wrote on April 26, attempting to console Otto and offering the suggestion that "perhaps with the passage of time and on longer reflection you will have a different feeling about what went on here." Should Otto ever be ready "to secure a good tryout of my play," or "to have it generally submitted," Meyer promised "to try to find a good producer."[1]

For the first time in more than three months, Otto broke his silence and on May 19 responded in a somewhat conciliatory voice. "I am pretty sure that our views in the matter still differ to a great extent," he acknowledged, though he, too, was disappointed that recriminations had arisen on all sides. "You know that I hate to hurt your feelings. I would have liked the atmosphere around the dramatization of Anne's book to be a better one." Nor was he now as certain of what had actually happened in the last weeks. Having "spoke[n] to a number of well known people," he had become "very careful in what I am doing. I certainly will not urge matters," he concluded, without, however, making any reference to Meyer's offer.[2]

"I can't help saying again that my actions in the whole matter of the play were the only ones consistent with my conscience as a writer," Meyer responded. "One can only try to do what is right by one's own conscience, and hope that others will see the whole case. If this is a mode of conduct that brings one into difficulties and unpopularity, it has its rewards in a certain personal sense of integrity." In this he spoke not only for himself. "Few writers would have behaved otherwise," Anne included.[3]

McCullers' decision in early June not to go forward with the adaptation, a decision Crawford considered "wise," opened the door for Meyer, as it did for

Hellman and Bloomgarden.[4] Meyer quickly renewed his search for a producer, without considering how Otto might respond should he be successful. But few would now chance becoming involved. In mid-June, Billy Rose wrote Meyer that "a careful look" had found his play "a workmanlike job which you may well be able to nurse into a hit." Unfortunately, his own schedule for the fall was too full even to consider another project.[5] No other responses have survived.

There was little reason for Bloomgarden to appear too eager now that the field had been cleared, and so, throughout the summer, he and Hellman remained silent, allowing Meyer's bid to run its course. With no other interest apparent, Otto responded to Meyer's May letter on July 30. "Just a few lines to keep in contact," he began, speaking mostly of family matters before briefly mentioning the *Diary*'s success in Japan.[6]

As Otto intended, Meyer felt encouraged by his "friendly letter." When he responded late that August, he claimed to have intended to do so "without any involvement about the play," but "fate did not will it so." He had received a telegram the previous day from a young producer, Terese Hayden, expressing her interest in his script. After meeting with her, Meyer was convinced of her sensitivity to the material. She proposed "to do it at once on Broadway," he informed Otto, knowingly adding that "she saw the universal implications as all-important."

Mermin, of course, had already refused to consider her proposal, claiming that a "big producer who has not yet selected an adaptor" would soon make Otto an acceptable offer. Meyer complained that the pattern seemed to be repeating itself. Here he was with a firm offer from "the best of the young producers," with four Broadway credits and other productions to her name. "She is, in short, one of the most energetic and talented of the up-and-coming group. To deny her is to deny the future itself." Worse still, "it would be the same as denying Anne." Why wait for one of the "big name" producers who had "all but wrecked the American theatre by their bad taste and slavish addiction to commercialism," witness the previous season's worst record ever? "I beg you not to deny us. I beg you not to take a lawyer's judgment in a matter of art." Instead, Meyer asked only that Otto trust his own ability to decide, knowing that he had a script and a producer "this season . . . rather than to wait for a promised adaptation that may again never materialize." To do otherwise was to deny the "murderous" nature of the theatrical world whose "complexity of motives" was "impossible to explain."[7]

That same day, Hayden sent her own appeal to Otto. Mermin's "cold and negative response" might have led her "to drop all of my desire," had she not been so "in love with the script." Admittedly young, she was "on fire and anxious," and hopefully asked Otto to consider her "firm offer to give your play an immediate first-class production on Broadway." Meyer's script, "faithful and well-conceived dramatically," could be ready for rehearsal after only minor changes.[8]

Angered by Mermin's response, Meyer asked why he had refused to consider Hayden's offer now that Crawford's withdrawal had removed all "moral obligations" to eliminate his script from consideration. "Could it not be that some personal feelings are distorting a view as to what might be best for Mr. Frank in this matter?"[9] Two days later, when Meyer sent a second appeal to Otto questioning the "basis" for Mermin's decision, he had still heard only unconfirmed rumors that contract talks were under way with one of Broadway's "big names."[10] It was, of course, by design that word had not yet been released concerning the progress of these negotiations.

Uncertain how to respond to Hayden and Meyer, Otto shared their letters with Zimmerman, who asserted that Meyer had now resumed "the same old pressure and nastiness again," though she failed to offer any specific instances in her two-page, single-spaced letter. Instead, she characterized Meyer's remark about lawyers as "not only unrealistic, but rather crazy," the product of "a pathological hatred for successful people," and the real reason for his inability to accept the judgments of Crawford and Mermin. Nor could someone "in his right mind" have suggested Hayden over Bloomgarden, Zimmerman added, having heard from "a friend of mine" that she was "generally unstable, inexperienced and difficult," as well as "*not* a particularly bright person." Finally, "everyone" she knew who had dealt with Meyer over the years had suffered "the same kind of treatment from him. He is the least trusted man in America next to McCarthy probably, and after all there *must* be something in it"—a rather curious logic given McCarthy's own use of guilt by innuendo and the awareness of his reign of terror upon those with whom Zimmerman associated in this matter. Though it was as yet unknown who the playwright would be, "we *have* to trust [Bloomgarden's] judgment, and put the fate of the play in his hands."[11]

Otto had not yet received Zimmerman's letter when he wrote to Meyer confirming Mermin's "serious negotiations with one of the well known producers," the details of which "I do not know . . . at the moment myself." He would say no more until he received further information from Mermin. "I never will talk from one to the other." Yet, whatever the final outcome, he assured Meyer that it would not have been reached without great deliberation and a thorough search "in different directions."[12]

Otto then repeated his claim to Tereska that without "reliable" information from different sources, he could not judge the latest proposal from Hayden and Meyer. Not that it mattered, he admitted, for Mermin's vacation was all that stood in the way of the "well-known producer" signing the contract. In obvious contradiction of his earlier statement alleging not to have "details" of the negotiations under way, he spoke of the offer as "very reasonable," though experience had taught him to be "very cautious."[13] He was, in fact, remaining noncommittal as before. Negotiations with Bloomgarden might still collapse.

The arrival of Zimmerman's letter two days later, on September 9, destroyed what little chance Levin and Hayden might have had in attracting Otto's support. As Zimmerman had feared, Otto was indeed beginning to lean in their direction and might have signed with them had Bloomgarden ultimately backed out. "The reaction of Miss Hayden gave me for a moment again the feeling of doubt: Are we doing right or wrong?" he had wondered. "But now, knowing that she has not the standard Levin is pretending, I am quiet again. You are right: a fine production or none." He further agreed with Zimmerman that news of these negotiations had to remain private, even after Bloomgarden's signing. They hoped to avoid angering Meyer, as Otto had thus far succeeded in doing by writing him "without much content."[14] With Zimmerman's reassurance now in hand Otto sent Mermin his approval of the contract with Bloomgarden.[15]

Not yet aware of this development, Meyer wrote Otto on Rosh Hashanah "with a full feeling of this as a solemn day upon which one seeks to determine true values." As he argued, "From all the evidence I have been able to gather, the predominant opinion is that my play is good and producible and faithful, and therefore it deserves production; the producers are ready, and I can see no basis for refusal."[16] Continuing to move cautiously, Otto sent Mermin a draft of his response to Meyer, along with a copy of Meyer's letter. "I think Mr. Mermin should know every letter I receive," Otto had written Zimmerman. Receiving Otto's material, Mermin determined that Otto ought not to forward a reply of any kind to Meyer at this point in the negotiations with Bloomgarden.[17]

But the lack of a response from Otto could not silence Meyer. Having shared a panel on Creative Expression as part of a three-day conference on moral standards held at the Jewish Theological Seminary, he told Otto that he could not allow his work to "be destroyed without raising [his] voice." Not to continue "putting forward my claims" would "be an act of cowardice" and surrender in "the question of 'control' in the arts," Meyer argued perceptively. "I am fairly ready to assume that Mr. Mermin has not confined himself to the same list to which I was confined." Meyer had agreed to the "controlled list of producers" under protest and without the advice of counsel, "as I had left the law office by which I had been represented, because they also represented Miss Crawford." There was still time to allow Hayden to attempt her production, he advised. "A young producer with sensitivity and sincerity is fully as good in a commercial sense as the 'biggest,'" though as Arthur Miller had stated at the conference, the producer's role in the theater had become a "constantly shrinking one." Surely Mermin's concern that he find a "better deal" for Otto would be protected.

Meyer closed his lengthy note to Otto that day as he had three weeks earlier, speaking of the Jewish history textbook he was writing for the Reform movement, of which Otto was a member. Touching upon Otto's expressed concern for the future of Israel, Meyer added word of his newest commitment, the writing of a weekly series of scripts for Israeli radio.[18] Each bit of news seemed calculated to remind Otto of those things he claimed to have put at the center of his life.

Though he had "not intended to enter into discussions" with Meyer, Otto could not allow these allusions to pass without angrily asserting that he was under no "moral obligation" to accept Meyer's script. Nor would he allow himself to be "urged or pressed," even by the passing of "personal feelings which I used to have towards you." Instead, it remained solely a question of the "*best*" possible script, which, based upon the reactions of Crawford and Bloomgarden, Meyer's was not. "That is what I want for Anne."

Nor would Otto accept any responsibility for the financial risk Meyer had taken on his behalf, claiming that there had been an agreement between Meyer and Crawford which did not involve himself. Otto knew that no such written agreement had ever existed and that Meyer's reference to the need for all to act in good faith had been well justified. "I am glad you started to work . . . now that you are no more worried about the choice of a producer," Otto had written encouragingly to Meyer the previous July in a letter that later disappeared from his own files. Now, "after long and earnest reflections and after having received reliable informations from different sources (not from Mr. Mermin)," he had once again decided to reject Hayden's offer and Meyer's script without further comment. "I am [too] tired to continue discussing," he told Meyer as he awaited final word of Bloomgarden's signing.[19]

Five days later, on September 26, Otto notified Hayden of his decision, indicating that the "difficulties" involving Meyer's script, even if current negotiations failed, had foreclosed the possibility of its being produced. Instead, he would wait for news of "further developments" from his lawyer and, if need be, longer still for the right script. There was "no hurry to see Anne's book dramatized on the stage."[20]

Less than a week passed before Otto received word from New York that Bloomgarden had signed, giving him the "sole and exclusive right to prepare and/or cause to be prepared a dramatic version of the book," including "the right to employ for such purposes a dramatist or dramatists." Otto would retain "the right of approval with respect to the selection of the dramatist," as he had previously, as well as the right to allow Meyer to have his adaptation produced in Hebrew translation in Israel, "subsequent to the opening in New York" of Bloomgarden's production. Aware that further trouble with Meyer might lie ahead, Bloomgarden had secured indemnification from "any claim, action, or other proceeding asserted or instituted by Meyer Levin . . . which challenges the right of the dramatist to write the version and to have the version pro-duced, or which in any manner challenges the right of the Manager to produce and present the versions." All such liability would be Otto's.[21]

Though Meyer heard of the contract's signing long before it was reported in the *New York Times* on November 22, several days passed before rumors began to reach him.[22] And so he pressed Otto further on October 2, admitting that "obviously we should have cooperated." But he had given so much of himself to the book and the play, only to be pushed aside "to make plans with others." Although he agreed that Otto might not be legally obligated to use his script, he did "not think that the mountain of correspondence that passed between us in regard to my writing the play would indicate that you did not know that I was writing it, and that you did not approve of my writing it." He would, therefore, most assuredly present his adaptation somewhere on stage and would withdraw it forever only "if the audience reaction is not good." The correspondence, Meyer claimed, demonstrated that Otto had given him per-mission to conduct such a tryout, "and a try-out I shall get, the best that I can find." This he promised as the "fundamental issue of a writer's natural duty to his work," adding with a bite that would sharpen in the days ahead, "I am sure your daughter would have felt the same way."[23]

By October 8 "rumors of another contract" had reached Meyer. "I do not know what your situation is now," but "this continuing atmosphere of secrecy and animosity does not help, either, for the past cannot be erased," he warned Otto. There could be little doubt that "I was overnight put in the position of an outcast whose usefulness had been exhausted." If not that he would become "a traitor to my function as a writer," denying his work "a normal life and a normal death," he would have written "the whole thing off as a bad experi-ence." But he felt about his work "exactly as you felt about your daughter." Both had been "created out of love." Neither should have been "put to death by Nazis or their equivalent. . . . Those who would destroy [the script] before it can reach any public are no better, in their authoritative attitude, than the persons who destroy human life without trial, but simply on their own whim."[24]

Confirmation that it was indeed Bloomgarden with whom Otto had signed brought a long letter from Meyer to the new producer a week and a half later, asking that his script "come to an audience test" and that, if well received, it be permitted its "moral right" to a life on the stage. Having "never 'protested' my legal position, and out of sympathy for Mr. Frank allowed myself to be pressured into signing a contract which I protested most vigorously as unfair," he sought only to prevent Bloomgarden and Otto "from doing an injustice, not only to me but to the original book." (He was, in fact, "ready to waive any royalties . . . to a memorial for Anne Frank.") After so many positive reactions, surely Bloomgarden understood that his reading of the script had been clouded by Crawford's assessment, and that now "a different impression might result."[25]

Meyer, of course, was as yet unaware of Hellman's influence upon Bloomgarden's judgment and of the larger conflict it represented. And so he continued to hope that a sense of fairness would be exercised. If not, he promised to do all he could to see that it was. "I believe that any writer who considers an adaptation, in the light of the circumstances around my own work, would have the fullest opportunity to know my side of this situation from me, so that any future complications that might lead to a moral problem for such a writer might be, to whatever extent possible, avoided." Bloomgarden would not respond to Meyer's letter, nor to a second sent on October 31, which he gave to his attorney at Paul, Weiss.[26]

Meyer's active role in McCullers' decision not to write the script had been a clear signal to all that he did not intend to remain idle during this latest search for a playwright. The selection would have to be far from the reach of Meyer's moral arguments, less emotionally vulnerable than McCullers, and dependable through close and personal ties to the new producer and his silent backer. The first step was to try once again to shut the door on Meyer's unyielding hope for his script. On October 23, Otto wrote Meyer that his script would never be given a tryout. Nor was there any moral question involved. "[I] repeat that you did not write on my instigation," Otto insisted, contrary to the many letters both he and Meyer had before them. Moreover, he chastised Meyer for his "too serious and too egotistic" comparison of the treatment of his script with Anne's death. "I regard your point of view highly exaggerated," he protested. "It is not a crime" to be rejected, nor treasonous to his function as a writer to "quiet down." "You seem to forget that the dramatization, which you did so faithfully to Anne's book, is not a pure creative work." In spite of its admitted fidelity to the Diary, Otto simply refused to revisit Meyer's work. "I got to the decision that it is my duty to have another script written."[27]

Unable to accept Otto's advice or his moral judgment, Meyer responded as a victim of "the stupidity that I and every other writer must deal with throughout life," and as Anne would have, "had she lived to continue her career." It was arguably an unfortunate parallel to draw. But Meyer was more desperate than ever, knowing now that his position was doomed. Never had Otto listened to those who had been "moved" by his work, Meyer wrote passionately. Instead, "You have been used against me. But it is no use arguing with you against the weight of the big shots of the theatre whom you have involved against me." Meyer was, however, willing to accept some of the responsibility for having consented to the list of "chosen producers," but he had done so only "because of your anxiety." "I have been taken advantage of by legal tricks and maneuvers," he wanted Otto to admit. "To suppress the play on these flimsy grounds is to me and always will be a scandalous piece of arbitrary manipulation," about which he could not remain silent, though he again promised to take no legal action against Otto. "My restraint in this situation is due entirely to what you are and what you have been through." But "I do feel that it is questionable to force me to extend my feeling for you to a producer by giving him your protection against me."[28]

Three weeks later, on November 19, Leah Salisbury, theatrical agent for the screenwriting husband and wife team of Frances Goodrich and Albert Hackett, contacted her clients to tell them that Bloomgarden "would very much like to have you consider adapting [the *Diary*] for the theatre." The offer had come with Hellman's recommendation to Bloomgarden that "you would be ideal."[29] The Hacketts had earned well-deserved reputations in Hollywood, with some thirty-two films to their credit. Writers mostly of musicals and light comedies (*Easter Parade*, *Naughty Marietta*, and the like), they had adapted the highly successful *Thin Man* series, based upon the work of Hellman's longtime friend and lover, Dashiell Hammett, and had scripted the now-classic *It's a Wonderful Life*.[30] But while three of the Hacketts' comedic efforts had found their way to the stage, the best of these had failed to win the critics' praise. Hellman herself suspected that the last of these, *The Big Doorstep*, had been something of a "struggle" for them to write.[31]

Successful on the screen but not in the theater, the Hacketts at first seemed an unsuitable choice for Hellman to make. No one was more surprised, or concerned, than they. "I wish we were as sure that we were the people for the job as we are sure that it will make a fine and moving play," they responded to Salisbury with excitement, gratitude, and apprehension. "It seems to us to lend itself admirably to play form with its tense drama, the possibility of great intimacy in the scenes . . . and moments of lovely comedy which heighten the desperate, tragic situation of the people." But they worried that their conception of the *Diary* might not be Bloomgarden's.[32]

They need not have been concerned. Hellman knew exactly what she wanted for the play, and whom she could count on to write it—with her ongoing help. With McCullers gone, Otto had asked that Hellman write the script herself, but she had refused, insisting instead that Bloomgarden use the Hacketts. Bloomgarden was amenable, having himself worked under Shumlin when he had produced the Hacketts' last Broadway play. In excusing herself to Otto, Hellman had cited her inability to work with someone else's material. It was an odd disclaimer, given that The Children's Hour had been lifted from an eighteenth-century British court case, while Watch on the Rhine paralleled the story of a woman and her family whom Hellman had met shortly after their flight from Europe to America. Her next project was itself an adaptation of another playwright's work.

Having been hauled before HUAC the previous year, and having in March experienced the banning of The Children's Hour by the United States government from two hundred of its Information Service Libraries, Hellman wisely declined Otto's request out of concern that the Diary would suffer from her open association with it. After spending the summer fearful of a second HUAC subpoena and possible arrest, she now wished to maintain a behind-the-scenes posture, in order not to jeopardize all that she had intended to accomplish with the Diary. "There are certain things you should never tell anybody," she advised a friend who had raised the issue of Communist affilia-tions during this period.[33] What she needed was a writer willing to take direction, someone whose thoughts were similar enough to her own that her suggestions, made directly or indirectly, would be accepted—someone whose experience was perhaps elsewhere than in the theater and who was therefore open to help at every turn.

Meyer, with his objectionable politics, socialist and Zionist, and with his ethnic focus upon the Diary, could not be manipulated. At best, he would accept help in staging a script whose contents he would refuse to change if it meant giving Anne a different posture. He felt loyalty only to the victims of the Holocaust, and certainly not to Hellman, whose views on basic questions he knew to be fundamentally at odds with his own.

The Hacketts, malleable and willing to follow Hellman's direction, would unknowingly provide the "front" she needed. They had first met two decades earlier at MGM, had formed a circle of friends whose conversations often turned to discussions of Communism, and together had struggled to establish, direct, and then reestablish the Screen Writers' Guild after the studios had attempted to destroy it with charges of radicalism in 1936. These charges were not without some basis, given the central influence of Hellman and Hammett (himself long a Party member). In the coming years, she continued to wield this influence in some forty other organizations, some of which were clearly established as Communist fronts. Hellman, who was at times more actively involved than Hammett in Party affairs, had in fact initiated several of these groups. Thus, while Hammett enthusiastically responded to instructions from the Party, Hellman's had been the more combative spirit. She had first com-mitted herself to the fight that year as a member of a special, loosely organized group within the Party, and then openly joined after attending its Tenth National Convention in June 1938.[34] As early as 1929, Hellman had been a member of the John Reed Club in New York, a Party-sponsored group then under the supervision of the Party's future leader, Earl Browder, whom Hellman would urge to come to Hollywood in 1936. (He returned the favor in 1948 by counseling her active participation in the presidential campaign of Henry Wallace.[35]) And when Goodrich panicked, fearing that "a group of writers" allied with Louis Mayer were "probably going through our mail everyday," Hellman merely grew more strident.[36] Hackett recalled that "while the rest of us considered various tactics against the studios and the dangers involved, Lillian would contemptuously brush such caution aside and say something like, 'They're bastards. Let's clean them out.' . . . She was somebody wonderful to have on your side, but then you were afraid she'd go too far."[37] As Hellman's former husband, Arthur Kober, noted in his diary in 1935, "Lil talks Revolution."[38]

As officers of the Guild's Board (Goodrich was for many years its secretary), or as financial contributors to "some other organizations" later alleged by HUAC to be Communist fronts, the Hacketts had themselves come under investigation as part of the committee's continuing Hollywood witch-hunt. Though never subpoenaed by Congress, they had nonetheless been compelled to respond to the committee's charges against them during the fall of 1952 and the early winter of 1953 in order to remain working in Hollywood. They repeatedly denied ever having been Communist Party members, though many of their friends were, Hellman among them. It "didn't matter to us," Hackett later asserted. Thirty years later, they still refused to speak to anyone who had cooperated with HUAC. For them, Hellman's stance during her testimony before the committee remained "a wonderful thing."[39]

Hellman knew the quality of their work from the *Thin Man* films and had called upon them again in 1943 to condense her *Watch on the Rhine* for use by the United States Armed Forces. "It's an extremely skillful job, and God knows I am grateful to you for it," she had told them, before asking for additional changes, knowing that they would comply without objection.[40]

In a word, the Hacketts were safe. They could be depended upon by Hellman to deliver a script with the proper ideological focus, properly deethnicized, and with the Holocaust itself lightened with touches of sweet comedy to mask the particularism of the horror out of which the *Diary* had emerged. From the first, Bloomgarden would make it clear that he didn't want the script "wringing tears out of people," that "the only way this play will go will be if its funny. . . . We said always that we felt, get them laughing, and that's the way its possible for them to sit through the show." There could be none of the "breast beating" that had characterized the "awful" script already rejected, Bloomgarden told them during their first meeting.[41] And they would comply, ever distorting the larger picture as each subsequent revision moved the script further from the *Diary* itself. As Hellman later assured them, "What you write will be true."[42]

With time and the repeated intervention of Hellman and Bloomgarden, and of the director they eventually chose, the Holocaust's presence in the play would be diminished to the point where one British critic later wrote that "the text of 'The Diary of Anne Frank' does not give us . . . the sense that this particular crowding was due to the menace of racial persecution." The critic had emerged from the theater "totally unmoved and even uninterested," thinking that aside from a few hints at the underlying cause of the overcrowd-ing, they "might have been piled on top of one another by a housing short-age."[43] Joseph Schildkraut, who played Otto on the stage, acknowledged three months into the initial Broadway run that the "Diary of Anne Frank is not primarily a Jewish play. . . . In this adaptation, the sectarian nature of the story is not emphasized. These people could be any refugees, not just Jews."[44]

Brooks Atkinson praised the lack of reference to the Annex inhabitants' ultimate treatment by the Nazis and to Anne's murder in Bergen-Belsen as an instance of "taste rare in the theater." He further observed that "in fact, they do not dwell on the shocking conclusion to Anne's brief career in human society . . . [in this] record of what happened in the lives of some refugees and in the heart of a maiden. It is a record of homely things and human reactions— gratitude for sanctuary in the garret, the disciplines needed to keep their presence a secret, petty irritations, rebellion, treachery, ridicule, callousness, love, forgiveness. It is basically a portrait of Anne keeping alive her interest in life, her faith in the sweetness of the passing moments and her confidence in the future." Atkinson was pleased to see that "at rare intervals along Broadway, something happens that puts the theatre on its mettle and animates everyone into doing a little more than he is capable of doing," for "suddenly, something has happened that has transformed them all [the Hacketts, Schildkraut, and Garson Kanin, the play's director] into dedicated artists with a mission."[45]

The Hacketts later declined offers to adapt several other Jewish books for the stage and screen, believing themselves "not right" for the material, or finding the story to be "too remote from our experience."[46] Perhaps under-standably, they turned down the offer to write the script for *Marjorie Morn-ingstar*, another tale of an adolescent Jewish girl, stating simply, "We don't want to do another Jewish story."[47] As an increasingly observant Jew, the novel's author, Herman Wouk, would certainly have demanded more Jewish content than had been allowed in the *Diary*'s script.

"We are more than ever convinced that it will make a good play," the Hacketts had written Bloomgarden on December 4, 1953, confirming the pre-vious day's telegram, in which they had spoken of their desire to do the script. They had already completed a second reading of the *Diary* and had "started to block out . . . scenes."[48] On the eighth, Bloomgarden cabled that he would be in Los Angeles in four days to begin their discussion, confident that they shared a common vision for the play.[49] The Hacketts then sent Salisbury word that they were "in agreement with Kermit about the book" and would soon meet with him. "The reason he wanted us," they told her, "was that he wanted comedy . . . and there is certainly a great deal of comedy already in the book."[50] Yet they knew that because their "last venture in the theatre was disastrous," it would be difficult for Salisbury to command the contract terms she hoped to negotiate for them with Mermin, particularly the removal of the "final approval" clause Otto had insisted upon in any contract.[51]

At 8:30 on the morning of December 12, Bloomgarden met with the Hacketts and began by telling them that Hellman had "suggested [them] for the job." After Bloomgarden left two days later, they wrote Salisbury that "we talked and talked about the play. We were in agreement on every point he made, and he seemed satisfied with the way we thought of the play." He had also convinced them not to worry about the "final approval" clause demanded by Otto. Reassured by Bloomgarden's description of Otto's character, they felt certain that "such a man will never be unreasonable."[52] Certain that they would accept the contract being negotiated by Salisbury, the Hacketts notified their Hollywood agent that the "deal" was "all set" and that they would need a six-month leave of absence from MGM. They then sent their thanks to Bloomgarden "in appreciation . . . [for] wanting us," to which they added a final "little note to Lillian, thanking her for speaking of us."[53] Their obligations now completed, they rushed off to a bookstore to purchase materials on Holland, Jewish history and culture, and "teen-agers," in preparation for the start of work the next day. Seasoned writers, they would work into the late afternoon, trusting that with Hellman's producer as their own, they could begin without a contract in hand.[54] On the eighteenth, Bloomgarden would support their trust by telling them of his belief that they were "so right for the job."[55]

Anne Frank at Montessori School, 1941 (ANNE FRANK STICHTING)

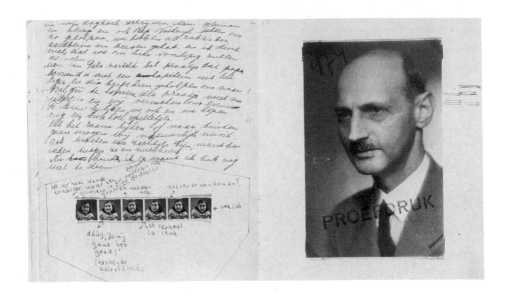

Otto Frank's photo on a page of Anne's diary (ANNE FRANK STICHTING)

Meyer Levin as a war correspondent, 1945
(COURTESY OF JO BASISTE [ELI LEVIN])

Tereska Torres, c. 1970 (COURTESY OF JO BASISTE [ELI LEVIN])

Cheryl Crawford (SMITH COLLEGE ARCHIVES)

From left, Harold Clurman, Elia Kazan, and Maxwell Anderson
(PHOTOGRAPH COLLECTION, HARRY RANSOM RESEARCH CENTER,
UNIVERSITY OF TEXAS)

Meyer Levin, c. 1953 (COURTESY OF JO BASISTE [ELI LEVIN])

Herman Shumlin (WISCONSIN CENTER FOR FILM AND THEATER RESEARCH)

Kermit Bloomgarden (PHOTOGRAPH COLLECTION, HARRY RANSOM RESEARCH CENTER, UNIVERSITY OF TEXAS)

Lillian Hellman (WISCONSIN CENTER FOR FILM AND THEATER RESEARCH)

From left, foreground, Frances Goodrich, Albert Hackett, Otto Frank, and Garson Kanin in front of Anne Frank House (PARTICAM PICTURES/MARIA AUSTRIA INSTITUTE)

Frances Goodrich and Albert Hackett (WISCONSIN CENTER FOR FILM AND THEATER RESEARCH)

Susan Strasberg and Joseph Schildkraut as Anne and Otto dancing on Broadway (PHOTOGRAPH COLLECTION, HARRY RANSOM RESEARCH CENTER, UNIVERSITY OF TEXAS)

Peter and Anne confront one another on stage (PHOTOGRAPH COLLECTION, HARRY RANSOM RESEARCH CENTER, UNIVERSITY OF TEXAS)

From left, foreground, Frances Goodrich, Albert Hackett, Otto Frank, and Garson Kanin in front of Anne Frank House (PARTICAM PICTURES/MARIA AUSTRIA INSTITUTE)

Frances Goodrich and Albert Hackett (WISCONSIN CENTER FOR FILM AND THEATER RESEARCH)

Susan Strasberg and Joseph Schildkraut as Anne and Otto dancing on Broadway (PHOTOGRAPH COLLECTION, HARRY RANSOM RESEARCH CENTER, UNIVERSITY OF TEXAS)

Peter and Anne confront one another on stage (PHOTOGRAPH COLLECTION, HARRY RANSOM RESEARCH CENTER, UNIVERSITY OF TEXAS)

Otto Frank, c. 1970 (ANNE FRANK STICHTING)

Meyer Levin, c. 1970 (COURTESY OF JO BASISTE [ELI LEVIN])

Last photo taken of Meyer Levin, 1981 (COURTESY OF JO BASISTE [ELI LEVIN])

Lilly's Suggestions Will Work Out

News of the Hacketts' agreement with Bloomgarden reached the *New York Times* on December 19, and Meyer, reading that they were to begin work immediately in preparation for an opening in the fall of 1954, wasted no time in offering to provide them with details of "the circumstances surrounding the dramatization of the book . . . in fairness to yourself as well as to me."[1] To this note of a single short paragraph, he added a more pointed appeal to Otto the next day, reminding him that his own script had been rejected in search of what was, as Otto had repeatedly claimed, "best for Anne." The Hacketts, Meyer argued, "can scarcely conform to this description." He was now "more than ever convinced that personal reasons rather than valid judgment" had worked against him. "For reasons of moral principle," he would continue "to combat the decision to the limit of my ability. . . . I must do what I think is right." "My play cannot be withdrawn without some kind of audience test," Meyer demanded, accusing Otto's "representative" of suppressing not only his play but "even a discussion of what happened."[2] Otto responded briefly a week later, noting that while he could neither convince him nor "go into details," he still wanted to reassure Meyer that both decisions had been purely professional. If anything, their "personal relations" had complicated matters for Otto, though "my conscience tells me that no injustice is done against you."[3]

After ten days of work, the Hacketts, "walking on air . . . however smoggy . . . since you left," sent their first thoughts to Bloomgarden, nearly all concerning the set design. The basics were in keeping with Bloomgarden's general outline, to which they had added some of their own plans. Any that were "contrary to [the] reality" of the *Diary* were designed to "stress scenes" that involved Anne, "since this is a dramatization of Anne's diary." In what constituted a fundamental distortion of Anne's experience, but not of the general directive given them by Bloomgarden, it was their intent to have Anne go to Peter's room "for their intimate scenes . . . not he toward her. . . . We now think it is important for Anne to move toward him, both physically and spiritually." Peter would be made to vehemently argue against Anne's growing sense of her Jewishness and of her deepening understanding of the special role God had assigned the Jews in their suffering, historically and in her lifetime. It seemed to matter little to those now legally in control of the *Diary* that this new script would so severely distort its focus.

The Hacketts planned to write Otto, "gently at first," telling him of their "deep feeling for his child," before raising the more painful questions.[4] The following morning, December 27, they introduced themselves to Otto by letter and spoke of how "very honoured and very humble [they felt] in approaching the task. It is a very beautiful, and very moving, book. . . . We pray that we may be able to capture its quality . . . the spirit and indomitable courage of your daughter."[5] Though Otto knew that they, like Meyer, had begun to write without a contract, he answered them with encouragement, approving of the "spirit [with which] you approach the dramatization," pleased to "see how deeply moved [they] were by Anne's Diary." He pledged his assistance in any way it might be needed, "persuaded . . . that it is my duty to propagate Anne's ideas and ideals in every manner."[6]

The Hacketts had also written Meyer that day in response to his offer to share the details of his story with them. "Our hearts went out to him," they had told Bloomgarden, having first sent a copy of Meyer's letter to him for clarification.[7] But Bloomgarden's negative reaction had left them somewhat less sympathetic toward his "unhappy and frustrating experience." There was little they could do, they wrote Meyer. "An understanding had already been reached." Sending their "best wishes," they apparently hoped never again to hear from him.[8]

But Meyer could not let go. In a four-page, single-spaced, narrow-margined letter, he told the Hacketts how he had "been pushed around on the whim of a couple of producers," while Otto, "frightened and subjected to a good deal of pressure talk in which I was presented [in 'a whispering campaign'] as someone who was trying to take advantage of his property," had sided with them, refusing to allow even a "test reading" of his script. It was "the old story of the writer against the people who control access to the audience." In censoring his work, they had so distorted their own refusal to provide "an objective judgment" that it now appeared as if it were merely Meyer's own "personal issue." Somehow, he would have that public reading, even if it required a public challenge to Bloomgarden.[9]

Not knowing how to respond to Meyer's objections, the Hacketts sent his second letter to Bloomgarden. "I feel a deep moral obligation to him, as a writer," Goodrich wrote, noting, however, that her husband thought Meyer "selfish and a villain." "If what he says is true, he has had a pushing around," she continued. "But since there is such a division of feeling between Albert and me, we must leave it to your good judgment."[10] Yet they would seek further confirmation of Hackett's assessment from Salisbury the following day, despite their longstanding awareness of how unsympathetic she might be toward someone like Meyer.[11] As far back as 1936, Salisbury had in a letter to Goodrich characterized one of her own clients as "Jewish and egotistical."[12] Two years later, she had told a producer with whom she was negotiating a client's contract that he was being "kikish" and then related this conversation to Hackett without remorse or embarrassment.[13] She had spent much of her professional life with Hellman, Bloomgarden, and others whose vision of reality was fixed elsewhere. So much so, in fact, that even years after the *Diary* had opened in New York, Salisbury could still find herself shocked, as a Jew, to discover anti-Semitism in her world. "Can this really be true?" she wrote Otto with the disbelief of someone to whom the Jewish experience was virtually unknown.[14]

Before Meyer followed through on his threat of a public notice, he first offered Otto the courtesy of foreknowledge and the opportunity to remedy his grievance. Amid the repetition of old claims, Meyer noted how Mermin's statement that neither he nor Otto had judged the merits of the script was clear proof "that certain producers gave you bad opinions. . . . It is because of this that I repeat to you that you sometimes have been manipulated. You were talked to by people of imposing influence [who] for one reason or another . . . didn't like my play." The skewed chance to find a producer after Crawford's withdrawal was merely further proof of this fact, Meyer having found after inevitable failure that he "had been cleverly manipulated into a position where it was claimed I had no legal rights." He had been "swindled." Equally shocking, he had been usurped by "a couple of Hollywood writers!" He could not rest, he promised Otto, but would continue to demand a test reading, "even if I have to pass out leaflets in the street."[15]

Negotiations between representatives for Otto, Bloomgarden, and the Hacketts, which had begun in earnest on December 10, had continued into the new year, with various counteroffers being made on the issues of script approval. At a meeting with Salisbury on December 21, Mermin had stressed Otto's reluctance to give up this right for fear that he might "open the door to additional complaints from Levin by giving new dramatists more favorable rights for their script than he gave Levin." Although Salisbury understood Otto's position, she nonetheless advised the Hacketts to hold out as long as possible against his insistence. "Mr. Frank should be willing to rely on the judgment of Bloomgarden," she argued. Nor would she accept the one-month extension, similar to that given Meyer, should Bloomgarden withdraw. Instead she proposed a period of four months, "and some intelligent way of agreeing on the producers to whom we would be allowed to submit it." However "dangerous" it was to make these demands, Salisbury knew how unfairly Meyer had been treated.

Salisbury was further dissatisfied with the protection offered against the theft of "any new character, new situation, or new plot . . . not found in the book," should their play prove unacceptable. "Scenes, sequences and dialogue" would have to be added. But Mermin refused even to recommend this emendation to Otto, having already broadened his client's liability by allowing Meyer the one-month extension. Fully aware that plagiarism was not uncommon in the theater, Salisbury worriedly wrote her clients on January 14 that "when I am on the side of the dramatist I do not like it."

Salisbury was equally displeased with the proposed extension to the Hacketts of Otto's agreement to indemnify Bloomgarden from any liability connected with Meyer. Despite Mermin's claim that "no reputable lawyer would accept his case," she worried that it might ultimately have some legal merit, and she therefore wanted greater protection for her clients than an amount limited to Otto's royalties. Meyer's challenge to Bloomgarden for a public tryout had by now appeared in the *New York Post*, while Salisbury's own conversation with Meyer's agent had left her deeply worried that the Hacketts were indeed vulnerable. As Salisbury admitted to the Hacketts, Meyer had in fact written a "much better than average dramatization" that had left several producers "very impressed." Howell's assessment that "Frank owes Levin a debt of gratitude" could prove troublesome. Should the Hacketts be sued, they would be forced to retain their own attorney.[16] "Naturally we are very much disturbed about Mr. Levin," Goodrich responded. "He evidently wants no percentage. . . . He wants his play done, and that's that."[17]

The Hacketts had every reason to be upset. They, like their agent, had learned of Meyer's public statement challenging Bloomgarden to give his play a public hearing. "Is it right for you to kill a play that others find deeply moving, and are eager to produce?" he had demanded in the *Post*. "My work has been with the Jewish story. I tried to dramatize the *Diary* as Anne would have, in her own words." "The test I ask cannot hurt any eventual production from the book," he argued. "To refuse shows only a fear my play may prove right. To kill it in such a case would be unjust to the *Diary* itself. This question is basic: who shall judge? I feel my work has earned the right to be judged by you, the public," whom he now asked to petition Otto.[18]

But Bloomgarden had already told the Hacketts that he would not respond to Meyer's advertised challenge. "It would be beneath my dignity." Instead, he added to the campaign of character assassination by telling them how everyone in the theater thought Meyer "ridiculous and laughable by his unethical attachment to the book." Turning Meyer's contribution to the book's promotion on its head, he accused him of accepting the *New York Times* review assignment for personal gain, a charge he later brought before the *Times* itself.

More significantly, it had been clear from the start "that any producers wanting to have a dramatization made of the book originally would have had to take Mr. Levin or there would be no sale," Bloomgarden told the Hacketts. "This was the position that Cheryl Crawford found herself in," he noted, lending credence to Meyer's claim that she had merely used him to get to Otto and the *Diary*. "I agree with Albert," Bloomgarden concluded with unconscious irony, having himself profited from this deception. "This man is a villain," he said of Meyer, "and no further attention or thought should be given to him."[19]

Long out of the picture, Price now resurfaced as Otto's contact at Doubleday following Zimmerman's marriage and departure. It had been Mermin's hope that Price would merely "continue the close contact which Barbara made possible."[20] Instead, he sought to embolden Otto by placing some of the blame for Meyer's continuing disruption at Otto's own feet. "I feel that in many ways your own gentleness of spirit has allowed this matter to go on to the point where it has reached this impasse." Fearing that Otto was not firm enough in his resolve to reject Meyer's claims, Price raised the spectre of the Hacketts' possible withdrawal for the very reason he claimed McCullers had departed, "Meyer's accusations." Fully aware that the Hacketts had no such intention, Price nonetheless told Otto that "a second honest and intelligent attempt to produce it has probably been killed," all in the service of "the personal vanity of a paranoic man . . . [who] is not more concerned with the book at all, but purely and simply with himself and his own problems." To this end, "he has sacrificed all considerations for Anne's diary and has literally done everything in his power to prevent its production as a play."[21]

Unaware of the Hacketts' progress on the script and concerned that they might actually withdraw, Otto wrote them two days later, speaking of "the nasty ads placed by Mr. Levin in the N.Y. Post" and of the "*idée fixe*" Meyer had "formed" in order "to make trouble without any real base." He reassured them that their work was secure as long as Bloomgarden found it acceptable, for it was Bloomgarden, together with Crawford, upon whose opinions of Meyer's script he had based his own decision. "Never would I try to impose a writer to a producer," he insisted, though he continued to negotiate through Mermin for the right of final approval of the Hacketts' play.[22]

"We have finished our first rough, so very rough draft of the first act," Goodrich would proudly report to Bloomgarden that day, noting how they had made "amazingly fast progress for us." They planned to go ahead with a second draft that would include the entire story, after which they would be able to get "a good look at the whole."[23] "Starting back at the beginning," Goodrich wrote in her diary that January 21. "This is not like any other job we have done. Terrible emotional impact. I cry all the time."[24]

A week later, the desire for authenticity in their script brought the Hacketts to a Los Angeles rabbi whose daughter had known Anne in prewar Amsterdam.[25] In choosing to use the *Diary's* Hanukah scene, they needed to know "what liberties [they] could take without offending anyone." But they soon discovered that Meyer's appeal for support in his nationally syndicated weekly column in the Jewish press had made it "rough going," forcing them to first show the rabbi Otto's letter of introduction before he warmed to them slightly. A similar coldness then greeted them at a Jewish bookshop where they had gone that afternoon to purchase additional materials. "I am afraid for the play," Goodrich wrote Bloomgarden on January 30. "Will this man be able to marshall all the Jewish people against us?" Perhaps they were trespassing in someone else's world, not in terms of Meyer's claims, but regarding the subject of the *Diary* itself. "The worst thing is that we can understand their resentment against two goys."[26] Underestimating Meyer's determination, and having heard nothing further from his playwrights, Bloomgarden would respond nearly two weeks later that "I am very pleased for all our sakes that the Levin business seems to have quieted down temporarily."[27]

As promised, Otto was pleased to give the Hacketts "every detail" he could recall concerning the Hanukah celebration in the Annex. Otto described the traditional religious background of Dussel, the dentist, and spoke of the adherence by Mrs. Frank and Anne's sister, Margot, to the more liberal practices of "progressive" Judaism. He was himself "not educated in a religious sphere," though his marriage and the Holocaust had left him "more conscious as a Jew." As for Anne, "the forms or ceremonies did not seem to impress [her] very much," he asserted, while again admitting that "one could not make out much of her feelings," however much he continued to wish to see her redrawn in his own image of her. If she stood beside him as the Hanukah candles were lit and the traditional "Ma'oz Tzur" was sung, and if years later he revealed that she had observed the Sabbath each Friday evening while in hiding, he still could not admit to Anne's deepening Jewish religious consciousness as chronicled in the *Diary*. For if in the beginning Anne, when asked to read several prayers, had objected to being made "to act so religious and devout . . . just to be polite" to her mother, a year after entering the Annex she had grown to understand and experience the relevance of prayer itself. And although it was not framed according to tradition, the content and spirit of Anne's prayer belied Otto's image of her. "Merciful God, comfort her, so that she at least won't be alone," Anne had pleaded on behalf of a friend "as devout as I am, maybe even more so," whom she dreamt had fallen prey to the Nazis. In their final days together, Anne would note with sadness that without a religious consciousness, Peter had become "so lonely, so scornful, so wretched." "Though I'm not Orthodox either," she felt herself as a Jew "blessed with the ability to believe in a higher order."[28]

The Hacketts sensed this "strong religious feeling" in the *Diary*, but they, like Otto, could not see the role that Judaism had played in her thoughts. Instead they focused on those "heavenly things" about which she had also written,[29] and which Otto had identified as the essence of "her religious feelings." This spiritual sensitivity could be found only "in her diary," he wrote them in late February. "There you can see it, that she really had it," however much he refused to endorse its presence on the stage.[30]

He was not alone in this, for ultimately none of those involved with the Hacketts' play would seek to portray Anne as she had become. Instead, they pursued their own conceptions of her, or the one they were given. Otto's discussion with Goodrich that day could therefore turn toward the lesser issue of his growing impatience with Bloomgarden. Although he had written to him some time ago, he had yet to receive a single letter. "I resent it a little," not because it was "a business matter to me, though business is connected with it, but everything relating to the book is real life. . . . Anne's Diary is a link between those who work on it . . . and myself and it creates a certain personal feeling."[31] Under the pressure of Meyer's latest assault, Otto needed a word of reassurance from Bloomgarden. But Bloomgarden rarely wrote. In looking for materials four years later, his secretary would question "whether we had anything on file. . . . It's very possible that the whole business was verbal—over the phone, lunch, etc."[32]

While Otto waited to hear from his producer, support continued to come to Meyer from around the country, much of it addressed directly to Otto through Doubleday, including numerous offers to hold a test reading. Even Rabbi Judah Nadich, one of Dwight Eisenhower's advisers on European Jewry at the close of the war, was now demanding a hearing for Meyer's script.[33] With the help of an editorial hand (Mermin's?), Otto cautiously worked through two draft responses before directly addressing Meyer on March 10. In the earlier draft, Otto had used Meyer's extensive public support as further proof of the need to diminish the role of Jewish identity in dramatizing his daughter's *Diary*. "My work has been with the Jewish story," Meyer had written in his open challenge to Bloomgarden, but for Otto, the *Diary* was to have served as a means toward raising the more universal issue of tolerance. "Nearly all the letters I received came from Jewish persons or organizations, who know you, your articles, your books and admire your work for the Jewish cause. They wrote about your knowledge of Israel, the concentration camps, your war reports and your fight against Nazi-Germany. This is their reason for support-ing you. Of course Anne's book and a play based on it have a special impact on Jews, but it has a far greater mission to Non-Jews." Upset and clearly defensive, Otto asserted that "there is more involved in the question of dramatization," although "only a few [had] asked about my point of view."[34]

Otto's final response to Meyer dropped all mention of this "far greater mission" and dismissed his strong public support in a single sentence, charac-terizing it as mere sympathy from those who did not know the full story of his "manipulations."[35] Otto never again aired the Jewish question. Perhaps he feared fueling Meyer's challenge. Rather than provoke further confrontation, he appears to have preferred the stage as the forum in which to argue his position, hoping thereby to win support of his own. "I am fully conscious of the message [the *Diary*] contains and have taken my decisions with the view to keep this message alive and effective," he wrote in a letter widely circulated among those who had written him on Meyer's behalf.[36] "I know that Anne's ideals and example have found an echo in many countries and I consider it my mission to spread her ideas as much as possible," he added in mid-April, in response to a request from French radio to produce a play based upon his daughter's work.[37]

But if Otto hoped to end the debate over the proper understanding of Anne's *Diary*, Meyer desired precisely the opposite, even invoking her ideals in his own defense. "You write me that I am going against Anne's wishes, as she hated dispute," Meyer began his challenge. "Is not this rather your own inter-pretation on what would have been more important to her? She also hated injustice. I too hate disputes, but where an injustice is involved and it is necessary to undertake a dispute, I believe there can be no question as to which is the more important. You understand Anne as her father; I understand her as fellow writer. These are areas in which, unhappily, even a parent cannot enter."[38]

Otto was clearly angered by Meyer's claim to a better understanding of Anne than his own and, in a draft response, characterized it as a worthless attempt "to construct Anne's point of view." But in keeping with Mermin's vain efforts to dampen Meyer's passion, Otto never sent the response.[39] There were, after all, more important matters to deal with beyond the objections Meyer had repeatedly raised. As before, this disputatious exchange had con-tinued against the background of ongoing contract negotiations. The issue of "final approval" had ultimately been settled in the Hacketts' favor. Only Otto, and not his estate, would "exercise the veto power," and once rehearsals began, he would have to be present to make changes, which everyone knew would not happen. Doubleday would have "the first opportunity to publish the play," while the Hacketts' right to an extension, should Bloomgarden fail to produce the play "due to reasons other than the merits of the script," was to be more narrowly construed than previously with Meyer. On March 8, Salisbury sent the Hacketts this best possible contract. It was, she warned, "by no means perfect . . . because of Mr. Frank's disastrous experience with Levin." Still, she had secured their right to fill in the date of submission, advising that it be later than they might now anticipate.[40]

It proved to be sound advice. Finishing the first full draft of the play on February 26, Goodrich noted in her diary that she was disappointed with it. "N. G. So afraid of making people unsympathetic that we have not made them human."[41] On March 20, the Hacketts wrote Otto that they had made further progress. "We are now on our second writing of the script. The first was very rough. Now we are adding scenes, changing, amplifying." They were including the Hanukah celebration, "but very briefly," having modified their original plan after receiving his "explanation of Anne's feelings." They pressed further, wanting to know whether "Anne was herself to the very end . . . courageous, generous, full of spiritual faith?" It was their intention to complete this next draft, and then do another rewrite, hoping "to have the first real effort finished by July first."[42]

But the Hacketts found the process of revising their work "a very very difficult one technically. We hope we have a play." It had become "a curious job" for them, and though they had "just as much (if not more) enthusiasm and belief in it as when we started," certain that there was a play to be found in the *Diary*, they were no longer convinced that they could "dig it out." They would finish the "second run-through" in a week or two, they wrote Bloomgarden on April 3, "take a few days off to get some kind of perspective," and begin again.[43] Their frustration with the material had already spilled over into a "bad fight" between them.[44] They were determined now to be done with the script after the "third run-through," and would submit it to Bloomgarden, "hot or cold."[45]

In the midst of their revisions, Otto sent the Hacketts a copy of Anne's essay "Give," as an example of the "rather childish idealism" that was "typical for Anne."[46] It was a curious remark, but they were too busy to respond immediately as they pushed to complete the third draft by the date promised. On April 22, Hackett commented disappointedly that because the "first thirty pages [were] lacking direction," they would soon be "starting again from [the] beginning."[47] The momentary break between drafts allowed Goodrich to respond to Otto's disparaging characterization of his daughter's idealism. "It is naive, I suppose. But somehow I cannot believe that such gifts of love and the understanding that she pleads for might not well be what is most need[ed] in these chaotic and terrible times."[48] Having based their several previous drafts upon Anne's belief that true tolerance was based upon the recognition of differences among peoples rather than on an attempt to diminish them, Otto's comment must have left them confused as they began once again to work on her *Diary*.

In mid-April Otto made one last attempt at reaching a peaceful resolution with Meyer. "You sure will realize that all the differences I have with him are very painful to me," he began in a letter to Tereska, then in Paris without Meyer. "People are not always sincere and do not tell . . . their real opinion," he suggested, as "in the case of Mr. Clurman," who, Otto maintained, had never really shown a firm interest in Meyer's script beyond a possible second reading. As evidence, he cited a meeting he had had in Paris with Clurman's sometime coproducer, Whitehead, who had not liked the script.[49]

Tereska forwarded Otto's letter to Meyer for comment, but Meyer, "against the advice of a friend who is a lawyer and who feels that this entire matter may yet come to court," could not respond to her note without sending Otto his most blistering defense to date. As yet unwilling to openly discuss the agenda of those who had wanted the *Diary* for their own, he alluded to the existence of "other factors" fueling "the vindictive nature of these people" and condemned Otto for not "perceiv[ing] their motives," as Meyer himself had perceived Otto's true attitude toward writers. "Your cavalier treatment of the writer who undertook the first translation" exactly paralleled Meyer's own experience. "You encourage writers to go ahead, you are ready to reap the advantage of their work for you, while feeling that you are not really in any obligation to them," Meyer protested, threatening not to rest until his play had received "a fair hearing," if only, as a last resort, "before a courtroom audience."[50]

There was no immediate response from Otto, nor any communication between them for some time. Goodrich, however, wrote Salisbury five days later with the news that their last revision would be on its way to Bloomgarden by early June. It was their plan to send a second copy to Hellman "for her criticism. She has been an angel and offered to read it for us. I can think of no one whose criticism would be more valuable."[51]

Goodrich wrote in her diary on May 14 that they had had "a great day . . . working hard. At last we see [the] end for the play."[52] A week later, they were relieved to report to Bloomgarden that "we have finished our play, if play it is." They had made a number of changes "since our conversation," but only one that was truly significant. The narrator's voice would be Otto's rather than Elli's, as previously discussed. As the one "responsible for Anne's development," it seemed more appropriate that he give the play its "unity" from scene to scene. "We have tried therefore to have their relationship a continuing, unifying thread throughout the story." Goodrich hoped that Bloomgarden would find this in his reading of the script. If not, "we are indeed lost."[53]

Copies of the script were soon being prepared for mailing on May 27. The Hacketts would be in New York on June 1 and were looking forward to seeing

Hellman, to whom they owed an explanation for this major change in the script. They had deviated not only from Bloomgarden's instructions but from Hellman's, with whom he had apparently mapped out the play before his visit in Los Angeles. "We will explain to Lillie . . . who was so wonderful in offering to help . . . and who got us the job, that we are trying to beat a deadline" and had therefore gone ahead without first receiving her approval.[54]

The Hacketts' doubt over the quality of their work grew more acute during this interminable wait. On the twenty-fourth, Goodrich wrote Salisbury that although Otto would be sent a copy, they were more concerned that Bloomgarden's "very very high" standards would not allow him to accept the script. "I do not believe that Kermit will produce this. I am not at all sure that it is what he wanted." Perhaps it would be best to secure Otto's endorsement before sending it to Bloomgarden. "He may be shocked at the amount of comedy we have in it . . . but I think it is true to the character of Anne . . . and consequently in the spirit of the book."[55] But their question had come too late. Plans to meet with Bloomgarden in New York were already set. Salisbury agreed with their strategy of first securing Otto's support for the draft, but they could no longer delay Bloomgarden's judgment.[56] Both copies would be sent at once.

"We submit it to you in all humility," the Hacketts wrote Otto on May 28, cautioning him that they had made "changes in time and in the chronological sequence of events" and had "combined characters" as well. Yet they hoped to reassure him that "we have always tried to keep the lovely spirit of the Diary."[57] Otto's initial response arrived two weeks later. "How much would I like to meet you and to discuss many points with you! As this is not possible I prefer in the present situation to await the decision of Mr. Bloomgarden in principle before giving my view."[58]

It was not at all the response they had hoped for, but by now, Otto's reluctance no longer mattered. "Lunch with Leah, conference with Kermit, drink with Lilly," Goodrich had recorded in her diary on June 2. "All hate play. Devastating criticism. Kermit won't pick up option, but willing to read it again after rewrites." They had already found an apartment in New York, where they would remain until the next draft had been completed.[59] "We have talked it over with Mr. Bloomgarden and agreed on certain changes," the Hacketts wrote Otto on June 10. "Better to be here, where we can be in touch with him and with others in the theatre," they added, promising to meet with Otto in Amsterdam after the play had been rewritten and accepted.[60]

Bloomgarden had raised a number of objections concerning the more technical aspects of staging the Diary—the placing of Peter's room, the "overuse" of Otto's reading, and the like. "I am sure that we are in agreement on this," or "in accord on that," he would add, concluding his tightly written three pages of comments with a compliment and a note of expectation to ensure the

Hacketts' continuing efforts. "I think thus far you've done an extraordinary job with extremely difficult material and that if you agree with me on the reservations I've raised and want to tackle them we will have the play we want."[61]

Throughout his critique, Bloomgarden had played a single note, that the focus of the play was to be on Anne's heroic triumph over the normal problems of adolescence as "heightened by the abnormalcy of the situation. She is virtually a prisoner. She has been shut from the light of the skies—like Shaw's Joan." Yet Anne had offered her own critique of Bloomgarden's one-sided vision of her as a heroic archetype, and of the overemphasis by him and the Hacketts upon Otto as Anne's mentor. Less than three weeks before the S.S. and the Dutch Green Police violated the Annex, carrying all but one of its occupants to their deaths, Anne wrote in her *Diary*, "The final forming of a person's character lies in their own hands. . . . Daddy tried everything possible to check my rebellious spirit, but it was no use. . . . How is it that Daddy was never any support to me in my struggle? . . . I didn't want to hear about symptoms of your age, or other girls, but as Anne-on-her-own-merits and that Pim [Otto] didn't understand. . . . This is a point that gives me much thought: why is it that Pim annoys me, so that I can hardly bear him teaching me, that his many affectionate ways strike me as being put on!"[62] Even Otto knew that he could not dismiss Anne's true feelings, and thus his own edition of the *Diary* had included these lines almost without change, however much he might have wanted to see his daughter in the archetypal role later assigned to her. Nor could he dismiss her characterization of the *Diary* as a record primarily of "how we lived, what we ate and what we talked about as Jews in hiding." As she noted only weeks before their discovery, "the Jewish question . . . is discussed by everyone in the house."[63]

Nevertheless, Bloomgarden wanted the Hacketts to fully develop this image of a young girl's reliance upon her father as one of several matters of "greater psychological truth" at the center of the play. How else could attention be so sharply diverted from the reason for her imprisonment in the Annex? Certainly not by allowing the "irritability" between them to be "softened considerably." And though he understood the Hacketts' desire "to avoid the danger of a collection of disagreeable people on stage and too much of the depressing atmosphere of nightmare and horror," all of which "I go along with" (though Anne wrote in the final days of hiding, "I hear the ever approaching thunder which will destroy us too, I can feel the sufferings of millions"), he urged them to use the *Diary*'s most negative images of those in hiding with Anne in order to emphasize her alleged victory over despair. "I don't think we should worry too much about reactions to showing oppressed Jews in an unfavorable light." Instead, the Hacketts were to make the characters conform to his notion of what made them appear truly human. "In wanting not to have

Mrs. Van Daan be a thoroughly objectionable nuisance . . . you have given her as a character a little too much of the best of the bargain." He would later be pleased with her reinvention as a shrew, of her husband as a thief, and of Dussel, a kindly, educated man, as a clownish figure.

The most telling of Bloomgarden's comments are those concerning his displeasure with the handling of Anne's changing relationship with Peter. "I think we must know clearly what her attitude is to him at first, and how and why it changes." Here was "one of the main roads to our understanding of the inner Anne Frank and her conflicts." Surely the Hacketts could not have wanted to portray "an interrupted romance . . . blighted by tragedy" when its better use lay in highlighting Anne's "intensity of . . . feelings" and their change through "self-realization."[64]

But this was precisely the Hacketts' intent, in keeping with the *Diary*, for tragedy does cut short their relationship—Peter's resentment of his Jewishness as the cause of his suffering diverges sharply from Anne's embrace of it as the means by which she finds meaning in her experience of the Holocaust. Anne could not accept Peter's sorrow for having been born a Jew or his intention to hide his Jewish identity once they emerged from hiding. "He would have found it much easier if he'd been a Christian and if he could be one after the war," she had noted with deepening disappointment. "This gave me rather a pang. It seems such a pity that there's always just a tinge of dishonesty about him."[65]

Having sensed this estrangement and having attempted to portray it in their script, the Hacketts saw it become diluted and distorted as one draft moved into the next in the coming year. It is perhaps not coincidental that Bloomgarden was throughout this period producing Hellman's adaptation of Jean Anouilh's *L'Alouette*, a play from which Hellman had replaced the religiously based nationalism at the center of Joan of Arc's struggle with lighter, more humorous touches in an attempt to focus upon her execution as an instance of undifferentiated political oppression. In spite of imprisonment, torture, and eventual execution by fire, Hellman's hero in *The Lark*, like Anne, somehow retained her optimistic vision of a better world to come. "Shut from the light of the sky" by the HUAC hearing, frightened but determined, Hellman imposed upon Joan a portrait of her own heart and mind.[66] Five years earlier, Hellman had said of her adaptation of Emmanuel Robles's *Montserrat*, similarly manipulated to promote her politics, "If you're a creative writer you can't do what is merely a glorified translation."[67] That she redefined Joan as she did Anne is not surprising. As she worked with Bloomgarden on *The Lark* and the *Diary* simultaneously, the same vision and intent had consumed both.

During rehearsals for *The Lark*, Hellman had questioned why Julie Harris's Joan prayed on her knees. When Harris replied that it was how people prayed,

Hellman responded, "Oh, I guess so, but I do hate it"—as she hated the remaining religious material that she had cut from the original Anouilh text. Hellman portrayed Joan not as a religious and nationalistic visionary but as a young secular woman, contemporary in voice and demeanor (sounding distinctively American, like the Hacketts' Anne), a Hellmanesque "political creature," once again withstanding the forces of oppression. She had, in short, created a figure not unlike the Anne Frank she hoped to see reconfigured by the Hacketts.[68] "Joan is not just a French girl. She is everybody's girl. She belongs to the world," Hellman told a reporter days before *The Lark* opened in New York.[69] The Hacketts' inclusion of religious and particularistically Jewish material was simply too alien and too objectionable.

In the earliest surviving draft of the Hacketts' play, the one distributed that May, it is Mrs. Frank who first speaks of God's protectiveness toward the Jews, asking those in hiding with her to "pray that God in His infinite mercy will spare us, as He has spared us in the past." In lighting the Hanukah candles, a ceremony given its fullest treatment in this draft, Otto is made to recite the traditional blessing, "Praised be Thou, Oh Lord our God, Ruler of the Universe, who hast wrought wondrous deliverances for our fathers in days of old." Here again the Hacketts chose material that spoke of the Jewish experience of persecution and of their salvation by God's hand, a theme repeated a third time as the scene moves back to Mrs. Frank's explanation of the holiday as a remembrance of the Jewish struggle "against indifference, against tyranny and oppression," and of the need to "ever look unto God, whence cometh our help." Otto then recites Psalm 121, reminding those gathered that "He that keepeth Israel doth neither slumber nor sleep." Immediately following the candle lighting, conversation turns to news of the house-to-house search for Jews by the S.S. that Elli and Dirk, the Franks' Christian helpers, had witnessed that day.[70]

This focus upon their victimization as Jews received even greater emphasis in the second act, where Peter objects to Anne's finding comfort in her deepening spirituality, against which he argues that the very reason they are "caught here, like rabbits in a trap, waiting for them to come and get us!" is "Because we're Jews! Because we're Jews!" It is for this reason alone that Anne tries again to share the source of her peace with Peter, telling him that they are not alone in their suffering. "We're not the only Jews that've had to suffer. Right down through the ages there have been Jews and they've had to suffer," she records on the first day of Passover, paralleling one of the *Haggadah*'s central themes, and one crucial to many in the concentration camps, that "in every generation they stand up against us to destroy us, and the Holy One, blessed be He, saves us from their hand."[71] There is no mention in the *Diary* of a Seder at which this would have been read, but given Dussel's religious training and Mrs. Frank's own inclination, it is not unlikely that some form of a Seder was held, perhaps with the recitation of portions of the *Haggadah* from memory, as was done in the camps.

It is in the context of her understanding of the Jewish experience and her belief in God as a moral force that Anne finds the faith needed to utter the statement which, out of context, became the cornerstone of the play's ultimate message, and the bromide that it has remained, that "in spite of everything, I still believe that people are really good at heart."[72] But Anne was not a naïve, innocent, adolescent spirit. Nor was it in some blue sky that Anne ultimately found her strength. That is why Meyer, quoting more directly from the *Diary*, placed this same expression of faith in human goodness within the larger dialogue with Peter that encompasses Anne's final declaration of Jewish understanding and belief as the play ends.[73]

After spending nearly three weeks integrating a portion of the comments they had received from Bloomgarden and Hellman, the Hacketts told Salisbury that it would take at least two months, "and probably more," to rewrite the script. "It is more than half of the play which must be rewritten," Goodrich wrote, in a tone of frustration and resignation. "And new stuff, not just rewriting. It took us five to do it at first, and this is just as tough."[74] The tension boiled over through the heat of the summer as the Hacketts pushed themselves day and night to produce a script that would ensure their continuing role in the project, unaware that they would be given an almost unlimited number of opportunities to meet the needs of those who had hired them. "Bad fight with Hackett," Goodrich again noted in her diary on July 24. "He says I am killing us both with work."[75]

Nor had the Hacketts any real need to worry about Otto's "blue Monday" critique of their script. Strikingly similar to Bloomgarden's and Hellman's, in the end it required little further adjustment from them. "I have a lot to object," Otto wrote, commenting at length on the "rather humoristical touch" in the first act, the lack of emphasis on the tension between Anne and her mother, the troubling portrait of Margot as "snappish," the "too compressed" treatment of Anne's relationship with Peter, and the failure to demonstrate adequately Anne's "optimistical view on life." They had, in sum, failed to address "the inner feeling of the young generation," who, he believed, composed the *Diary*'s greatest audience. (Miep Gies, the *Diary*'s Elli, and Anne's childhood friend Hannah Pick-Goslar, Lies Gossens in the *Diary*, both later objected to Otto's repeated emphasis on Anne's statement concerning the goodness of people.) "I know how devoted[ly] you worked on the play, praying to succeed in catching the spirit of the book," he told them with apologies for speaking frankly and sounding "harsh" at times. But the play had failed to "do justice to circumstances."[76] He felt "desolate" now, no longer certain that "the points I raise could be corrected," though nowhere did he mention the near-absence of the Jewish backdrop against which the story occurred. Two years later, as he negotiated to retain his right of approval for the film script, Otto "point[ed] out" to Mermin how the "first script the Hacketts wrote . . . though it was based on the book, had an entirely wrong approach."[77]

Otto had, of course, sent a copy of his comments to Mermin, who forwarded them to Bloomgarden.[78] The Hacketts, in response, thanked Otto and promised to write "a better play!" They would reduce the humor ("we shall do the play more seriously"), and more fully develop Anne's relationships with her mother and Peter. A "fresh eye" had helped them to realize how "wrong" their perspective on "the spirit of the Diary" had been.[79] But had they so badly misunderstood the *Diary*, they wondered? Before they had sent the script, several people knowledgeable about the "Jewish angle" had read and "raved about it. That is why we were a little stunned by the avalanche that fell on our heads the first day in town," they wrote Bloomgarden in mid-July. Their belief that the material needed only minor changes had been a "complete miscalculation," forcing them to take "some time to adjust our minds to all of the changes." They were now rewriting nearly the entire play, hoping to complete the next draft by September 1. That would leave "two weeks for Kermit to turn it down." Their confidence all but gone, they planned to return to Hollywood and their lives at MGM.[80]

Bloomgarden took the Hacketts' loss of confidence seriously enough to send them a three-page outline of the changes he had recommended, fearing that they might flounder without close supervision. The solemn Hanukah observance marking past Jewish persecution would be converted into a holiday of celebration, using a "song of joy" to replace Psalm 121's promise of divine salvation. Bloomgarden further suggested the invention of a scene in which Dussel would be found stealing bread as a demonstration of the "demoralization" caused by prolonged confinement. Against this dark background, the triumphant light of Anne's spirit was to shine in the next and penultimate scene. "Anne and Peter [draw] closer: Anne has come to believe that people are really good at heart," he directed the Hacketts. Deeply moved, Peter would then declare his will to live restored, only to have it shattered by their sudden arrest, after which the play would close with Otto recalling "his daughter's final testament: her faith in the good of mankind."[81]

As the Hacketts rushed to complete their script, Meyer renewed his effort to win Otto's approval for a public reading of his own. But no such test would be granted without a fight. Otto had "repudiated every suggestion," Meyer told him, leaving "a court of law as the only recourse." In this he was supported by "the whole history of civilization and particularly of Jewish civilization," whose essence was "the growth of means by which justice can be determined"—and by the tradition out of which Anne had spoken and found meaning in her confinement. "I do not believe that your daughter would have found it in herself to deny a hearing to anyone," Meyer asserted in her name. Further overstepping the bounds of propriety, he added that through his suffering, Otto had perhaps "learned a little too well to live by one-sided decree."[82]

Otto refused to respond, but Meyer wrote again on August 18 after the *New York Post* reported that the Hacketts were on their "millionth re-write" because of the difficulty of capturing Anne's "inmost thought" on the stage. "It may never come out," Goodrich had told the reporter. Deeply shaken by Goodrich's confession, Meyer repeated his earlier protest, "that the writing of Hollywood comedies is scarcely a greater recommendation for the adaptation of the Diary than my record. It makes one want to cry or to commit murder to see how people who have only a money-getting record in writing are given a year to play around with the Diary, when I was given a few months." Anne had spoken of her father as a just man. Meyer challenged Otto to prove that he still was.[83]

"I see by the Post that you are unsure of your adaptation," Meyer then wrote the Hacketts, telling them with certainty "that mine manages to bring onto the stage the 'inmost thoughts' of Anne Frank." Why not put aside "personal motives" and allow his play to be tested?[84] But Meyer's plaint was already too late. With clear evidence of an outside hand at work, the fifth draft was completed the following day.[85] Years later the Hacketts wrote an admirer that "with Anne's diary we were doing something that was 'real' . . . something that actually happened. Therefore we were not permitted the freedom to create as under ordinary circumstances. Our task was to re-create theatrically Anne's impressions . . . using her own words whenever possible . . . and finding a way to have her speak her most 'secret thoughts.'"[86] But under the pressure of those who had brought them to the *Diary*, its content was slowly being redefined.

To lend a more serious tone to the *Diary*, the Hacketts had chosen to add several graphic descriptions of Jewish suffering. Most of this new material would ultimately be removed, but for now they spoke of "an S.S. truck filled with Jews . . . old people, children . . . women with babies," whose cries of "help me! Help me!" reached out from inside, and of other Jews being "marched through the streets, driven by S.S. guards" and "shipped to Germany in freight cars . . . crowded in like cattle, under indescribable conditions." Yet alongside this portrait of victimization, a new element had been introduced. "It is not only the Jews who are suffering," the audience learned, but "the Dutch as well."[87] In subsequent drafts, this inclusiveness would be further broadened to encompass all of humanity, negating the particularism of the event and of the *Diary* itself.

The Hacketts had added other scenes of Jewish religious expression to make the play's tone more serious, but these scenes were similarly reduced in later drafts. But for now, their script included a prayer from Chronicles pleading for the redemption of a suffering Israel. "Save us Oh God our salvation, and gather us together, and deliver us from the heathen," it read, a passage that was soon replaced with a more universal and optimistic message.[88] Already the deaths of Mrs. Frank and her daughters were removed so that the play would end on a redemptive note, however illusory.[89] Instead, Anne turns and waves goodbye to Otto, as if she is still with us in spirit, and for the second time in as many pages, the salvific incantation is recited as proof of Anne's triumph over evil—"In spite of everything, I still believe that people are really good at heart."[90]

On August 23, copies of the new draft were sent to Salisbury, Bloomgarden, and Hellman. The following day, Bloomgarden called the Hacketts with a more enthusiastic response than before, but at lunch on the twenty-sixth, he asked to see "more spiritual lift for Anne" before agreeing to do their play. "I am down in [the] depths," Goodrich told Hackett afterward, "so blue about [the] play [I'm] ready to cut my throat." But Hackett was at last confident that they could satisfy Bloomgarden, and he flew to Martha's Vineyard with his wife to see Hellman on September 5. "She was amazing. Brilliant advice on construction," Goodrich wrote afterward in her diary, having returned to New York for a final set of instructions from Bloomgarden before beginning a sixth time.[91]

"The diary is a symbol of . . . the war and all its misery and pain and wasted hope," Bloomgarden told them. Nowhere in four pages of additional comments did he ever mention the Holocaust, coming closest only when speaking of the "gravity" of the situation facing those he characterized as being in "self-enforced imprisonment." "There is no reason that the original [*Diary*] must be followed so closely as to restrict the independent creativity and point of view of the playwrights," he advised the Hacketts in prescribing for them the central theme of the play, a theme left unspoken by Anne herself. "The play is about the fear of death. The intensity of Anne's will to live is the core of the drama. Everything that happens is colored and heightened, intensified, put in perspective, by her intense will to live. She insists that there is a future in everything she does, in each relationship. The depth of the inner struggle and the true nature of her inner thoughts manifests itself in the exaggerated off-centre approach to each situation and person. What is important is what she has not said in the diary. It is this that makes her tragedy so vital and meaningful to us, and why its impact is so shattering."[92]

Bloomgarden ended, as before, on a positive note, evaluating "the extent and quality of the work . . . [as] tremendous" and inestimable. Even so, it was his "strong feeling" that unless these recommendations were followed, "you will not be doing justice to yourselves and to the story we all feel equally strongly about." On September 11, after apparently meeting once more with Hellman, Goodrich recorded in her diary, "Starting again. . . . Feel Lilly's suggestions will work out. Have agreed to give Kermit re-written version by Octo. 15th. He agrees to make up his mind then."[93]

CHAPTER EIGHT

A Production That Isn't Faithful

Work going quite well," Goodrich noted midway through September. Hand-delivering the sixth draft to Bloomgarden's office on October 8, she returned home to learn that he had already telephoned with his acceptance of the script. "I [was] too numb to take it in," Goodrich later recalled.[1] At lunch the following day, Bloomgarden told them of his wish to begin working on the production immediately. He spoke of casting possibilities, and for the director he suggested Garson Kanin.[2] The Hacketts attempted to reach Kanin a week later, unaware that Bloomgarden had already contacted him, though Otto had yet to give his approval to the script.[3]

"I am chewing on a few bones," Kanin wrote Robert Sherwood as part of an extended conversation that year concerning the nature of the theater and of playwrights.[4] Feeling himself blocked while at work on his next play, *Do Re Mi*, Kanin had earlier declared that "the function of a writer in the middle of the 20th century, as well as his stimuli, subjects, aims, problems, are part and parcel of his being. In our time a new human being exists and we require a new sort of writer to describe that being."[5] This new writer had to write out of his passions. "What are they?" he had asked. "What are the things that irritate you? What people? What sort of people and what particular people? What ideas and movements do you despise? Which do you love? What makes you mad? What inspires you? What is your faith?"[6] Each of these was to find an answer in his work on the *Diary*, upon which he would put his stamp alongside those of Hellman and Bloomgarden. By October 18, the Hackett play was on its way to Kanin in London.[7]

Otto had felt that "slight changes . . . necessary in [the] interest of dramatic effect" would be acceptable as long as the "spirit of the book is preserved and . . . the play works on the audience as the book on the readers."[8] On

October 25, he sent the Hacketts his approval, "deeply impressed" with their efforts. Aware of "the hard strain, the frustration and the exhaustion it has given you," he thanked and assured them that the script had "all the qualities which we all wished to be realized." Whatever suggestions he could offer would surely concern only minor details and would be "of no importance as a whole." The Hacketts, he acknowledged happily, had essentially captured "the spirit of Anne."[9]

Faithful to his promise, Otto wrote again on November 5, after several more readings of the play. "The more I get familiar with the details the more I admire the way you caught the spirit of the book." Even the invented scenes fit well, he told them. Attached were two pages of such minor details that he doubted whether anyone other than himself would detect the errors they were meant to correct. The option to disregard them was, of course, the Hacketts'. Only one issue greatly concerned him. Dussel's theft of bread had been transferred to Mr. Van Daan, whose brother was living in New York. Otto feared a potential "legal situation," though he made no mention of moral concerns.[10]

Kanin cabled the Hacketts on October 29 that he was "vitally interested" and sent a seventeen-page critique of the play ten days later, a set of "reflections" intended to make "a manuscript as good as this one . . . great." The possibility to do so existed, he assured them. "I see and sense it thus, somewhere within me." Much of what Kanin wished to discuss concerned the "staging" of the Diary, but his most serious concern was the same issue that troubled Hellman and Bloomgarden, the identification of the Holocaust as a specifically Jewish event.[11]

Bloomgarden was "excited and pleased with [Kanin's] notes," while the Hacketts responded immediately by reducing Dussel's description of the hardships experienced by Jews and non-Jews to simply, "No one in Holland has enough to eat." The traditional religious material was similarly trimmed by the removal of the Sabbath prayer of salvation offered by Mrs. Frank in the previous draft, though "Ma'oz Tzur," with its mention of "raging foes," was retained as a part of the Hanukah ceremony.[12]

But these changes were too minimal for Kanin. And while the Hanukah scene was ultimately changed several more times in an effort to use song and light comic relief to diminish the horror—and thereby the specificity of what befell the Jews—it was Anne's comment that Jews had suffered throughout history, an essential realization in the Diary, that Kanin objected to most strenuously. On this issue, the only one within the seventeen pages designated as a "serious point," he insisted upon "basic agreement":

> Anne says "We're not the only Jews that've had to suffer. Right down through the ages, there have been Jews and they've had to suffer." This strikes me as an

embarrassing piece of special pleading. Right down through the ages, people have suffered because of being English, French, German, Italian, Ethiopian, Mohammedan, Negro, and so on. I don't know how this can be indicated, but it seems to me of utmost importance. The fact that in this play the symbols of persecution and oppression are Jews is incidental, and Anne, in stating the argument so, reduces her magnificent stature. It is Peter here who should be the young one, outraged at being persecuted because he is a Jew, and Anne, wiser, pointing out that through the ages, people in minorities have been oppressed. In other words, at this moment the play has an opportunity to spread its theme into the infinite.

Sending the Hacketts only half his notes, Kanin invited them to join him in London for further revisions, after which they would go to Amsterdam and meet with Otto, providing "deal and dates" could be worked out between Kanin and Bloomgarden.[13] Arriving three days later, on November 15, they immediately set to work, writing each day until late afternoon, and then visiting with Kanin all evening to discuss their progress and the next revisions. "Garson wonderful," Goodrich added to her diary on the twenty-second. "Right feeling for the material." They set a new deadline of December 4, after which they would travel to Holland to "see the rooms, etc.," and to meet with Otto, who had telephoned on the nineteenth to confirm these arrangements, despite his concerns over what the Hacketts explained were merely "small changes" based upon the comments that he and Kanin had made. None would "affect the spirit of the play," they promised.[14]

Without asking to see this newest script, Otto responded with his approval, pleased to hear from the Hacketts that the play's essence had remained unchanged.[15] In truth, the revisions had been "very very extensive," as they told Bloomgarden. Though the basic outline had not been altered, "practically every page" had felt the effects of Kanin's hand. "We have agreed on most of the things which Garson suggested in his notes." Had their ideas not been "in accord . . . it would have been impossible for us to work together and for him to direct." But this had not been a problem. "So perfect [was he] for our play" that they were willing to arrange the next few months of their lives according to "his plan" of London, Amsterdam, and then back to the States for rehearsals.[16]

Kanin confirmed their assessment, reporting to Bloomgarden on November 27 that "the Hacketts and I are getting along famously." After countless hours of discussion, they had all remained "in pretty general agreement," though the longer they worked, the more apparent became the need for additional changes. They planned, however, to keep to their scheduled meeting with Otto in Amsterdam, where they would photograph the Annex and discuss the years in hiding with those who had assisted the Franks. Kanin had suggested Joseph Schildkraut for the part of Otto and was seriously considering Susan Strasberg for the part of Anne. Bloomgarden's plan for a tryout in Philadelphia had met with Kanin's approval. It would require only three weeks of rehearsal if the actors knew their parts when they arrived.[17] Yet a week later, Kanin was still questioning the project's viability, privately telling Sherwood that he was at work on something that was "not absolutely certain."[18]

At 10:20 P.M. on December 5, the Hacketts completed their seventh script and prepared to leave for Amsterdam the next morning. Bloomgarden had cabled that day with news that rehearsals were to begin on January 10, heightening everyone's enthusiasm for their meeting with Otto.[19] When the Hacketts arrived at their hotel, Saint Nicholas Day gifts from Otto awaited them. Later in the day, they met with Otto and Kanin and set an itinerary for the four days, including a tour of the Franks' prewar apartment and Anne's school as well as the Annex. Lunch with Louis de Jong of the Netherlands Institute for War Documentation led to his offer to read the script for "mistakes in documentation," out of which came a number of "constructive suggestions." During their brief time in Amsterdam, a photographer spent two days in the Annex recording "every detail" for the work ahead in designing the set. Recordings were purchased of the Westertoren bells and of the street sounds below— traffic, bicycles, tram, children at play, and street organs—"and always questions, questions, questions to Mr. Frank," Goodrich noted in her diary at the end of their stay.[20]

On the eve of their return to London, the Hacketts wrote Bloomgarden that in spite of the "big re-write" before the trip to Amsterdam, the script would now "have to be corrected for historical inaccuracies."[21] After lunching with Otto on the eleventh, Kanin and the Hacketts flew back to London feeling "really spent."[22] The next day, Otto was pleased to report to Bloomgarden that although "a great deal of details" would have to be added now that his "very sensitive" collaborators "had undergone the influence of the hiding place . . . the spirit of the script will not be changed."[23]

Nowhere, however, did Otto speak of the impact of these changes on the "spirit" of the *Diary* itself, as if the Hacketts' script had become the authoritative source for Anne's thoughts. Of the changes confirmed by Otto's approval of their seventh draft, none had more dramatically altered the sense of Anne's *Diary* than the scene imposed moments before the play ends, in which Anne is made to declare that they are suffering not because they are Jews, as Peter had claimed, but because such suffering is the essence of the human condition. In the *Diary* she had affirmed the particularity of Jewish persecution through the centuries; in the play she was forced to assert: "We're not the only people that've had to suffer. Sometimes one race . . . sometimes another."[24] Motivated not by commercial considerations but by an ideological stance he shared with Hellman and Bloomgarden, Kanin had succeeded with the one "serious point" of his critique. As "the most important project I have ever tackled," he had given it "full attention, complete concentration, and extra sensitivity."[25] Otto may never have conceived of this posture for his daughter, despite his assimilationist sentiments. Yet he did not dispute this radical change. Perhaps he, too, was pleased that the script had moved even further from being "too Jewish." Nor would either Hellman or Bloomgarden suggest a return to the previously approved wording of "We're not the only Jews who have had to suffer" now that the script more closely conformed to their own personal beliefs. When the eighth version of the play was completed on December 19, this distortion remained untouched, as it would thereafter.[26]

In time, Kanin altered even Peter's cry against being persecuted as a Jew. But such additional changes would have to wait, for on the following day, Bloomgarden cabled the Hacketts that it was now too late to bring the play to Broadway during the current theatrical season. Rehearsals would instead begin in late August 1955. With nothing to be done with the script until then, the Hacketts cabled their agent that they would soon return to Hollywood.[27]

Meyer was unaware of the changes made to the Diary when he sent Kanin a copy of his play on the day the Hacketts had finished their latest script. "Believ[ing] there are things you might later on wish you had known," Meyer offered to tell him what had happened "in the Anne Frank matter. . . . To me, the issues are of an ethical nature; I find it hideous that a question of injustice should have been allowed to arise around this girl's legacy, and I am therefore all the more determined to see that question resolved."[28]

Meyer had already petitioned Dorothy Schiff, owner of the New York Post, for a hearing. There were two issues involved, one "a very special animosity toward me . . . that has a political bearing which I would be glad to explain to you in private," and the other, which he hoped to air publicly, the principle that the Diary was "a party [to] the Jewish people's experience . . . rather than a commercial property." In this latter question, who more than he deserved such a hearing? "I have devoted most of my adult life to telling the Jewish story. . . . As much as any other American writer, I have gone out to bring this story to the public, in novels, in reportage, in war coverage, in films." Without Schiff's help, he had but one recourse.[29]

On December 30, Meyer's attorney, Samuel Fredman, filed suit on his behalf against Otto and Crawford in New York State Supreme Court, alleging that Otto had breached their agreement to allow him to write or collaborate on the script, for which he had received Meyer's services as his otherwise uncompensated agent; that Crawford had breached her agreement by not allowing Meyer to work with a collaborator after her refusal to enter into the standard Dramatist Guild's contract; and that they had fraudulently used the name of Elia Kazan to ultimately secure Meyer's removal from the project. As relief, Meyer asked for monetary damages against Crawford, and for Otto to "perform" as agreed, allowing Meyer's participation as writer or collaborator.[30]

In forwarding Meyer's pleadings to Otto on January 5, 1955, Mermin wrote of his own plan to file a motion of dismissal. As a resident of Switzerland technically not "doing business" in New York, Otto could not be served legal papers through his attorney. Yet even if the motion were successful, they would have to respond to the suit once Meyer's attorney discovered the proper procedure. Mermin asked Otto to prepare a response to Meyer's charges in the interim and to have Doubleday send all royalty payments to an address outside New York State so that Meyer could not attach his money while the suit was being litigated.[31]

Otto responded five days later, denying each of Meyer's claims. Even Meyer's involvement as his agent had been minimal, he insisted. Having "neglected his duties to a high degree at the time," Meyer should not now be rewarded with a production of his play. "Never would [I] allow it," Otto promised. Nor was there reason to. The Hacketts' play was simply "far better." Otto's only concern was whether he would be able to receive "reimbursement from the opponent" for legal fees anticipated in the months ahead.[32]

Two weeks later, after receiving Mermin's assurance that the dismissal motion would be filed, Otto agreed to separate his own case from Crawford's, believing this to be in his own best interest. Though he would "back her as far as I know the case," he admitted that she might, in fact, be guilty of misconduct. "It is not clear to me why this agreement [between Crawford and Meyer] never was made. Is it the fault of Meyer or of Miss Crawford?" he asked, claiming to be ignorant of the matter. Why else would Meyer have charged them both as he had, for certainly he had never made such a promise? Though his 1952 telegram had read, "Desire Levin as writer or collaborator," it had merely suggested a preference. "Levin understood it the way I intended it," Otto assured Mermin, who might one day have to argue this point.[33]

Meanwhile, Kanin wrote the Hacketts that he had received a copy of Otto's notes on the latest script but that he was largely disregarding his suggestions. "I think all is handleable, don't you? I just glanced at them, y'unnastan?"[34] This attitude of dismissal persisted throughout the project. In May he wrote them that he was in frequent contact with Otto, "usually about nothing."[35] Yet Otto had succeeded in capturing his attention, and that of Salisbury and Bloomgarden, over the issue of allowing Meyer to produce his play in Israel. "We all know that Mr. Frank did, as a conciliatory measure, promise Mr. Levin something about Israel," Salisbury had told the Hacketts on January 12, but there was a potentially large Israeli market, stage and screen, which Meyer's play could take from them. Agreeing that "it was dangerous" and could not be allowed, the three had already turned to Mermin, asking that "various changes in the foreign contract" be negotiated with Otto. It was their opinion that Otto had "too much control . . . and that all steps within our legal rights should be taken to prevent such a thing from happening."[36]

Yet Otto, concerned that the Hacketts were upset at the news of Meyer's suit, had written to assure them that he was not overly disturbed by Meyer's "silly and invented arguments distorting completely the facts." Rather, he was saddened by Anne's involvement in such a suit. Both he and his daughter "hate[d] quarreling and disputes."[37] The Hacketts, in turn, offered him their support, but Otto felt confident that the matter would be dropped because of the technical violation in serving the complaint. As to the substance of the pleadings, he assured the Hacketts that "the whole matter misses every serious base."[38]

Meyer had similarly invoked Anne's memory that January in appealing to Kanin for a reading of his play. "It would be the greatest pity for any unfair act to be done in the name of her work," he asserted. As the victim of "a few individuals . . . acting more out of vindictive anger than out of art[istic] judgment," he had had no choice but to institute legal proceedings, however obsessed by it all he had become. "The sheer arbitrary nature of the behavior toward me has been so embittering as to invade my thoughts at all times," he readily admitted. Yet he could not abandon the struggle. His very life as an artist was threatened. "There are many ways to kill a writer, and to kill his work without a fair hearing is one of them."[39]

"What is all this with Meyer Levin?" Kanin wrote Bloomgarden after receiving Meyer's letter in early February. "Is there any danger that if some arrangement is not made with him, some sort of injunction is possible?" Anticipating that all would be handled by the attorneys, Kanin had already written Meyer that he would not read his script, as it might prove confusing once he had begun to rehearse the Hacketts'.[40] Bloomgarden, in turn, advised Kanin not to respond to any of Meyer's letters. "The man is wacky and quite an unethical character," he added, applauding Kanin's decision not to read Meyer's play, though he had done so himself.[41]

But Otto, like Meyer, knew there was far more involved here than art or legal maneuvering. "For me it is not a play," he would tell the man who was to portray him on the stage, "but a very essential part of my life."[42] Joseph Schildkraut, who was to win recognition for his portrayal of Otto, would echo this sentiment several weeks later, writing to Bloomgarden that "each time I think or talk of 'our play'—(don't laugh, Kermit, please)—I get an almost sacred feeling inside me."[43] A photograph of Otto's "sensitive, fine, cultured face" had so inspired him that he and the Hacketts ("an exemplary couple of the human race!") had already auditioned a young actress, Natalie Norwich, and had found her to be "Overwhelming!—Unique!" a *"dark-haired—dark-*

eyed, Jewish (not Yiddish!!) Julie Harris. This is our girl!!!!!! . . . this *revelation for 'Anne'!!!"*[44]

On March 30, Otto's motion "to vacate service of the summons and complaint" was granted by the New York State Supreme Court.[45] A month later, Mermin reminded Otto that the court's decision had not reflected upon the merits of Meyer's cause of action, nor had it precluded further action by him. Meyer was, after all, clearly unpredictable. Should he file again and find Otto in New York at some point, proper service of the complaint could be made and Bloomgarden's production possibly enjoined from opening. It was Mermin's recommendation that Otto not return to New York. Nor did he believe it advisable to respond to Meyer's latest appeal for a trial production, published the previous week in the *National Jewish Post*. "It would only play into his hands if he were able to develop a debate in newspaper columns which would attract further attention."[46]

This, however, had not been Meyer's only attempt at seeking satisfaction after his court defeat. On April 2, he had written to the American Committee for Cultural Freedom (a group founded in 1949 to oppose Stalinist ideology) concerning "questions of culture control." Materials "dealing with a representative folk experience" must remain free in order to allow the particular community to select its preferred expression, Meyer argued, "regardless of the version that a commercial producer may wish to impose on them." The individual writer, he insisted, must be accorded the "normal freedom" to submit his work "on the open market." These freedoms had been denied him by "the manipulation and control exercised by Mr. Frank's local advisers." And when "such practices strangle cultural expression," Meyer added bitterly, they dangerously distort the truth, as they had with the *Diary*'s basic message.[47]

"As a war correspondent following 'the Jewish story,' I had the gruesome distinction of becoming the 'expert' on the camps," he wrote several days later on the occasion of the tenth anniversary of the liberation of Buchenwald. Since that fateful day, he had witnessed the world's avoidance of this reality. He feared that without the lesson of the death camps, it could all so easily happen again, somewhere, to some people. It was this universal message that he hoped could be communicated out of the tragedy that had fallen most specifically upon the Jews. "The negative meaning of the camps has not been fully explored. We have cataloged the horrors, the torture, the sadistic inventiveness of commanders and generals. But we have not found any explanation for this vast ghastly rift in the pattern of human behavior. We know that millions of people today, in other lands, are subjected to labor camp slavery. And we feel in our souls that the additional step—to mass murder—could take place. . . . Yet some day this awful gap, this abyss in human behavior, will have to be fitted into the entire pattern of man's activity."[48]

In late April, the American Fund for Israel Institutions contacted Meyer

with a proposal from the Ohel Theatre to produce his play in Hebrew translation in Israel. The request soon became legally clouded by the fund's desire to
have exclusive rights in Israel, raising the concern of Bloomgarden and his
colleagues that Meyer's play might preclude the Hacketts'. But for the moment, Meyer remained encouraged by this unexpected prospect and by Ohel's
request for Kazan to direct. It would be a challenge to produce the play before
an audience composed largely of Holocaust survivors, he promised Kazan,
adding that his involvement with the *Diary* would "help to bring out its full
meaning to the world." Although Meyer knew nothing of the Hacketts' play,
he doubted that "big-money writers" would be equal to the task. Fearing that
Kazan might reject his offer because of the "good deal of gossip and misin-
terpretation" now circulating about his relationship to the *Diary*, Meyer reassured him that all such allegations fell "under the heading of character assassination." This had been generated by his own refusal to step aside in favor of
Bloomgarden's choice of playwrights, after having first advised Otto to decide
in Crawford's favor for fear that a threatened HUAC investigation of Bloomgarden might harm the *Diary*. All of this had now become a "vengeance
point."[49]

At the same time, Fredman contacted Mermin concerning the American
Fund's request for "exclusive rights to produce 'The Diary of Anne Frank' in
Israel."[50] The granting of such rights, Mermin reminded Fredman two weeks
later, was beyond the scope of the agreement reached between Otto and Meyer
and would therefore need the approval of both the Hacketts and Bloomgarden.[51] It had been Meyer's understanding, Fredman responded, that the
agreement had, indeed, referred to this type of arrangement, though admittedly it was "patently ambiguous."[52] Mermin, of course, could not agree,
arguing instead that Otto had not intended to allow Meyer to effectively ban
his own authorized play. Meyer would therefore have to apply "in writing . . .
to enlarge" what had been previously permitted "by contract."[53]

The text of the November agreement drawn up by Mermin had, in fact,
been ambiguous, granting Meyer "the opportunity to make arrangements for
the presentation of a Hebrew version of your script in Israel . . . subsequent to
the New York opening of a play based upon the book," without ever specifically mentioning the fate of the "New York" play in Israel.[54] But however it
may originally have been understood by either party, this latest difference,
after two years of frustration, shattered whatever remained of Meyer's reserve
in dealing with those who had blocked his every effort. "I have held on, in this
struggle for my play, and fought for it, through these long months of attrition,
hoping that some saving force would appear before it was finally doomed to the
pit," he wrote that June in ending his eighteen-page "Dear Anne" letter.
Having lived with her innermost thoughts for so long, he now hoped to share

his own with her, speaking of how, in the closing days of the war, he had come upon the survivors "and the open mass grave in your own Bergen Belsen, and long afterward when I read your diary I could not remove from my mind's eye the image of that great well of bodies, where you lay. Because I saw all this without preparation, it had perhaps a stronger effect on me than on others who were to read of these things. During the ensuing years, I could not rest from the sense that the world had been unable to absorb the enormity of all this extinguished life. Even today, I feel humanity dazedly unbalanced, like some individual who has as yet failed to assimilate an amputation." He, too, remained dazed, unbalanced, fighting for "the right of my play to live," crossing boundaries of propriety he might not otherwise have violated had the need to tell the Holocaust's victims' story been less compelling.[55]

"I was shocked at the action of Meyer Levin in sending you an extract from his article in *Congress Weekly* with his marginal notation," Mermin consoled Otto in early June, angered by Meyer's renewed campaign to see his play upon the stage. It was, in fact, not the first such clipping Meyer had sent Otto, having several weeks earlier forwarded Shumlin's advertisement for his critically acclaimed production of *Inherit the Wind* in an effort to demonstrate how wrong he had been to reject Shumlin's offer. "Obviously, he cannot possibly stand any frustration," Mermin concluded. He planned to meet soon with Fredman to discuss the matter fully. There was reason to believe that until then, Meyer's interest in seeing his play produced in Israel would temporarily silence him.[56]

But Meyer refused to be silenced even by negotiations whose outcome might be in his favor; from a hospital bed he accused Otto on June 3 of causing his physical and emotional collapse. Claiming to have knowledge "of the content of the Bloomgarden version," he expressed astonishment that Otto could permit such a distortion of the *Diary* and promised to wage a "Warsaw Ghetto resistance . . . [against] a production that isn't faithful."[57] Meyer then sent Otto a long list of rabbis who had indicated their desire to see his play on the stage by responding to the several appeals he had placed in Jewish publications.[58]

Mermin found Meyer's latest foray "almost beyond belief," but agreed with Otto that it was best to leave it unanswered. He had already met with Fredman and had responded negatively to Meyer's demands for exclusive rights in Israel and for limited access to religious and other noncommercial audiences in the States. Certain that the latter of these was "dangerous and damaging to the normal exploitation" of the property, Mermin suggested to Otto that it might be prudent to trade the Israeli rights for a written promise from Meyer that he would "discontinue all his activities against you and the production." Should Meyer violate this new agreement, "his ability to put forth additional propaganda which sounds plausible would be very much hampered." For Meyer was expanding his campaign and within the past several days had circulated a letter to potential investors in such a production. Going even further, he had advised Simon Rifkind, a senior partner in Mermin's law firm, that "the slightest degree of human consideration, in your office, could have avoided all this embarrassment for your client, and all this unfairness to me."[59]

Otto refused to agree to such a proposal, and he grew ever more intractable as Meyer continued his pursuit unabated throughout the summer. By July 1, he had written Otto of Bloomgarden's "vengeful spleen," and had called Salisbury "a pretentious and conceited woman" who was taking vengeance against him for having earlier declined her offer to represent him concerning the Diary. In each case, Meyer argued, the motives behind their attacks had "nothing to do with the real issue" of the Diary's adaptation and were therefore particularly "shameful, when connected with your daughter's work." "You will understand, then, why this matter drives me to distraction, but I despair of your understanding anything" or of ever showing "the slightest concern over the ruin of all my time and efforts" and the hardship it had caused his family.[60] News that the Hacketts had collected a settlement of twenty-five thousand dollars for their rejected film adaptation of Fanny only fueled Meyer's rage, as did the thought that they had been given "a year to play around with the Diary, when I was given a few months."[61] Fredman's continuing failure to win any concessions for his client's script in Israel or America finally led Meyer, on August 1, to notify Otto of his firm intention to sue as widely and deeply as possible.[62]

Tereska had meanwhile remained in France with their children throughout these difficult months, hoping that Meyer would "come back to [his] senses." The arrival of Meyer's letter announcing his plan "to go on with this fight, for some neurotic, morbid reason of your own," as she characterized his decision, had led to her own ultimatum of "this A. F. play, or us." She had previously spoken of divorce; "this time I mean every word of it. . . . Forget forever this madness or you leave me and the three children." They had all suffered enough. If she remained willing to consider a simple legal battle, it would have to be without "any kind of scandal, exhibitionism, [or] disturbance about that play," or she would seek "immediate divorce on grounds of insanity." She pleaded in vain: "Come back to us, to your real work. If you have any love left for me, and at least, if you love the children, you can't do that to them."[63]

But it was already too late, the wound too deep to be healed. Shumlin had recently revealed that he had been told by Mermin in December 1952 of the intent by all involved to be rid of Meyer. Shumlin was now encouraging Meyer to move forward with his suit. "Go ahead. I will confirm that I made the offer." Meyer forwarded Shumlin's remarks to Fredman for evidence on August 5, as

Tereska's promise of divorce arrived to confront him with an added challenge.[64]

Two days earlier, the Hacketts had met with Bloomgarden and Kanin to discuss the production, its set, costumes, audition schedules, and casting possibilities.[65] Beyond the designation of Schildkraut as Otto, Gusti Huber had already accepted the role of Mrs. Frank. It was a curious choice, at best. In mid-July, Bloomgarden had received a letter from another actress, Lotte Stavisky, informing him of Huber's "former Nazi affiliation and special friendship with Josef Goebbels." Stavisky had refused to be a part of any postwar production employing Huber or other former Nazis.[66] It is uncertain how seriously Bloomgarden took this accusation but he appears to have shared it with his playwrights and perhaps with Kanin. The Hacketts, either from personal concern or because they had been deputized, wrote Otto about her. He replied in early September that his Viennese wife did not recall Huber's participation in that city's theater but that she "would be very interested to know more about her."[67] In time, Mrs. Frank's suspicions would be confirmed by others who were outraged at seeing Huber in this role.

The *Playbill* given to the *Diary*'s theatergoers on opening night included a biographical account of Huber that implied an abrupt end to her career coinciding with the German annexation of Austria, there being no mention of her activities until after she came to the States in 1946 as the bride of a U.S. Army officer. Huber's first appearance on the American stage some years later had been in George Tabori's "tragic story of the displaced people in Europe," *Flight Into Egypt*.[68] The Jewish press, however, soon ran stories of her wartime career as an actress in Nazi propaganda films, while Meyer's investigation in the *Almanac of German Films* uncovered additional evidence of such activity. Had she not openly supported the Nazi regime, she would not have starred in so many roles "at the very same time Anne was murdered in Bergen Belsen," he reported. "Surely it is sacrilege to engage in such [casting] practices in the name of Anne Frank, whose young soul cried out for truth. For her to appear in this role is an affront to the public. All who are connected with the lie that made this possible are equally guilty." He was outraged to find "the Nazi technique of the audacious lie revived amongst us."[69]

Nor was this the last time that Bloomgarden would hear of the matter. In January 1957, during casting for the filming of the *Diary*, Herbert Luft, a journalist in Hollywood who had been in Dachau during the time that Huber was performing on screen as a member of the Nazi Actors Guild, sent Bloomgarden a copy of his latest column. It included a reproduction of a Vienna newspaper clipping dated July 1, 1935, citing Huber's refusal to associate with "Non-Aryan artists [who] would endanger her stature in Nazi Germany." Luft wrote with obvious skepticism that he was certain that Bloomgarden was "unaware of Miss Huber's background." How else could someone with such strong "anti-Semitic leanings prior to the incorporation of her homeland into the Greater German empire . . . have worked with performers such as Joseph Schildkraut and Susan Strasberg, [or] with director Garson Kanin. Yet, today she has the nerve to utter the word 'Shalom' from the stage."[70]

Ultimately, Otto alone seemed truly concerned that the production be fitting in every way. "I pray that the spirit of Anne's book will be transferred to the public," he had told the Hacketts in August 1955. Though "the whole idea of having all represented on the stage is depressing me always," he was prepared "to bear it for the GOOD."[71] And so he had asked that the details be as accurate as possible, writing to the Hacketts on September 7 that the men had worn "hats during the prayers" for the Hanukah candle-lighting ceremony.[72] But now, more than two weeks into rehearsals, there was no longer a contractual obligation either to consider Otto's suggestions or to seek his approval for changes being instituted by Kanin and the Hacketts. Had Otto known of the many alterations, significant and otherwise, being made to the script he had approved, his concern would undoubtedly have deepened. (Had Kanin waited until now to make certain changes for this reason?) It was perhaps something of a relief for them to read Otto's letter of September 15, written the day tryouts began in Philadelphia, announcing that he would not be attending the play's opening night in New York. It was simply too "painful" to watch. Instead, he would send his best wishes for a successful production, together with his hopes "that the message which it contains will, through you, reach as many people as possible and awaken in them a sense of responsibility to humanity."[73]

"I'm besotted about this play, and can hardly wait to get my hands on it," Kanin had written Sherwood back on May 11.[74] Rehearsals had finally gotten under way on August 22, using a "Master" copy of the script that had been "corrected [as of] August 16, 1955." "This is not a play in which you are going to make individual hits," Kanin told the cast that first day. "You are real people, living a thing that really happened." But as they read through the script for the first time, it became evident that there was, as Goodrich noted in her diary, "Something wrong with our second act. But what?" By September 7, more than two weeks into rehearsals, she recorded "feeling more and more strongly that something [was] needed. . . . [We] sit watching [the] play, worried."[75]

Yet the following day Bloomgarden, Kanin, and the Hacketts met to discuss a different concern. "Bad news," Goodrich wrote in her journal. "Haven't been able to sell any benefits for N.Y." The play was apparently "too serious." Ticket sales were being adversely affected. Something would have to be done. After the next day's rehearsal, the four met for another "big conference" at which further changes were discussed and decided upon. They were to be ready for the Philadelphia opening.[76] It was now Friday afternoon. The Hacketts had the weekend to give the play a lighter tone and to make the *Diary* conform to a vision of what all four had agreed would be more appealing to audiences. They would spend the weekend with Hellman, reshaping the material to be presented in Anne's name.

There were, of course, the play's backers to consider, and the need to seek their support for future productions. But how necessary had it been to remove most of the remaining Jewish material in order to give the play the less serious tone they sought? New York's vast Jewish population, however acculturated or upwardly striving or reactive to the heightened anti-Semitism of prewar America and its postwar echoes, nearly always provided the majority of Broadway's audience and was certain to do so again. Sufficiently diverse in outlook and consciously Jewish in the aftermath of Israel's successful struggle for survival, they presented no real marketing concern. Given the success of other dramatic treatments of anti-Semitism in the postwar period, most notably the critically acclaimed films *Crossfire* and *Gentlemen's Agreement* six years earlier, it seems unlikely that further reductions in the *Diary*'s Jewish content and theme were motivated by these considerations alone. Other reasons and other hands were clearly at work. Kanin told the *New York Times* three days before the Broadway opening that the *Diary* was neither a sad play nor about war. "This play makes use of elements having mainly to do with human courage, faith, hope, brotherhood, love and self-sacrifice. We discovered as we went deeper and deeper that it was a play about what Shaw called 'the life force.' Anne Frank was certainly killed, but she was never defeated." Throughout Kanin's extended remarks that day, remarks that seemed to echo Hellman's own concerning *The Lark*, not once did he make reference to the Holocaust or to the Jewishness of its victims.[77]

Nearly thirty years after the last changes to the script had been made, Hackett emphatically denied ever having received any help from Hellman. Instead, he continued to claim only to have discussed the fear he shared with Goodrich that they "were getting away from Anne" and "that [Hellman, Bloomgarden, and Kanin] wanted some things that we didn't want."[78] But this had not been the case, as the Hacketts themselves acknowledged only months after the play opened in New York. "It turns out on the highest authority that Lillian Hellman had a considerable part in helping to fashion its ultimate triumph," the *New York Times* reported in May 1956. "Miss Hellman, before she grabs the telephone or her typewriter to demand a retraction, had better pause. The credit was paid to her the other day by the play's adaptors themselves. . . . 'We don't know what we would have done without Lillian. And if she denies it, ask her about those long week-ends last summer.'"[79]

From the time that Crawford involved Hellman as an adviser and possible collaborator, through the rejection of Meyer's script, the suggestion of Mc-Cullers as playwright, Crawford's departure and Bloomgarden's entrance, the choice of the Hacketts, and their calling upon Hellman for assistance throughout the long process of writing and rewriting the play, her hand had been ever present. The final changes to the script that she had so carefully and radically altered were now ready to be made. Though Bloomgarden was pleased with the play he saw that first night in Philadelphia ("It was just wonderful. We got every laugh"), the Hacketts had continued their daily routine of making "small changes" and "tightening scenes" under Kanin's guidance.[80] But when they returned from their "long week-end" with Hellman on Martha's Vineyard, they carried with them a new set of revisions and a "new scene" that would fulfill her agenda.[81]

Throughout the script, tension was reduced as nearly all talk of war, illness, arrest, deportations, frustration, conflict, and fear was either diminished or eliminated, and more joy was introduced.[82] Without the details of the Jews' persecution that would focus attention on them as victims, separated from all others by their victimization, the image of this suffering as undifferentiated could more easily be supported. Just four days before opening in New York, Anne's long monologue in the first scene of act two, in which she speaks of "feel[ing] like a songbird whose wings have been clipped, hurling itself in utter darkness against the bars of its cage," was cut and replaced by talk of the "miracle that is taking place" within her as she menstruates. "I think that what is happening to me is wonderful. . . . Each time it has happened I have a feeling that I have a sweet secret. And in spite of any pain, I long for the time when I shall feel that secret within me again."[83]

Kanin's own demand that the Hanukah scene be transformed from a plea for God's salvation to a "sweet celebration" further added to Hellman's latest distortions of Anne's legacy. Violating the call by Otto for accuracy in all details, Kanin was now free to remove "Ma'oz Tzur"—which had been sung by a thousand women in Auschwitz, where Anne was imprisoned after her capture—in favor of an upbeat Hanukah tune then popular among American Jews. A week before the New York opening, Jack Gilford, chosen to play Dussel, was sent by Kanin to find such a song; he returned with "Oh, Hanu-kah" and its lyrics of gathering to feast "in complete jubilation" at this "happiest of seasons." Gone now was all mention of the "raging foes" who "furious . . . assailed us."[84]

For above all else, there remained the need, prompted by Hellman and shared by Bloomgarden and Kanin, to deemphasize, if not eliminate, the Jewish particularism of the Holocaust. In order to universalize the theme of human suffering after their own fashion, they had, throughout these final weeks, accelerated the process of removing nearly all references to the Jews as objects of persecution. With the playwrights' complicity, fundamental distinctions between Jew and non-Jew, between victims of the Holocaust and all others, were washed away, sanitizing the script of the disease that had brought the *Diary* into being and had taken away the life of its author.

"Would anyone, either Jew or non-Jew, understand this about me?" Anne had asked in a line that was eliminated six days before the play reached New York.[85] A week earlier, the comparison between the Jews' fate in the camps and the relatively mild punishment of those who had hidden the Franks had been similarly cut. ("It wasn't a concentration camp as you know it, Mr. Frank," Miep tells him. "And it wasn't for long. You can't say we suffered.")[86] And now, with Anne's discussion of Jewish suffering having months earlier been transformed into the suffering of all peoples, and with only hours remaining before the Broadway opening, one final and deeper cut had to be made. The last clear reference to the Jews' unique experience, Peter's outrage at having to suffer "Because we're Jews! Because we're Jews!" was slashed from the script, leaving Peter and the audience without a true understanding of why nearly all within the Annex, and six million other Jews throughout Europe, were murdered.[87]

The morning after *The Diary of Anne Frank* opened in New York, Goodrich recorded in her own diary, "Every notice good! Walking on air! . . . We only wish that Anne could have known."[88]

CHAPTER NINE

Successfully Blocked

I have seen the play," Meyer wrote Otto on September 24. No longer able to await its Broadway opening, he had gone to Philadelphia while final alterations were being made and had been appalled to see much of what he had created being staged with radically changed dialogue. "I need hardly tell you that it is very much like the play I wrote . . . except . . . that in my play the characters are more fully and truly developed."[1]

Adulatory notices in the popular press greeted the play's opening in New York. Even the *Daily Worker* praised it as "a story of the Nazi terror as seen through the eyes of a wonderful girl as she hid out with her folks and others hounded by the gestapo." Once the story had been stripped of particularistically Jewish elements, Zionist among them (Israel now being viewed by Moscow and its minions as an arm of American imperialism), the Communist Party in America could break the silence it had maintained toward the *Diary* when first published three years earlier. The reviewer recognized the play as a useful weapon against the new alliances America had made with former Nazis in an effort to defeat the Soviets, and he noted how Anne is seen to "grow to womanhood . . . wise, beautiful and strong to the very end," as Hellman and the others had intended.[2]

But other voices shared Meyer's concern and criticism, demanding something "more faithful to the Diary," as he would that October in pleading with Otto "to return to doing what is right."[3] "Seldom do we glimpse the Anne Frank of the real diary," *Commentary*'s reviewer protested in pointing to her "Broadway metamorphosis into [an] American adolescent." The voice that is heard reading passages from the *Diary* as a device to tie scenes together "is the voice of a girl who has never really listened to the *inner* voice of Anne Frank." It was not her fault, however, but that of the playwrights. "These incoherent halts seem only to heighten the effect of superficiality and inarticulateness that renders the script so poor, does pitiful injustice to the diary, and proves too much even for those of the actors who try to make up for it." But all of this would have been "forgivable . . . if the spirit of Anne herself had survived . . . [that of] an unaffected young girl, exceedingly alive, deep, honest—experiencing more, and in a better way perhaps, than many of us do in the course of a whole lifetime. . . . That it did not can only turn us back to her real diary for the kind of memorial she requires."[4]

"There are things which are holy and thus Broadway has to let them alone," the first Dutch press review argued angrily. "Nothing is perhaps sadder than that . . . 'The Diary of Anne Frank' is without a doubt a big success in New York . . . because what has been the innermost thoughts of an extraordinarily sensitive girl . . . has now become an article of amusement." Distorted by the script, Anne's ideas appeared as "deformed creatures" and "ridiculous." In such a state, the *Vrij Nederland* asked, "who can understand what these people must have endured? . . . The entire performance is sacrilege, sacrilege to all those who were tortured." The reviewer cried in anguish, "I cannot have it, I cannot support the expectation of these well-fed people entering the theatre, I cannot hear their laughing." Anne should never have been brought to the Broadway stage, he declared with outrage. "Anne Frank is not to be looked at. Anne Frank means to be quiet or to pray for her . . . on a wide field where the sun is setting or at the Synagogue on the J. D. Meyersplein."[5]

"The terrible plight of the Jews, who live in constant fear of deportation and a fate worse than death, never crystallized," wrote the reviewer for the *B'nai B'rith Messenger* in February, certain that "the attitude of the diary has been changed." More potentially damaging to the play's financial success, however, was the *Messenger*'s public exposure of Gusti Huber as "a top stage and screen star in wartime Nazi Germany" who had "discovered her concern for human suffering" after starring in the comedy, *A Thief in the Night*, "at the very time Anne was murdered in Bergen Belsen."[6]

Meyer's own critique had, of course, preceded these others, appearing barely a week after the play had opened in New York. The play lacked substance and direction, he had written in the *National Jewish Post*. It had, in fact, evaded the *Diary*'s truly "universal theme" by denying Anne her separate identity, an element common to us all:

> To me, the depth of the entire drama lay in the self-doubt it generated in every heart. What Jew in the entire world has not faced that same doubt, every day: Is it worthwhile to remain a Jew? What human being has not asked himself, is it worthwhile to remain honestly my own self? This is the universal theme. And the Jews of Europe faced it under the most dreadful circumstances. In that tiny house in Amsterdam where the Franks and the Van Daans were hidden, this question

existed. . . . This discovery was also the event that brought Anne her maturity. She emerged . . . able to become objective and free. This remarkable drama is, of course, completely absent from the Hackett play. . . . Is this fair to Anne? And to the Jews who perished for the sake of their identity? And to the world, owed something of this understanding this girl found?[7]

In a last attempt to avoid further litigation by Meyer, who was now ready to add a new charge of plagiarism, Fredman wrote Mermin seeking "a just settlement . . . especially since now everyone connected with the Diary of Anne Frank will be amply rewarded for their efforts with the exception of that person who first recognized its potentialities and first toiled so hard in its behalf." He further suggested that Mermin's clients take Meyer seriously, and that they understand that any settlement discussed "cannot be on the basis of something for nothing," for each of the scenes now being praised by the critics could be found in Meyer's earlier script.[8]

Mermin's response was to send a copy of Fredman's sharply worded letter to Otto, along with his judgment that Meyer's claims were "thin." Still, their "nuisance value" suggested a sound "business reason" for a settlement. The charge of plagiarism and the uncertainties of litigation could easily affect the sale of the *Diary*'s film rights. Nor might Otto have service of this suit so easily vacated now that he was enjoying a New York income. "Such a lawsuit would, of course, involve you in expense," he further noted, and would, perhaps, require personal testimony. Mermin recommended that a settlement be attempted, the cost of which he hoped the Hacketts would share. (He recommended, as well, that the *Diary*'s translator sign an "estoppel letter," effectively removing her from all film-related financial considerations.)[9]

Otto countered by questioning the wisdom of such a settlement. Meyer's contention was simply an attempt at blackmail, he maintained, however nicely Mermin had tried to recast it. "He will always ask more and more." Worse, payment "will make him think that he has certain rights." However distasteful "on account of all the excitements and the publicity," Otto was willing to face litigation, even if it meant an appearance in an American court, he worried that the Hacketts might otherwise be sued for plagiarism in his stead. "For my person I would risk his litigations, but I hate the idea of the Hacketts being involved in the matter." Nor did he believe in their sharing the cost of any potential settlement. Perhaps Meyer would simply accept his half of the agent's commission. There was, in fact, ample "justification, for . . . Levin was the first to write me about his view" concerning stage and screen possibilities, and had "worked . . . to find a producer," however unnecessary given the normal response of producers to any successful book. Angry and frustrated, and still unable to admit, even to his attorney, that he had in fact promised

Meyer the opportunity to write the script in lieu of an agent's fee, Otto found "all this . . . rather depressing," and ultimately insisted "that Anne's belief that people are really good at heart is not appropriate to Levin."[10]

"I have tried to understand you for some years, Mr. Frank," Meyer wrote hours later, having had no direct contact with Otto for some time. "Now perhaps you should try a little to understand me," he argued, desperately drawing an outrageously offensive analogy between Otto's confinement in the Annex and the camps and the injustice he himself had suffered as the *Diary*'s first playwright. "Over and over in your mind the question kept asking itself, why, why, why, why have they done this to me?" Meyer was certain. "Why could they simply take and do these to me, because they are more powerful?" After three sleepless years, he, too, was left asking, "Why, why, why. Why should Mr. Frank do this to me? Did I ever injure him? . . . Because some men were powerful, should they take away and destroy what I have in all honesty done?" With "every scene that was singled out for praise exist[ing] in my play . . . the entire affair resembles the arbitrary way in which the Germans took away some business that a Jew had created, and simply handed it to one of their own onhangers," he maintained. Despite discussions of a settlement, Meyer was determined to seek full justice in the courts, "all because you did not have the faith to stand by a friend and an honest writer." "Oh how your daughter would weep for the evil use to which you have allowed her work to be put," he charged. "How tasteless she would find a success gained at the expense of such needless cruelty."[11]

Four days later, Meyer wrote Otto "that my experience with you has shaken what was left of my faith in humanity. If someone of your supposed probity and considerateness could take such advantage of me, and prove himself so callous, then I no longer know in whom one may have any trust." There was no alternative but "to go to the very end of this experience, no matter at what cost, in order to find somewhere that there is consideration and justice left in the world." In this, he had the support of Norman Mailer and James Farrell, who, in characterizing his situation as "a striking case . . . of suppression," had publicly affirmed that "Mr. Levin has a creator's right to reach an audience, just as the public has a right to see his play. As it is now, a serious and faithful work has in effect been suppressed. We suggest that Anne Frank's Diary, a legacy to humanity, be viewed as a literary work rather than a commercial property. It is not uncommon, indeed it is stimulating for more than one adaptation of a book to be offered to the public. We urge that qualified productions of Mr. Levin's play be permitted in recognition, so appropriate to the Diary, that not only human beings but their works have a right to life."[12] (Herbert Gold's endorsement of this position quickly earned Hellman's lasting enmity.[13])

In a separate mailing, Otto received a copy of Meyer's *National Jewish Post* article on October 27. He had been forewarned of its contents by the Hacketts, who had earlier written that Meyer had distributed copies of it to New York's theater critics even before the play's Broadway opening. Perhaps not fully understanding the concept of plagiarism, Otto responded by writing Mermin that Meyer had severely damaged his claim in noting the Hacketts' failure "to have stressed enough the Jewish point of view."[14]

On November 10, Meyer sent Otto yet another demand that he "make some amends" (which Otto interpreted to be monetary), attaching a copy of the *Commentary* critique for support.[15] This letter, like the several before it, remained unanswered. Meyer did, however, receive a response to a copy of the article that had accompanied his second request that Kanin read his play. Although he disagreed with *Commentary*, Kanin nevertheless told Meyer "how sorry [he was] about all this unpleasantness." Still, he judged it best not to read Meyer's play "while continuing to deal with the present version" or to "become involved in your dispute" with Otto, Crawford, and Bloomgarden, to whom he, of course, sent copies of his response.[16]

Kanin's reply predictably generated yet another letter from Meyer to Otto, demanding a public reading of his script, together with a copy of the critical review of the Hacketts' play that had in the meantime appeared in *Commonweal*.[17] "Does he think there is still a chance to produce his play?" Otto asked Tereska ten days later, as the year drew to a close.[18] There was simply no possibility of allowing such a reading, however great the support he had generated from writers like Mailer and Farrell. With the play grossing $28,000 per week by December, there was just too much money at stake.[19]

"May I pause for a moment before going into business to tell you that I read the book as soon as it came out in this country—I took all of you Franks to my heart—and loved you and suffered with you," Salisbury wrote Otto on December 1, hoping to broker the film contract as his agent, as she had once hoped to do for Meyer. Anne's words "fell on fertile ground in me," she continued, relating the stories she had heard from her own Jewish immigrant parents, of pogroms and conscription in Russia and "hiding from Cossacks," all of which she claimed "prepared me for the dedication I have from the beginning felt for this play." This same "personal dedication to the property" was shared by all those producers who had already approached her, she assured Otto. "We all hope of course that the final deal will assure us the Hacketts as the screen writers and Kanin as the director," she continued, advising that he "not under any circumstances permit readings on radio or presentations via television in any country whatsoever."[20]

As calculated, Otto was appreciative of Salisbury's "warm personal interest in everything concerning Anne's Diary." It was for that very reason, because "the play means more to you than business," that he hoped she could understand why he disagreed with her recommendation to ban all further public exposure for the *Diary* until after a film contract had been negotiated. "I cannot see any harm in case parts of the book are simply read."[21]

Nor did Otto see any reason to hire Salisbury as his agent, however "tremendously . . . impressed" he had been by her letter. "He is a very frugal man . . . and I think he will think twice before paying 10%," the Hacketts told her. A "curious mixture of great emotion and business," who "gives his money away" while taking care to secure its source, he remained "unable to speak of the Diary without crying" and yet was open to invention and change concerning the script. "I think we helped him to realize the necessity for certain changes, and helped him visualize and understand the performance." As the agent negotiating their role as the *Diary*'s screenwriters, it was crucial that Salisbury fully appreciate these diverse qualities in Otto. They had worked hard to cultivate the relationship. It was time to reap what they had sown.[22]

But the course of negotiations soon proved more difficult than anticipated, and by January 9, 1956, the group's feelings toward Otto had changed. "I thought I was the only one who dreaded his visit," Hackett wrote Salisbury in anticipation of that day. "He lives in the past and gets talking about the diary, the play or Anne, and very soon he has reduced Frances to tears."[23] For Salisbury, Bloomgarden, and Kanin, Otto's willingness to freely grant others "various things in connection with the foreign production" of the play, and its potentially negative impact on "the current film situation," had proven highly disturbing. Suddenly, their hold over the material no longer seemed secure, heightening their concern over Otto's vision of the *Diary* and of the dramatization they had spawned.

For Van Daan's theft was not the only change Otto had found difficult to accept. Having so cavalierly dismissed his opinion on this and other aspects of the play, they now feared his use of the contractual right to change the script in its foreign production. However strongly they might argue for their dramatic value, there were errors he might no longer wish to accept. "I put this before them as something to deal with carefully," Salisbury told Hackett of the group's meeting, "as Mike [Mermin] has been asking for various changes in the foreign contract I had submitted to him which seemed to me would give Mr. Frank too much control." She was not alone in this opinion. "Kermit and Garson agreed with me completely—said it was dangerous and must not be allowed to happen," as did the Hacketts, whose "own qualms regarding Mr. Frank's approval of adaptors" had first prompted Salisbury to convene the meeting "to hold this down." No contracts for foreign productions could be signed "until this thing of Mr. Frank's approval is straightened out." Although the delay was causing significant financial loss, they still could not chance entering into a film contract.[24]

After two additional weeks of renegotiations with Mermin over foreign production rights, Salisbury could report to the Hacketts that they had reached a point where, if she was successful, her "revised wording will make it impossible for [Otto] to insist upon changes in the American text, or the sequence of scenes," or to "impose his ideas regarding deletions or additions because the play is 'too glamorous' for Europe." Meyer's repeated mailings had undoubtedly helped him understand that the image of his daughter had been overly Americanized. Salisbury hoped that Otto would misperceive her "wording" and would agree to the proposed contract changes, "unless he is determined to deviate from your dramatization, which no one else wants."[25] On February 2, Mermin inexplicably consented to her terms, believing that Otto would soon follow his lead.[26]

Still unresolved, however, was the ongoing dispute over the Israeli production of Meyer's play. "We also discussed the likely bad effect of a production of Levin's version in Israel," Salisbury had written the Hacketts that January. "We all know that Mr. Frank did, as a conciliatory measure, promise Meyer Levin something about Israel, but the three of us remembered that surely Mr. Frank's attorney, in permitting such a promise to be made, must have limited the time—or specified the conditions, and should not have left out the fact that Mr. Frank himself or Kermit or others would need to approve permissions on the contract—or casting—or something." Here again was a potential threat to their absolute control, about which Bloomgarden would soon meet with Mermin. "I hope something constructive will come out of it."[27] (Actively engaged in the ongoing fight to prevent Meyer from ever staging his play in Israel, Salisbury wrote the Hacketts in late 1965 that Meyer "must be eaten up inside!"[28])

Salisbury's discussions with Bloomgarden and Kanin, and her approach to Mermin, had come in the midst of protracted negotiations between Otto's attorneys and Meyer's. Though somewhat disillusioned with the Broadway script, Otto still could not bring himself to allow Meyer to present his more accurate dramatization. Ill will and profit had fueled Otto's refusal to issue a statement concerning Meyer's "exclusive rights" in Israel, leaving Israeli theater companies fearful that the Hacketts' play might present undue competition, which they could ill afford. It was a clever ploy, allowing Otto to subvert the agreement that he had signed three years before his financial success on Broadway. But Fredman made it clear to Mermin that any such interference would be seen by Meyer as "inconsistent with his own rights" and cause him to "look to Mr. Frank for redress."[29]

And so, on January 15, Otto sent Mermin his authorization to allow Meyer to produce his play in Israel, provided a specifically defined period of time could be agreed upon. The contract of November 1952, he noted, "contains our moral duty to make it possible for Levin to have his version produced by not offering and giving the rights for the Hackett version at least for a certain period." Still, however much he may have wished to honor his agreement with Meyer, Otto's apparent change of heart was predicated as well on the belief that "the financial results from Israel will be very unimportant" and that once Meyer's production had closed, the Hackett play could be presented for years thereafter. More significantly, he believed that by "exercis[ing] the right the contract gives him," Meyer had made "an acknowledgement of the whole." Here, Otto thought, was the perfect defense against all present and future litigation.[30]

But Otto was no longer a free agent in the handling of his daughter's *Diary*. The property was now shared by those who continued to block not only Meyer but Otto as well. And even as negotiations continued regarding issues of foreign production and film rights, Meyer sought further support for his right to give his play a "hearing." He circulated an appeal throughout the American rabbinate in accordance with "our tradition which emphasizes every man's right to issue a call to judgment." In a second request to those who had not yet signed his appeal by February 14, he stressed how his work had been "suppressed out of personal motives" that had "omitted . . . the question of Jewish identification," thereby taking from the audience "the full value of the material. . . . Peter's desire to 'pass' if he survived, Anne's avowal of faith, her sister's wish to become a nurse in Israel, all are absent."

"There are two ways of destroying Jewish life," Meyer reminded the rabbis. "One is physical extinction as practiced by the Nazis. The other is extinction of Jewish identification." The latter, in a covert reference to what he would soon declare publicly, was being practiced "in some countries . . . through the extinction of Jewish culture," as it was in America by those who would suppress his play. After "the catastrophe in Europe, it is owed to Anne, it is owed to the Jewish community, that her answer be voiced."[31]

Without waiting for this additional response, Meyer sent Otto a copy of his appeal together with a list of the one hundred rabbis who had already signed it.[32] The next day he sent a series of excerpts from the supportive letters that accompanied these many signatures.[33] Eight days later he wrote Otto that among the more than one hundred and seventy rabbis who now supported his "petition" were two with whom Otto had spoken in Paris the previous summer in an effort "to convince them I was in the wrong." They had now "given me their moral support for a hearing." He wanted Otto to realize that the issue of an Israeli production had still not been settled ("Your attorney has again put off a request for a meeting, this time for another ten days"), and that others had raised the question of "someone who was popular with the Nazis to the very end of the war portray[ing] your wife." To this he added news of criticism recently leveled against Bloomgarden by the renowned theater critic George

Jean Nathan for having "cast aside" Christopher Fry's far better adaptation of Anouilh's L'Alouette in favor of the "far worse translation made by Lillian Hellman," a decision identified by Meyer as "a parallel example of Mr. Bloomgarden's brutal authoritarianism in the arts."[34]

Meyer had also sent a copy of the petition to Bloomgarden, who, like Otto, had refused to respond, as had the Hacketts, to whom Meyer had written "as fellow-writers, and in the interests of Anne Frank who was a writer."[35] With little recourse remaining beyond the courts, Meyer called a news conference, hoping to avoid further litigation by sharing his story and the signed petition. But only one reporter appeared, a staff writer from the New York Times who later telephoned Meyer to tell him that his story had been "killed upstairs." Meyer's subsequent approach to the Saturday Evening Post yielded a similar end. He then tried again to secure the assistance of Simon Rifkind, a founding partner in Mermin's law firm whom Meyer had met in Europe when Rifkind had served as Eisenhower's adviser for Jewish affairs in the American Zone of Occupation. At first Rifkind failed to recall their earlier meeting, and when he discovered that Meyer intended to criticize one of his fellow attorneys at Paul, Weiss, he escorted him from his office.[36]

On February 23, 1956, Meyer filed suit in New York State Supreme Court, naming Otto and Bloomgarden as codefendants.[37] Four basic causes of action were delineated: that an agreement had been reached with Otto "that in sole consideration" for Meyer's agency in seeking a theatrical or film producer, he "alone would have the right to write a dramatic adaptation of the Diary or to have others collaborate with him for that purpose"; that Bloomgarden, having learned of Crawford's withdrawal, "wrongfully, knowingly, intentionally and maliciously induced, persuaded and enticed the said defendant Frank to violate, repudiate and break his said agreement with plaintiff"; that in violation of an additional agreement with Otto following the initial rejection of his script, allowing for its Israeli production, Otto had "constantly and still does refuse to permit" Meyer to "arrange for this production"; and that Otto and Bloomgarden had, subsequent to reading Meyer's script, "consulted and collaborated" with "those other persons [who] prepared an adaptation of the Diary."[38]

Before making this final charge, with its implication of plagiarism, Fredman had himself conducted a detailed "structural comparison" of the scripts, concluding that "a study of both scripts will show that the crucial question of choice key incidents is solved in virtually exact parallel. The same incidents were chosen. . . . About nine-tenths of the structural content in the Hackett play may be traced to Levin's radio script and stage play." With similar scenes similarly framed in nearly the same sequence ("The material, in point of timing on the stage, falls almost exactly into the same place"), and with Anne's voice similarly used as a "link" between scenes, "one may well ask what was the contribution of the second adaptors? Their work would seem to be analogous to what is done in Hollywood when one team of writers follows another writer on a script, cutting, polishing, transposing." The Hacketts' play clearly differed from Meyer's only in its disregard of "much more material from the Diary about religious feeling and about Jewish identity—such as the desire of Anne's sister to become a nurse in Palestine." The playwrights, "in omitting such material," appeared "to be studiously following a pattern of avoiding discussion of Jewish identity, the essence of the drama."[39]

In a deposition given by Meyer the following day in pursuit of "a warrant of attachment" upon Otto's income from the play because of his foreign residence, Meyer summarized the causes of action against him as "fraud . . . breach of contract . . . [and] wrongful appropriation of ideas," made all the more inexcusable because of the play's content and purpose. "It seemed to me that the Diary contained the elements by which the world could finally and clearly absorb the enormity of the mass murders perpetrated by the Nazis," he testified. In detail after detail, Meyer chronicled how Otto, in spite of his assurance that his agreement with Crawford had secured Meyer's own role as the Diary's adapter ("as my agreement with him provided"), had "carefully skirted any mention of any change in the setup between Crawford and myself." Having devoted his efforts to the adaptation, only to have it rejected and himself removed from the project, he had then been forced by "a series of threats and pressures, of false representations and frauds," to accept an Israeli production as the sole outlet for his play, and had then seen this coerced agreement ignored as well. He had "tried to resist vigorously," but it was all in a losing cause. Frank and his associates were adamant; they would settle for "no less than eliminating my interests completely." As subsequent actions had demonstrated, "any moral rights I may have had, let alone legal rights, were not to be recognized. I was successfully blocked."[40]

"I find Mr. Levin's disputations hard to understand," Bloomgarden wrote that same day in response to an inquiry from Samuel Silver, director of public relations of the Union of American Hebrew Congregations, regarding Meyer's petition to the rabbinate. His play simply "does not live up to my concept of the potential of the underlying work." Bloomgarden argued that Meyer was merely "trying to convert his private disappointment into a public moral issue" when no such issue existed. The Hacketts' play was clearly superior, "not only good theater but . . . also an inspiriting communication which carries forward the spirit and the message of [the] Diary." Using Anne as a shield, he concluded that Meyer's attempt to "injure this production" was indeed "a disservice to her spirit."[41]

The effort to secure a warrant of attachment had in the meantime halted all negotiations concerning Meyer's Israeli production. "Fredman's timing was unfortunate," Ephraim London, an attorney asked to mediate the dispute, told Meyer on February 27, though he believed that "a reasonable chance" might still exist for Mermin to approach him if no "additional pressures to compel an adjustment" were applied.[42] Meyer could not follow this freely offered advice; instead, he wrote Otto two days later that Mermin had "broken off negotiations."[43]

Otto's response to the charges brought against him by Meyer continued at length throughout the spring of 1956. "I can only say that from the whole correspondence one can see that I never wanted to give Levin any commitment to write," he asserted early in the process, accusing Meyer of irresponsibly starting his script "without fulfilling his [agent's] duties" of first securing a contract for him with Crawford. Meyer had, in fact, caused his own problems, Otto asserted. "Before he started writing he ought to have seen to it that a written agreement would have been made as is usual in every case of this sort (as the Hacketts did with Bloomgarden)." (In fact, Otto knew, contract negotiations had dragged on long after the Hacketts had begun to work on their script.) Further deflecting all responsibility for his decision to reject Meyer's work, he emphasized how Bloomgarden's negative response to Meyer's script had "made a big impression on me" and had convinced him not to accept it, as had the absence of any interest by other important producers. Offers by Shumlin and Clurman—"directors not producers"—had been unacceptable, he insisted, though two months earlier, in a letter to Tereska, he had referred to Shumlin as a producer from whom "there was no offer."[44]

"I never saw so many lies," Otto wrote the Hacketts of Meyer's suit on March 8. "I can easily give evidence against his statements," which he characterized as "the meanest insinuations."[45] A month later he referred to Meyer's suit as "this disgusting matter."[46] Rejecting all possibility of a quiet out-of-court settlement, he demanded to see "Levin withdrawing it and publicly declaring that his accusations were wrong."[47]

It was a vain hope. Meyer was already taking his fight further into the public arena by writing the New York *Daily News* of "the contempt that the management of 'The Diary of Anne Frank' has had for the public, particularly the Jewish public." The fight against "the suppression of [his] version of the Diary" was not for the sake of money, he insisted, but an effort to give voice to "the deeper and more essential ideas of Anne Frank . . . omitted from the Broadway version of the play." No one, he argued, had "the moral right to decide to hold back any of her material," least of all an ideologue like Hellman, whose spectre he now publicly raised for the first time. "There is a very real clash in point of view between myself and Lillian Hellman, whose political connections up to 1949 are not denied. It was Lillian Hellman, on the admission of the Hacketts, who masterminded their version of the Diary after choosing them to write it for her producer, Bloomgarden. The question arises as to whether there is not a very slick job of propaganda by omission, here."

Nor had anyone the moral right to steal the work of another, he added as a final issue in his attempt to build wider support for his script. "My lawsuit, incidentally, charges appropriation of ideas, citing many structural similarities between the Hacketts' Pulitzer Prize play and mine, written two years earlier. Could the reluctance to allow any production whatever of my play, even now that the commercial values are virtually exhausted in the Broadway run, be due to an apprehension that a stage production would show up, very forcefully, such similarities?"[48]

"What's wrong with you is that you are a very obstinate man and that you *must* believe that you are *always* right," Tereska wrote Otto that March after receiving his "very angry letter" condemning Meyer as "childish." She had believed Otto the previous summer when he promised to allow Meyer to produce his play in Israel, "without conditions," and had continued her efforts to convince Meyer "to go back . . . to his own creative work instead of losing all this time and energy in lawsuits." But Otto had not kept his word and was now asserting that she had fallen under Meyer's influence and had abandoned her own "set of ethics."[49]

Otto drafted a response for Tereska but never sent it.[50] His attorneys had now taken charge of these matters, and unlike Meyer, he listened carefully to their counsel. It was their hope that the large cache of correspondence Meyer had sent Otto through the years, which Otto in turn had passed along to them, could now be used as a weapon against him once the "peculiarities" of the case had been subjected to legal analysis and a defensive wedge had been found. But thoughts of "a program of procedural attack on Mr. Levin . . . to make it clear to Mr. Levin and his attorneys that we intend to fight this matter right down the line," as Mermin's assisting attorney, Edward Costikyan, sketched the strategy for Otto on March 12,[51] were suddenly dropped less than two weeks later. Such tactics "would add up to a delay, but would not dispose of Mr. Levin's claim on the merits," Costikyan admitted reluctantly. In place of an endless stream of motions, Paul, Weiss was now recommending litigation. The firm would make a final attempt to negotiate a binding settlement, "if only for public relations purposes." But "delay works against you," Costikyan advised, for "the longer we delay matters, the longer it will be before royalties will again be paid."[52]

CHAPTER TEN

Too Jewish

O tto spent the next several days composing a seven-page, single-spaced set of "remarks" in answer to Meyer's successful warrant of attachment, sending them to Mermin on March 26. Mermin later called these notes "extremely important" in helping to prepare Otto's defense. But they have proven significant and telling for reasons other than Otto had intended. Meyer, by Otto's own account, had raised the issue of Jewish identity from their first meeting in Paris in the spring of 1951. "The greater part of our conversation was personal," Otto recalled five years later. "Levin mentioned his activities in the Jewish field, he wanted to know more of my experiences." But Otto would add nothing more of this discussion to his notes, perhaps too embarrassed to tell his attorney that he had been unable to respond in much detail. Instead, Otto refuted numerous other issues raised by Meyer's affidavit, including the assertions that he had acted as Otto's agent and had written his script with Otto's approval. Nor had Meyer, through his efforts on Otto's behalf, earned the right to adapt the *Diary*, Otto further argued. "If Levin pretends that he acquired legal or moral rights because he had worked for years to interest people for play or film, he exaggerated highly his activities. What did he do? In the time before the book was published, he did send manuscripts to several producers or film people," Otto admitted, but "this was a work next to his work as a journalist and writer, just as I did the work for the book next to my work in business."[1]

"All the difficulties which arose were caused by the negligence of Levin as my agent," Otto wrote Costikyan the following day, denying any role in the matter aside from that of a victim of Meyer's failure to secure a contract with Crawford. Why, then, should he be forced to appear in court? Hoping to avoid an open inquiry, Otto fell back on his celebrity as Anne's father, claiming that coming to New York "would be a tremendous strain not mainly in connection with the lawsuit, but my visit would be known all over, and I could not escape many people wanting to meet the real Otto Frank after they had seen the play and this would be very emotional."[2] He hoped, instead, to respond only in writing, as he did again two weeks later, using excerpts from Meyer's own correspondence to attack him.[3]

Otto remained unaware that these negotiations were, in part, designed merely to delay the suit's adjudication. As the Hacketts had written Mermin, Kanin, Bloomgarden, and Salisbury after they had met several times to discuss the Israeli staging of Meyer's script, "If the suit can be postponed until we have had several European productions . . . that will definitely lessen Mr. Levin's chances of hurting us with the production of his play in Israel. . . . We only regret that in the contract between Mr. Frank and Mr. Levin there is no time limit to Mr. Levin's 'opportunity to produce.'"[4]

Bloomgarden similarly denied Meyer's many allegations, briefly and carefully nuancing his response to conceal the sequence of events that had led to his having "declined to produce" Meyer's play. Missing from Bloomgarden's "Answers" was the fact that it had been at Crawford's suggestion, following her weekend with Hellman, that Meyer had brought the script to him and that he had given Meyer a decision only after first discussing the matter with both Crawford and Hellman. Nor did he mention his own earlier attempt to secure the *Diary* with Hellman's assistance. Instead, he told the Court only "that at some time in the fall of 1952 plaintiff showed this defendant a dramatic adaptation of the Diary, which he had read with the permission of Cheryl Crawford, and that he did not believe the adaptation warranted production." Bloomgarden similarly admitted to having "consulted with persons selected by him to write an adaptation of the Diary," but denied having "collaborated" or given them "the ideas in the plaintiff's radioscript and adaptation . . . for the preparation of such adaptation."[5] Meyer, of course, had already demonstrated the probability of both in materials filed with the Court.[6]

"Let me respectfully say that the facts you set forth are for the most part inaccurate," Fredman wrote Costikyan six days later. He had little patience left after receiving Costikyan's opinion that a negotiated settlement would be nothing more than the "buying off [of] a nuisance lawsuit." Fredman had taken this as a "personal affront" and, in castigating Costikyan, told him that "we can only conclude that Mr. Frank, in taking this view, is unaware of the seriousness of our claim." "Personally disappointed" in opposing counsel, he stressed to Costikyan that "the onus of breaking off negotiations must fall upon you."[7]

In late May, Otto offered the Court a response to Meyer's pleadings that was nearly identical to Bloomgarden's.[8] There was now little possibility of reaching an amicable conclusion to the dispute, as Meyer and Otto had continued their threats and counterthreats during the intervening weeks, each disclosing to the press the other's alleged wrongdoings.[9] And although Meyer amended his original suit against Otto and Crawford by dropping all monetary claims against them, he did all that he could to fan the passions of his supporters in calling for Otto to allow his play to be seen—as did Otto, through his attorneys, to ensure that it would not.[10]

But theirs were not the only voices to the conflict. The play received the New York Drama Critics Circle Award for the season's best American production, but a Dutch critic in Amsterdam's *Het Parool* published a scathing attack upon it, asking why the *Diary* had not been allowed to speak as Anne had intended it, "as a characteristic document of our time." In the reviewer's judgment, "the writers deviated too far from the book to have the right to speak about a stage adaptation from it. . . . A diary is a particularly private writing and theater is an especially public matter. Therefore I doubt if one can ever adapt a diary for the stage. These 'adaptors' scarcely tried it. Even the passages of the Diary which are read by an invisible Anne are not citations but fabricated by Miss Goodrich and Mr. Hackett. Their play is a new product which is sailing under a false flag, trash which I hope we shall not see here."[11]

Nevertheless, the Hacketts were awarded the Pulitzer Prize for drama on May 7. "The miracle of the playwriting is such that the sense of doom is never as important as the will to live," the prize committee noted, in contradistinction to the reality Anne had intended to portray. The committee, which viewed the play as "a tragedy that also happens to include comedy and a romance," found it "more than . . . a brilliant and poignant reminder of the agonies through which the world has recently gone." It seemed "a statement, courageous and immensely human, of the need of a people in their daily lives to live not merely with death but above it"—a far easier task for those living with abstractions than for the Jews whose experience had been so terribly distorted.[12]

It is not surprising that few newspapers reporting that the Hacketts received the Pulitzer Prize mentioned Anne's Jewishness. Even the *New York Times* failed to note this fact, citing instead how "a young girl's sweetness, courage and confidence in the future . . . during [the] Nazi occupation of the Netherlands [had] contributed to a memorable evening in the theatre."[13] The question of whether it was a "Jewish play" was answered in the New York *Sunday News* with "an emphatic negative. It is a drama about human beings. They happen to be Jewish because those were the people who had to hide from the Germans in all of Europe, but their race and religion are incidental details of the drama."[14] Goodrich herself confirmed this by telling one reporter that "Anne Frank seemed to be typical of . . . American girls."[15] (Otto's own approach reflected much the same attitude. In deciding against its production in Yiddish translation for a Jewish audience in Argentina, he expressed his preference for "the native language," the play's content presenting little that might otherwise jeopardize its broader reception in the "representative the-aters of the country."[16])

"The most crucial defect of the play," a critic in the Zionist journal *Midstream* protested, was that as a "result of omission . . . it insufficiently projects the tragedy." Instead, "there is a distortion of emphasis . . . and a falsification of the diary." As "largely a sequence of quarrels foolish enough to be funny . . . [the play] could almost be a comedy of any people isolated in unpleasant quarters anywhere, for whatever reason."[17]

Meyer could hardly remain silent while this "surface drama," devoid of any concern for "the deeper psychological aspects of Jewish identification in the hidden Jews and the survivors," was "winning prizes." Here was a case where the "Hollywood treatment" had "reach[ed] in advance to Broadway," preclud-ing all others by its success, regardless of how "wrong" it was, he told the *Village Voice* in early May.[18] In Israel that June, a critic for the newspaper *Haaretz* called for an end to the Broadway monopoly over the *Diary* so that a more accurate portrayal could be presented.[19]

On May 24, two days after filing his "Answer" with the Court, Otto sent a lengthy note to Mermin concerning his own growing reservations about any further handling of the *Diary* by those who had already distorted it on the stage. In the midst of negotiating a film contract, Otto suddenly expressed his concern that while the Hacketts had "inserted a number of ideas of their own which were wonderful," and though he could accept "anything that would fit into the pattern," he could not allow the *Diary* to be used for a film that "would not contain the mission of the book."

Nor was Otto comfortable knowing "that some of the characters would be represented in a wrong light. How could I face the reproaches of my con-science, of my family, of Miep, Kleiman and the others who never understood that I gave away the rights to get money without any promise from the producer to respect the quality of the material." Surely his own attorney knew that his "personal feelings and . . . conscience would not be at rest when in a film in which my family and my friends are represented, characters or situa-tions would be falsified."[20] But Otto did not know that for some time, Mermin had been forwarding his confidential correspondence to Salisbury, with whom he was negotiating on Otto's behalf, and that she, in turn, had kept the Hacketts fully informed of Otto's feelings, thus enabling them to advise him that he would "never be able to sell the play for pictures if he insist[ed] on approval of the script."[21]

Torn between the commercial potential of the *Diary* and the need to keep faith with his daughter, Otto "consent[ed] in principle" to W. W. Norton's "idea of using the *Diary* as [a] textbook for American students" but withheld his final approval until he could read the author's manuscript and perhaps "offer a little help."[22] But no such reservations remained for those involved with Otto in the theater. On June 8, Kanin sent a memo to James Proctor, the play's publicist, asking that they meet for "another one of our exploitation sessions."[23] (Proctor was later brought before HUAC in 1958 as part of the committee's final attack upon the entertainment world.[24]) It was Kanin's plan to "aim a little more directly at the Jewish Community," particularly now that so many would be vacationing. "I am told that about four and a half million people go to the various Catskill, Berkshire, and Adirondacks resorts. . . . I have a feeling that there's gold in them thar hills." A vigorous advertising campaign was planned, using the many statements they had received from prominent Jews— Leonard Bernstein, Edna Ferber, Herman Wouk, Edward G. Robinson, Richard Rodgers, Danny Kaye, Milton Berle, and Phil Silvers, among others.[25] Proctor further suggested adding a "direct mail campaign," using the Federation of Jewish Philanthropies list of sixty thousand who had contributed at least fifty dollars to its last fund drive, "the plushiest list we can aim for," though how he would obtain the list "will have to be not quite legitimate."[26]

Yet they still could not bring themselves to speak of the specifically Jewish victimization central to the *Diary*. Few references to the Nazis or to the camps found their way into the excerpted statements prepared for the play's latest promotion, nor had those elements been prominent in the advertising copy written earlier by playwright, producer, director, and publicist. To the Hack-etts, Anne had been

> A young girl like other young girls who wriggled, giggled and chattered. . . . An eager heart unafraid to speak frankly of the delightful tortures of falling in love for the first time. . . . A sprite who managed to live a full, rich life in an atmosphere tense with the conflicts of personalities and the ever-present sense of danger. . . . A captivating, bright spirit whose self discoveries of the joys, sorrows, terrors of adolescence was always leavened with wit and humor. . . . A young girl with the same hopes and dreams and foolish romantic ideas, the same moments of serious-ness and yearnings and bewilderment that all boys and girls have. She might have been your neighbor's teen-aged daughter—or your own. Her's [sic] was a real life lived in a real and sometimes terrifying world.[27]

Expanding on that characterization, Bloomgarden noted that "what made 'The Diary of Anne Frank' altogether unique and remarkable as a book was the frankness with which Anne portrayed her own feelings, day by day, as she changed from a child to a young woman, sentimental and humorous, witty and alive, wise beyond her years." As a play, it had become "an extraordinary picture of adolescence . . . [and] a theatrical experience that is so real it might be your own."[28]

For Kanin, the *Diary* was as much "the honest telling of a breathlessly exciting story . . . a thrilling observation of Anne's necessarily swift, yet magical, journey from childhood through adolescence to passionate young womanhood," as it was "a lesson in living together; a chronicle of the dignity and nobility of common people; a salute to the great spirit of man alive." Why Anne's spirit had been challenged, or why her maturation had become "necessarily swift," was never mentioned.[29] Instead, here was "a story of a young girl whose spirit could not be imprisoned or thwarted," a dramatization, according to Proctor, "authentic with the fidelity of Anne Frank's own words and emotions . . . words that have bubbled with amusement, love and self discovery, words so wondrously alive, so near that one feels it might be the people living next door to you."[30]

In June 1956, Proctor again claimed that "although the story has been dramatized, it has not [been] fictionalized. The characters and situations of the Diary are the same . . . [as] recorded by Anne Frank during an exciting two-year period." Yet "the story itself is not what makes it distinguished," but rather its "remarkable recording," he maintained in advertising copy approved by Bloomgarden and Kanin "for the direct selling of 'The Diary'" in "Jewish summer resort areas" that summer.[31]

Small wonder that we discover Bloomgarden noting in his "Production Daily Log" that the play's emphasis was still "too much on [the] German section" and that sudden displays of anger were to be preferred over the more constant "lachrymose" state to be expected of those in flight and hiding—or that, with apparent approval, he had repeatedly recorded the audiences' laughter, particularly with reference to the words, "Our Damned Jews."[32] Nor is it surprising that Otto's growing discomfort with those distortions had become a deepening concern for those who wished to retain their hold on the *Diary*. In this atmosphere, any suggestion of a return to greater authenticity could hardly have received a sympathetic hearing, as Otto soon discovered in questioning the choice of Hanukah songs for the film.

It was Otto's fear that "if the usual Chanukah song would not be used . . . it would make a very strange impression among all Jews and those who know a little about Judaism." Upon receiving Otto's request that "Ma'oz Tzur," "the song . . . in all European countries," be reinstated and sung in Hebrew, Salisbury immediately forwarded it to Kanin, who fired off two letters in response. "The choice of the present song was neither personal nor arbitrary," he wrote Otto, "but rather dictated by the special needs of the moment." If he wished to suggest something "spirited and gay," Kanin would consider it, but not a "hymn-like song" that would give "the wrong feeling entirely. . . . Or if it has the sound of an anthem, then I feel it would be a very great mistake."[33]

"I had hoped that this subject was closed forever," Kanin wrote the Hacketts, soliciting their aid in dealing with Otto. "The ending of the first act will be flat as a latke unless the song which is sung there is a gay one." To sing in Hebrew would be a "great mistake" as well, Kanin argued, for it "would simply alienate the audience." Deputizing the Hacketts, he encouraged them not to "be afraid to speak firmly to Frank" but to remind him how "damn foolish" it was "to horse around" with what he himself had identified as the only version of the play that had succeeded. Salisbury had offered similar encouragement a few days earlier. "What you say will influence Mr. Frank—if anyone can influence him on this point."[34]

"It is the very childlike gaiety of this song that gives the tremendous dramatic effect," the Hacketts wrote Otto in an attempt to convince him that the song should not be changed. Here were "people with death hanging over their heads" still capable of "happy celebrations." Otto's song had left the first act "without any emotion," they argued, while Kanin's choice was "the great reason for the success of the play." Through this happy song, "the whole spirit of the play, the poignancy, the indomitable courage of these people came to us. This is the dramatic high point, the spiritual high point of the play," they insisted, though Otto may have thought the arrest of those in hiding of far greater moment, dramatic and otherwise.

Echoing Kanin, they insisted that to sing in Hebrew would be to "set the characters in the play apart from the people watching them." Rather than enabling their identification with those who shared the Annex, as the Hacketts had "striven for, toiled for, fought for throughout the whole play," the audience would not have been made to feel "that, but for the Grace of God, [that] might have been I." They had written "not only a play for the Jewish people . . . but for everyone . . . whatever religion . . . faith . . . race," they asserted ever more strenuously as they stripped the event of the very specificity without which it would not have occurred.[35]

But Otto knew all too well why his family and friends had been murdered and had grown more insistent upon a contractually secured voice in the film's creation. Unable to silence this demand, Mermin turned to Salisbury, who advised him to convince Otto that in all matters of "taste" the Hacketts and Kanin could be "depended upon." Should this fail, then only the most basic elements of the story—"the family must be Jewish, in Holland at the time of World War II, and all except Mr. Frank must die in concentration camps"— should be allowed into the contract so that the needs of those whom she represented could be met and a film produced which would not "go off the theme or ideology."[36]

That August a series of meetings between Fredman and the opposing attorneys raised the possibility of a settlement, but Meyer would no more relinquish his right of production than Otto would countenance it.[37] Meyer had made these negotiations more difficult by telling Otto that he suffered from what the Dutch psychologist and concentration camp survivor Eli Cohen called "the barbed wire sickness," wherein former inmates "are extraordinarily small-minded and always aiming at their own advantage," unable to "bear the slightest contradiction. You seem to insist that you will show who is stronger," Meyer observed, though "our accusations are equal, and only the rankest egotist will assume that his accusation has more value than the other person's." More important, the hatred Otto had displayed toward him in his letter to Tereska was eroding his character. "Your behavior," Meyer told him, was not that of the man portrayed in Anne's *Diary*. "The one good line in the Hackett play is the last one in which you say, of your daughter, 'she puts me to shame.'"[38]

On August 13, Kanin and Bloomgarden appeared before a writing class at Columbia University to discuss the play, reconstituting history as they spoke. "I tried several people," Bloomgarden said of his search for a playwright, until "Lillian Hellman suggested I send it to the Hacketts." He had then "had a discussion" with them before they began to work, but their first draft had so "terribly disappointed" him that he "almost gave up." Only his "feeling . . . for these writers" had enabled him to give them another chance, and another. "There is nothing in the play that is not in the diary," Kanin further claimed, "nothing in the play that did not in one form or the other happen." With Otto consulted at each turn, Kanin asserted, the script had undergone five additional rewrites since he had accepted the role of director. "Mr. Frank's requirements" had to be met.

"When I read the book I got more of the message of the problem of being a Jew, and the play seems to emphasize more the universal nature," a student noted in response. "Was this a transformation for audience or box-office appeal?" Neither, Kanin insisted. But the play had been "a cooked goose before it started." With no expectation of commercial success, the Hacketts' responsibility to "somehow mov[e] beyond the words on the printed page" had become his. "I'm astonished you didn't feel it in the play," Kanin retorted, emphasizing the use of the "Chanukah feast" as "the great climactic scene . . . worked out by me and two rabbis." The conversation with the students then ended abruptly. "I feel someone tugging at my coat so we'll have to adjourn."[39]

A final attempt to negotiate a settlement with Meyer was begun in late August. "I have a feeling that there is a possibility (however slight) of a settlement," Mermin advised Otto, "but if we cannot conclude a settlement at this time, we will have to go to trial."[40] In the end, the accord foundered as much on matters of personal pride as on those of fact, particularly over the joint statement that was to declare all differences "settled in mutual understanding." Convinced that Meyer would "try to have a formulation which is face-saving," Otto insisted that the release be written so that it would be "face-saving from my side."[41] Meyer, resentful that a settlement was being sought by Mermin merely "to spare Mr. Frank the necessity of coming to the U.S. to testify," was further angered by the characterization of his suit as a mere "nuisance claim." He protested, "I cannot proceed on that basis. The very least they could claim is that the differences are the result of a series of compounded misunderstandings. Until and unless they adopt a respectful attitude there can be no discussion of a settlement."[42]

Of these differences, one remained nonnegotiable on both sides—Meyer's role in dramatizing the *Diary*. "I am not optimistic about prospects for settlement," Mermin wrote Otto on September 11. "It appears that Meyer Levin now has the idea that he should write the movie script as the price of peace."[43] Twelve days later, Meyer told Fredman that he would neither "drop the claim to freedom of production" nor relinquish his right to prepare the film script "in furtherance of our original understanding that my work was required in order to 'guarantee the idea of the book.'" Rather, "Whatever has intervened," Meyer added, "I want it on record that I am faithful to this."[44]

The *Diary* "pleads for the right of every human being to live his life as he is created," a plea highlighted by "the destruction of six million Jews for being created as Jews," Meyer wrote two days later. "As though all literature does not teach us that universality comes through the highest particularization," those in possession of the *Diary* had attempted to argue "that a more 'universal' version" could be based upon "the suppression of individual traits." Was the *Diary* not the story of Anne's "self-realization as a Jew?" How, then, could "a play about the death-experience of Jews . . . appropriately be dismissed as 'too Jewish'"? What "tragic irony that arbitrary and authoritarian methods should be used in connection with a work such as the Diary, which is itself an example of the ghastly result of such methods!"[45]

On October 1, Otto wrote Salisbury that he found the possibility of publicity concerning a lawsuit between Jews, "especially in connection with the name of Anne," particularly distasteful, and that he was now prepared "to make some concessions," there being "certain obligations to give [Meyer] the opportunity [for an Israeli production of his script] in my contract with him and in the Bloomgarden contract." Surely, it "would be much less costly," Otto assured her, for "Israel is not interesting at all and as the Hackett play will be produced in so many countries this season, a later production of the Levin version in Israel, if it will be produced, can never hurt the Hackett version."[46]

Nothing ever did dampen the critical and popular reaction to that play, but the reputations of those involved with it were suddenly endangered from within their own circle by publication of the Hacketts' account of the long process out of which the play had arisen. Without first consulting their attorneys, the Hacketts had given their "Diary of 'The Diary of Anne Frank'" to the *New York Times*, which published it on September 30.[47] Perhaps feeling free of the burden of being defendants, they issued a detailed outline of the script's history. Horrified and angered that the Hacketts had compromised their clients' defense, Allan Ecker wrote Salisbury of the "sense of distress" felt at Paul, Weiss. "While engagingly written and interesting to read, this article—with its details as to the six versions, and the time and assistance given to the Hacketts—will probably exacerbate Levin's bitterness and may fortify his case." It was the hope of Paul, Weiss "that any further articles of this kind be shown to us for our comments on their possible bearing on the litigation and the settlement."[48]

Insulated by faith in themselves, the Hacketts and Bloomgarden were "distressed" by the "unfortunate tone" of the letter. Ecker, given the task of writing on behalf of his firm, suddenly found himself having to apologize for what "sounds much more peremptory than . . . intended," as he wrote the Hacketts on October 19. "Certainly, I did not mean to suggest, in any way, shape, or form, that we set up a lawyers' censorship over your writing in or out of the press." But "the Litigation Department felt—and feels—that the article might serve to remind Mr. Levin anew, and in chronological detail, of the fact that he was given (as he sees it) only one chance by Cheryl Crawford, under an acute time pressure, to dramatize the play, whereas you were permitted and encouraged to do eight versions over a longer period of time. The Litigation Department felt that this might well dampen Mr. Levin's readiness to settle, by heightening his old sense of grievance; and also, that in a lawsuit, the article might affect the sympathy of the jurors towards Mr. Levin." Because of the inferences that could now be drawn from the Hacketts' own account, it was the suggestion of Paul, Weiss that their clients "check in with us as to further articles that might bear upon the facts in dispute." They were, of course, "entirely free to go right ahead and have the articles printed anyway, even if you disagreed with everything we said." That, Ecker concluded for the benefit of the Hacketts and their associates, "is the difference between advice and censorship."[49]

But the advice had come too late. "Lillian Hellman, it has lately come out, picked the writers . . . and supervised the writing of the play," Meyer had already concluded. The Hacketts' "Diary of the 'Diary'" only "confirmed what was almost a conviction to me through the whole period—that I was the victim of the communist blacklist." "Ideological difference was the real motive for 'getting rid of Levin,'" he told fellow writer James Farrell, who was himself familiar with the American Communist Party.[50] (Six years earlier, Hellman had dismissively characterized his critique of Communist-bound writing as "a violent and dull attack on something he called Stalinist art"; she found his reference to "Irish art and revolution," a violation of her ideological orthodoxy, equally offensive.[51])

"It was not until I saw the [Fund for the Republic's *Report on Blacklisting*] that characterized 'omission' as the current communist method in the U.S., that I caught on fully" why references to Jewish identity were all but absent from the Hackett script. The Soviet policy of murdering or imprisoning individuals expressing "Jewish Nationalism" had been translated in America into "kill[ing] my play" and making him "the object of an organized character assassination effort," which he claimed to have traced back to Proctor, a "known commie" acting as Bloomgarden's agent. "The timing—this happened in 1952—was correct," he noted, referring to its parallel with the Doctors' Plot murders. Meyer, of course, knew that all of this "may seem a far fetched idea," but he assured Farrell that he could "fill in many details" of what was "more . . . than an attack on the pitiable Mr. Frank. . . . The play as finally produced is a subtle job of adherence through omissions to the communist line. Every psychological impulse toward Jewish identification is eliminated in what was presented to Mr. Frank as a 'more universal' way of using the material."

"All of the foregoing is for the present confidential," he told Farrell.[52] In the next several weeks, Meyer produced two additional "confidential" accounts of his attempt to dramatize the *Diary*, but he published neither. "The entire entourage of the production, from press agent to company manager, seems to be in the communist field, and doubtless some of the investors are, too," he wrote in one.[53] Hellman, in fact, was among this latter group as well.[54] In both accounts written by Meyer that fall of 1956, it was Hellman who had played the pivotal role in "one of the strangest stories of Communist intrigue ever to happen here, the story . . . [of] the virtual professional martyrdom of a best-selling American author," all because he had included in his dramatization of the *Diary* "material in which Anne Frank expressed what the Communists call 'nationalist' sentiments."[55] Ideologically offensive, this could not be allowed once "the Communists saw in the Diary a potential world-wide success, and wanted it done their way." Meyer continued: "It is my belief that Lillian Hellman read my play through her intimate connection with Cheryl Crawford, advised Miss Crawford that it was 'too Jewish' because of the religious and cultural material I had taken from the Diary, and advised Miss Crawford to get rid of me. Miss Crawford found the situation too complicated and withdrew, while recommending Mr. Bloomgarden—Hellman's producer—to Mr. Frank. Mr. Bloomgarden made it a condition that I be eliminated. The Hacketts were eventually selected as playwrights since they would collaborate fully with Miss Hellman's ideas."[56]

Hellman's intimate involvement in all of Bloomgarden's decisions was confirmed by Bloomgarden himself that fall in a situation not unlike the rejection Meyer had experienced. Feeling stabbed in the back by "the same kind of knife [that] put us up before the House Committee in '51," John and

Marguerite Sanford wrote Bloomgarden on September 25. The Sanfords, whose careers as playwrights had been destroyed by HUAC, were angry over Bloomgarden's unexplained change of mind regarding their script, which he had first accepted for production, then precipitously rejected. "We have the theory that somebody has done the complete shiv-job on us, blade, hilt, and right arm. We have a right to hear about that, and we insist that you tell us. We don't care a pinch of owl-shit whether you ever produce a play by us . . . but we do care about getting it in the back."[57] Bloomgarden denied the involvement of anyone besides himself in this decision and expressed surprise at their "vituperations." Never had he produced anything that was not his choice alone, he insisted. "The only person I have used to read a play that I am considering has been Lillian Hellman, and each time I have submitted a script to her, I had already decided to produce the play."[58]

CHAPTER ELEVEN

Damn His Soul—That Levin

tmost confidence in you as writer of [the] script. Trust to be allowed consulting rights even if not legal," Otto wired the Hacketts on October 24, concerned that he might be losing control over the *Diary* as it moved on to Hollywood. "We understand each other so well," he added in a lengthier note the following day. "I know how dear the meaning of Anne's message is to you."[1] While Otto was pleased that negotiations for the filming of the *Diary* were progressing, he remained fearful of their outcome. Salisbury had managed to secure a proposed contract from Twentieth Century Fox that would leave "the theme or basic ideology of the Play" intact.[2] But Otto knew that the Hacketts' play had already deviated from his daughter's work and that his control over the *Diary*'s further adaptation was all but gone. As he conceded to Salisbury that day, he would have "to rely on the judgment of the Hacketts and Kanin now [that] a decision has been taken."

Otto was aware as well of just how dependent he had become upon Salisbury's goodwill, and as with the Hacketts, he attempted to remain in her good favor. "You certainly achieved a splendid deal after having several deceptions," he wrote, praising her business prowess. "Now we can only hope that personalities chosen will create a picture worth the play and the book."[3] Yet, for all of his efforts to placate the others involved in the project and to maintain a position of some moral authority over the *Diary*, he continued to "bedevil" those whom he most needed, as the Hacketts wrote Salisbury in early November.[4]

The prospect of a film based upon a play which itself was in part a distortion of the *Diary* proved even more disturbing to Otto now that Meyer's suit was reaching its most critical phase. Thirteen months after opening in New York, all royalties from the play remained attached by the Sheriff's Department, pending outcome of the suit. In response, Otto's attorneys had prepared a counterclaim that November, asking for a judgment against Meyer for damages resulting from the attachment, as well as for payment of all legal fees incurred. The Hacketts had clearly "prepared a completely original adaptation," Otto's counsel argued in further asking the court to have Meyer "permanently enjoined and restrained from doing or causing to be done any acts" that would continue their public debate over the right to present his own adaptation.[5]

To quash all discussion, even in the courts, Otto's attorneys served Meyer with a motion for summary judgment concerning the attachment.[6] But Meyer would not be silenced and, on December 7, gave a detailed account in his "Bill of Particulars" of the alleged manner by which he had been fraudulently denied his promised role of writer or collaborator. Each point was supported by copies of correspondence between the parties to the dispute. To this had been added another point-by-point "structure and content comparison" between the Broadway play and Meyer's radioscript and adaptation. One third of the "Bill of Particulars," some eleven pages, was concerned with this analysis, concluding that, "While much other material existed in *The Diary*, the incidents chosen for high points, the incidents given as curtain effects and some of the curtain lines are the same."[7]

Nowhere in Otto's detailed response to these allegations, written for his lawyers' eyes alone, did he discuss this textual comparison. Instead, he attempted to prove that Meyer had not been fraudulently dealt with by himself or Crawford, but, rather, had been allowed to act as his agent, and to write a script out of friendship and because of his deep feelings for the *Diary*, without Otto ever having expressed any commitment to him, oral or written.[8]

After examining Meyer's evidence and Otto's response, Costikyan informed his client on January 11, 1957, that he would soon file a new motion for a summary judgment.[9] Otto's affidavit in support of this motion, however, clearly misrepresented the facts. Although Otto had not met with Meyer between March 1951 and September 1952, they had maintained an extensive correspondence, which was now largely disregarded in order to support the claim that the "plaintiff never relied on any alleged material representation of facts."[10] Left out of this presentation to the Court was Otto's cable to Doubleday on June 18, 1952, stating that one of the "conditions to any sale of . . . film and play rights" would be "Levin as writer or collaborator in any treatment."[11] Otto's further claim that Meyer had "never advised me" of his having given "a written authorization of agency to one Howard Phillips to act as Levin's and my agent" was patently untrue. Though the court was assured that Otto had first learned of this agreement from his attorneys some time afterward, the copy sent to him by Meyer in 1952 still lies within his files.[12]

Salisbury had meanwhile informed Twentieth Century Fox on January 9 that the Hacketts "had never seen Levin's version" and therefore should not be contractually obligated to indemnify the studio against any claims Meyer might make against them.[13] As Salisbury told the Hacketts the following day, Meyer had already approached Fox with the assertion that they had "plagiarized his version and . . . had ruined the ideology."[14] Otto and Bloomgarden had responded to this charge by merely annexing copies of the Hacketts' and Meyer's scripts to their motion for a summary judgment, but Salisbury perceived that the issue could not so easily be dismissed and insisted, in her letter to the Hacketts, that "if this point should ever be brought up to you, I want you to stand firmly with me on the position I have taken."[15]

The forcefulness of Salisbury's demand raises the question of how familiar she was with the Hacketts' receipt of parts of Meyer's scripts throughout their months of writing, though without their knowledge. So, too, does it raise the question of how suspicious they themselves may have become by this point in the process, and of their fear of the consequences. For the Hacketts were not strangers to the issue of plagiarism. Goodrich had received a "substantial settlement" from Alexander Korda in a suit involving his film *The Private Life of Henry VIII*.[16]

The depth of the Hacketts' concern can be measured by the subsequent "work we did in documenting our play from the book," as they told their own attorney, Lloyd Almirall, in a letter accompanying this detailed analysis. "Everything that is in our play is implicit in Anne's book," they asserted. "We have no 'new characters,' no 'new situations,' no 'new plot.'" What might appear to be borrowed from Meyer had been developed by them out of "only a line in an entry in the book."[17]

Otto himself employed a related defense in a letter to Costikyan accompanying his signed affidavit. "As a whole it is natural that every dramatist takes the dramatic events from the book and it is not astonishing that in many cases the Hacketts chose about the same events as Levin." Yet Otto was not at all certain that Meyer's material had not been misappropriated and could only assure Costikyan that he had not shared or discussed it with the Hacketts, having limited his own conversation to "details of facts and happenings." Although he was pleased with Costikyan's "personal note . . . about the righteousness of the case," he could temporarily allay these suspicions and take some odd comfort only by acknowledging that "Levin [had] kept closer to the book and stressed more the Jewish background."[18] Years later, long after the case had been settled, Otto advised a teacher to "induce your pupils to read the Diary itself" rather than rely upon the play, as "the many thoughts and ideas [Anne] confides to her diary are not used in the dramatization," among them "one of the sources of [her] confidence and strength . . . her faith."[19]

It was these very omissions, tardily acknowledged by Otto, that had so exercised Meyer and about which he continued to speak out publicly. He now added to the debate the one element that he had long withheld from it, the allegation of a Communist origin to this suppression of Anne's thoughts as expressed in his adaptation of the *Diary*. Two months earlier he had stood before the Boston Jewish Book Month Committee and had declared, as he had previously written in his "confidential" and unpublished analysis of the events, that a "propaganda by omission is operating in the legitimate theater in this country. . . . References to ethnic and cultural nationalism, particularly as they refer to Jews, are being systematically cut out of Broadway productions. . . . The works of Jewish writers are being killed in this country by this treatment in a manner reminiscent of the actual killing of Jewish authors in the Soviet Union." In responding to the charge, the Dramatists Guild, upon whose governing council both Hellman and Kanin sat, had demanded "evidence that this has happened," which they promised to place before the council so "that if anything so shocking has happened in the past . . . it [would be] impossible for such outrages to occur in the future."[20]

But Meyer persisted, nonetheless. "By your remark about Lillian Hellman's having left Voltaire's satire on Utopias out of her Candide," he wrote Brooks Atkinson in December, "I gather you are aware of the implications of propaganda by omission. . . . Perhaps then you will understand why I have put up, and am putting up such a bitter fight against the omission of the more significant Jewish material from the Diary of Anne Frank." Might he not "recall a group that rather systematically uses character assassination as a weapon?" Meyer asked, referring to the *Report on Blacklisting* and the Soviet murder of Jewish writers as "clues."[21]

Meyer was less oblique three weeks later when, in writing to an attorney whose assistance he hoped to solicit, he noted that "broader aspects" were embodied in this "too-ironic example." Here was a "case [that] happens to sum up the great problems that confront us today. I tried to point out that the difference in my treatment and the Broadway treatment, subtle as it may seem through the slick job done by the Hacketts and Hellman, nevertheless epitomizes the difference between 'their' thinking and 'ours,' between the communist world and the democratic world. I realize it may be difficult to present. All the more reason to show it, and to show up the devious routes taken by communist propaganda." Having left Hollywood when the war began "to come into contact with the real thing," having spent those years and seven more "on the Jewish story," and given "the all-important political significance" of the issues involved, he could not countenance "a couple of slick technicians who never wrote anything creatively important on their own, and who get a Pulitzer prize out of Anne Frank's body" by perpetrating "the phoney and the specious."[22]

"There has been a consistent hush-up of my two-year struggle on the Anne

Frank play," Meyer wrote columnist Walter Winchell three weeks later, on January 20, 1957. According to "reliable sources" in the press, Proctor had been claiming that Meyer was "a crackpot, and [an] incompetent writer, etc." The court battle itself was mired in "legalistic discussions" designed "to prevent the real issues" from coming before a jury.[23] (Costikyan advised Otto two days later that "in order to prevail on the motion [for summary judgment], we must be very careful not to raise questions of fact. . . . We hope to be able to dispose of Levin's claims on the law without going into the question of whether or not you showed the radio script or the stage play to the Hacketts."[24]) It was Meyer's hope that Winchell would "break the story," for "Anne's understanding that people have a right to live the way they are made by God, as Jews, as Hungarians, as Americans" was among the "key issues in the world today," witness the Hungarian revolt against Soviet authority. It was this very "theme that has been toned down in the Broadway show." Had the "Bloomgarden-Hellman combination" controlled the *Diary*'s publication, they would have removed this same "Jewish depth material" by similarly convincing Otto that a more "universal" treatment was needed. There was certainly nothing random about what had happened to the work "of this Jewish girl who represents six million Jewish dead, and whose deeper words on the Jewish experience have been suppressed through the suppression of my play!"[25]

Two weeks later, Meyer appeared on Mike Wallace's *Nightbeat*, eager to continue his discussion of this suppression. Indemnifying Wallace, the television station, and the show's sponsors, he was willing to risk all "because it goes to the very roots of my life as an artist, as a writer, and as a Jew." While his pending lawsuit would not allow a detailed accounting of the "peculiar things" that had happened, he would not be silenced on the ethical issues, particularly on the audience's right "to hear those portions which were left out of the Broadway production." For it was "the Jewish material in the *Diary*," and not its exclusion, that had truly made his play the "more universal, just as the Hungarians trying to be Hungarians are doing a universal thing in the world today" in their opposition to the Soviets.[26]

Meyer's anger was evident the following night on Barry Gray's radio show when he spoke of Otto's failure to honor his contractual obligation to allow him a first Israeli production. The Hackett play had now opened in Tel Aviv's Habimah Theatre while his own had continued to be suppressed.[27] (Otto had sought to close the Hackett play until Meyer's claim to prior Israeli production was settled, recognizing that "the clause about Israel in the contract being without time limit was a mistake."[28]) Without directly raising the spectre of Communist suppression, he spoke again of the universality of the struggle for "self-determination, the right to be oneself . . . as the Hungarians are trying to prove with their blood right at this time," and of Hellman's role in the Hackett play's "construction." As Salisbury's notes on the interview pointed out, "Levin wanted to make it completely Jewish—Broadway play diminished the Jewish angle."[29] When asked by Gray whether the world had learned anything from Anne's efforts, Meyer could only respond with grave doubt. It was for this very reason that he was "so bitter and adamant about keeping up this fight . . . until somewhere, somehow, my version will be heard," for "her words, the real deep words, that might have taught them something" were being censored.[30]

Undaunted, Meyer made a third radio appearance on the Tex and Jinx McCrary Show on February 18. "I am suing to uphold the beautiful faith and truth that Anne Frank had in her book and wrote about so strongly with the purity of a young girl," he declared emphatically. Those who had seen the play without first having read the *Diary* had been left without "any understanding of what the Jews were thinking about, during all this persecution." Having become a war correspondent to "find out the fate of the Jews in Europe" and having offered up "the very, very first [descriptions] of the death camps," he had remained "strongly taken with the need to make the world feel what had happened to the Jews." Those now opposed to the production of his play seemed so "fanatically devoted" to this end that without either a literary or commercial purpose to their opposition, "one can only assume that there are other reasons for their peculiarly powerful resistance to having anyone ever see my version."[31]

The response from Bloomgarden, Otto, and their attorneys was swift; transcripts, notes, and correspondence began to circulate among them the morning after the first of these interviews. Paul, Weiss hoped to find something "damaging" to Meyer's charge of plagiarism and to his interest in the Israeli production of his play. He had at least compromised his claim as designated playwright, they believed. In a memo to Costikyan after the Gray interview, Ecker assured him that Meyer's account of Otto's alleged promise would be seen merely as "some friendly words" and not as "approval in the context of a dispute as to rights to produce it."[32]

Otto once again concurred, insisting that he had never "accepted . . . [Meyer's] first draft," and not "because it was too Jewish," as Meyer claimed. Yet, Otto went on to note that Meyer's use of "Jewish elements in the foreground" of the radio play had been "right" because it had been written "for the Holy days"—as if to say that this emphasis was out of place in a dramatization for the larger world.[33] In this context, the "importance" that Meyer had placed on Margot's declaration of Zionist commitment became unacceptable. Though many of her surviving peers had already left Holland for Palestine, Otto remained nonetheless confident that "she would not have done so." Such "an occasional remark," Otto assured his attorneys, was "not to be taken seriously."[34]

Bloomgarden's response to his attorneys' request for a reaction was to propose a press release prepared by Proctor. After reading its sharply worded attack upon Levin, Ecker advised Proctor that the "form and content" would have to be revised in accordance with the "ethical canons of the Bar Association." Paul, Weiss, in fact, advised against release,[35] but Bloomgarden refused to allow Meyer's remarks to go unanswered. Hellman was even less pleased than Ecker with its wording, Proctor reported, though he was taken aback by how "violent . . . Lillian's reaction" was. She preferred "to use much stronger language in characterizing Levin, and wanted to cut out what she regarded as 'legal double talk.'" Ecker then suggested that a second draft "along Lillian's lines" be submitted for review by Paul, Weiss. Proctor, in turn, told Bloomgarden of his "own feeling . . . that Lillian has gone a little overboard," and advised a cooling-off period before "the three of us, or you and Lillian, can discuss it in a thoughtful way."[36]

But the revised press release, issued on March 18, nevertheless bore Hellman's heavy stamp. In her hands, what had read initially as "the act of a disappointed writer who tried his hand at dramatization of a great book and failed to write a good enough play" became simply "the act of a disappointed writer who wrote a bad play from a good book." Meyer's "unsatisfactory" talent was similarly changed to "bad," and the lengthy discussion of Meyer's rights to an Israeli production was removed, with the Hackett play's production in Tel Aviv used as proof that the amount of Jewish content in the play was not the issue. To further support this position, Bloomgarden's original denial that Meyer's play had been rejected because of "its emphasis on the Jewish aspects of the book" was altered by Hellman to read "supposed emphasis," while repeating that Meyer's script had not been "discriminated against because it was 'too Jewish.'" It followed, then, that the praise given by Bloomgarden for the Hacketts' ability to "have captured the universal meaning of Anne's story" had to be altered to include "not only the Jewish but the universal meaning," and that Meyer's persistence reflected his inability to "reconcile himself to the established custom and law of the theatre, that a rejected adaptation has no right to open shop in competition with the successful."[37] Meyer had simply "dragged into his public statements all kinds of extraneous issues," none of which merited discussion, Otto similarly noted that month after reading the first draft of the release.[38]

All of this was standard Hellman. "When you are too fooled by people it has to be your own fault," she had said of Hollywood "slickness and colleague-double-crossing" three years earlier.[39] Besides, what precisely was the truth about anything? In 1967 she wrote from Communist Budapest, "One cannot tell the truth when one writes about one evening, or even about years. . . . Fiction is the truth more often than fact."[40] "What is true in one time may change or be pushed aside in another," she had asserted two years before, sadly unable to find the anchor she thought she had once possessed. Perhaps she, too, had finally become a victim of all that she had helped, in her way, to propagate, and of all that opposed the freedom in which to do even that. "I believe in involvement—but whose involvement, when and how?" she wrote in the Soviet Union's *Literary Gazette* when asked to comment on "the responsibility of the writer to the world in which he lives" for an issue commemorating the twentieth anniversary of the war's end.[41]

A second release issued by Paul, Weiss on April 26, 1957, reflected the original draft's less inflammatory language. Reversing Hellman's substitution of "bad" for "unsatisfactory," it focused instead on the issues in dispute and on Meyer's renewed challenge to Bloomgarden to allow the "people of the theater" to decide the merits of his script. The attorneys preferred to engage Meyer in such matters of business, particularly his continuing assertion that he held rights to the Israeli production of his play, which they claimed had "lapsed," leaving him with "no rights" at all. Conscious of the public relations factor in the case, they ended their release with an attempt to discredit Meyer's petition by claiming that "so many responsible people" had signed only because they had not heard "the other side of the story."[42]

Perhaps it was the support unexpectedly given Meyer by Eleanor Roosevelt that had pushed the attorneys in this new direction. On April 2, Mrs. Roosevelt wrote Otto that she quite agreed with Meyer after meeting with him and hearing "the story of his long struggle." Having lent her name to the *Diary*'s publication, she was now concerned that "a long drawn out suit which would bring out so many disagreeable things, such as why you moved to Switzerland, would be harmful to the feeling people have for you and for the play and particularly the diary." Rather than continue this very public dispute, she counseled Otto to consent to arbitration, as suggested by Meyer.[43]

In response, Otto vigorously protested Meyer's "distorted" and "onesided report" of the facts of the "law suit which has no base at all." Though he had never been opposed to arbitration or to a "reasonable settlement," all attempts had failed "owing to Mr. Levin's insistence on his highly exaggerated and unrealistic demands," none of which dealt with the *"case as such,"* Otto disingenuously claimed, but solely with *"the quality of the script."* This, of course, had become a nonnegotiable element after "Mr. Bloomgarden's statement had convinced me that Levin's version was not the best I could get for Anne." It was now too late for negotiations, he told Mrs. Roosevelt. "Only a decision of the Courts can free me forever from his unjustified attacks," among these, the notion that his move to Switzerland had been at all motivated by a desire "to avoid high Dutch taxes." And although "this matter has nothing to do at all with the merits of the case," he nonetheless felt compelled to answer the charge, insisting that he would not engage in such acts of "fraud and deceit" as Meyer, "a man who does not even keep an agreement he signed," had committed against him. Wisely, Otto made no mention of the dispute over Israeli production rights. Instead, he referred Mrs. Roosevelt to Hellman's harshly reworded press release as demonstration of the "true facts" in the matter, "leaving it to you to form your own opinion . . . on Mr. Levin's behaviour."[44]

But Otto had no intention of leaving this solely to Mrs. Roosevelt's un-aided judgment. Even before writing her, he had solicited outside help from Francis Price, "know[ing] how close you feel with me in regard to the Levin matter." They had recently met in Paris, at which time Otto had reported fully "on the mean methods he is using to influence people against me," including his approach to Mrs. Roosevelt, who "only listened to his side of the story." More "disappointing" was her failure to realize that "Levin's allusion" to his move to Switzerland was an attempt at "blackmailing" by threatening "to hurt my reputation." He feared that Meyer was having some success. "I am very much disturbed that Mrs. Roosevelt seems to be doubtful about my character, believing in the righteousness of Levin's case." Otto asked Price to write Mrs. Roosevelt, with whom he was "well acquainted" after arranging for her intro-ductory remarks for the *Diary*, "telling her a little about me and the bad character of Levin."[45]

Otto may have discovered that Price was away from Paris before writing to Nathan Straus four days later, asking him "to inform Mrs. Roosevelt about my person and the integrity of my intentions." He regretted having "to accuse her . . . of having not acted impartial," but he had found her letter "rather hos-tile."[46] Straus, upon whose radio station Meyer had been interviewed by Barry Gray, later told Otto that he had immediately "set to work to draft as effective a letter as possible . . . for Mrs. Roosevelt's enlightenment."[47] In five long pages, Straus recounted his long relationship with Otto, dating to their student days at the University of Heidelberg in 1909. "It is scarcely necessary to have me add the statement that Otto is an unusually fine, sensitive human being," or that "a bitter and disgruntled man has seen fit to attempt to besmirch a fine and dedicated life, oblivious alike to the mandates of justice and to the poten-tial injury to the message carried by the play." Surely, "Otto would seem to have suffered enough without being forced, in his old age, to endure character assassination, slander—and, worst of all, loss of respect of fine people." Straus concluded by urging Mrs. Roosevelt, "in old friendship," to send Otto a "com-forting letter."[48]

Mrs. Roosevelt responded to Straus's lengthy plea as he had hoped she would. Retreating from her initial position, she quickly sent Otto a letter of apology for having "distressed" him by accepting Meyer's account. "I have read the material you sent and I think you are probably right in your stand," she wrote in wishing him well in the court battle ahead.[49] Otto was pleased with the effectiveness of Straus's letter and thanked his old friend for "the right influence" his "elaborate letter" had had upon her, certain that Mrs. Roosevelt "regrets to have acted on the base of one-sided information."[50]

Her reversal, however, brought an appeal from Tereska some weeks later. Responding to it on June 5, Mrs. Roosevelt wrote of her inability to judge between the parties, having "no doubt that both of them think they are right." Yet, she had chosen to side with those who were a part of her world and whose opinions she had long trusted. Having received not only Straus's letter but a message from Lloyd Garrison on behalf of Paul, Weiss, "a firm of lawyers . . . whom I also deeply respect," she felt certain that Otto could not have moved to Switzerland "to escape taxation, as your husband told me." Nor was there any reason for further arbitration, she stated matter-of-factly.[51]

Tereska thanked Mrs. Roosevelt for her "patience" in the matter but felt it necessary to clarify the two issues she had raised. Contrary to Otto's denial, the question of his move to Switzerland to avoid Dutch taxation was both indisputable and central to the case before the court. In Meyer's files was Otto's letter discussing the tax issue as a motivating factor in his decision to leave Holland. Otto had used this as his reason for not signing a contract with Meyer at a time when he knew that Meyer was already preparing a script for Crawford. "This started all the trouble," Tereska explained to Mrs. Roosevelt, "as Meyer went ahead without a signed contract being certain Otto Frank would keep his word." He had not, nor had he ever been truly willing to accept arbitration, though Meyer "really desires" it and would accept a decision "of integrity chosen by a neutral party." In fact, after ruling on the latest motion, the judge in the case had privately advised both parties to negotiate a settlement, offering himself as mediator.[52]

Meyer responded to Mrs. Roosevelt's disturbing note to Tereska by advising her that "it never struck me that [Straus] could have taken the most active part in the entire affair, as it would now seem." How "embarrassing" it must have been for her to have him "bring a complaint that turned out to be against someone who had been so close," he added. Never, however, did he offer an apology for having approached her with this matter.[53]

Tereska's efforts could not possibly have countered those of insiders like Straus and Garrison, members of a social order shared by Mrs. Roosevelt, as Meyer had correctly judged. "Please tell Mr. Frank I never believed most of the things Mr. Levin told me," she wrote Price on July 10, claiming to have been "simply telling him what Mr. Levin told me."[54] Price's characterization of Meyer's struggle as a "long series of harassing actions," the reasons for which, Price readily admitted, he had "never been able to understand," had added weight to the attack of the others. Little wonder that she accepted Price's explanation that arbitration was tantamount to "blackmail" in a case that Garrison's firm overconfidently believed was already won.[55]

Others, however, came forward to argue on Meyer's behalf, among them Jacob Weinstein, a rabbi from Chicago whose "Betrayal of Anne Frank," appearing in *Congress Weekly* on May 13, had earned a strong reaction in print from Bloomgarden's and Otto's attorneys and a response from Meyer. "Does the Jewish people have a right to its own cultural material?" Weinstein opened his questioning. Was there "a pattern of omission in the Broadway version that reflects an ideology opposed to strong Jewish identification?" Was it true, as Levin contended, "that the sentiment attached to the girl's diary has been exploited by persons whose actions do not show them in full sympathy with her ideas?" If so, Weinstein concluded, "then the control of the Diary as it is presently constituted is a bitter travesty on Jewish fate. . . . The possibility that a writer was forced out of a Jewish work because he was Jewish is sickening." There were two courses of action to be taken—the "rights of performance" for Meyer's play had to be secured, and "the important ideas left out of the play" had to be reinstated by Fox.[56]

The challenge posed by Weinstein had to be addressed by opposing counsel, if only to forestall the Jewish community's insistence upon a more culturally Jewish approach to Anne's work in the forthcoming film. Samuel Silverman of Paul, Weiss was first to respond, declaring that Weinstein, *Congress Weekly*, and the American Jewish Congress had been "libelous in the extreme" by charging Bloomgarden "with anti-Semitism."[57] Two weeks later, Ecker published a second rejoinder in *Congress Weekly*, this time over Bloomgarden's name.[58] "My sole reason for declining to produce the Levin version," he had Bloomgarden write, in words echoing Hellman's harsh treatment of Meyer, was that "I regard it as a hack job, a bad play, what we call in the theater a 'turkey'"—and not because the play was "too Jewish." As proof, Ecker offered Hellman's press release and a letter written for Otto by Paul, Weiss to the president of B'nai B'rith that had portrayed the dispute as an attack by one Jew, Meyer, upon another in "disregard [of] Anne's message of hope, faith and understanding." Had Weinstein first spoken to Bloomgarden, the Ecker letter noted with a familiar voice, he "would have absolved himself from the unfairness of purporting to write an impartial article about a controversy after consulting only one party to it"—precisely what had been written to the president of B'nai B'rith in an appeal to use his "influence to prevent Jewish community groups from supporting" Meyer.[59]

In reply to the *Congress Weekly* statement, Meyer noted that Bloomgarden had attacked his ability as a playwright "while carefully avoiding the basic issue raised by Rabbi Weinstein." If he were indeed "bad" or a "hack," why had his radio script been so well received in *Variety* and *Billboard*, and why had its "story-telling method" been used by the Hacketts, whose first draft had, nonetheless, been rejected while his had received Otto's initial acceptance? That they had been allowed to continue to work on a script after he had not been indicated "that considerations unrelated to ability were in force." Furthermore, "Scores of persons who saw the [Hackett] play have told me that they felt it lacked the Jewish quality of the Diary," among them the American Zionist leader Israel Goldstein, who agreed with Meyer that universality was best expressed through the particularity of a people. "No more important issue than that of the national feeling of identity, of peoplehood, of the right to be what we are, faces the world today," Meyer assured his readers. "My play endeavored through Anne's own words to remind the spectator strongly of this essential idea."[60]

In June, B'nai B'rith published "The Facts About Meyer Levin's Case Against 'The Diary of Anne Frank,'" an article assigned by the editor of the organization's National Jewish Monthly to Charles Angoff. His account proved to be the most balanced to date. After considering the public statements of both sides, he had submitted a series of questions to Meyer, Bloomgarden, the Hacketts, and Schildkraut. Only Meyer answered his inquiry into Hellman's role and Huber's Nazi past, and whether anyone had attempted "to keep some of the Jewishness . . . of the book . . . out in order to make the appeal of the play less 'nationalistic' and more 'universal' so that the ideology of the play would comply with some political philosophy."[61] Frightened by Angoff's questions, the Hacketts quickly contacted their lawyer, who judged the inquiry to be inappropriate while a suit was still pending.[62] Two weeks later, in writing to Otto to refute the claims of "Liar Mevin," they claimed "never [to have] had a lawyer before!" though both had been parties to prior suits in Hollywood.[63]

Wishing "not to infringe upon matters that properly belong to the courts," Angoff instead chose to discuss those "that are apart from the law," the "moral-cultural issues" raised by the events in question. "If the Hacketts' version falsifies the Diary of Anne Frank, as Mr. Levin charges, must their 'falsification' forever remain the only permissible adaptation on the stage?" he asked. This question was particularly troubling now that a film based upon the Hacketts' previous work was certain to "have a more permanent effect on the public at large." Setting all personal and legal issues aside, Angoff asked how the play, as a dramatic work, held up under normal standards of criticism. While most critics had praised the Hacketts' play, several of equal prominence had judged their adaptation to be "a shabby and shallow work, missing most of the grandeur of the original." Though he was neither a producer nor a director, Angoff felt qualified as a Jewish writer to state that Meyer's "version is much closer to what Anne Frank put on paper, and it is certainly more Jewish. Further, it seems to me that as sheer drama it is also superior to the Broadway version."[64]

A writer in the Los Angeles Jewish weekly Heritage was far less measured some weeks later when he wrote, "It is not for Anne Frank's father, nor Kermit Bloomgarden to decree the literature that must flow from the epic story of Anne Frank. For indeed they do not own the timeless voice of Anne Frank, speaking in eternal beauty from a mass grave." Angered that "only one bit of Jewishness breaks through" the Hacketts' play, he condemned the harassment Meyer had suffered and exclaimed that while "it may be legally correct to bar life to the Meyer Levin version, morally, it is reprehensible."[65]

The impact of these outside critics and journalists was ultimately felt as the film neared production, though Meyer never accepted this partial vindication as a sign of recognition for all that he had struggled to change on behalf of the Holocaust's victims. For what changes were affected by public pressure paled against what he believed could have been accomplished by a faithful retelling of Anne's story.

Perhaps others, too, had sensed this loss, for even before the contract with Fox had been signed on May 20, Otto had made a request that "Ma'oz Tzur" replace the Hanukah song that had usurped its place. "This is the song Mr. Frank always wanted in the service," Goodrich wrote Salisbury. Otto believed "that no other song would be acceptable to the Jewish people," she wrote, describing how she and her husband had explained to him that their use of a "gay, childish song" would be more dramatic. But now the Hacketts were themselves no longer certain of this for the film, having learned how "tremendously effective" "Ma'oz Tzur" had been in Holland and Germany, where it had substituted for the distinctively American "O Hanukah."[66]

Not that they were suddenly willing to abandon their notion of universality. (In fact, they credited the play's success in Germany to its willingness not to point a finger of blame directly at its audience.[67]) "If we were to do as you suggest," they wrote Rabbi Max Nussbaum of Hollywood on August 8, and "read the [Hanukah] service in Hebrew, this identification of the audience with the people in hiding would be shattered . . . [and] they would be alienated." Once again they had argued naïvely and at length against acknowledging the centrality of the very distinctions that had created the opportunity for them to write their play. "What we all of us hoped, and prayed for, and what we are devoutly thankful to have achieved, is an identification of the audience with the people in hiding. They see them, not as some strange people, but persons like themselves, thrown into this horrible situation. With them they suffer the deprivations, the terrors, the moments of tenderness, of exaltation and courage beyond belief."[68]

A month later, the Hacketts shared their perspective with a group preparing the Paris opening of their play. Problems with the script had developed, and Otto had suggested that they seek the assistance of a "Jewish personality."[69] Having grown fearful that the film might further distort the *Diary*, he had recently told the Hacketts that "you will understand that in my innermost

I cannot feel happy about it as long as I do not know how matters will develop further."[70] Salisbury, too, had grown concerned that those in hiding were being portrayed so negatively "that audiences would end by hating the family, and the Jews . . . that the final effect is a kind of anti-Semitism," though she would never admit that the fault lay in the script that she later asserted had "merged in popularity with the book."[71] The Hacketts, without these concerns, found someone outside the Jewish world to assist the French production. Changes were made, they reported to Otto in late September, without "Zionists in to decide the whole matter. We had refused to have any such people. . . . We wanted the play judged only on the basis of the *theatre*."[72]

But those responsible for its cinematic success, unlike the small theater circle that had pursued an ideological tilt, had no choice but to attend to the criticism being heard with increasing frequency from influential Jews, the Jewish press, and individual Jewish communities throughout the States, together constituting a significant portion of the film's potential market. It is even possible that George Stevens's experience filming concentration camps immediately after their liberation had added to this commercial sensitivity. Stevens, the *Diary*'s director, submitted a copy of the Hacketts' screenplay to the Los Angeles Jewish Community Council in late December 1957, just before filming began. Generally pleased with the already revised script, the council made particular mention of its clearer portrait of "the terror and the peril" that had forced those in the Annex to seek its refuge. Where the Hacketts and their associates had previously deemphasized this element as a way to universalize the story, a somewhat enhanced awareness of Jewish victimization had now become the means by which "a more 'universal' meaning and appeal" could keep "the tragic world situation alive and horribly vivid."

But the council then moved beyond mildly encouraging the addition of several similar scenes and strongly recommended a number of changes that would have significantly enhanced the Jewish element of the film. Two of these stood in direct opposition to the spirit of the play. "In the light of current history," it was important for the audience to understand that Hanukah was a commemoration not only of physical deliverance but of God's "strengthening of the spirit to endure suffering" in the struggle for the *"freedom of worship."* Without this emphasis, "The main idea of the celebration in Mr. Frank's speech is entirely omitted." Its importance for the story extended beyond the Holocaust's attack upon "our culture and our faith." Echoing Meyer's repeated reference to Soviet repression in Hungary, the council emphasized that this was "a very important concept especially today when there are still peoples struggling to win the same freedom." To remedy this oversight, they asked that Nussbaum's earlier suggestion of using "Ma'oz Tzur" in place of "the song of good cheer" be adopted.

Of still greater significance was the council's request concerning the exchange between Anne and Peter over where they would go if escape from hiding became possible. Anne asks Peter, who plans to go to England and join the Free Dutch, but he does not ask her, though "she has some good lines in the diary itself," where "she speaks of Palestine." This, the council suggested, might "make for a more poignant scene—a parting that may separate them for ever." Because his assimilationist response was wholly incompatible with her Zionist answer, this crucial distinction needed to be emphasized. "Peter's is actually the feeling and thought of one who has been assimilated—while Anne's is one of greater dedication to her faith." It was because "this diversity is important today" that they asked Stevens to "please look it up in the diary," and to consider what Meyer had found far more troubling—the still egregiously altered scene in which Anne is given to proclaim Hellman's "universal" message. Here, too, were "a few good lines in her diary," the council understatedly noted for Stevens's benefit.[73]

Yet few suggestions ultimately were heeded, beyond the change of a word here and there for greater textual accuracy, as in the prayer for lighting the Hanukah candles.[74] From the very beginning, in Hollywood as on Broadway, "the mission of the play or film is prevalent," as Otto himself could still maintain that spring of 1957. Even the threat of a lawsuit by Dussel's widow for libeling her husband could not alter this conviction.[75] "In general, I do not wish my husband to be shown in the film as a psychopath," she had angrily written them. "I think it enough that this has been done already in the play."[76] But the "mission" remained sacrosanct, and all that was needed to accomplish it inviolable, even if that meant falsifying the story itself. "She is demanding from a film historical truth. This she cannot ask, nor does the public expect it," Otto tried to convince himself. Still, he nervously told the Hacketts, "I can only pray that everything will turn out the way that you and I hope."[77]

As, of course, did Salisbury, whose advice in dealing with Dussel's widow was to be "clearly evasive. . . . Don't admit anything and don't encourage her."[78] Their response was further edited by their attorney, "always cutting down on any sympathy for her claims or any admission of our sympathy to her."[79] After being advised by his own lawyer in Holland that "she had no rights at all," Otto spoke directly with Dussel's widow, asking that she "not be so childish as to believe that the Hacketts had not taken every information from the legal point . . . and that they knew perfectly well what they were allowed to write."[80]

With Hellman and the others exercising such total control over the *Diary*, supported by an unshakable belief in their own infallibility, the "universal" message that continued to distort Anne's vision could only remain intact.[81] With no room for negotiation, the course toward an extended court battle was set. Yet in preparing his defense, Otto acknowledged (if only to his attorney)

that a contractual understanding had, in effect, existed between the parties—
that he knew by mid-July 1952 that Meyer had "started to work, so as not to
lose time," and that he had himself "answered in my letter of July 21, (after
Miss Crawford was appointed as producer) 'I am glad you started to work'"—
though he, of course, was not to blame for what had subsequently happened.
"As Miss Crawford had made her agreement with Levin, as she had written to
me and as I had given her my word to be the producer, I did not worry much
about the formality of contracts."[82] If Meyer's charges of breach of contract
and of fraudulently using this breach to gain access to the *Diary* were ultimately dismissed for lack of prima facie evidence, Otto knew differently. But
without a written contract or corroboration beyond a disputed interpretation
of the relevant documents, his attorneys could argue in court that Crawford
"never made any agreement with Levin to be the adaptor" and that "all the
facts belie this alleged oral contract."[83]

Meyer was fully aware of the nearly impossible task that lay ahead, and in a
statement distributed on November 15 at the National Conference on Jewish
Writing and Jewish Writers held at the Theodore Herzl Institute of the Jewish
Agency in New York, he protested that he would soon "go on trial . . . as a
Jewish writer," but that the struggle extended far beyond personal interests:

> The case involves another Jewish writer, Anne Frank. In her death she exem-
> plified the eternal life of a people, through expression. Other Jewish writers have
> been killed more selectively in recent years, as witness the fifteen Jewish writers
> extinguished in the Soviet Union for doing what we do—writing about Jews.
> There is a third way to kill a writer—by keeping his work from the public. It is this
> that I shall really be contesting in this trial, concerned with my own dramatization
> of the Diary of Anne Frank, which preceded the version shown on Broadway. It is
> the right of Anne Frank to a full interpretation of her work, that includes the
> material of Jewish identification, which she so deathlessly expressed. It is the right
> of the public to hear that material on the stage.

"There will be attempts to confine the issues to legalistic technicalities," he
assured his readers, "but I shall try to bring out the deeper matters involved, for
when necessary we must fight for our culture, which is our enduring life."[84] As
Meyer had written that year in an unpublished essay, the basic issue was "the
right of the Jewish community to its own cultural material. It is the right of the
voice from the mass grave to be fully heard."[85]

In dismissing all but the charge of plagiarism on December 30, Judge
Samuel Coleman set out clear guidelines for the attorneys to use in presenting
their case in this final matter, specifically, whether ideas from Meyer's scripts
("new plots, characters, etc.") had been appropriated, and whether they had
contributed to the Hacketts' play in ways that had significantly improved the

script. Only after hearing this presentation would Coleman decide whether this last cause of action should go to the jury. It would then be their task to assess whether damages were warranted after all the evidence had been presented.[86]

Detailed testimony by numerous witnesses and parties to this remaining issue helped to establish that Meyer's material had been stolen. The Hacketts found their time on the stand particularly distressing. "We were stumbling, utterly unprepared for this ordeal," Hackett later noted inside the cover of his copy of the trial transcript. "We had come East to be witnesses for Mr. Frank and Mr. Bloomgarden in the case brought against them by Meyer Levin. The charge was breach of contract. But when we got in the stand the issue suddenly and mysteriously became one of plagiarism. Things went very badly for a while."[87] They had, in fact, feared the worst and had received extensive counsel from their own attorney before giving testimony.[88] After repeatedly denying any knowledge of Meyer's scripts, the Hacketts finally admitted that Hellman had assisted with the play's construction. As Hackett explained, she had said "that we had been too literal . . . holding more to a moving picture technique than the drama form."[89] She had encouraged invention, suggesting ways in which she would have written certain scenes, like Dussel's entrance into the Annex and the Hanukah celebration.[90] Though Meyer might have wanted to ask the Hacketts whether Hellman had suggested any textual changes of an ideological nature, his attorney held to the issue of plagiarism, convincingly securing their admission that Anne's reading from the *Diary* for continuity and emphasis, a central element in Meyer's scripts, had been added to the play only after their fifth draft had been accepted and critiqued by Kanin. Kanin was himself in touch with Hellman and, like Bloomgarden, with whom he had consulted on this decision, had thoroughly read Meyer's work.[91]

Witnessing all of this testimony, Otto wrote out for himself a series of comments, several of which were predicated on the possibility that Bloomgarden had, in fact, shared Meyer's ideas with the Hacketts, as the evidence now seemed to indicate. Reacting to Meyer's testimony that he had discussed the construction of his play with Bloomgarden, Otto noted that "Bloomgarden never has been asked if this conversation really took place. But suppose it took place, then whatever the Hacketts would have written would have been taken from his ideas." Why then, Otto wondered, should he have to pay damages?[92]

On the witness stand, Otto at first denied speaking of the play with the Hacketts beyond the brief mention of "historical facts." He claimed as well to have given Meyer's radio script only a cursory reading, to have set it aside without recalling precisely where he had put it, and to have read only a small portion of Meyer's revised play script during his New York visit in the fall of

1952. Meyer's attorney responded by setting before the court evidence to contradict these claims, forcing Otto to retract his initial statements and to acknowledge having made more extensive suggestions to the Hacketts during their visit to Amsterdam. As for the claim of not having read Meyer's revised script, Otto was asked how he could have rejected Meyer as the *Diary's* adapter, which he then credited to Mermin's advice.[93]

After twenty days of testimony, Coleman ruled on January 7, 1958, that enough evidence existed to allow the jury to deliberate. Ten hours later, they returned a 10–2 verdict in Meyer's favor. Refusing to accept their judgment of $43,750 plus 25 percent of all future film royalties, Coleman sent the jury back to reconsider the amounts awarded, whereupon they returned with a fixed figure of $50,000. A motion to set aside the verdict was immediately filed by the defense, followed by Coleman's announcement that he would reserve his decision until after hearing opposing arguments.[94]

Samuel Silverman, the trial lawyer representing Otto and Bloomgarden, was so upset by the verdict that, while still in court, he spoke of leaving the bar. Coleman reminded him that hundreds of rabbis appeared to concur with the verdict. Silverman "shouted back that he did not think much of American rabbis." In reporting the incident to Rabbi Israel Goldstein of the American Jewish Congress, Meyer thanked Goldstein for his words of support following the trial but noted that an appeal would probably cost him that portion of the jury's award not already spent on legal fees. It was possible that the defendants might elect to drop all further court action, fearing that it would bring attention to the plagiarism finding, which the press had largely overlooked. But Meyer was not at all hopeful, as long as the verdict remained a goad that could not be ignored. Perhaps some pressure from Jewish leaders could help preserve a portion of the award for donation to "good causes," Meyer suggested. So much money had been used by both sides in this "senseless court battle," though he had tried to settle the matter "quietly through arbitration."[95]

"Damn his soul—that Levin," Salisbury wrote the Hacketts two days after the verdict had been reached. "Everyone is in a state of shock as I guess you are too." Her best advice for her clients was to separate themselves from the verdict and from all feelings of financial obligation toward Otto, despite the damages he had incurred as a result of the plagiarism verdict. "Please don't do anything foolish—or impractical—don't quickly make the kind of gesture I know OF is expecting you to make, i.e. since everything else was thrown out, it is just the Hacketts' script which brought about this decision." Instead, she advised them to retain their own attorney, "a *brilliant* one." "I'm sick, just sick, and am going home and take a stiff drink to try to care a *little* less."[96]

"We are all in a state of shock," Hackett wrote Kanin on January 11, still disbelieving the award of "FIFTY THOUSAND DOLLARS," the jury having believed that "all of us . . . Otto, Mermin, Frances, me, Kermit . . . were lying." Worse still, Mermin now thought that Meyer might begin to sue everyone connected with the play and, like Salisbury, had advised them to retain counsel. "We have already got hold of Lloyd Almirall" (who had represented them in their previous lawsuit concerning the film *Fanny*). There was little else to report, other than that a heart attack had prevented Bloomgarden from giving testimony at the trial. It was a curiously brief statement, matter-of-factly mentioned in passing, with far less concern expressed for his health than for the possibility that Fox, now "having jitters," might back out of their contract.[97] Or had they, too, heard the rumor that Bloomgarden's illness had been one of convenience?

A week later, Goodrich asked Salisbury whether she honestly thought that Otto would be asking them to share the damages awarded to Meyer. "Did you feel this? Did you think he really expected anything? I can't believe it." Should he present such a demand, they were prepared to abandon Otto to the situation he and his attorneys had undoubtedly created. "You'd only make such a gesture if you felt guilty. And this, I must say, we don't."[98] They had long maintained that similarities between the scripts had been the result of their common origin in the *Diary* and had failed to understand why Mermin had blocked Meyer's attorney from introducing his script as evidence.[99] But Mermin knew that introducing Meyer's draft would have clearly demonstrated the truth of his claim, as it would have belied the notion that changes had been made by Meyer after he had seen the Hacketts' play, as they had been told. "Why why why didn't they let Levin put in evidence the fake script, written after seeing our play?" they asked. "If the lawyers knew this a year ago, why was nothing done?" The loss of the suit was therefore neither their fault nor their responsibility, they asserted, their consciences clear. Still, they had spent the first nine days after the verdict "documenting our script . . . i.e. putting references beside each line of our play, to similar lines in Anne's diary, or lines which suggested a scene," preparing for their defense, if needed.[100]

Abandonment of a colleague was apparently not at all unusual for the Hacketts. Six months earlier they had similarly forsaken Jack Gilford, the play's Dussel, when he sought to repeat his role in the film. Gilford's struggle to save his career from being destroyed in a HUAC-tainted Hollywood was apparently insufficient reason for the Hacketts to risk financial loss. "If he has been in trouble with pictures," they had written Salisbury, "I am afraid he may still be."[101]

Nor were they alone in this practice. Hackett wrote Kanin two weeks after the verdict that Bloomgarden was in Hollywood, "but we have not seen nor heard from him," though they had sent his and Otto's attorneys copies of their annotated script. "We had offered to do this for them while we were in N.Y., while the trial was going on, but they were so cocksure of winning they said no," he added angrily. Further still, if Kanin's "lovely telegram" had "cheered" them at a moment when they "were feeling low and a little discouraged," no such encouragement had come from Otto.[102] Instead, he had intimated in a letter to Salisbury, the essentials of which she had passed on to them, that "the only thing that was wrong was the authors." Had Otto and Bloomgarden not agreed contractually "to protect us!" Hackett protested. "It's beginning to sound as though Otto Frank believes we stole Levin's play!"[103]

CHAPTER TWELVE

The Struggle Is Not Over

A brief in support of the defense motion to set aside the verdict of plagiarism was filed with the court on January 27, 1958. The attorneys for Otto and Bloomgarden claimed that Meyer had failed to present evidence of "willful and unlawful appropriation." Nor had he proven that the "defendants had anything to do with the copying if copying there was."[1] One month later, Judge Coleman set aside the fifty thousand–dollar judgment awarded by the jury that he had charged with the task of making this determination. "You are just as much judges as I am and . . . even more important as judges after a while . . . because the final decision rests with you," he had told them as the trial began.[2] But Coleman now claimed that "guides were lacking" in the presented testimony by which damages could be assessed. Without such guidelines, the members of the jury (among them two bankers, two doctors of philosophy, a librarian, two insurance executives, an advertising copy writer, and a television technician) were incapable of making such a determination based upon moneys earned by the defendants from the use of Meyer's script. Meyer's lawyer, in response, promised either to appeal the ruling or retry the case.[3]

Although Coleman had ruled in the defendants' favor, the matter of plagiarism remained open, and to the Hacketts, defense counsel appeared undeservedly overconfident in their ability to win. There was good reason for worry. As one attorney at Paul, Weiss wrote Bloomgarden a day after the verdict was read, "everyone concerned, flabbergasted."[4] "I think that Mr. Mermin is at least satisfied that something must be done about the kine of the Diary," Goodrich protested angrily to Salisbury. "Aren't they terrible those boys in the Wharton firm? I wish to heaven that Kermit and Otto would quit them."[5] Even a final court victory, she realized, would still leave her and Hackett unprotected. "We want now to hear from Levin what he means to do." Would Meyer "appeal the judge's decision, or sue us directly?" she asked Salisbury, convinced that he would pursue the latter.[6]

Goodrich's fears were well founded, for on the very day that she wrote Salisbury, and only three days after the film script was completed, Meyer's attorneys were already notifying Fox that following the jury's "finding in substance that the authors . . . wilfully appropriated into their adaptation new situation, new character or plot created by Mr. Levin . . . any use by your company of such material without providing compensation to Mr. Levin will be regarded by him as inconsistent with his own rights and he will look to you for damages." A copy of this letter was forwarded as well to the Hacketts, who sent copies to Salisbury, Bloomgarden, and Mermin, despite their feelings toward him. Otto alone was not directly given a copy.[7]

Meyer ultimately sued neither the Hacketts nor Fox. Instead, two weeks later he filed an appeal, asking "for reargument and reinstatement of the jury verdict," a motion whose ruling was postponed by Coleman as he awaited the outcome of negotiations.[8] "The repercussions of this case, as they have been revealed to me by the attorneys, are many and varied," Coleman wrote a year later, disappointed that his efforts at mediation had in the end failed.

In April 1958 there was still reason to be encouraged. Meyer's attorney had agreed to a major concession, that a public statement to be jointly issued as a part of their settlement would specifically exonerate the Hacketts "of any wrongdoing or moral culpability." Meyer had come to realize, as his attorney had told Coleman, "that they had innocently received and made use of suggestions from Mr. Frank and others which, in fact, without any knowledge on the part of the Hacketts, had been gleaned from [his] script."[9] But negotiations dragged on throughout much of the year as the parties argued primarily over the text of this public statement.[10]

During this period, relations continued to sour among those who had benefited from Meyer's dismissal from the project, with emotions fraying as the fight for ideological control turned ever more toward the immediate goal of accumulating wealth. So hungry had the principals grown that permission to perform the Hacketts' play was denied even to amateur groups. Performances "in the vicinity of a stock company . . . practically rules out such stock rental . . . which are sources of considerable profit," Salisbury told one such inquiry that February, though by early January the play had already grossed more than $2.6 million, while the *Diary* had sold 825,000 copies worldwide.[11]

Otto had intended his profits from the play to be used by his Anne Frank Foundation to restore the Annex as the Anne Frank House and support related educational programs. The building itself had nearly fallen prey to a developer's plans to construct an office complex on a larger site of which it was a part. The daily newspaper *Het Vrije Volk* had protested in late 1955 that "the plan to demolish the Secret Annex must not continue! If there is one place where the fate of Dutch Jewry is most clearly revealed, it is here."[12] It had been saved, but it remained in a deteriorating state while Otto's funds were held in escrow awaiting settlement of the lawsuit. Among those who had similarly profited from the *Diary*, only the Hacketts had promised even minimal assistance. In July, Otto asked them to honor this pledge. "Is this not fantastic?" Goodrich wrote Salisbury, angered by the sudden request of "our generous, open-handed friend Mr. Otto Frank" to fulfill their commitment. Yet they would send him six hundred dollars, hoping that it might "ease" his "bitter[ness] about us in regard to Levin (that we did not pay a part of that)."[13] "Infuriated," Salisbury chided her clients, "Surely you didn't expect anything else when you offered them such an easy out," as if so small a contribution to the source of their growing wealth were somehow improper.[14]

Having helped to distort his daughter's thoughts and image only to have his own role in the affair become more narrowly circumscribed, Otto now found himself without the financial support he had allowed himself to expect from those with whom he had made this alliance. But Meyer had found more faithful allies in his struggle, and although he could not regain control over his play, he could at least depend upon others to carry forth the message of what had been done. On June 6 the "Strange Case of Anne Frank" covered nearly a full page of the *Jerusalem Post*. "To those who wrote and produced the play which was finally presented, and to a company of men which includes, strangely enough, rabid Jewish assimilationists, many well-intentioned liberals, and the Communists, the Anne Frank story is a 'human' story in which the Jewish element has to be toned down or presented as merely 'religious,' in a cultish sense," Moshe Kohn noted after seeing the Hackett play's Israeli production. "The Anne Franks who spent years in gruesome concealment or whose remains evaporated in crematorium smokestacks left their most glorious legacy in their [Jewish] affirmation." Anne's pleading with Peter to remain a Jew and her sister's pledge to emigrate to Palestine were evidence of this heritage for those who would learn from their example, but "none of this is heard in the play." Instead, "Only pity is aroused, but no understanding, and without understanding the work remains superficial, almost a travesty." It is a play in which Jews seem almost ignorant of the holiday they are celebrating, Kohn complained, and not, as in Meyer's, where Anne "speculates, as she does in her diary, about what it means to be a Jew." Kohn urged his readers to understand that "it is for this reason that Levin has been fighting, the legal issues merely being the means for fighting the moral issue—an issue which contains the very meaning of Jewish history and experience."

"Dejudaized hence dehumanized," Kohn concluded, choosing to mention only briefly the connection between the Soviet persecution of Jewish writers and the attack upon Meyer as a "Jewish nationalist."[15] But privately, the publisher of *Maariv*, Israel's leading progressive newspaper, felt no such restraint. As an old friend of Nathan Straus, he wrote him on July 27, having recently learned through independent sources that Meyer's claims were solidly grounded. It was Ben Ami's hope that Straus would intervene with Otto. "It is my conviction that Meyer Levin has been persecuted for reasons of being sincere, honest, and 100 per cent of Jewish aspirations," Ben Ami told Straus.

> I have heard from well-informed sources that the campaign against Meyer Levin comprised the pattern known as the communistic character assassination scheme; he was anathema to the communists because they considered him a Jewish national writer. This episode started in 1952 when Jewish writers were executed in the USSR, and in coordination, the communists of the USA set forth to destroy Meyer Levin as a Jewish national writer. The people who were influential in the dismissal of Levin from the Diary project, who chose the Hacketts for the authors, and who guided the writing of the play, were Lillian Hellman, a known communist up to 1949, and Kermit Bloomgarden (Hellman's producer), known at the time for his extensive communist front affiliations. His press agent, James Proctor, only a few weeks ago revealed before the Congressional Investigation Committee that he had been a member of the communist organization right up to the present time. Tales about Levin have been traced to this same Proctor, and to communist front circles. I have even heard some of these same stories here. I happen to know how unfounded they are, but others do not, and the damage is immeasurable—to a man who simply asked for justice, and was upheld by a jury. Meyer Levin is not fighting for material gains. We in Israel do not know how it came about that Mr. Frank should fight Levin's request that more of the Jewish material of Anna Frank's Diary should be heard. Nor do we understand how Mr. Frank can fight Levin through the influence of a bunch of enemies of the Jews, or even allow such people to use Anne Frank as a shield for their attack on a good Jewish writer.[16]

Perhaps the answer lay in the statement made by Otto during an interview that appeared a month later in Ben Ami's newspaper. When asked whether the many letters he had received had helped him "to continue with your fight against antisemitism," Otto responded, "No, not against antisemitism, but against discrimination, against lack of human understanding, and prejudice. Antisemitism is the primary example of these three. To fight antisemitism one has to touch the root of the evil."[17] But Meyer's response in *Maariv* the following week asserted that Otto had "been convinced by the Hacketts and those around them that [the play] will be 'more universal' if they do away with these Jewish chapters." Promoted by Hellman, this political agenda was but a part of the same "persecution of Jewish culture" that had driven so faithful a member as Howard Fast from the American Communist Party after more lethal attacks in the Soviet Union.[18]

"I believe that you have been used by others," Meyer stressed in a letter to

Otto calling for a just resolution to their differences before the eve of Yom Kippur, the Jewish Day of Atonement. Not that Hellman was necessarily acting on "party orders," Meyer tried to explain to Otto, though he realized that Otto continued to "dismiss as nonsense" the evidence he and others had repeatedly presented about her background. But Hellman's reaction to his script had been "other than objective," given her opposition to what she had defined since her days as a Communist ("by her own admission—I am 'exposing' no one—until 1949") as "nationalism," an ideological stance which "shows no change."[19] Otto responded that he could "not agree at all with [Meyer's] argumentations," and declared "further correspondence between ourselves . . . without value."[20]

But Otto's waning faith in those who had helped him to define the "universalism" of Anne's message (however he continued to defend them in his response to Meyer) soon took an ironic turn that caused his Anne Frank Foundation to suffer further financial losses. In early February 1959, without first discussing the matter with him, Fox determined that the "universality of the picture [would] be stressed" as a marketing tool, and that rather than reserving all benefit performances in the States "exclusively" for the Foundation, as Otto had expected, the studio would allow a variety of other charitable groups to sponsor these showings. "I know how very disappointed you will be to hear this," the Hacketts wrote Otto, while assuring him that there would be other performances "in Holland and abroad" to compensate for this loss.[21] But before Otto had a chance to respond to this news, Spyros Skouras, president of Fox, announced to the press that there would be no opening benefit for the Anne Frank Foundation or for any other Jewish organization. "This isn't a Jewish picture," he declared emphatically. "This is a picture for the world."[22]

It was, after all, how it had been written and filmed, and when it opened in March, the critic for the Hollywood Reporter trumpeted its "glowing promise of universal sisterhood and brotherhood." Here on film was "Anne's final philosophy [as] expressed in her diary—that other peoples have also suffered persecution but always there have been some people . . . who have taken a stand for decency. This proved to her that the world is fundamentally and enduringly good." "Every second of [the film] rings with the fresh-minded tone of veracity," the reviewer concluded, mistaking the film for truth, as Hellman had intended.[23] Anne's voice had been effectively silenced, raising erroneously based sentiments that have been echoed repeatedly over the years since. Some months later the president of Vassar, in defending her acceptance of a gift to the college in Anne's name, declared her "a symbol of the endurance, courage, and indomitable spirit of young people and families during the most disgraceful and barbaric period of modern times," while neglecting to draw the distinction between Anne's suffering and the experiences of those who had been free of anti-Semitic persecution.[24]

Nor was this misperception to be rectified in court. "I am now advised that negotiations have reached an impasse," Judge Coleman had written that February in ruling against Meyer's motion for reargument and reinstatement of the verdict. Rather than rescind his decision, he called again for a new trial in order to evaluate the monetary damages suffered. For this, he demanded expert testimony on the value of the property stolen by those who had used Meyer's ideas, which Coleman was satisfied had occurred. Only "technical" matters stood in the way of a final court determination. It was, as Coleman noted in his decision,

> a question of the value of plaintiff's work, of his contribution to a play. It was presented to the jury on that theory. How was that value to be determined? We are dealing with a special kind of property, literary property, and the contribution by the plaintiff to a play adopted from a book available to the plaintiff and the accredited playwrights. The jury could determine for itself without the aid of experts that there had been a breach of the agreement. For that purpose objective comparison between the two versions may suffice and the jury decided in the plaintiff's favor. But the question of the amount of damage is a different matter. For that question I thought that we needed to have more than the amount the accredited playwrights received and that it could not be left to judge or jury, without any other standard, to say what the money damage was. . . . Granting the integration of the plaintiff's ideas, in breach of contract, in the final work, the property is of such a nature that the damage to the plaintiff can be measured, it seems to me, only against a measure and in a balance supplied by those accustomed to measuring it, by means, that is to say, of opinion testimony of experts.[25]

On March 2, an order for a new trial was entered.[26]

Meyer, of course, objected to this purely "technical" view of the issues involved.[27] In a letter circulated among the American Rabbinate two weeks after Coleman's decision, he wrote that "the case cannot be limited merely to the legalistic aspects, which are now confined to a measure of my monetary damages, to a haggling over Anne Frank's grave." Rather, "The real question in the Anne Frank case is the motive for the bitter and obstinate refusal to allow Jewish groups to perform a version of the Diary which they prefer because it is attentive to Jewish values. This question must be fully explored. I contend that political and ideological motives are involved." With an "immeasurable aggregation of wealth and power" arrayed against him, he once again appealed for their support. "My charge is serious. . . . Moral force is my only weapon."[28]

He had last approached these same Jewish leaders in late November, informing them of the attempt made in court to have him enjoined from even discussing the matter publicly, an effort of suppression made "in the name of Anne Frank, who cried out for every human freedom!"[29] Now, in March 1959, he was asking for "more than your signature." He needed them to speak out in public and write to others in positions of influence.

In signing the printed pledge of support that accompanied his letter, many added their own messages of encouragement, reflecting the anger and frustration that they, too, felt at not being able to offer their communities the more Jewish Anne Frank. None was more eloquent than Richard Rubenstein, whose own book, *After Auschwitz*, was to play a central role in opening the Holocaust for discussion in the decade ahead. "I believe you are absolutely right in stressing the Jewish issue. I am particularly interested in this because my wife is a Dutch Jewish girl of exactly the same age as Anne Frank, who lived in Amsterdam until the invasion. She came from a background which was entirely devoid of Jewish contact and the war especially led her, as it did so many of us, to her self-discovery as a Jew. I want to add my word of encouragement to your struggle. I know exactly the kind of thing you are contending with."[30]

"I have been heartened that there is still an element in our world to cry out for ethical and creative values," Meyer wrote in gratitude for the support he had solicited. Nevertheless, he was discouraged to see so few others, particularly fellow writers, joining him "as Anne Frank would have, in this struggle for their own preservation."[31] Yet however much he wished to struggle on, Meyer realized that the force of this imperative had grown far beyond what he could manage emotionally. Fearing for his sanity and the disintegration of his family, he suddenly announced the formation of a committee of three prominent Jews who were to represent him in negotiating a settlement. He would sue no further. Assigning power of attorney to Joachim Prinz, president of the American Jewish Congress and a signer of Meyer's petition; Abraham Katsh, director of New York University's Institute of Jewish Studies; and the author Charles Angoff, Meyer announced his "hope that mediation will be achieved."[32]

Trusting their judgment, and with complete faith in their ability to reach an equitable settlement, Meyer placed the fate of his work in their hands. Some three hundred rabbis had now signed his petition calling for mediation, and with their moral force behind him and his charge of plagiarism already proven in court, Meyer left for Israel, where he would settle and await the committee's decision in Kfar Shmaryahu, a town populated in the mid-1930s by refugees from Hitler who had come to build "a homeland."[33]

On July 10, Fredman wrote Meyer that the committee was in effect "blocking me out from knowing what it is that they are going to write to Frank until after it has been written." He was, however, still in contact with Angoff, and had spoken a dozen times with William Maslow, an attorney and staff director for the American Jewish Congress whom Prinz had asked to assume the role of chief negotiator for the committee. Their offer, Fredman told Meyer, would "be an attempt to rest on the moral issue as a fait accompli, taking the position that the jury verdict cannot be taken away from you and stands as permanent buttress for your position." With the specific terms of the proposed settlement being kept from him, there was little more that Fredman could add, aside from the hope that all would end "satisfactorily" for Meyer, including his current trouble with Darryl Zanuck over the writing of a screenplay based on Meyer's own best-selling novel *Compulsion*. "It is a foregone conclusion that some of us must go through life involved in problems, even those that repeat themselves, steadily engaged in the kinds of situations which undermine morale and destroy what would otherwise be the good things of life," Fredman wryly counseled Meyer. "That you are 'blessed' in that direction is obvious."[34]

Meyer received Fredman's letter three weeks later and responded the following day, August 1. He had by now seen the public statement proposed by the committee as part of the settlement and was objecting to it on several basic grounds—that he was being asked to acknowledge as "fair" terms that were not, that it was untrue to declare further public discussion of the matter detrimental to the Jewish community's best interests, and that a statement rescinding all injurious claims by him against Otto was not being reciprocated by a similar statement from Otto. Although Meyer repeated his intention to abide by the committee's settlement, he told Fredman that it would be "hard for me to have it come out over my name," preferring, instead, "that it appear to be the statement of the committee to whom these things may not be lies." He could agree to call Otto "an honorable man" only if Otto would agree to add "that no reflection on Mr. Levin's talent or capacity as a dramatist was ever intended." All "obstacles" could then be described as merely "contractual in nature."

Meyer's greatest fear, however, was that regardless of the statement issued and the monetary terms agreed upon by the committee and the plaintiff's attorneys, it would remain "quite likely that individuals in the diabolic gang on the other side will not let the matter drop, but will now engage in a kind of word of mouth campaign." Worse, still, was the "terribly expensive . . . sad lesson about justice" he had learned, that "even when you prove yourself, instead of being sympathetic with you at a continuation of the injustice, people are annoyed against the victim. . . . I hope I can someday understand it in a good light."[35]

Nearly twenty years later Meyer learned that the terms of the settlement, including the accompanying public statement that had worked against his interests, had been reached in violation of the agreement he had entered into in good faith—that the full committee had never met, nor had all of its members ever seen this final agreement, let alone approved it.[36] And there was more to this process that he never discovered. Otto, for example, knew Prinz before these negotiations and had asked Costikyan to intercede with him personally and outside of the parameters of the committee and the power of attorney granted it by Meyer. And while Prinz, on behalf of the committee, asked Fredman to draft a proposal for submission to Costikyan that was to be kept "in confidence" from Meyer and to be matched by another from Costikyan for Fredman's consideration, he also asked Maslow (who later called Meyer a "contract breaker" when he questioned the agreement) to draft a third proposal for Costikyan's approval, which Fredman knew nothing about.[37]

Nor did Meyer ever discover that he need not have agreed to statements exonerating the Hacketts or Bloomgarden, that these had been added by Costikyan at their insistence, though they had no legal standing in the matter.[38] Throughout these negotiations, Bloomgarden was kept informed by Costikyan of developments, often receiving copies of correspondence addressed to others.[39] The initial public statement, the purpose of which, Costikyan told Bloomgarden on August 3, was to "have the effect of minimizing the impact of any subsequent statement which Levin might make," had mentioned only Meyer and Otto. "Despite his differences with Mr. Frank which are now disposed of," it read, "Meyer Levin takes this opportunity to state that he believes Otto Frank is an honorable man and that nothing that Meyer Levin has ever said should be construed to the contrary."[40] Bloomgarden objected to this wording, and although he acknowledged having "no rights in the settlement," he nonetheless argued, successfully, that "something should be said about my position and the Hacketts' position. I believe your statement leaves him open to attacking us ad infinitum," he told Costikyan on August 5, as if "Mr. Frank is the angel and we are the villains."[41]

To support his position, Bloomgarden may have contacted the Hacketts, for on that day, Almirall wrote Paul, Weiss that although the Hacketts did not "have or desire any standing to participate in these discussions, we are very much concerned that any public statement . . . specifically exonerate" them.[42] Salisbury had, of course, been equally insistent on this matter and had advised her clients that it was their right, given the trouble Otto had caused them, to demand a similar exculpation so that Meyer "would never bring any charge or suit or accusation." Without it "you personally might still have trouble with this bastard."[43] (The Hacketts' feelings toward Meyer were, of course, as fierce as Salisbury's; in writing to Otto several weeks later, they characterized him as "just as evil as ever."[44]) "It was never your fault that Otto Frank had this relationship with Levin," she counseled them, "and when he finally gets Levin off *his* neck, he also owes it to you to get him off your necks and at once."[45]

Within a week of Bloomgarden's and Almirall's letters, Costikyan recommended a far more inclusive draft. "Despite his differences . . . Mr. Levin takes this opportunity to state that he believes that both Otto Frank and Kermit Bloomgarden are honorable men, that nothing Mr. Levin has ever said should be construed to the contrary, and that he regrets that the Hacketts received unfortunate publicity as a by-product of the dispute. Both Mr. Frank and Mr. Bloomgarden take this opportunity to state that nothing they have ever said was intended to be a reflection upon Mr. Levin's talent or capacity as an author or playwright."

But for all of the concern raised by this statement, neither the Hacketts' nor Bloomgarden's public exoneration was ever Costikyan's greatest worry. As he explained to Otto, "the whole basis for a settlement in our minds has been a termination of the dispute and relieving you of this constant barrage of communications from ignorant people who are stimulated to action by Levin's writing." It was for this reason that he had modified the draft to read that "both Mr. Levin and Mr. Frank have accepted and approved the settlement recommended by the committee. They consider it an honorable and final solution [!] to the dispute, and join in the committee's recommendation that there be an end to private and public controversy."[46]

As all feared, Meyer rejected this wording as another attempt to silence him and thereby to silence Anne. "The revised statement is in some ways worse than the previous one," he responded angrily to Fredman in mid-August. "The most repugnant part is the thought-control suggestion." He could agree to end all debate concerning his personal differences with Otto, but Anne's Diary, and the adaptations drawn from it, had to remain forever open to "literary discussion." He insisted: "I will not join in a public statement recommending thought control," nor agree to "bar a discussion of the content of Anne Frank's Diary as it appeared on the stage and screen!" Should Otto refuse to reach an agreeable settlement, he would "be forced to carry on the discussion" of the dispute as well. Nor would he even consider exonerating Bloomgarden. "I think this makes the whole statement a farce." Meyer was less resistant to including the Hacketts, though he believed that their desire to be mentioned was "unwise as it only reminds people."[47]

Fredman presented Meyer's objections to Costikyan, who had stepped into the committee's role in order to protect his client. Costikyan offered to remove all references to a ban on literary discussion, as long as Meyer privately agreed that all "overt tactics," such as "the circulation of the rabbinate," would forever cease. He was willing to bargain for this added security and the continued inclusion of Bloomgarden and the Hacketts in exchange for a similar assurance to Meyer that no ban on the discussion of the contents of the Diary or its stage and screen adaptations would ever be imposed.[48] Costikyan then sought Otto's approval for this change and informed Fredman of his acceptance.[49] Fredman, in turn, presented it to Meyer as a reasonable alternative and recommended his approval. "I feel gratified," he told Meyer, "that the two lines to which you so strongly object are able to be deleted."[50]

The final statement would be accompanied by a separate and more clearly worded "stipulation of settlement." In it, Meyer promised not to "circularize rabbis or any other groups or persons on the Anne Frank subject or stimulate either public or private controversy about the Diary or my part in relation to it." In turn, he would retain the "right to discuss any literary questions relating to the Diary," as long as this discussion did not raise the question "of whether or not the stage adaptation of the Diary which I wrote should or should not have been produced."[51] Otto and Bloomgarden, now joined in a single settlement of the case pending against both, issued their own stipulation, agreeing not to raise "either public or private controversy about [Meyer's] capacity as a writer, or [his] part in relation to the Diary."[52] All parties, however, ultimately violated their stipulations.

The final settlement assigned to Otto, "irrevocably and forever," all rights claimed by Meyer to his radio script, stage play, and "the Hebrew language dramatization . . . if any such now exists," thereby precluding the production of his script anywhere at any time in the future. Similarly, Meyer gave up all rights, "without limitations," to undertake "any actions" not only against Otto and Bloomgarden, but against the Hacketts, Fox, and Doubleday. To further strengthen these prohibitions, he was specifically disallowed from ever "claim[ing] an infringement if any other dramatist or dramatists willfully makes use, or has made use, of any new character created by the Assignor or any new situation or plot"—a clear response to the jury's finding of plagiarism that read like a silent admission of wrongdoing.[53] To settle the claim for damages, Otto paid Meyer the sum of fifteen thousand dollars, barely enough to cover the legal expenses incurred during his long years of battle.[54]

On January 13, 1960, Costikyan wrote Otto that with all necessary signatures secured and moneys exchanged, "the settlement has now become effective, and the lawsuit is over." There remained only the question of whether to publish the public statement over which so much debate had occurred.[55] Paul, Weiss worried that its release might raise questions by the press and that any response by either Otto or Bloomgarden might be used by Meyer to pursue his mischief while asserting that he was simply responding to the latest attack.[56] It was a difficult position for the defense to be in, for Meyer had already demonstrated his eagerness to continue the public debate, having lectured and written about the case even while the settlement papers were in the process of being signed and, therefore, not yet binding. So seriously had Otto taken this "violation" that he had withheld his own signature for several days.[57]

Uncertain and in need of independent counsel, Otto contacted an attorney outside the firm of Paul, Weiss whom he had known for some time. Max Grossman suggested that aside from the Hacketts, no one in the States "is particularly interested" in the case. "These matters have a short public life. Interest dies out pretty quickly." Why "revive a controversy that should remain dormant," particularly when the unusual stipulations in the settlement could "make people wonder what's behind it all?" Nor was there anything to be gained by arguing against Meyer's "opinions as to the lack of 'Jewish emphasis' in the play," which "cannot be counteracted by the stipulation. The Diary, the play, the movie stand on their own merits," he counseled. "People will draw their own conclusion."[58]

Otto agreed with Grossman's assessment and chose to "wait and see" as he tended to other matters relating to the *Diary*, including his suit for libel filed against a German schoolteacher whose questioning of the document's authenticity ironically had its roots in Meyer's critique of the play's distortion of Anne's text.[59] The *Diary* itself would have to be subjected to graphological and literary study by German authorities before Lothar Stielau would offer Otto his apology in October 1961 and Otto could withdraw his complaint.[60]

In the end, Otto was never free of the controversy that he had helped to create. Nor would he ever be able to rely on the support of others, not even that of his codefendant. Freed by the terms of the settlement, Bloomgarden saw no reason to offer the Anne Frank Foundation that portion of his income from the play which Meyer would otherwise have been paid. With the foundation's work of restoring and opening the Anne Frank House nearing completion that spring, money was once again growing exceedingly tight. Shocked by Bloomgarden's sense of "fairness," Otto suddenly admitted to Mermin his own belief that, as Grossman "had always told me," Bloomgarden was "responsible in a certain way in the question of plagiarism."[61]

The Hacketts, whose primary concern was the damage Meyer might cause to their reputation, again offered Otto little more than had Bloomgarden, remaining fixed upon this threat despite Otto's having reached a settlement as favorable to them as they had hoped. For Almirall was not certain that Meyer had been "permanently quieted" and had advised his clients to allow him to retain all of their materials relating to Meyer and the *Diary* "until we can have a reasonable hope that Mr. Levin has turned to other pursuits."[62] And though Salisbury assessed the Hacketts' position more positively, asserting that they should "certainly be happy and relieved" to hear of Meyer's signing ("So— 'after many a summer dies the swan'—what a lot of heartache, worry and money this demon caused us all"), she nonetheless continued to characterize Meyer as "a man *sans* ethics" who might well continue his "usual vitriol."[63]

The Hacketts had taken seriously both Almirall's warning and Salisbury's and had asked Almirall to retain their documents as he had proposed. "Like you, we believe that there is no truth in Levin." They felt "particularly sorry" for Otto, who was to go to Israel soon on behalf of the foundation's charitable work there. "He is walking right into the enemy camp. . . . When Levin is suddenly confronted, in his own country, with Mr. F bringing gifts, nothing will keep his mouth shut," they wrote Almirall, implying that Meyer's Zionism had superseded his U.S. citizenship.[64] Almirall responded only that they should be comforted by the knowledge that the releases Meyer had signed did indeed afford them "protection against any future claim," legal as well as literary.[65]

Otto had by now discovered that Meyer would not be silenced. Five days earlier, on January 21, 1960, he had promised Otto that "while the legal phase of our encounter is over, the moral phase is not done." He admonished Otto: "Your behavior will remain forever as a ghastly example of evil returned for good, and of a father's betrayal of a daughter's words." How could a truly "honorable man stoop to vindictive, vengeful, underground and destructive behavior against another man, particularly against a man he has wronged," he asked, further accusing him of being aware of "the pro-communist element's . . . underground character assassination attempt" against him, and of using his "money and influence" to deprive him by "legalistic devices . . . of the full enjoyment of a jury verdict." Still, the true victory was Meyer's, for, as he explained to Otto, "the moral verdict stands, no matter how many dollars you saved; the moral verdict that you, Otto Frank, wronged Meyer Levin remains ineradicable. Consider simply that Meyer Levin would not haggle with you over your daughter's grave as to the financial amount of the damages, for these wrongs cannot be measured in money. The greatest of them is your suppression on stage and screen of your daughter's greatest perceptions."[66]

Fredman, as Meyer's attorney and friend, was, of course, appalled at this clear violation, "strictly as a matter of law," of the agreement not to "stimulate" further controversy. He understood Meyer's desire to go forward with the struggle but was "grieved . . . by its having taken place" and hoped it was merely "a last ditch blowing off of steam." Such outbursts could only prove detrimental to Meyer himself, should Otto want to bring it before the public, together with the settlement's stipulation. "I do not choose to see you dragged down into the mire where certain of your enemies would like to put you."[67]

"If you had not sent my last letter to your attorneys, you would not have provoked this one, which doubtless you will send on as well," Meyer wrote Otto, in total disregard of Fredman's advice. "You did not 'buy my silence' with the so-called settlement," he warned, welcoming the opportunity threatened by Otto's attorneys, "for they will open the real issue of the case, which was and has always been political" and which "your attorneys fought so hard to keep from the ears of the court. . . . I am ready to test it in court and before the public at any time." Meyer once again went on to recount "the course of this tragedy," how he had repeatedly tried to make Otto understand that he had been "manipulated by a pro-Communist group" and had "suppressed the deeper Jewish content of your daughter's work when you followed their advice to oust me—for in their eyes I was a 'Jewish nationalist.'" Only Otto's "blind obstinacy" and "sense of high-born pride and 'honor'" had kept him from admitting what "ample evidence" had proven—that the Hackett play was "the radio play in essence . . . with the Jewish material minimized." Despite its legal status, "this is still an open question, morally and culturally." Meyer challenged Otto by "suggest[ing] that you could best honor your daughter's memory by seeking an absolutely impartial investigation of this whole affair, and guiding yourself accordingly."[68]

Otto did not take up the challenge, nor did his attorneys choose to go back into court. They attempted instead to isolate Meyer by ignoring his efforts, allowing Otto to pursue the work of his foundation. In early March Otto issued a pamphlet designed to raise funds for the next phase of its work, the creation of an International Youth Center adjacent to the Anne Frank House. Yet not once did the words *Jew* or *Nazi*, or anything that could be directly identified with the Holocaust, appear in his pamphlet. Rather, such phrases as "the suffering of Anne and 2,000,000 other children," "enemies of humanity," and "a period of immorality and injustice" were used to stress the "universal" theme, permitting the distortion of Anne's experience and thoughts to stand. "The Diary of Anne Frank is a demonstration of the human experience, that in times of distress one learns to know one's true friends and that in the end the powers of evil are not equal to good will and mutual understanding." Otto was determined to make of Anne "the symbol of an adolescent believing in the future" and "a symbol for the whole world." But he believed that "young people of all creeds and nationalities have been inspired by the young authoress of the Diary" because he had left Anne's own religion and ethnicity in the shadows of the past as he sought to build "the suitable place . . . for the ideals of the Diary."[69] In May he "tearfully" repeated this expression of faith, officially dedicating the Anne Frank House as "a building in which the ideals of Anne will find their realization."[70]

Meyer could not have disagreed more with this approach. "The success of [the film] 'Exodus' shows that the general public does not find any lack of universality in the Jewish theme," he had written several weeks earlier in "An Open Letter to Otto Frank," published in the *Jerusalem Post* during Otto's tour of Israel. A reporter sailing to Israel on board the *Theodore Herzl* had met Otto and in the course of their conversation had been told by him that Meyer's script had been rejected in favor of "a more 'universal' treatment" of Anne's

Diary. After the reporter had related this conversation to Meyer at the home of a mutual friend, Meyer had spoken of it in his "Open Letter," explaining how this admission had contradicted the trial testimony, in which the sole reason given for the script's rejection had been its writing, not its contents. It was, for Meyer, further indication that he had accurately assessed what had happened, and it was one more reason to speak out, particularly now that Otto was among those who could better appreciate what was at stake in the questions being raised. "Yes, I am and will be a troublemaker for Jewish cultural rights," Meyer promised Otto and the *Post*'s readers. "I contend that it is not 'universalism' to have a German actress portray the mother of Anne Frank. I contend that it is not 'universalism' to exclude from stage and screen the expressed wish of Anne Frank's martyred sister to live, if she should survive, in a Jewish land." Meyer had hoped that here, in Israel, an "appropriate body" of writers, or perhaps someone of the stature of the world-renowned philosopher Martin Buber, could at last arbitrate "the serious issues I have raised . . . in the name of all that Anne Frank stood for."[71]

At the only press conference Otto gave in Israel, he announced the establishment of a fifty thousand–dollar Youth Aliyah scholarship fund, and then, "in a voice choked with emotion," denied ever having made the remark attributed to him by Meyer. Fully aware of the facts, he misleadingly spoke of the fourteen American producers as having rejected Meyer's play simply because of his inability to create a workable drama—proof enough, he claimed, that his assessment of it was correct and that Meyer's allegation was without merit.[72]

But in truth Otto had made the statement, and when he attempted to clarify it once he returned to Basel, the reporter, Edwin Eytan of the Jewish Telegraphic Agency, confronted him. Eytan explained that in speaking with Meyer, he had merely recalled his stating "that one of the reasons for rejecting the play was that it was not universal enough." The reporter emphasized that he had kept his promise not to use "our private meeting as the basis for any press article or information, according to your requests" and that "at the time . . . had no idea that Mr. Levin was going to use our private conversation for publicity reasons"; but he must surely have known how provocative such a remark would be for Meyer. Could he have naïvely expected Meyer not to use it publicly? Or had he counted on Meyer to do what he himself could not?[73] Otto thanked Eytan for his explanation, but in doing so he made a partial admission that he had, in fact, said precisely what Meyer had reported. In a face-saving effort, he alluded to the "misunderstanding [of the remark] which gave Mr. Levin a base for his article."[74]

That April an extensive critique of the work done by the Hacketts, Bloomgarden, Stevens, and the others appeared in the American Labor Zionist

journal *Jewish Frontier* under the title "The Vanishing Diary of Anne Frank."
Its author, Martin Dworkin, who had been among the American troops to
enter Buchenwald and Ohrdruf, understood how difficult it was to make "the
very size of the horror the Germans had perpetrated . . . into something that
could be known." Like Meyer, he knew as well the importance of finding "an
articulate vision, as in a work of art, [that] can create the conditions of
knowing, giving form to the inaccessibly, bewilderingly complex and various
realities that must be grasped." It was with a profound sense of this need, "of
bringing all who can care to the state of personal bereavement," Dworkin argued, "that we must read and judge the diary of Anne Frank, and consider its
dramatization on stage and screen." What he found there, however, was "simply
untrue to the spirit of the book," an attempt at "popular comprehension"
achieved by "a grievous loss in spiritual complexity—and in fundamental credibility." The Anne of stage and film was nothing more than "a signally American
figure of thoughtless American youth," not the Anne whose *Diary* was

> profoundly, passionately intellectual, emerging from the intellectual and spiritual
> vitalities of a Jewish family which talked and read and sang together in several
> languages, wrote poetry in honor of festive occasions, argued about judgments of
> history and works of art, fought throughout its vigil, in constant fear, discomfort
> and privation, to preserve not only its existence and essential virtue, but actually
> as well as symbolically the entire humane tradition of knowledge and humility,
> intellect and spirit, laughter and charity. . . . Out of what must be seen as a
> carefully considered effort to universalize the imagination of a particular young
> girl, there emerges a picture of an imagination that is recognizable because it is all
> too familiar. The particular Jewish girl, born in Germany and raised in Holland,
> deeply, if still youthfully educated in the European literary tradition, with the
> meaning of her Jewishness vivid in every instant of her life, emerges as an apo-
> theosized, yet theatrically conventional adolescent. The person of the play and
> film is knowable, but not in any way ambiguous, as is the author of the book. As a
> dramatized cliché, she may induce an illusion of recognition. But the very ease
> with which the audience is enabled to know her every mood and manner measures
> the mystery that is evaded—and enters a new doubt that so carefully common-
> place a character could have created so richly individual a work, that has become
> the torch to light up the faces of all the unknown dead in the dark spaces of our
> hearts.

Such "evasions" could not lead the "vast proportion of those seeing the play
and film [who] know little of even the facts of the extermination of six million
Jews by the Nazis" to any knowledge of the event. Although both productions
might have theatrical value, he argued further, "what they make of the heroine
can have no more than fictional bearing upon the true tragedy of Anne Frank,

the little girl who died, one among millions." Whatever the worthiness of Meyer's script as drama, it had raised the issue of "alternative dramatizations," without which there would be nothing more than "progressive theatricalism carried over to the screen from the stage . . . a melodrama with an implied tragic ending, around a conventionally central love story . . . [with] a familiar soft-drink flavor."[75]

"In the end, Anne Frank was betrayed by a determined group of persons, of hardened ideology, who wanted their 'universal' version, clear of all inner Jewish reference, to represent her," Meyer told the members of the Anglo-Jewish Association in October 1960, nine months after he had signed the final settlement papers. "The surface 'message' of the Diary is, obviously, its plea against genocide." But there was a more positive side to Anne's work which this "determined group" had worked hard to suppress, a catharsis amid tragedy achieved by "her self-discovery as a Jew." After engaging in "the self-agonized debate that went on ceaselessly in every Jewish soul," Anne had elected to remain a Jew. If there was a universal message in the Diary, he argued once again, it was "that even in the most dreadful of circumstances the complete self could emerge, and that a girl of fifteen could understand that every individual had a right to live as himself, whether Jew, Hungarian, Negro, or Englishman." He asked rhetorically, having long ago found the answer for his own life, "Can any 'faithful' adaptation of the Diary pretend to value, if it completely ignores this question?" Could it claim to be "faithful . . . if it does not give Anne Frank's triumphant answer?" Declaring that "the struggle is not over," he promised to fight on so that "more than one dramatic version of this work [might] be allowed a hearing," as Dworkin and so many others, including the five hundred American rabbis, signatories to his petition, had insisted. "I can never recede from this demand, which morally supersedes any commercial arrangements made by her father. Can anyone doubt what side Anne Frank would be on?"[76]

Meyer could not. "You must write it all down, how you lived and what happened to us all, so it will be known. You must write down everything exactly as it was," the hero of his 1959 novel was told by her mother as the Holocaust closed in on them.[77] "I wrote Eva as a culmination of fifteen years of trying to understand and explain what had happened to the Jews of Europe," Meyer commented shortly after finishing this "essential human story." In it, he had put "all that I have learned since I went to Europe as a war correspondent in 1944 to find out the fate of the Jews," though he knew that his work was far from completed. "It was my sad distinction to be the one writer bearing this assignment. Today, fifteen years later, I am still trying to fulfill it." Out of this search for answers, and from the hundreds of survivors he had met, "a single theme was to emerge . . . the search for identity," a theme of contemporary universal importance, of the commonalities of human needs and not of a specious leveling that sought to draw unfounded equivalences between disparate experiences. "It was the 'Who am I?' that comes so sharply to the individual who has survived a thousand near-deaths. It was the Who am I that echoes in every one of us, and that rings so loud in the entire world today."[78]

Eva: A Novel of the Holocaust was, in fact, the real-life story of a woman who had approached Meyer shortly after he had settled with his family in Israel (and perhaps the first book to use the term "Holocaust" in its title).[79] But in telling her story, Meyer tried to give Anne the voice she had twice been deprived of. And though Anne had been murdered, as Eva she lived through the horror so that she might fulfill the promise of the *Diary*, choose to live a fuller Jewish life, and thus take on the task Meyer had assigned to Anne when he brought her face-to-face with Peter's assimilationist fears in the pivotal scene that had been "universalized."

"Being Jewish. What did it mean?" Peter's counterpart in *Eva* asks contemptuously in the weeks immediately following the war's end. "What is it? In time Jews would be absorbed, assimilated," he asserts with those who had reduced Anne's Jewishness to a cultic Hanukah ritual. "What good was there in keeping alive this separatism? It had brought only agony, and mass murder, and bestiality. For what? For an outmoded religion, a cult in which no enlightened person believed?"[80]

"But then what of Palestine?" Eva asks as "a strong memory of the Zionist atmosphere" of her childhood suddenly sweeps over her—an allusion to the opening page of Anne's *Diary*. "Surely people have the right to be their own selves in the world. If not, all the turmoil, the strife, the war, the victory had been for nothing." She will go to Palestine and fight for Israel's independence and survival. "This was our way, by our own choice." Why then, Eva asks as Meyer forges an even stronger link between himself and Anne, has she even "gone again among a strange people?" She will leave Poland "to find my own," Meyer has her proclaim, as he himself slowly adjusted to his new life in Israel, declaring through her final words, "I'm home."[81]

CHAPTER THIRTEEN

An Unrepentant Stalinist

I n November 1961 *Time* reported that Stalin's "campaign against Jewish 'nationalism'" had "sent hundreds of Jewish artists and intellectuals to jail and killed many others."[1] Meyer sent a copy of the story to Otto, together with a letter he had written to those who had responded to his *Congress Weekly* article of the previous month, "Another Kind of Blacklist." After a year of silence on the matter, Meyer had once again spoken out publicly on the "character and career assassination campaign deliberately set in motion years ago by a powerful clique. . . . Mention the name of Meyer Levin in theater, film, or television circles, and someone will almost certainly make a quip about lawsuits." Yet for all the humor engendered, he noted in his letter, the campaign had proven "deadly in its effect," robbing him of assignments in the various media.[2]

Harry Golden, whose *Only in America* (1958) and other works on Jewish life in the States had brought him a national reputation as a journalist and humorist, had been in Jerusalem several months earlier to cover the trial of Adolf Eichmann, one of the chief architects of the Holocaust. While there on assignment for *Life*, Golden was asked by the U.S. government to cover a story in Korea. He had suggested to his editor that Meyer take his place during this absence, but the request had been denied. "You have a great problem," Golden wrote him on April 30, 1961. It appeared to Golden that Meyer had "made the public relations mistake of the century" when he sued Otto. Still, "to blacklist a writer is a very great crime and other writers should not stand for it," Golden insisted.[3]

Meyer, in fact, had been given this assignment before Golden, only to be "mysteriously dropped" by *Life*.[4] "Your letter was a real brightener," he told Golden. "I am glad—the wrong word, let's say it helps to know that you followed through on the proposal to have me fill in for you, and thereby got a direct confirmation of my tale of woe." Yet the blacklisting itself was not the result of a "public relations mistake," he told Golden, but rather "the other way around." "The average reaction" to suing Anne's sainted father, Meyer argued, "indeed, your own, I'll bet, would be 'a man like Levin doesn't sue an Otto Frank unless there is very good reason.'" The jury verdict should have confirmed this suspicion. But because "Frank's gang saw that it was bad public relations *for him* to have an obviously blameless writer sue him," they had spread the rumor that Meyer was simply "a nut who sues everybody! . . . They could not base this character-assassination campaign on my suing him, alone."

This "vindictive plague" had so "poisoned" his and Tereska's lives, that "as the case went on, and Tereska finally saw what [Otto] was really like," she had tried to drown herself in the Hudson River. Friends had advised Meyer to turn all of this into a novel, but he could not. "Some things cut so deeply that one can't write about them." Instead, he would use an invitation from *Congress Weekly* to write "a piece on what it feels like to be blacklisted" in order to break the silence maintained by the press, even after Albert Camus, himself a witness to the persecution of Jews in Vichy France, had signed a petition demanding an end to this suppression. Only then could he hope to "counter-act a whispering campaign" that had consistently portrayed him as a "troublemaker."[5]

Meyer had also written that May 9 to Arnold Forster, attorney for B'nai B'rith's Anti-Defamation League, telling him what Golden had discovered so that he would "know what I am really up against."[6] But when this appeal yielded no assistance from Forster, Meyer asked Golden to use his media contacts to attempt to "persuade the bigots who have murdered my reputation that I am indeed a decent person." Living in Israel, he needed someone in America to champion his cause. Only if he exposed "the blacklisting campaign . . . as vigorously as possible" could there be any possibility of change, Meyer assured Golden. "I was always taught by my mother . . . [to] raise my voice against evil. I have tried to do this, and believe I should continue to do so even in a world of hush-up, and even when the evil is an evil done to me." With Golden's support, he hoped to convince liberals like Forster, whose protests had succeeded in ending the blacklisting begun by HUAC, "that it is sometimes as liberal to defend a liberal as it is to defend a communist."

He hoped as well to enlist Jewish writers and the Jewish press in his fight, "hav[ing] given my life to the cause of Jewish culture through writing. It is inescapable that I have now for eight years been persecuted because of that very same devotion." If "bitterly disappointed" during this struggle, he had previously been able to excuse their lack of support. But now that claims which once appeared "so extreme . . . have been proven," such abandonment was unconscionable.[7]

Meyer had thus begun that November to distribute copies of his letter to his *Congress Weekly* readers, together with the clipping from *Time*, as a means of explaining "the motive for these attacks." No longer omitting their ideological roots, he feared only that he might be misunderstood as "a red-baiting reactionary."[8] ("I was never a rabid anti-Communist, and was as far from McCarthyism as every decent liberal," he had written a friend that June. "But for many years I have been down in the Communist blackbook as a Zionist writer. I think you know how far they will go on an ideological slant."[9]) With the respected backing of *Time*, he now spoke more openly of "this hideous affair" as "a strange international projection of Soviet culture-control." The blacklisting begun in 1950 with his criticism of the Communist attack on Zionism in his autobiography *In Search* had made his dismissal from the *Diary* inevitable once "Broadway's pro-Communist clique [became] determined to capture it for the stage." And when he protested against "the doctrine-dictated omissions . . . of the Jewish content of the Diary," he had been "promptly smeared as a 'troublemaker.'" Since his court victory on the issue of plagiarism, "the attacks [had] redoubled," forcing him now to call upon his readers, "in the name of the decency for which Anne Frank cried out," to help "put an end to these politically inspired slanders."[10] As he had written in his "Blacklist" article, "I ask every decent person to help halt this campaign . . . and to demand not only that it be stopped, but that some effort be made to undo, when yet possible, the harm done to a writer whose sole 'crime' was to fight with all his strength for literary integrity and cultural freedom."[11] In forwarding this letter and the *Time* clipping to Otto, Meyer bitterly scrawled only the briefest message across the top of the page, "Proud of yourself?"[12]

"Some of my friends in that organization have expressed outrage at the fact that Levin is still getting an audience for his nonsense," Costikyan wrote Otto in reaction to Meyer's *Congress Weekly* article. If they had chosen to ignore "these explosions" in the past, a point had now been reached where a public response from the American Jewish Congress appeared necessary.[13] Costikyan had composed a long letter to the journal's editor, Samuel Caplan, quoting extensively from the settlement stipulation concerning Meyer's promise not to "stimulate either public or private controversy," while alleging that the article was "so loaded with false assertions that it would be impossible to list them all."

Costikyan sent a copy of the letter to Prinz, seeking his permission to quote in it from a private letter Prinz had sent him some months earlier. Prinz had written of his disgust with Meyer's "complete dishonesty" and of his "hope that Levin's behaviour [was] due to emotional disturbances for which he might not be responsible."[14]

With Otto's approval and Prinz's authorization, Costikyan sent the letter. Caplan had already phoned Costikyan to ask whether he wished the letter to be printed in a forthcoming issue of the journal when Prinz suddenly reversed himself, asking instead that the journal simply issue "an editorial comment" in order to avoid the "start [of] a polemic with our friend Meyer Levin."[15] A week later, on December 27, Prinz unexpectedly advised Costikyan that as president of the American Jewish Congress, he wished to withhold even this response from the congress's journal, believing that any comment "would begin an endless discussion which would benefit nobody and aggravate all of us."[16]

Costikyan could not, however, leave his clients exposed to Meyer's charges. Instead, he allowed Caplan to revise the letter and remove Prinz's comments so that it could be published in *Congress Weekly* after he had approved these final changes. Costikyan demanded as well that Caplan pub-lish "an independent statement by the magazine in which the appropriate regrets and apologies are to be given." But before granting Caplan permission to publish the revised letter, Costikyan sent it to Hellman and Bloomgarden for their approval. Accompanying Bloomgarden's copy was yet another letter that Meyer was now circulating together with copies of his "Blacklist" article, which Costikyan had received from Hellman.[17] In it, Meyer had further expanded his argument by explaining that his play had been "jettisoned on the advice of Lillian Hellman, whose ideological formation is well known." She had "then supervised the writing of another version in which material inimical to this ideology is omitted." All of this, he noted, had occurred during and subsequent to that period when "the Stalinist campaign against Jewish culture had reached its height, with the execution of many Jewish writers."[18]

On February 13, 1962, Costikyan sent Caplan permission to publish the revised letter, while making it clear that Hellman and Bloomgarden "greatly prefer[red] the original" and that "an independent statement was still re-quired," particularly given the use to which Meyer had put the article he had published. Among the many people to whom Meyer had mailed copies were Hellman's colleagues and friends at Harvard and Columbia Universities.[19] Costikyan's revised letter appeared in *Congress Weekly* a month later, alongside an editor's note "deplor[ing] the fact that Mr. Levin is circulating reprints of the article with a personal letter which contains an unjust attack upon Lillian Hellman and renews the controversy about the Diary, although he had signed a pledge not to do so."[20] Paul, Weiss, having outlined the contents of this statement for Caplan, sent an advance copy to Hellman with the hope that she would find it acceptable.[21]

With this statement's publication, a period of relative peace fell to those against whom Meyer had struggled for the *Diary*'s integrity. "We had an evening with Lillian" helping her to edit Dashiell Hammett's writings into a single volume, Goodrich wrote Salisbury that spring—repayment for Hell-man's assistance with the *Diary* and other projects.[22] But Meyer could find no peace. "Every social discussion, every conversation leads to the subject he knows he must avoid," Meyer wrote of himself in the novel that grew out of his struggle to put it all behind him in the months following *Congress Weekly*'s disclaimer.[23] "I know I get obsessive," he had told Golden the previous year, noting some months later that "it seems I can never have enough of the books about the Jewish fate in Europe." In the aftermath of the Eichmann trial, he argued in *Congress Weekly* that "not only the generation . . . but the entire world has to be taught and re-taught."[24] Anything impeding this process had to be opposed. And so he had to write again of the Holocaust and of the attempt to distort its reality, now using fiction as his weapon, though as he admitted in its earliest draft, "I have tried not to write this book. I have tried to turn to one subject or another, but always I find myself staring fixedly at the page on which the lines have petered out, while in my mind there obsessively intervenes a series of scenes from this history. . . . I recognize, I have freely recognized for some years, that this is indeed an obsession." He would attempt to move past it all with this final accounting, but only by "try[ing] to tell everything straight. . . . I see no other way, perhaps because I am a writer."[25]

The Fanatic (originally titled *Obsession*) was from the start a worrisome retelling of this struggle. Meyer's editor at Simon and Schuster, Robert Gottlieb, wrote him after a first reading in early January 1963 that the publisher's attorney, Ephraim London, "tells me that the problems are immense; that with characters so identifiable to anyone who knows more or less what took place, the libel problem is huge." Not that he doubted Meyer's account. Gottlieb himself had lived through Meyer's fight to retain control over the Broadway production of *Compulsion*, seeing how hampered he had become by the character assassination campaign that had branded him a "troublemaker" and "litigious." "I was a witness to your participation, and in that matter I *know* that you behaved properly, and were treated shabbily." Still, there were "legal doubts" that had to be addressed. "One thing is certain," he concluded, "I'm glad you wrote it, told it, and possibly relieved your feelings somewhat."[26]

Meyer found it exceedingly difficult to let go of these feelings of disappointment, betrayal, and anger, and he questioned why he continued to subject himself and those he loved to this unending pain. (After all, he admitted in *The Fanatic*, "in the theater everyone is an enemy."[27]) Still, he ultimately made some compromises with his text so that the basic story could be told. There was no choice, London assured him, for once Paul, Weiss learned of the book's existence, the firm would threaten to sue to stop publication on the grounds that Meyer had violated the settlement's terms by once again "stimulating controversy" over the *Diary*. And if suit were brought, he felt certain that "the Court will be sympathetic with the person suing," particularly now that Silverman, Otto's attorney at the *Diary* trial, had been appointed to the New York Supreme Court, where the case would be heard. To better judge the likelihood of a suit, London promised to reread the book, while asking Meyer to write a prefatory disclaimer.[28]

This all came as a "bombshell" to Meyer, who had not "construe[d] 'stimulating controversy' as prohibiting me from writing." It all seemed but the latest "wearing-down technique to squeeze things out of me that would in the end deprive me of my basic rights." He would "have to fight all the harder for it now," he realized, though he was prepared "to write the sort of preface" London requested. "As to Silverman," Meyer added defiantly, "even if he becomes a justice of the Supreme Court in Washington, his character will remain as he revealed it in the trial."[29]

Meyer continued to write Gottlieb over the next few weeks as he awaited London's decision, arguing his case for freedom of expression with increasing desperation. "No matter what the legal position, I am convinced it is morally my duty to do all I can to have this book published. If the Anne Frank case must persist as a test of my beliefs, I can't draw away." Should Simon and Schuster balk, he was prepared to publish *The Fanatic* himself, as he had years before with *In Search*, believing "that in the end it would be seen that I was no less right." Four days later, on July 14, he wrote that "my tension is mounting and I don't know how long before it reaches some point of explosion." He needed an immediate decision. The next morning he added that "Tereska went into a serious depression over the prospect of further protracted legal tortures from the Frank crowd," the first such relapse since they had left New York. "I'm not in such a good state either," he wanted Gottlieb to realize. "Some of my shoulder and arm pains have returned." Yet he and Tereska were in agreement that the fight for this book had to be waged, though the courts were the wrong arena. He pledged instead to undertake a "hunger strike against [Frank's] efforts to suppress me. . . . I have no other choice."[30]

London ultimately cleared the book for publication, but with a carefully worded preface designed to satisfy the attorneys at Paul, Weiss. It was his belief that they would accept this statement rather than reopen the case before the public. After a six-month publication delay, *The Fanatic* appeared in January 1964.[31] But however strongly Meyer pleaded with each of his readers "to confine his feelings and his judgments to these fictional characters alone," the reviewer for the *New York Times* wrote of this "novel of obsession" that "despite the usual disclaimers, 'The Fanatic' would seem to have been inspired, at least in part, by Levin's own experiences." There could be "no gainsaying its raw power and the hypnotic grip of its obsessed hero."[32] "Again and again the whole story breaks out of him," Meyer wrote of his protagonist: "the ideological motive, the campaign against Jewish writers in the Soviet Union, the whole cabal existing right here, from the playwrights to the press agent, and even as he speaks, [the] words resound in him like the raving of some fanatic anti-Communist who wildly flings accusations about. And he grows accustomed to seeing that old, opaque look that appears in his listeners' eyes. He knows then that he ought to stop, to change the subject, but instead finds himself pouring out more names, additional proof."[33]

Several weeks later, Zimmerman's recently established *New York Review of Books*, whose stated purpose was "to suggest, however imperfectly, some of the qualities which a responsible literary journal should have," issued a relentless attack upon Meyer in the guise of a review of *The Fanatic*.[34] As "the work of an ambitious mechanic who thinks he can bruise and shove his way through reams and reams of paper to Apocalypse," the novel was said to demonstrate "the difference . . . between art and perspiration." The preface itself was criticized as both too lengthy and suffering from "Levinesque weight." Here, ultimately, was a "clumsily earnest but eventually spurious novel. For Levin is the kind of author whose sententiousness and poor writing derogate his doubtless sincere work to the level of the big books on 'important' subjects cynically contrived by fiction-mongers."[35]

If *The Fanatic* had failed to release Meyer from the survivor's guilt he had carried with him since his earliest experiences in the death camps, it had at least fulfilled his moral obligation to speak out "as though the living of each life, the very enduring of life was for this: that the world should know! . . . That our experience at the hands of man should not be lost. That perhaps there could still be a minute portion of benefit, a learning, and that perhaps this alone was the intention."[36]

Some two years after writing this passage, Meyer acknowledged in the *Jerusalem Post* that such learning had at last begun, if only in a limited way. "Are we beginning to comprehend that what happened to the Jews was different in meaning from even the highest accumulation of atrocity?" he asked in marking the twentieth anniversary of the liberation of Buchenwald.[37] Not that Holocaust denial had ceased. Months earlier, he had drawn a character in *The Stronghold* who had argued that the survival of a single Jew was "proof that all these tales about their gassing all the Jews were false, or at least heavily exaggerated."[38] But Meyer could at last see some recognition developing, however slowly. "It has taken these two decades of hammering at world consciousness for even the extent of the atrocity to be accepted," he noted, though as early as 1943, and "as far away as California I knew, and everyone knew, from sporadic reports, that some such thing was in progress, on an unimaginable scale." Having personally experienced its aftermath, he had been compelled to pursue the path he had taken. If "the comparatively few who survived that atrocity know that they are apart, that there is an area in their lives which we others will never truly comprehend," there were "some of us who came close enough to peer for an instant into the rim of the volcano, and that shock alone was enough to dominate the rest of our lives."[39]

And so, despite *The Fanatic*'s publication and its exploration of the issues involved in his fight over the *Diary*, Meyer could not rest until his play had found its way onto the stage. It alone might satisfy the questions that remained unanswered when he wrote *The Stronghold,* a dozen years after adapting the *Diary:*

> What could he give of himself? he wondered, refusing to give in to despair. What could he consecrate in the last of his years? How could he find the lever on which to exert his remaining strength, in some way, in some infinitesimal way, to help the poorly evolved nature of man, so slowly, so painfully, detaching itself from chaos, in learning to control the dread energy of life itself? Something urgent, something possible that he could do, seemed almost on the point of appearing to him. He hardly dared lift his eyes as the question echoed through him: What can I do? It was the same question he had cried out in past years when perhaps he could have done something, when, if he had gone one step further, if he had exerted one more ounce of will against all who counseled "No," so much might have been averted. But that way, in such speculation, lay eternal guilt. What can a man do? What can I do? What must I do?[40]

Although the potential threat posed by *The Fanatic* had proven too marginal for Otto and the others to chance public embarrassment in the courts, they continued to do all that they could to stop the performance of Meyer's play, whatever the circumstances of its production. In the spring of 1966, Peter Frye, the Canadian-born director and head of Tel Aviv University's drama department, received Meyer's permission to use his script for the initial production of the newly formed Israeli Soldiers Theatre. By May 2, Frye had put together a cast of mostly amateur performers and theater students and was hard at work doing what he could to see that Meyer's work received the best possible production. "The play deserves more," he lamented, for however good these newcomers were, their performance would not be "really enough" for a work of far greater significance than the Hacketts'. "The longer I work on it the more firmly am I convinced that yours is the more important play. Notice I don't say better because 'better' is a subjective evaluation, a matter of taste, a matter of the level of cultural development. For example, in terms of American show business theirs may be the 'better' play because it is easier, slicker, more sentimental. But in terms of literary and cultural importance the yardsticks are, perhaps, more precise and one can more easily prove the merits of one work as opposed to another."[41]

A critic for the newspaper *Maariv* concurred after attending Frye's rehearsal. Meyer's play stood in sharp "contrast with the much less dramatic version . . . approved by Mr. Otto Frank in order to insure a 'universal' success with non-Jews." In stressing "the Zionist conviction of Anne Frank," Meyer had populated his version of the *Diary* "with living human beings," not merely with stereotypes. With this portrayal of a more Jewish Anne, Frye hoped to bring "the message of the play (Jewish consciousness, history, and consequences) to the young generation." And he had succeeded, the critic noted, for even without the use of costumes, sets, or lighting, "the audience sat tensely through the presentation—as if it were a perfect dramatic experience," finding in it Anne's true thoughts. "Why should it be possible to have many dramatic versions about the life of Jeanne d'Arc," he asked, "and not be able to educate our young generation on the basis of the spiritual heroism and the human vision of this wonderful apparition called not Yohanna [Joan], but Anna?" Why was Meyer being censored?[42]

On November 26, Meyer's play opened in Tel Aviv. Each night that it played, the audience wept as Meyer sat wishing that Otto or the Hacketts or Costikyan could have witnessed their response. The Israeli press spoke warmly of the play, calling it a "display of mastery" where "artistic and theatrical value" could be seen even "without the lesson of the Holocaust that it brings." A "profound experience," wrote a second reviewer, while the *Jerusalem Post* concluded that "it hews closer to the original" and was, "on the whole, a more honest dramatization than the slickly professional one we have seen before." Still another judged "every sentence rich in meaning, every word appealing to the mind and to the heart," while the head of the Israel Association of Drama Critics added that it was "infinitely superior to the Hackett version, which put aiming for a hit above faithfulness to the sources."[43]

Yet the play had only a limited run as Paul, Weiss moved swiftly to shut it down after the *New York Times* trumpeted this "first breakthrough for Mr. Levin" in his fourteen-year fight to have his play produced. With its stage-worthiness now tested, Meyer told a radio interviewer of his plan to push for an American opening. "The 'Diary' has had its run, as far as the Hackett play is concerned. But it [Anne's Diary] should be a permanent institution in the theatrical literature in every country, particularly where Jews are numerous, and I think that my play and not the Hackett play will be the one that can become that permanent institution."[44]

Paul, Weiss did all it could to prevent this from happening. Cabling Meyer, Frye, and the Israeli army on December 6, the firm demanded an immediate halt to all future performances on the grounds that Otto's rights had been infringed and that Meyer had violated the agreement not to "stimulate controversy." Failure to cease immediately would bring a lawsuit.[45] Meyer's Israeli attorney, H. J. Brodie, countered with a request for additional time to study the agreement, hoping that Otto might yet waive this restriction on "good grounds" should it prove that Meyer had, in fact, signed away his right to an Israeli production of his play in Hebrew. For if Otto's earlier objections had been artistic, as he had repeatedly claimed, then they should be dismissed now that the critics were "unanimous in their opinion that the Levin play is much superior to the Hackett play. From the reviews it would appear indisputable that by including the aspects of Jewish significance contained in the Diary but omitted from the Hackett play, the present production is more inspiring and does greater honour to the memory of Anne Frank." Would the Hacketts then "stand in the way of the obvious strong Jewish feeling to see the Levin play?" Brodie demanded.[46] There was no money to be made from an amateur production, so why should Meyer's more faithful rendering of the Diary not be staged?

The army, hoping to preserve its expanded schedule of daytime performances for school children and its three months of bookings throughout Israel, offered to pay Otto for the use of Meyer's play. Yet Otto continued to demand that the play close. Even the offer of a six-month tour of the States and several publishers' requests to issue Meyer's play, all of which were potential sources of income for Otto's foundation, could not change his mind. Davar, a leading newspaper in Israel, objected to the order to desist, arguing that "The Diary of Anne Frank is not the private property of her heirs." Legal action against Meyer was in this instance shameful, it declared.[47] Brodie even attempted to convince Paul, Weiss "that when it comes to the story of Anne Frank . . . there are certain considerations which rise above the right of both Mr. Frank and Mr. Levin," and therefore "an extraordinary non-legal approach to the differences between the parties" was warranted.[48]

But there was simply nothing that could be done, and after fifty performances, the tour ended on January 18, 1967. "No one could understand why it should be suppressed," Meyer wrote Prinz of the final audience's reaction.[49] The decision to close was "scandalous," even if he had mistakenly signed away his rights. "The Diary represents the suffering of 6 million persons, among whom was Anne Frank," he told a reporter for the New York Times. "Otto Frank doesn't have the moral right to make a decision in the name of all the dead."[50]

Meyer was not alone in expressing his outrage at the play's closing. "I was distressed to learn that Anna Frank is again condemned to oblivion," the celebrated author and Holocaust survivor Yehiel Dinur (Katzetnik) wrote Meyer that day. "When I saw your play . . . I felt the magnetic pull between the audience and Anna Frank on the stage. It is a shame that questions of a non-literary nature can sometimes come between an artist and his audience in expressing the human condition. You have my deepest sympathies."[51] "What a pitiful post-scriptum to the Diary," Elie Wiesel added a few days later. "I fail to understand the behavior of Anne's father. That he should speak of 'rights' and 'agreements' and 'trials' is beyond me. Your play is what it should be: an outcry. Many years ago I have seen the Broadway production on the same subject: good entertainment. Needless for me to say that I would gladly and willingly do whatever possible to put back Anne Frank in her true light."[52]

A week later, Newsweek carried the story of the German trial of the S.S.

general and members of his staff who were responsible for the deportation and death of 87,000 Dutch Jews, Anne Frank among them. It had taken twenty-three years for justice to be attempted. In reporting the upcoming trial, the writer concluded with Anne's own words, that "a quiet conscience makes one strong."[53] Meyer himself had quoted this passage on a number of occasions, though he had never experienced this inner quiet. But he could now take strength from the support of Dinur and Wiesel and the critics, and from his own vision of Anne.

Once again, he vowed to fight on. In open defiance of Otto's attorneys, he signed a contract with the Israeli publisher Akim for a Hebrew edition of his play. "I do not believe that I can be denied the right to print and give away my own work" for the sake of "literary discussion," Meyer said of his free distribution to libraries, universities, and theatrical groups of both the published Hebrew edition and the English, which he had printed at his own expense. Having received monetary prizes from the Jewish Book Council in America for the past two years, he had decided to use the money to finance this work. In the preface to both editions he gave a lengthy retelling of the conflict, concluding that "this argument is not merely between a version that contained more, and a version that contained less of the Jewish content of the Diary. What a paradoxical argument, when the Diary was accepted as the outstanding Jewish document of the Holocaust! No, this is a case of the cold suppression of what is acknowledged to be the superior literary work, a suppression resulting from underground political influence. If I am obsessed it is because to me this ranks among the literary atrocities of the period of Dr. Zhivago!"[54]

"The spirit of suppression and hush-up is symptomatic of what I have to contend with in the long and unequal struggle for the right to live of this work," Meyer wrote several weeks later in his longest appeal for outside support. Should those who opposed him possess forever "the moral and artistic right to monopolize . . . and to enforce exclusivity over . . . a version that is deemed truer to the original Diary" simply because he was, "to their political thinking, a 'nationalist,' a 'chauvinist,' a 'Zionist-Imperialist'"? How utterly outrageous that Jewish audiences should be barred from seeing his work performed while the "expurgated stage version of the Diary was then heavily to be 'sold' on Jewish sentiment."[55]

After speaking with Costikyan about this latest appeal, Prinz sent Meyer a strong letter scolding him for "misbehaving." Confident that this would silence Meyer and "mark the Israeli episode as closed," Costikyan planned to use Prinz's letter to "prepare a form response" to the many rabbis requesting permission to stage Meyer's play as a result of his latest petition for redress.

Costikyan had meanwhile secured a promise from Prinz to speak with the other members of Meyer's committee about these latest violations and to raise with them the concerns that Tereska had addressed to Prinz in confidence, which Prinz had nonetheless shared with Costikyan, who, in turn, had related them to Otto—that Meyer had become "paranoid, totally out of control, [and] unwilling to take psychiatric help." Costikyan had written Otto in January, "Of course we have known for many years that Mr. Levin was a paranoid," to which Otto responded by assuring Costikyan, "Nothing can change him." More than ever, he realized how important it had been to have Meyer relinquish the copyright to his scripts.[56]

The *Diary* had nearly destroyed the Levins' marriage and family. It had been Tereska's hope that the committee could help bring some reason back into Meyer's life.[57] But Prinz contacted neither Katsh nor Angoff, as Tereska had pleaded with him to do and as he had promised Costikyan. Nor could he have done so under the circumstances. That March, Katsh confirmed what Meyer had suspected some years earlier, that he had never been a party to the settlement.[58] Meyer told Katsh that he was "not surprised to learn you were never consulted on the agreement," but that his name was still being used "in what I consider unscrupulous efforts by Frank's attorneys to hush up the barbaric act of suppression in which he is engaged."[59] Several more years passed before Meyer could confront Prinz directly with this knowledge.

In September the *Ladies Home Journal* published a long article by Otto entitled "The Living Legacy of Anne Frank." Only once, in describing the school she was forced by the Nazis to attend, did he use the word *Jewish*. For Otto, Anne's legacy was to be found in the work of the International Youth Center established by his Anne Frank Foundation and in its attempt to explain "how the Nazi barbarities were possible in our century." Yet rather than answer this question with the specifics of Anne's story, he wrote of the center's work in helping "to establish as many contacts as possible between young people of different nationalities, races and religions"—prophylactic work for which Anne had become a "symbol . . . when the play, and later the film, based on the diary were produced."[60] As Otto told a Dutch reporter two years later, "We must not flog the past. We must know the past, but we must build for the future. And the future is the Anne Frank Foundation," which he characterized after another two years as "perhaps the most important response to the diary."[61]

It was left to the *Journal*'s editor to offer a corrective, however skewed by the recent Six-Day War, that through the *Diary* Anne had become a far different "symbol of the Jewish past" and that events recorded in her diary were now a part of the "national memory that built the State of Israel. . . . There could be no more martyrs. Dead heros, if need be, but no more Anne Franks. That is her living legacy."[62] Only in private, nearly a year later, did Otto speak of the specifically Jewish character of the Holocaust, admitting to a young

Jewish woman that "when I returned from [the] concentration camp alone, I saw that a tragedy of unexpressible extent had hit the Jews, my people, and I was spared as one of them to testify."[63]

Weeks earlier, in May 1968, Meyer had sent John Wharton, a senior partner of Paul, Weiss, a copy of his play, hoping "that I might awaken a reasonable curiosity in some members of your firm, with its liberal tradition, and that you might examine this matter afresh in its literary, as well as legal implications." They were free to consign his work and his appeal to the trash, "but I feel it is my duty to the memory of Anne Frank to try to get you really to see what happened to her work on the stage," particularly "in the light of the brave fight of Soviet writers and the victory of Czech writers against culture control." These same "methods of culture-control were projected onto Broadway and Anne Frank," he told Wharton, whose firm, he asserted, had been used to attack him as "an ideological outcast, a 'Zionist.'"[64]

"It is not the suppression of Meyer Levin but of Anne Frank that is in question," he wrote Morris Abram, the president of Brandeis University, in early November. With the *Diary* now widely taught in the schools of America, should "the Stalinist version remain the permanent, exclusive image of Anne Frank on the stage?" Meyer called upon Abram to add his name to those hundreds of others, now including Isaac Singer and Bruno Bettelheim, who had signed his appeal for a noncommercial production of his play. Perhaps "those who control the Diary" would finally be persuaded "to overcome their intransigence, their personal hatreds, and to act in accordance with the ethics of the *Diary* itself."[65]

Meyer had once shared the dangers of a newspaper reporter covering the Spanish Civil War with Martha Gellhorn and Ernest Hemingway, whom she married after the war. Meyer had since maintained a friendly relationship with her. "Let me try to explain little old Meyer Levin's obsession," he wrote a week after his appeal to Abram. "I have tried with two analysts and am on the third so probably incurable." But "the real issue" was "political," he told Gellhorn. "In Moscow they would simply have put me in a writers lunatic asylum and here I am branded as paranoid. . . . But maybe now you understand a little better. I am sick with this because my whole being as a writer revolts at any act of censorship." Even worse, having first "swiped it from me," they had copied the "whole staging, the structure, etc.," only to leave out "the Jewish heart."[66]

Gellhorn, however, counseled him to abandon the play and to cease causing his family such "murderous" pain. Not that she was unaware of the horrors he felt so compelled to address with the *Diary*. "I never get over the Nazis and the Jews," she wrote Meyer in response. "That is the permanent nightmare of my generation surely. . . . They started me fearing the human species: one has ever increasing cause to fear same," she added out of the pain she felt in the shadow of Vietnam and the civil rights struggle in America. "But the likes of us, Meyer, are privileged beyond belief. . . . Disaster for disaster, we are as new-born babes, untouched." It was time to set the entire affair aside. "Find your way back to being a brave, disinterested man! . . . You used to be quite a funny guy; such a waste, to degenerate into this."[67]

Gideon Hausner, the Israeli prosecutor of Adolf Eichmann, offered Meyer similar counsel in March 1970, urging him to "let bygones be bygones—even if it is hard on you." The "assignment of rights is unequivocal," he advised. Even if it could be proven that fraud had occurred, the time had long since passed when a court battle over this issue could be waged. Nor would provoking a lawsuit by the copyright holders for an unauthorized production of his play be successful. "Perhaps there is some consolation in the fact that after all, the authentic Anne Frank's diary is available to the public and has made an infinitely stronger impact than the muzzled version produced on stage."[68]

But Meyer remained inconsolable, taking little comfort from the caring support that served only to fuel the fires within. The following month he was awarded the World Federation of Bergen Belsen Associations' Remembrance Award "for excellence and distinction in literature concerned with the Holocaust"—an award made more poignant by its presentation on the twenty-fifth anniversary of the camp's liberation. The distinguished jury awarding this "Special Citation for the high merit of his writings on Jewish life and on the Holocaust, and particularly for his memorable dramatization of the Diary of Anne Frank," included many of the world's leading writers, among them Saul Bellow, Emil Fackenheim, Saul Friedlander, Abraham Heschel, Alfred Kazin, Primo Levi, Maurice Samuel, Andre Schwartz-Bart, George Steiner, and Elie Wiesel. Many were themselves Holocaust victims who had become important voices for the murdered. In presenting the award, they made particular note of Meyer's long struggle to have Anne's true voice heard, and appealed for an end to the ban:

> There has been a long controversy over the two dramatic versions of the Diary, the first written by Meyer Levin, and barred from production, the second written by Albert and Frances Hackett under the supervision of Lillian Hellman, produced on Broadway and the world over. There is no need to enter into this controversy. Millions of spectators have been moved by the Broadway play. But through the years and until today, many community theatre groups, some of whom had already presented the Broadway play, have asked for and been refused permission to present Meyer Levin's version. It is the owners of the commercial rights who refuse. This cannot be regarded as merely a commercial matter, since Anne Frank's Diary has become part of our culture. The Broadway play notably omits any reference to the Jewish homeland, yet Anne wrote of Margot's dream to go there as

a nurse if she survived. Nor does this play reflect the spiritual search that Anne voiced, nor her remarkable affirmation of Jewish faith. . . . We appeal to Otto Frank, Kermit Bloomgarden, and Albert and Frances Hackett to disregard all personal animosities that might have developed in this controversy, and in respect for Anne and Margot Frank, and all the dead, to give their consent to any qualified requests for the rights to perform Meyer Levin's adaptation of the Diary of Anne Frank. We appeal to the distinguished law firm of Paul, Weiss, Goldberg, Rifkind, Wharton, and Garrison to advise their clients to this end. Anne Frank's voice, like that of our spirited youth of today, cried out in rebellion at the strife among adults, at destruction and horror in the world that was made for them by man. We feel that this protest comes out more powerfully in Meyer Levin's play, and that through it, Anne would come to life again as her true self, for an entire new generation. It would be the most fitting celebration for this anniversary of our liberation to free Anne Frank from any last vestige of censorship and suppression.[69]

Yet in spite of this recognition, the international writers' association, PEN, still refused to hear Meyer's case. "We conclude that no action by PEN is warranted," they informed him several weeks later—and time and again over the next decade.[70] Another two years passed before a group of students at Brandeis University, without concern for the politics involved, staged the unauthorized American premiere of Meyer's *Anne Frank*, two decades after it had been written. (A year earlier, a suburban Boston synagogue had presented a reading of the play, but the Brandeis production, with its full staging, was to be its "official" premiere.[71]) "Legal or not, we were among the very few who were fortunate to see this rather remarkable stage adaptation," the reviewer for *genesis 2*, a decidedly progressive Jewish journal, wrote of Meyer's play that April 1972. The play had illuminated for her the part of the *Diary* "that was obscure to me as an adolescent." Meyer's work had touched a chord within the hearts of those struggling with their Jewish identities in a way that Otto's efforts could not—particularly among the youth whom Otto had tried hardest to reach in his own way:

What makes this version so different and in a sense faithful to the original diary, is the presentation of Anne's search for herself as the search of an adolescent Jewess, and the struggle of the people living in the attic as a . . . struggle for Jewish identity, in addition to their struggle for elementary survival. Their scream for justice and peace is in a sense the uttering of the sacred words of the Shemah. So, excuse me Mrs. Hellman . . . but I don't like your shmaltzy sale of universal messages through identity genocide. Universal messages are all right with me, insofar as they are concerned with a humanism in Judaism or in blackness, but not behind them. In Anne Frank we have the Jew who retains a pride in her Jewishness even after Anti-Semitism in its most virulent forms has been manifested, while her friend Peter wishes to lose even the last remaining traces of his Jewish self; he adopts the principles of the brutal world which he rejects, and becomes a self-hating Jew, his identity completely vanished. Margot, Anne's sister, is a dedicated Zionist in whom the war serves to reinforce strongly held beliefs. Being different from Anne, she doesn't believe in cosmopolitanism or in the possibility of being a creative Jew anywhere but in Palestine. These three figures come very close to representing the ideological alternatives which face many young Jews today.[72]

Meyer had at last seen his play produced in America. It had received the hearing he had fought for and had proven worthy, though it remained an illegal performance of what another writer characterized as "perhaps the only work of samizdat literature both in the USSR and the USA."[73] And as the ban continued, so, too, did Meyer's inability to let go of the struggle to see it lifted. "In the middle of life I fell into a trouble that was to grip, occupy, haunt, and all but devour me, these twenty years," and from which he could not liberate himself—but which theater people, like *Fiddler on the Roof*'s Joseph Stein, knew to have a ring of truth, finding in Meyer's "fascinating" telling of *The Obsession* "an inside look at a unique show biz story."[74]

With the Brandeis success a year behind him, Meyer had decided to offer a full account of this struggle to the widest readership possible, and without the cover of fiction. Whatever hesitations he had felt over the issue of Red-baiting, or out of reverence for Anne's father, were now gone. "The prolonged fight, though dreadfully consuming in time and energy, deepened Levin in his individualism and in his justice absorption," the publisher's promotional literature later noted. Such tenacity was characteristic of Meyer. Even as a war correspondent, he had been "known in the press camps for his Jew mania, riding in his jeep sometimes ahead of the tanks that first entered the concentration camps."[75] The "mania" had simply continued unabated long after the war. In a passage later deleted from *The Obsession*, Meyer said of his initial reading of the *Diary* that "the appearance of the teller came with the shock of revelation. At once I began to proselytize."[76]

In the fifteen years since the settlement of his suit, the obsession had never left him, "not for a day, not for a night, nor can I say it has left me now, in this second attempt to write it out of myself." Nor had it left "the other side," he asserted, witness "their incredible efforts to keep this work suppressed,"[77] as they had again on January 17, 1974, when Costikyan had sent Simon and Schuster a five-page detailed retelling of the play's history, suggesting "in the light of the foregoing facts . . . that you investigate the accuracy of the statements made by Mr. Levin in his book before releasing it for publication."[78]

"Mr. Meyer Levin has begun the red baiting all over again," Hellman reported to Joseph Rauh less than a week later. "I don't think I can really answer him," she admitted, frustrated that for all but one minor point he had raised about the HUAC hearing, there was simply no response to be made in her favor.[79] Meyer had merely repeated his earlier assertion that she was an ideologue rather than a Soviet operative, and that she had chosen to act as she had out of her own volition. "I don't imagine Hellman was getting orders from Moscow to see that Meyer Levin was removed as adaptor of the Diary! But if you believe in a certain set of ideas, your actions follow, regardless."[80] (Levin didn't know that months after the *Diary* opened on Broadway, Hellman had received a $10,000 check from the Soviet government for an unspecified reason.[81]) Much as the Soviet memorial to the thousands of Jews massacred at Babi Yar had spoken of them simply as victims of Fascism, purposely deleting their identity and the reason for their murder, "millions of spectators the world over" remained unaware that with the Hacketts' play, they too had been "subjected to idea-censorship" through a "brazen example of the inversion of a dead author's words," and to "the programmatic, politicalized dilution of the Jewish tragedy." Here, again, was "the whole process of image deformation and of the subtle manipulation of ideas." In the conclusion to *The Obsession* Meyer wrote, "Through all those years of horror, I had striven to make heard the Jewish cry of affirmation"—for "in the Jewish conception, the era of justice and peace is not to be brought about by lies, suppression, or even power. Our Jewish Messianic belief is a belief in universal illumination."[82]

Hellman's view of the world had remained otherwise. "Nothing is true altogether," she wrote a few months after sending her note to Rauh, "nor does it matter."[83] And if she told the graduating class at Barnard College the following spring that it was their "absolute duty" to oppose the suppression of those "who did nothing more than express their democratic right to say what they thought," her opposition to such "spitball malice" had always been rather selective.[84] She had remained silent when the Smith Act was used to attack those of the American left who had violated Soviet Orthodoxy and when the Soviets assassinated Leon Trotsky and his family. Later, she failed to protest the censoring of other American writers during the McCarthy years. And while the United States agonized over the Vietnam War, Hellman continued in silence, even hypocritically befriending many key players in this tragedy in order to win social acceptance rather than remain marginalized—a fact overlooked by those who lionized her as a part of their own iconography of selective protest.[85] Having told an intimate friend in 1965 that "I can't get it out of my head that Stalin was right," she wrote in *Scoundrel Time* that Stalin's purges, while limiting personal liberty, were justified by "the necessity of a tight rein after any revolution."[86]

Scoundrel Time thus became Hellman's only "answer" to Meyer, at once an attack upon the witch-hunts of the 1950s and a defense of her own actions toward the perpetuation of a lie. "You thought, all those years, that you had nothing to conceal," she had written a dozen years earlier, in a fictional rationalization of her political past. "But you did have something to conceal, all of us have."[87] After a lifetime of fabrication, it seemed of little consequence that *Scoundrel Time*, allegedly true, had followed in this vein. Had she not been allowed by Hammett himself to lie to the press four decades earlier, telling a *Herald Tribune* reporter that he had only made suggestions for the fourth draft of *The Children's Hour*, when he had in fact critiqued the script throughout its six revisions?[88] What had begun in childhood as a "self-constructed suit of armor" against the vulnerabilities at the core of her fragile sense of self had thus been confirmed early in her career and had become a lifelong pattern.[89] "There's not a word of truth in this," an intimate friend had said of her earlier volume of memoirs, *An Unfinished Woman*, a reaction echoed by Shumlin and others, and later by a critic who spoke of *Scoundrel Time* as "an exercise in self-justification" conditioned by "political amnesia."[90]

"No doubt we still differ as to whether one had to choose *either* Stalinism *or* McCarthyism, or whether it was not only possible but necessary to take one's stand against both," the historian Arthur Schlesinger Jr. wrote Hellman in response to *Scoundrel Time*, aware that his critique would place him, as he subsequently told Rauh, on her "Enemies List too!"[91] The socialist writer Irving Howe was undoubtedly on that list as well, having publicly asked Hellman how "someone who believed in such splendid things didn't trouble to ask friends and collaborators whether *they* lived by 'freedom of thought and speech, the right of each man to his own convictions.'" By the late 1930s, he wrote in his *Dissent* review of *Scoundrel Time*, the "essential facts were known . . . [that] the better [Soviet] world they wanted came down to a soul-destroying and body-tormenting prison." These facts had been "violently denied by many of the people with whom Miss Hellman worked," Howe noted pointedly. In their support of "Stalinism and its political enterprises, either here or abroad," they had "helped perpetuate one of the great lies of our century . . . [and] befoul the cultural atmosphere."[92] As they had in the case of Anne's *Diary*, for as Price had recently told Meyer, his play had been rejected not because it was "unactable," but because Otto had been repeatedly told that it "couldn't be done because it was too Jewish."[93]

As expected, when *The Obsession* appeared that January 1974, critical response was divided. "Ah, Paranoia!" the *New Republic* titled its review, though its reviewer had found the book, if "not always convincing," written with "candor" and without "malice"—"surely one of the most exciting and hard-punching tracts of its kind since Zola's of 1898, 'J'Accuse.'"[94] The more conservative *Saturday Review*, however, found the book "fascinating" and its claims credible. "One cannot doubt, for example, that the version of Anne

Frank's *Diary* presented to the world on stage and screen—the version Mr. Levin contested so bitterly—was divested of its strongly Jewish character and sent forth swaddled in that 'universalism' so well loved by the progressive mind. No one who knows the fatuities Anne Frank is made to utter . . . in place of the passages in the diary, which bespoke so profound an identity with her faith, can doubt that it is so."[95]

"What to conclude? Was there a conspiracy to keep Levin's play from being produced for Stalinist reasons? I don't think so," answered Victor Navasky in an extensive discussion of *The Obsession* in the *New York Times*. "Levin sees the world from the cave of his preoccupations. . . . What he is describing are the shadows on the wall. . . . Nothing Levin says documents his charge that Miss Hellman opposed his play for ideological rather than dramaturgical reasons." Meyer's book, Navasky felt certain, would unfortunately reopen old wounds and further dissuade Otto from granting permission to those who wished to produce his play, the banning of which Navasky criticized, nonetheless. "Why not? I say. Enough time has passed, Anne Frank's reputation is secure; the Levin version will never be confused with the official one, and he is willing to forgo profits."[96]

The final words, of course, belonged to the parties in dispute. A month later, the *New York Times* published letters from both Meyer and Bloomgarden. While Meyer offered a rebuttal to Navasky and a general plea simply to read his account, "not because of the Diary case alone but because it is an amazing example of hidden censorship and may serve as a warning," Bloomgarden spoke of the "incredible attacks" that he, Hellman, and the Hacketts had repeatedly suffered at Meyer's hands. Now, for the first time, he would "present the facts," for "Mr. Levin's deceptions . . . [were] greater than Mr. Navasky could possibly know." Yet Bloomgarden's account of the "entire extent" of Hellman's involvement was in clear contradiction to the record published in the Hacketts' "Diary of the Diary" and to the correspondence between the players themselves. "I asked Miss Hellman's advice about a possible adaptor. Together we came up with the idea of Mr. and Mrs. Hackett. I sent Miss Hellman the final version of their play and she made some very helpful suggestions." By asserting more than this, he argued, Meyer was guilty of "old-fashioned red-baiting under a pious claim of noble motives. . . . No politics were ever involved. Nor did any of us ever think of the play . . . as being 'too Jewish.'"[97]

Unlike the others, Otto refused to read *The Obsession*, having "had enough bad experiences with Meyer Levin in the course of the years," as he told a student with whom he had carried on a lengthy correspondence. There was little to be gained by exposing himself once more to Meyer's "point of view." If he could at last concede that Meyer had been "the first who saw a play in the book," having previously denied this fact under oath, he still vehemently refused to admit that he had rejected Meyer's script for being "too Jewish." Yet for Otto the Holocaust had remained a largely undifferentiated instance of prejudice. "The persecution of the Jews under Hitler, leading to the annihilation of ca. 6 million Jews, among them Anne, was a consequence of prejudice and discrimination of which antisemitism is one form," he still maintained, unable to see past his assimilationist perspective and into the true nature of the event.[98]

It was this very problem of how the Holocaust was to be understood that Meyer once more raised with Prinz, insisting again that the Hackett play was a product of the larger Stalinist anti-Jewish campaign "to diminish and denigrate the unique nature of the Holocaust." Meyer entreated, "Consider this: Lillian Hellman, the instigator and key to this whole affair, has emphasized in her own book, 'Pentimento,' and in television appearances, that 'Jews were not the only ones who suffered' from the Nazis. The very words were put into the mouth of Anne Frank on the stage though they never appeared in the Diary. They were substituted for her outcry, 'Perhaps through Jewish suffering the world will learn the good.'" Meyer pointed out to Prinz that "the insistence on equating other suffering with the Holocaust" had far greater implications, "as you well know," for this "was only the first step in a mind-manipulation program" that could be "clearly traced" from its anti-Semitic Stalinist roots to the argument that what the Nazis had done to the Jews, the Jews were doing to the Arabs. It was the very argument that the Soviets were using to promote the notion that "Zionism is Racism" in their bid to weaken U.S. support for Israel while enhancing their own influence in the Middle East. When Meyer later found literature in support of the Palestinians at Otto's International Youth Center, he drew this connection more sharply between the Diary's theatrical distortion and the campaign to destroy Israel.

But for now, there remained the more personal issue of Prinz's lack of support, upon which Meyer had once believed he could depend. As he had finally learned from both Katsh and Angoff, the committee charged with negotiating the settlement of his lawsuit had never met to discuss the agreement, nor had either of them ever been given a copy after it had been reached. Had he known this, he would never have consented to "the amazing conditions that were later presented to me as the committee's decision," to which he had felt bound by the good-faith arrangement into which he had blindly entered. Because Prinz had been "instrumental in wronging me, and the public, and Anne Frank," Meyer insisted that he now use his "position of influence" as president of the American Jewish Congress and a leader of world Jewry to "alleviate this continuing horror for me . . . [and] for Jewish culture."[99]

"Whatever you may think," Prinz wrote Meyer a month later, on June 20, 1974, he was "a rather innocent bystander in the whole affair," and one whose "sentiments of friendship" had remained constant. Meyer's doubts, he advised, were regrettable. Yet Prinz himself claimed to "report from a rather faint memory" with "hardly any recollection of meetings," while insisting that Meyer not take "seriously and literally" the little he could remember. With the equivocation of one who has knowingly violated the trust of another, he recalled "only that meetings did in fact take place" and that the committee had asked Maslow "to guide us" in what they believed was a legal and not a literary matter. "We then decided to continue our deliberations," he explained, "but it was impossible to get the group together because one or the other was not available and we simply gave up. No report was ever written. No decision was ever taken."[100] Fifteen years after committing this grievous injustice, Prinz still refused to admit his own wrongdoing.

Nor was Costikyan yet willing to admit that the terms of the agreement being used to bar Meyer's play had not been "worked out over a period of months by me and the Committee."[101] But by now Meyer knew that this was not true, and once again he approached both Angoff and Katsh for statements to the contrary. In a notarized affidavit, Angoff wrote that "the committee unfortunately never met, nor do I have any recollection of working out any documents with Costikyan or any other member of his firm, nor have I ever seen those documents, except in quotations in your book, *The Obsession*, and in the Costikyan letter."[102] Katsh similarly repeated his earlier recollection of never having met with the committee or with the attorneys involved.[103] Three years later, he, too, signed a notarized affidavit stating that he "was never apprized of any such meetings or consultations, nor consulted as to the agreement, and never was a party to any decisions setting the terms of any agreement in this matter." Katsh further noted that Meyer's protests against the barring of his play had further intensified after he discovered that he had been "persuaded to sign the settlement agreement on the assurance that it had been worked out and approved by our committee in conferences with the opposite side."[104]

It was on this basis that Meyer now unsuccessfully sought the assistance of the Israeli arm of PEN. Though American PEN had continuously refused to endorse his petition, many of its members had done so individually, "including such oddly assorted ones as I. F. Stone and Anaïs Nin!"[105] Because of the "false statement as to the participation of the committee . . . I have not felt bound by the 'silence' stipulation of the agreement," Meyer wrote the head of Israel PEN. Rather, he had openly "violated" its terms, as Paul, Weiss had repeatedly accused him of doing, but only "after I realized I had been swindled into believing the agreement was approved by my committee."[106]

Two years later, in the August 1976 issue of *Midstream*, a leading Zionist journal, Benno Varon—a Holocaust refugee, journalist, and former Israeli ambassador in Latin America—wrote that it was "beyond doubt . . . that the [Hackett] play dejudaized the book and tampered with Anne Frank's ideas. . . . What remains to be proved is the why and who of the tampering." The similarity between what Anne was made to utter on stage and screen and Hellman's statement in *Pentimento*—that "Jews are not the only people who have suffered"—was all too obvious, he asserted, echoing Meyer's earlier charge. "Who is plagiarizing whom?" he asked with noticeable anger. "The Hacketts Miss Hellman? Miss Hellman the Hacketts? The answer is clear: Miss Hellman plagiarized Miss Hellman. By clear evidence produced in court, she 'supervised' the Hacketts' adaptation; hence, we may conclude that she substituted Anne's reference to Jewish particularism by the vagueness of 'other peoples' and—swallowing the Nazi nonsense—'races.'"[107]

Stalin's murder of Jewish writers and artists and his order that "Soviet martyrs," not Jews, were to be spoken of when discussing Nazi slaughters at Babi Yar and elsewhere, Varon pointedly added, were of a piece with Hellman's efforts to "get rid of the Jewish author Levin, so as to give Anne Frank the Babi Yar treatment." By her own admission in *Scoundrel Time*, Hellman had "for a long time . . . mistakenly denied" Stalin's crimes. If not for this "belated confession," Meyer might never have been vindicated, Varon observed. There remained only the need to inform all those who "had been duped for decades by political bias masked as literary judgment"—and worse, by the derisive labeling of Meyer as "paranoid," which "should come as no surprise if the political leanings are recalled of those who singled him out." For "Levin, more, perhaps, than any other American-born Jewish author of his time, has fought for his Jewish values and the public deserves to know the real issue beneath the smears, the obfuscation and the denigration around his name."

Varon's article renewed the controversy after a period of relative public silence on the issue. For the next half year, letters poured into the editorial offices of *Midstream* and spilled over onto its pages on three occasions, eliciting replies from Varon to these and to the eightfold more that he had received directly. "At long last there is someone to speak up for Mr. Levin and denounce an injustice perpetuated by far too many for much too long," wrote one respondent, who asked, "Are there no others to speak up?" "The story needed telling," wrote another, "so now, why isn't something done?" The writer Peggy Mann found Varon's work to be "of genuine importance in bringing clarification . . . [to] the fact that this could be a much more deep-reaching affair than a simple feud between Levin and the Hacketts, Hellman and Co." Harry Zohn of Brandeis University praised Varon for the "real courage" he had displayed with his "outspoken article," while James Michener spoke of "the splendid job you did of giving another writer a serious review of his work and position," though he personally "lack[ed] the scholarship to judge the merits of the polemics." Myron Kaufmann, himself a Jewish novelist, noted more pointedly concerning Hellman that "no assimilationist, no matter how renowned, no matter how powerful, can be comfortable reading . . . [what] seems to challenge the premises on which he has built his life." Kaufmann had known Meyer not as the popular image of the "lonely and embittered" man but "as an uncommonly warm and compassionate individual as concerned for the reputation of others as for his own . . . a quality not often found among the scrambling and egomaniacal breed of creative writers."[108]

Varon, too, had known Meyer for some time but had long since tired of hearing his complaints, unsure whether they were well founded or hallucinatory. Confessing his own years of reticence, he admitted in response to these many letters that his article had been an "act of repentance" for having so belatedly come to Meyer's aid. "Like all his friends, I had let Meyer Levin fight all by himself his battle against real or imaginary enemies. I had been skeptical about his assertions, listened to his repetitive tales with an inner yawn, and was only slightly less callous to his endless tribulations than the whole Jewish community of America." Even while writing the piece for *Midstream*, there were times, he further confessed that January 1977, "when I wondered whether I had not been infected by one of Levin's 'paranoias.'" But each time "unexpected corroborations" appeared, the most startling being Hellman's own plagiarism of herself in *Pentimento*. "Here was proof of her authorship of the elimination and substitution of Anne's proud statement on Judaism . . . [that] did not fit in well with Hellman's Stalinist *Weltanschauung*," which, by her own admission, she had maintained long after the period in question. Whether or not she had been a member of the Communist Party "was completely beside the point," Varon noted, for though he was himself a Zionist, he held no membership in any Zionist organization. "She was a Stalinist, and certainly an unrepentant Stalinist when she destroyed what would have been the most gratifying achievement of Levin's life of toil."

In this deception, she had enjoyed the unintentional support of many, including the prestigious law firm representing Otto and the others. Was there a chance that such "distinguished men" would finally step forward and acknowledge their error "despite a conscience . . . protected by thick layers of honors?" Varon had thought not when, in response to his article and to a prior letter of inquiry he had sent Paul, Weiss, Simon Rifkind wrote "with some sense of apology . . . that [the firm's] relationship to the Levin-Frank controversy was a purely professional one."[109] The duty of Paul, Weiss "in the adversary process" had been "to present our client's point of view in the most favorable light." But now, having "learned a great deal" from Varon's work, it was Rifkind's "hope that history will correct whatever injustices may have been done. That history, I am sure, will find a very large space for the genius of Meyer Levin."[110]

There was, however, "*one* injustice done to Meyer Levin, Anne Frank, and truth itself, whose correction need not be left to history," Varon insisted. "These words have a right to be heard from the stage," and Rifkind was perhaps the only person who could "sway" Otto to allow Meyer's play to be performed. The fate of Anne's message of Jewish self-assertion was now, in part, in the very hands that had helped her father to silence it.[111]

CHAPTER FOURTEEN

A Jewish Work of
Universal Importance

The renewal of public discussion caused by Varon's article afforded Meyer the unforeseen opportunity to widen his search for support, and he seized upon it with the knowledge that time was growing short for all of the players in this drama. In December he wrote to Irving Greenberg of the Jewish Community Council in New York, asking that his organization help to "expose this piece of anti-Semitic censorship." Meyer did not have the financial resources to carry the fight back into the courts, where he believed he might now find justice. Instead, he hoped that Greenberg would see the "great value . . . public attention around such an issue would have," and would join the struggle to overturn this "ideological anti-Jewish suppression." The details, he advised Greenberg, were to be found in *The Obsession* and in Varon's now–widely discussed article.[1]

"It is difficult to understand all this except that one must keep in mind that people hate those they have wronged," Meyer wrote one of Varon's respondents who had written directly to him. "We do live in a conspiratorial world," he added, "even the Nixon experience [Watergate] hasn't sunk in, apparently. . . . All the innocent schnooks like Meyer Levin will eventually get it in the neck if they don't learn the ropes and act accordingly." Though it all might remain "a bit mysterious," the search for facts, motives, for "the way things work" was essential—and not because he was, as some accused him, "a communist-hater, a red-baiter, or any of the rest," but because such instances of suppression had to be exposed, however "more and more difficult [it gets] in our conspiratorial world."[2]

In this, "the *Midstream* article has been of some help," Meyer noted further, "and particularly of help to my morale," though not all of the published responses had been positive, witness Irving Howe's dismissive treatment of him as an "undistinguished writer." "Can one doubt the verdict of a Distinguished Professor of Literature?" Meyer retorted, having recently "waded through the distinguished works of Lillian Hellman" for a *Jerusalem Post* article that "I think in a way . . . explains a good deal."

"Bitch Time," Meyer's response to Hellman's self-defensive *Scoundrel Time*, appeared on April 26, 1977. For two full pages, he berated the author of "this vindictive, self-pitying and carefully omissive memorial," offering his readers "a certain orientation" to the Stalinist background of her thoughts and actions, "as we are about to be inundated by paperbacks of this pamphlet" now that a "saturation campaign of television questing, puff interviewing, and culture-queen palaver" had made its hardcover edition a best-seller and Hellman an icon. So much so, in fact, that despite her political avowals, she had appeared in a full-page *Sunday New York Times* mink coat advertisement, unnamed but for the caption, "What becomes a legend most?"[3]

"Almost all of us, young novelists, playwrights, artists, were fervent united fronters and fellow travellers on the left during the Depression years," Meyer explained, but "many [had] jumped off the boat with the Stalinist purges, and more with the Stalin-Hitler pact." Those who had remained loyal to their Stalinist posture after the war had split the literary and theatrical worlds, particularly over the Zionist question that had played so pivotal a role in Hellman's falling out with Shumlin. Both her subsequent attachment to Bloomgarden and her later insistence upon Meyer's removal from the *Diary* project, in order to promote her "doctrinaire internationalist" ideology, were evidence that she had retained this earlier mind-set. Wrongfully blacklisted, Hellman had added an unyielding bitterness to her extension of these Stalinist beliefs into an "anti-Jewish blacklisting" that included "the suppression of the true drama of Anne Frank." Even as late as her 1969 memoir, *An Unfinished Woman*, she could speak of her visit to Maidenek, the second-deadliest Nazi concentration camp, without once mentioning that most of its victims were Jews. The omission recalled the four volumes of notes she wrote during the war for *Watch on the Rhine*, in which she had mentioned Jews but twice, and then, negatively; and the journal she had kept during a trip to Russia in 1944, when tales of Stalinist persecution of Jews were dismissed by her as "Jewish shopkeepers during a pogrom rumor," as if all talk of such attacks by the Soviets could only be mere fantasy.[4]

But by now Rifkind himself had at last grown uneasy with it all. Following Meyer's renewed plea for assistance against those "who have profited in the millions from the exploitation of the Jewish Holocaust," Rifkind urged his clients to lift the ban, only to be rebuffed or ignored. "It grieves me greatly to inform you that these consents have not been forthcoming," he wrote Meyer with sincere disappointment, adding, "what has complicated the problem is that the legal rights of so many people are now involved as a result of contracts made during the last twenty-five years that it is, as a practical matter, impossible to secure the necessary consents." But if Rifkind still honored the need to be protective of his firm's clients (a number far fewer than implied in his response), a greater responsibility seemed to weigh upon him as he scornfully revealed that "the silence of some and the refusal of others renders me incapable of doing that which you have asked me to do."[5]

In the years since tossing Meyer from his office, Rifkind, too, had deepened his awareness of how the Holocaust had been exploited. In his capacity as an adviser to Eisenhower, he had reported to the United States Congress in 1946 on those "Jews who have had the courage to endure, who are determined to live as Jews, who are prepared to pioneer and share again in a Jewish civilization" in Palestine, where they, as a group, "will again contribute [their] part to world civilization," despite the utterly wretched state to which they had been abandoned by that world. "If I live to be a thousand," Rifkind had told a group of new American citizens in 1974, "I will never be able to expunge from my mind the scene of human desolation, of human wreckage, of inhuman degradation, which opened before me" in the concentration camps visited not long after Meyer had witnessed a far worse scene. "Dante's description of hell is a picture of a joyous society in comparison to the horror-strewn panorama that I beheld."[6]

Along with an awareness of Holocaust distortion and denial, Rifkind now more fully understood Stalin's tyranny. Likening it to Hitler's, he had found both to be "overwhelming threats to human liberty, to human dignity, and to the human spirit." So, too, the threat to Israel from those "quarters [where] it has become politically attractive to be anti-Israel," a position which was, at best, the beginning of a plunge down the "slippery slope toward anti-Semitism." In its place, he offered the "elevation of consciousness with respect to ethnicity . . . [as] a potential for good." As chairman of the Board of Directors of the Jewish Theological Seminary, he had once summoned those who wished to "join hands in the construction of . . . a community so that our children and grandchildren may have cause to look back upon us with pride in their ancestry and with joy in the possession of the heritage we transmit to them."[7] Only now did he realize that he and his colleagues at Paul, Weiss had inadvertently opposed those very ideas, apparently forcing him to reevaluate the past and to attempt to right a wrong that could not be corrected after a quarter of a century.

With a recent change in leadership at the American Jewish Congress, Meyer again tried in June 1978 to enlist that group's support, even as a *Commentary* article entitled "Meyer Levin's Obsessions" threatened what momentum had built up in his favor by asserting the near impossibility of separating "alleged political motives from the crass imperatives of show business" and "objective truth from . . . hallucinatory delusions."[8] In response, Meyer argued that "few understanding Jews would deny that the suppression of Anne Frank's avowal of Jewish faith, in a drama still performed very widely in the schools, is a cultural crime." Given that the very agreement he had signed barring production of his play had been drawn up by the attorney of the American Jewish Congress at the request of its former president, "I should think it would be the function of the Congress to raise this cultural issue," and its "duty . . . to protest the blacklisting of Meyer Levin." But the congress again refused, deferring to Maslow, who cited Meyer's signing of the agreement as binding.[9]

This obsessive insistence upon maintaining total control over the *Diary* would soon take an ironic turn. Bloomgarden had died in September 1976, and now, two years later, his son was seeking permission to stage a musical version of the *Diary*, based not on the Hacketts' play but upon the *Diary* itself. In "going right back to the book," Goodrich told Otto in disbelief, the young Bloomgarden had "implied . . . really said, that we (Albert and I) were ob-structionists, keeping the story of Anne and the Diary from the world. That the world had a right to Anne's story." She found it "a very unpleasant accusation." "We do not understand what he thinks. . . . The play *is* the Diary, most of it word for word."[10]

Otto was in total agreement with the Hacketts in denying Bloomgarden's son access to the *Diary*, apparently satisfied that the play was a wholly accurate portrayal of Anne's thoughts.[11] Three years later in *Newsweek*, Kanin would concur. Writing on the fiftieth anniversary of Anne's birth, he would proclaim that "on stages everywhere, Anne lives on . . . challeng[ing] humanity to use her faith . . . 'that people are good at heart.'" There would again be no reference to the Jewish element of that faith which he and the others had removed nearly a quarter of a century earlier.[12]

"As many of us know from trying experience, censorship is not always governmental but may be carried out for commercial or political motives, in ways not easily perceptible to the public," Meyer had written in his last appeal to fellow writers. In recent years, Cynthia Ozick, Grace Paley, and Lawrence Ferlinghetti had added their names to the many others who had joined Meyer's protest.[13] In renewing his long-standing support, Norman Mailer had written Meyer in April 1979 that "Lillian Hellman is a good friend of mine and an old friend, but I don't think she's right in this matter, and I want you to know that you have my support, and can use my name if you want to circulate some petition of writers to . . . whoever the producer or office [it] is that prevents you from putting on *your* Anne Frank."[14]

In November, Meyer clipped Elie Wiesel's *New York Times* report of his recent visit to Eastern Europe. There had been meetings and ceremonies to

commemorate the war's dead, but when Wiesel raised the issue of the Holocaust victims' identity as Jews, he had met with strong opposition. There were,
of course, Jewish and non-Jewish victims of the Nazis, "but the Jews were the
victims of the victims as well," he had told his Polish hosts. "They, and they
alone, were fated to total extermination not because of what they had said or
done or possessed, but because of what they were; to ignore this distinction,
this essential fact about them, is to deny them." Earlier in the journey, Wiesel
had engaged in similar discussions in Kiev concerning the Babi Yar monu-
ment. He demanded that Soviet officials "not erase the Jewishness of the
Jewish victims," for "if the Soviet line were to prevail, history would be
distorted and forgotten in one generation or two." Here was the same issue that
Meyer had raised nearly three decades earlier, with Wiesel similarly arguing
against the notion that "by speaking of Jews, we were somehow turning our
backs on the millions of non-Jews the Nazis slaughtered." "Quite the contrary," he maintained, for "as we evoke the Jewish martyrdom, we also recall
the sufferings and deaths of the non-Jewish victims. The universality of the
Holocaust must be realized in its uniqueness."[15]

Like Meyer, the response Wiesel evoked had been less than equanimous, as
"often friendly" discussions "became terse only when we asked the inevitable
question: what about the Jews?" But unlike Wiesel, Meyer would never succeed in winning the support of a major organization, Jewish or otherwise. As
late as 1977, twenty-five years after his fight had begun, Arnold Forster, legal
counsel to the Anti-Defamation League, had responded to an editorial in the
Jewish Week criticizing the ADL's lack of support for Meyer by writing him that
his case was just one among many matters that were "peripheral to our central
concern," and that in such instances, "we never adopt an official policy."[16]
Only after another three years did Meyer find a modicum of organized support
from those who could no longer ignore what one writer acknowledged as a
"campaign to steal from the Jewish victims of the Holocaust precisely that for
which they were victims—their Jewish identity."[17] By February 1980 the
scope of the issues Meyer had first raised in 1952 had become so disturbingly
obvious that Forster, acting outside of his official capacity and together with
others, organized a Committee for Cultural and Historical Honesty, whose
"general objective [was] to expose and combat the increasing efforts to downgrade and generalize away the specifically Jewish significance of the Holocaust
and other distortions and misrepresentations of the Jewish experience." The
production of Meyer's play was to be at the top of its agenda, replacing the
"eviscerated version" that stood as a "blatant example" of this attempt "to
downgrade the Holocaust . . . to a footnote in the annals of Man's inhu-
manity."[18]

Yet even this type of pressure stood little chance of loosening the ideological and financial grip clutching the property Anne had created. At the same moment that a television production of the Hacketts' play was bringing them still more revenue, they could express their concern that since "every spoken word" of a recently performed cantata by Enid Futterman had been "a quotation from the book of the *Diary*, not the play," further exposure and expansion of this successful work "might be harmful to the already established production." They were, however, of two minds; Hackett wanted to block any additional performances, but Goodrich remained inclined to allow them, unable to even "think of stopping anything that gives Anne's message" now that the previously included "shouting song about being glad to be a Jew" had been removed.[19]

Otto's continued insistence upon control had, of course, been no less ill-founded over the years. "She wrote that despite everything, she believed in the goodness of people," he had continued to maintain as her legacy. "To work for the world and for people, this is the duty I have taken over from her."[20] But by 1980, Otto had grown too ill to respond to the Hacketts' request for his thoughts on the matter. Barely a week after his ninety-first birthday, Mrs. Frank wrote that "he becomes weaker and weaker from day to day." With Otto unable to formulate an opinion of his own, his wife merely restated his earlier objection that "he cannot imagine himself and his family singing the whole sad story."

But the cantata had raised far more serious concerns, she told the Hacketts that May, apparently unaware that her reservations concerning the cantata had been raised about the play itself. "I am not sure if the message contained in the book and the play comes through. . . . It mainly gives the feelings of people in hiding for a lengthy time." The same criticism had been leveled by many critics of the Hackett play over the years, among them Alvin Rosenfeld, who had recently noted in his study of Holocaust literature, *A Double Dying*, that to use its egregious image of Anne to strip away the Jewish identity of the Holocaust's victims was "not only to profane their memories, but to exonerate their executioners."[21] Nor did the cantata clearly delineate Anne's "development from child to young woman," Mrs. Frank felt, another persistent criticism of the Hacketts' treatment. "Quite impossible," too, were the Yiddish lullabies, "as none of the Frank family knew a word of Yiddish and singing it would falsify Otto's personality."[22] (Interestingly, a critic in Zimmerman's *New York Review of Books* had spoken of Rosenfeld's study as "passionate and perceptive," but "too Jewish for his taste. The same old problem again," Rosenfeld wrote Meyer a week after Mrs. Frank's letter to the Hacketts.[23])

Although the Hacketts told Mrs. Frank that they were in "complete agreement" with her feelings about the contents of this musical adaptation, they continued to differ over whether to allow its production. Goodrich was now willing to permit its performance by "religious groups," as long as Yiddish, "so completely alien to Mr. Frank," was not used, while Hackett remained un-equivocally opposed. They would, however, await their agent's advice on "legalities." In the meantime, despite their reluctance "to trouble [her] with business at this time," they were happy to report that their play had been transferred to the television screen "just as it has been played all these years . . . [with] no changes," though "we haven't got the money yet!"[24]

While the Hacketts' play continued to have success and others seeking to render new perspectives on the *Diary* were routinely dismissed, Meyer persisted in his efforts to present his script. Repeated failures, by letter, petition, and public statement, appeared to leave Meyer only one avenue for redress, a court-ordered nullification of the agreement that he had signed. His new attorneys, however, advised against taking this step. Even the affidavits from Katsh and Angoff were not likely to help, Shale Stiller assured him. "The fact that the Assignment [of copyright] was executed over twenty years ago and that no suits have been filed to attack the validity of the Assignment in that twenty year period will make a difficult case even more difficult." Instead, "the more fruitful approach" was to once again ask Rifkind to intercede. The chief litigator at Paul, Weiss had been a law school classmate of Stiller's at Yale. With Meyer's consent, Stiller would approach him as a means of access to Rifkind, arguing that those still alive had nothing further to gain by continuing to ban Meyer's play, while Meyer himself sought no financial return from its performance. "Most importantly," Stiller intended to assert, "it has only been in the last few years that the phenomenon of down-playing the Jewish role in the Holocaust has become a major problem." Since "the Hackett version falls right into this propaganda attack . . . Rifkind and everyone else who is involved with this should be appealed to on the basis of not permitting . . . rewrites of history to distort the record in so blatant a way."[25]

Meyer remained doubtful of his confident attorney's success, believing instead that Rifkind would merely advise him "to wait a bit longer," which Meyer could not do. With the years now running down, Meyer continued to argue for a new lawsuit, if only for the purpose of having "a public airing of the issue," even if the case could not be won. "It is more important to raise the issue as a clear textual demonstration of the Stalinist based and persistent campaign to dilute the Holocaust," he insisted. But Stiller retorted that such a "Pyrrhic victory" might just as easily be counterproductive. The loss would allow the public to "readily conclude that everything you were saying about a Stalinist campaign and about dilution of the Holocaust was as invalid as the lawsuit." Instead, he again advocated an "audience with Judge Rifkind," arranged by his former classmate, in which he would "pursue the effort . . . on the basis of his performing a mitzvah [good deed] for the memory of the 6,000,000 dead souls."

At the same time, he encouraged Meyer to seek out as many groups as he could find to perform his play. "I doubt that Otto Frank will want to institute any lawsuits," Stiller concluded on August 19, unaware that Otto was to die that evening.[26]

The obituary that appeared in *Jewish Week* on August 31 unexpectedly spoke of Otto's support for those who had eliminated "Anne's poetic tribute to Judaism . . . replacing it . . . with a univeralistic observation . . . denigrating [to] the importance of Jewish experience."[27] Accompanying this less than one-quarter-page coverage of Otto's life and death were four pages devoted to Meyer and his struggle to correct this omission, a tribute to him on the occasion of his upcoming seventy-fifth birthday. Half of this space was given over to Meyer to allow him to tell his own story, while the remainder was divided between an account of his career as a Jewish writer and a sharp criticism of Meyer's abandonment by the leadership of American Jewry.[28]

"The 'universalization' of the Holocaust is no minor issue in Jewish life," Philip Hockstein reminded those who had largely ignored this effort to de-Judaize the Holocaust. "If the Jewish people do not remember and if the world does not remember that the Holocaust was a climax to many centuries of anti-Semitism, the Six Million will have died in vain and all peoples, Jews of course at the top of the list, will again be in danger of genocide." The widening movement to portray this murderous act as merely "part of a nationalistic madman's elimination of all people who stood in his way" was political in nature and intent upon "lulling a threatened Jewish people and a threatened humanity." Among the immediate victims in the *Diary* case, Hockstein underlined, were "the insightful young Jewish girl who could not protest because she had gone up in smoke in one of Hitler's chimneys" and Meyer, who had been abandoned by American Jewish leaders who had "washed their hands of their moral responsibility by accepting the charges of Levin's enemies." It was now long past the time when "those Jewish leaders who have made only the weakest efforts . . . and those who have run away from the issue entirely should hasten to redeem themselves and organize their forces for a truly significant battle on behalf of a Jewish future."[29]

Reprinted for distribution in the thousands, these four pages would be used by Meyer as he redoubled his effort in this final year of his campaign to have Anne's true voice heard.[30] Yet the ban could not be broken, as the American Jewish Theatre learned when it attempted to stage a seventy-fifth birthday performance of his play at New York's 92d Street YM-YWHA that October. Still, there was comfort to be taken that day from a press release entitled "Meyer Levin's Summation at Seventy-Five": "Since the furor over Vanessa Redgrave in 'Playing for Time,'" it read, "there is better understanding of Levin's long one man fight against the 'Lillian Hellman Crowd' that gained control of the stage rights to the Diary." Fania Fenelon, the author of the memoir upon which the play of the same name was based, had similarly lost control of her work through a contractual oversight. As a survivor of the Auschwitz women's orchestra whom Redgrave was to portray in the play by Hellman's friend Arthur Miller, she had outspokenly objected to this choice because of Redgrave's vocal support of the Palestine Liberation Organization, which had denigrated the Holocaust and vowed to destroy Israel.[31] Meyer was, of course, not surprised at Fenelon's failure to be heeded, for as he had tried to explain while visiting her in Paris, those who "slant the material their way . . . exploiting the Jewish Holocaust experience . . . [were] eager to generalize that experience, to minimize the particular nature of the genocidal attack on the Jews," while "reaping large financial gains from [these] Holocaust exploitations."[32]

Meyer received numerous public acknowledgments of his accomplishments that October 8, highlighted by the awarding of the Maurice Stiller Prize at Baltimore Hebrew College for a lifetime of "literary achievement in Jewish belles lettres." But the recognition had clearly come at great personal cost. As a reporter wrote of Meyer after the ceremony, "Still formidable looking at 75, a hint of the old Chicago neighborhood evident in his laugh and his overall look of wariness . . . the old fire burning in his blue eyes . . . his battered bag in hand, a light bend to his back, he departed with a friendly Shalom, as ready as ever to pitch into those who would decline to face the truth."[33]

"Next month you'll be 75 years old," Tereska had told him some weeks earlier. "You still have a few years that could be saved. You can choose to save these few years for peace of sorts, for whatever happiness is available, or you can continue your own total destruction," by which she meant, as well, their relationship and his relationship with his children, all of which had continued to suffer by his pursuit. "How can you feel anything for me when you have taken out your heart and thrown it into the night," she had asked in desperation, trying to communicate her anger and sadness "for the hundredth hopeless time?"[34]

Her cry was clearly legitimate—the opposition would not be moved. "No need to think further on it," the Hacketts had written Otto's widow upon receiving one of Meyer's pamphlets that November.[35] They had no intention of ever releasing their tight hold over the *Diary*. Nor had Mrs. Frank, who, in a letter discussing yet another proposal for an opera, had agreed with the Hacketts "that you and I would absolutely want the right of approval should it come to a contract."[36] These were issues, of course, not only of content but of property.

Yet Meyer remained as unwilling as ever to abandon his insistence upon

the truth, however obsessively destructive it had become. In answering Tereska's pain-filled letter, the latest in a stream that stretched back over more
than twenty years, he spoke of the moral imperative that drove him, and of
how the need to pursue this matter had been so much more than a drive for
personal revenge over the loss of his play:

> At the beginning I of course did feel deeply hurt at a work that had been killed,
> but from the beginning as you know I already suspected the ideological and
> political structure of the whole affair. It took a long time to put together the
> pieces but it has by now for years been perfectly clear that I had been, and am,
> up against the basic issue of dogmatic Stalinist anti-Semitism. This is an issue
> that I would feel obligated to fight against in any example, and there is no way
> for me to turn from the fight just because the thing happened personally to me.
> The play long ago ceased to be a personal issue except in minor aspects, related
> to plagiarism by those dolts. . . . By now, quite a few serious persons, and out of
> no personal concern for me, see that what I saw so much earlier has proven to
> be the case. The campaign to denigrate the Holocaust has virtually succeeded,
> and as you know over the same misleading slogan about all people suffering.
> What was left out was not merely "a page" but the key statement about Jews
> and the Holocaust, purposively omitted, with the Stalinist slogan falsely inser-
> ted in its place. The omitted statement is the most quoted passage from the
> Diary, not merely a page. Nor, by being engaged on this issue, do I feel I am
> destroying myself. I have managed through all the years to produce my work, a
> body of work as extensive as that of almost any of my contemporaries. Whether
> it might have been better had I not at the same time been involved in this
> subterranean ideological fight, I cannot know. But such things are not volun-
> tarily shut off. . . . The falsification . . . is right at the application point of fas-
> cism and all authoritarian rule, and I would have no self respect if I had kept
> silent on it.[37]

In late December, Meyer asked the famed Nazi hunter Simon Wiesenthal
to "secure access" for him to Otto's files, believing they "would show how
Stalinism took over some of the anti-Jewish cultural role from Nazism." Soliciting Wiesenthal's assistance in his attempt to "expose this prejudice," Meyer
spoke of "the persistent and growing interest of the Jewish community in this
adamant manipulation of Anne Frank," particularly "in connection with the
entire picture of the Holocaust aftermath."[38] But like so many before him,
Wiesenthal chose to ignore Meyer's plea.

On May 27, 1981, the Jewish Academy of Arts and Sciences presented
Meyer with the first Joseph Handelman Award. In his comments that day,
Abraham Katsh, president of the academy, noted that "the body of Levin's
work contains some of the most authentic writing on Jewish life."[39] When

Meyer rose to accept the honor, he stepped forward to share what he had begun two years earlier, on the fiftieth anniversary of Anne's birth, as "a chain letter to persons who care about cultural freedom." He had asked those receiving it to copy and distribute it further, so that they, too, "will feel that there is still, in our world, an ethical linkage, through acts of this kind, that should not be broken."[40] Expanded and completed on Holocaust Remembrance Day, and in accordance with the centuries-old Jewish tradition of passing on to future generations the moral lessons of a lifetime, "My Ethical Will As to Authorship" now reflected upon what he saw as a state of "general moral decline in an era of massive slaughter."

In the world of writing, this decline "has its own evils," he stressed. "Today, as we all sorrowfully know, some of the world's most powerful states enforce conformity," demanding falsification under pain of imprisonment or worse for those writers who would not compromise their "innate authorial ethic. . . . Yet we must take into account another terrifying source of ethical erosion, that of the convinced, even fanatic ideologist who places dogma above truth, and will deliberately falsify, in the name of 'idealism.'" It was essential that the public have "a heightened awareness" of this development, no less than his fellow writers, for incumbent on all was the commandment, "Thou Shalt Not Suppress, nor Countenance Suppression." While Americans commonly regarded censorship as governmental in origin, Meyer stressed how "significant interference with freedom of expression is increasingly attempted in political and ideological spheres, and may be carried out by various forms of groups using power, intrigue, and conspiracy," as he himself had "long experienced" in his "twenty-nine year struggle."[41]

"The issue is not mine alone," he emphasized, "but everyone's as the example [of Anne's Diary] involves a Jewish work of universal importance." Nor was there a "time limit on fighting injustice. Not even mortality." He would use "this generous award" to pay for reprinting and distributing his adaptation of the Diary, "for in sum this is not my case but symbolically and literally the case of the young gifted authoress, Anne Frank, just as her life was the symbol of the lives of six millions." The continuing silence, imposed a second time by the "success [which] blinds the public to every moral imperative in art," had endowed this "grave example . . . with a double-suppression" that had to be overturned. "In the name of Anne Frank, her sister and mother and the millions more murdered Jews of the Holocaust, I call for a renewal of ethical human behavior, in all life, beginning in our most sensitive area, the arts."

Meyer's final words on the Diary were printed two months later as a memorial following his death on July 9.[42] Tributes poured in from around the world, none more compelling than the messages of grief of two younger writers whom he had befriended years earlier. "He shouted, he demanded bitterly that I help him mobilize writers in Israel for support over the great play *Anne Frank*," Aharon Megged recalled in the *Jerusalem Post*. "He was, it seems to me, like a wounded animal with the arrow still in his flesh: bristling with pain yet primed for battle." The ban on his play had "so incensed him that it destroyed his peace of mind. . . . [Yet], when I knew him better, I saw that this obsession . . . was not necessarily focused on the redemption of his personal honour. Rather, it was the kind of obsession that disturbed the tranquility of the prophet, the mad spiritualist who couldn't witness injustice and remain silent, who couldn't contain the fire in his bones, who was lashed by the whip of 'justice, justice, thou shalt pursue.'"[43] (Meyer would not have disagreed. In an unpublished essay from 1949, he had written that "the function of the writer in modern times is somewhat akin to the ancient Hebrew prophet."[44]) He was, in this sense, "a 'romantic' of the past," Megged stressed, "someone who believed in noble values and in the ceaseless war to defend them."[45] Meyer had "fought a hard fight . . . for the recognition generally of the suppression of Jewish writers," Myron Kaufmann added privately as he tried to console Tereska for her double loss. "I trust that that fight is not over, and that it will still be won."[46]

A year later, the *New Republic* became the first general mass publication to champion Meyer's struggle, raising once more the "basic questions about the true authorship of the Pulitzer Prize–winning play." "Why has there been so little clarification of the issues?" Stephen Fife asked in an article subtitled "A Note on Plagiarism," having concluded "after studying the two diary scripts and comparing them with Anne Frank's book . . . that Levin has a strong case."[47] (Meyer had, in fact, brought this matter to the attention of the prize committee the previous year, only to have it dismissed as a quarrel "not with us" but with "the authors and producers."[48]) Worse still, Fife maintained, was the Hacketts' violation of "the playwright's duty to the original material, changing the diary from a specifically Jewish document to something else, which the Broadway producers called 'universal.'" Yet for this, Otto alone was to blame, for without his compliance, the Hacketts could not have "sacrificed an aspect of his daughter's spirit which was very much a part of the diary, and which persisted in asking the question: 'Why the Jews? Why always the Jews?'" Should Meyer's play have been banned when "it was this side of Anne" that he had seen as "his own 'true task,' his own 'true destiny'" to portray? "Why shouldn't there be more than one interpretation of Anne Frank's diary," Fife demanded?

Meyer's play had its first professional theatrical production the following year, on Boston's Lyric Stage, and it was revived there in 1991.[49] But it could not counter the widely accepted distortion begun so many years before. In

1986, *McCall's* again spoke of Anne as "not only a symbol of the Holocaust, but, more important, a symbol of human hope."[50] And when Hackett died in 1995, eleven years after Goodrich and Hellman, his quarter-page obituary in the *New York Times* opened with a discussion of the Pulitzer Prize he had won for *The Diary of Anne Frank* and ended with the telltale reference to the goodness of the human heart, without ever mentioning Meyer's dispute and the issues it encompassed.[51] Nor did John Blair, the creator of the documentary film *Anne Frank Remembered*. "There are many who feel that the Holocaust was a uniquely Jewish experience and that Anne's story should be about the genocide of the Jews specifically," he told a *New York Times* critic in 1996. "I don't agree. I have firmly hooked my flag to Otto's universalist message," as had the group planning to return the Hacketts' play to Broadway in fall 1997.[52]

"Levin was not the victim of a conspiracy," Lawrence Graver had confidently asserted in his 1995 study of *An Obsession with Anne Frank*. Nor was Hellman "involved in an elaborate intrigue to sabotage his play," according to Graver's analysis. Rather, Meyer was simply "impaired by the opposition and mockery of those who did not respect his beliefs about Jewishness and his opposition to Russian Communism." But because Graver had failed to carefully study much of the extant documentation, he erroneously concluded that Hellman's HUAC appearance and her rejection of all that Meyer held dear had simply fed into his psychological instability, making her "a ripe candidate for 'villain' in Levin's tempestuous response to his misfortunes" and the central character in "one of Levin's most engrossing . . . stories, a story he in part created."[53]

Similarly unfamiliar with this documentation, several noted critics then helped to perpetuate the attack upon Levin by supporting Graver's ill-founded thesis.[54] How ironic for Graver to lay this charge against Levin, and for others to support it, when several years earlier, Elia Kazan had written of Hellman's reaction to his HUAC testimony, "I believe now that she wanted me to become the 'villain' I became. Life was easier for Lillian to understand when she had someone to hate, just as her plays were easier for her to construct when she had a 'heavy' to nail." And how disappointing that Graver would further fail to heed Kazan's confession concerning his and Hellman's awareness of the deaths of hundreds of thousands of Jews in Stalin's labor camps in the years after the war. "Lillian did know—hell, we all knew, and some even thought it justified."[55]

Only the critic of Blair's cinematic portrayal noted that "the diary was given a spin to make its particularity seem less important," thereby "highlighting an idealism that could never have survived the camps." It was this "aspect of Otto Frank's presentation of the diary and the play based upon it that riled the writer Meyer Levin," he boldly acknowledged amid the generally unquestioning applause crowned by an Academy Award.[56]

A newly translated edition of the *Diary* appeared in 1995, with much of the material removed by Otto restored. "The *Diary*, now 50 years old, remains astonishing and excruciating. It gnaws at us still," a *New York Times* critic commented in an unprecedented second front-page review.[57] An immediate best-seller despite the millions of copies previously sold worldwide, its crushing reality may yet give Anne back her true voice—and a new hearing to Meyer's struggle to preserve it against the force of Holocaust revisionism.

"My effort has been not only to encompass an obsession, but to resist suppression, overt or hidden," he had declared in the midst of his struggle.[58] Shortly before his death, Meyer argued for the last time that while "no one denies that all people have suffered . . . the Final Solution was not a common fate. A new word, genocide, had to be found for this mechanized mass murder that included the hunting down for destruction even of infants confided to non-Jews. Generalizing away the particular Jewish doom falsifies the Holocaust and opens the way for today's campaign of denials. It weakens the warning against genocidal methods that could indeed be directed at other peoples, or again at the Jews."[59]

But if there is reason to hope for a reassessment, there is greater reason to believe that the falsely crafted, ideologically determined image of an adolescent, stripped of her Jewish identity, naïvely proclaiming on stage and screen a simplistic and unwavering belief in the goodness of people, will remain fixed and unchallenged, denying the reality of the Holocaust—both the enormity of its evil and the very specificity with which those targeted for slaughter were hunted down and murdered. Even those who read the new *Diary* will not be free of this popularized image. How sad and frightening that Anne's voice has been so indelibly glossed and the horror of her last years, representative of the torturous end suffered by millions of other Jews, so terribly cleansed. The young woman whose deepening maturity allowed her to see the cruelty perpetrated upon her people as the fulfillment of an age-old hatred, however freighted with universal implications, remains hidden behind the mask imposed upon her, still awaiting discovery.

Notes

Archival Collections

Bloomgarden	Kermit Bloomgarden (Wisconsin State Historical Society)
Crawford	Cheryl Crawford (University of Houston)
Frank	Otto Frank (Anne Frank Stichting [Amsterdam])
Hackett	Frances and Albert Hackett (Wisconsin State Historical Society)
Hellman	Lillian Hellman (University of Texas)
Kanin	Garson Kanin (Library of Congress)
Levin	Meyer Levin (Boston University)
McCullers	Carson McCullers (University of Texas)
Melnick	Ralph Melnick (author's files)
Salisbury	Leah Salisbury (Columbia University)
Shumlin	Herman Shumlin (Wisconsin State Historical Society)

Correspondents

AF	Anne Frank
AH	Albert Hackett
BZ	Barbara Zimmerman
CC	Cheryl Crawford
CM	Carson McCullers
EC	Edward Costikyan
ER	Eleanor Roosevelt
FAH	Frances and Albert Hackett
FG	Frances Goodrich (Hackett)
FP	Francis Price
GK	Garson Kanin
HS	Herman Shumlin
KB	Kermit Bloomgarden

LH   Lillian Hellman
LS   Leah Salisbury
ML   Meyer Levin
MM   Myer Mermin
OF   Otto Frank
RM   Ralph Melnick
SF   Samuel Fredman
TL   Tereska Levin

Preface

1. ML to RM, 26 May 1979, Melnick.
2. ML to the Editor, *Jerusalem Post*, 5 March 1980, clipping, Levin.
3. ML to RM, 7 April 1979, Melnick.
4. ML to RM, 4 May 1979, Melnick.
5. ML to RM, 25 May 1979, Melnick.
6. ML to RM, 24 July 1979, Melnick.
7. ML to Isaac Imber, 10 December 1979, Melnick.
8. OF to ML, 8 January 1953, Levin.
9. OF to ML, 9 January 1953, Levin.
10. OF to ML, 28 June 1953, Levin; ML to RM, 26 May 1979, Melnick.
11. Tereska Torres, *Les Maisons Hantées de Meyer Levin* (Paris: Éditions Denoël, 1991).
12. ML to RM, 25 March 1980, Melnick.
13. David Barnouw, "Attacks on the Authenticity of the Diary," in AF, *The Diary of Anne Frank: The Critical Edition* (New York: Doubleday, 1989), 84.
14. David Barnouw, "The Play," ibid., 82.
15. Ruth Wisse, "A Romance of the Secret Annex," *New York Times* (2 July 1989).

Chapter 1. With My Own Eyes

1. ML, *In Love*, unpublished memoir, ms., 94, Eli Levin. Levin also reported from Buchenwald, Dachau, Nordhausen, and Ohrdruf.
2. ML, *In Search* (Paris: Author's Press, 1950), 291.
3. Thomas Mann to ML, 22 September 1950, Levin.
4. ML, *In Search*, 293.
5. ML, "Death Factory at Buchenwald Horrible Beyond Description," *Watertown Times* (2 May 1945), clipping, Levin.
6. ML, "Survivor's Guilt," ms., 7–8, Levin.
7. ML, *My Father's House* (New York: Viking, 1947), 92.
8. ML, *The Obsession* (New York: Simon and Schuster, 1973), 34–35.
9. ML to Messrs. Calmann Levy, 8 September 1950, Frank.
10. ML, *The Obsession*, 35, 7.
11. OF to ML, 19 September 1950, Frank.
12. ML to OF, 21 September 1950, Levin.
13. OF to ML, 25 September 1950, Frank.
14. Contract between OF and Ernest Kuhn, [1947], Frank; Ernst Kuhn to OF, 29 April 1949, Frank.
15. OF to ML, 25 September 1950, Frank.
16. ML to OF, 26 September 1950, Levin.
17. OF to ML, 29 and 26 September 1950, Frank.
18. OF to ML, 6 October 1950, Frank.

19. ML to OF, 6 October 1950, Levin.

20. OF to ML, 9 October 1950, Frank.

21. ML to OF, 15 October 1950, Levin.

22. ML to OF, 26 October 1950, Levin; OF to ML, 30 October 1950, Frank; ML to OF, 9 November 1950, Levin.

23. ML, "The Restricted Market," *Congress Weekly* (13 November 1950): 8–9.

24. OF to ML, 18 November 1950, Frank.

25. OF to Nathan Straus, 22 November 1950, Frank.

26. Janet Flanner, "Letter from Paris," *New Yorker* 27 (11 November 1950): 126.

27. OF to ML, 23, 24, and 29 November 1950, Frank; OF to Little, Brown, 27 November 1950, Levin.

28. ML to OF, 27 November 1950, Levin.

29. Ibid.

30. OF to ML, 18 and 24 November 1950, Frank.

31. ML to OF, 27 November 1950, Levin.

32. OF to ML, 29 November 1950, Frank.

33. OF to ML, 10 December 1950, Frank; ML to OF, 29 December 1950, Frank.

34. ML to OF, 29 December 1950, Levin; OF to ML, 11 January 1951, Frank.

35. OF to ML, 11 January 1951, Frank.

36. FP to OF, 14 March 1951, Frank.

37. FP to the Editor, *New York Times Book Review* [1972], clipping, Levin. Zimmerman and her husband, Jacob Epstein, had during the intervening years become powerful literary figures as editors of the *New York Review of Books*.

38. Ned Bradford to OF, 16 March 1951, Frank.

39. OF to FP, 21 March 1951, Frank.

40. AF, *The Diary of Anne Frank: The Critical Edition* (New York: Doubleday, 1989), 474, 526.

41. OF, *The [London] Times* (16 April 1977); Fritzi Frank, "Postcript," in Eva Schloss, *Eva's Story* (New York: St. Martin's, 1988), 222; Jane Pratt, "The Anne Frank We Remember," *McCall's* 113 (January 1986): 110.

42. AF, *Diary of Anne Frank: The Critical Edition*; quotations from, respectively, 266, 307, 237, 478, 518.

43. OF, *Israelitisches Wochen Blat* (16 February 1979), quoted in Alex Grobman, *Anne Frank in Historical Perspective* (Los Angeles: Martyrs Memorial and Museum of the Holocaust, 1995), 14.

44. FP to OF, 22 March 1951, Frank.

45. OF to Little, Brown, 27 March 1951, Frank.

46. OF, "Chronology," 30 March 1951, Frank.

47. OF to Clairouin, 3 April 1951, Frank.

48. Madame R. Tschebeko to OF, 6 and 27 April 1951, Frank.

49. FP to OF, 9 April 1951, Frank.

50. OF to Ned Bradford, 18 April 1951, Frank.

51. OF to [?] Warsaw, 27 April 1951, Frank.

52. OF to Nathan Straus, 11 August 1950, Frank.

53. OF to FP, 15 May 1951; FP to OF, 17 May 1951, Frank.

54. OF to Madame R. Tschebeko, 9 and 25 May 1951, Frank.

55. FP to OF, 9 April 1951, Frank.

56. ML to OF, 30 April 1951, Levin.

57. OF to ML, 5 May 1951, Levin.

58. ML to OF, 12 May 1951, Levin.

59. TL to OF, 9 September 1950; OF to ML, 17 May 1951, Frank.

Chapter 2. A Real Story of Jews Under Nazism

1. OF to ML, 21 September 1951, Frank.
2. OF to Donald Elder, 24 September 1951, Frank.
3. FP to OF, 2 October 1951, Frank.
4. OF, "Chronology," 5 October 1951, Frank.
5. BZ to OF, 17 October 1951; OF to BZ, 21 October 1951, Frank.
6. ML to Hanoch Bartov, [1973], Levin.
7. BZ to OF, 26 October 1951, Frank.
8. OF to BZ, 2 November 1951, Frank; BZ to OF, 5 November 1951, Frank.
9. Philip Nobile, *Intellectual Skywriting: Literary Politics and the New York Review of Books* (New York: Charterhouse, 1974), 108.
10. Jon Blair, *Anne Frank Remembered* (Sony Pictures Classics, 1995).
11. OF to BZ, ca. 1 January 1952, Frank.
12. BZ to OF, 4 February 1952, Frank.
13. BZ to OF, 11 February 1952, Frank.
14. ML, interview, 1979; Lawrence Graver, *An Obsession with Anne Frank* (Berkeley: University of California Press, 1995), 24.
15. OF to BZ, 12 February 1952, Frank.
16. BZ to OF, 15 February 1952, Frank; OF to BZ, 20 February 1952, Frank.
17. BZ to OF, 12 March 1952, Frank.
18. OF to ML, 6 March 1952, Levin.
19. ML to OF, 10 March 1942, Levin.
20. ML to OF, 14 March 1952, Levin.
21. OF to ML, 18 March 1952, Frank.
22. ML to OF, 23 March 1955, Levin.
23. OF to ML, 31 March 1945, Frank.
24. ML to OF, 28 March 1952, Levin; ML to Darryl Zanuck, 24 March 1952, Levin.
25. ML to OF, 28 March 1952, Levin.
26. OF to ML, 31 March 1952, Frank.
27. ML to OF, April 1952, Levin.
28. Ibid.
29. ML to Howard Phillips, 28 April 1952, Levin.
30. Thomas Orchard to ML, 9 June 1952, Levin.
31. *Variety* (18 June 1952), clipping, Frank.
32. OF to ML, 9 June 1952, Levin.
33. BZ to OF, 12 June 1952, Frank.
34. ML, "The Child Behind the Secret Door," *New York Times Book Review* (15 June 1952): 1–2.
35. ML, "A Classic Human Document," *Congress Weekly* (16 June 1952), clipping, Levin; Ludwig Lewisohn, "A Glory and a Doom," *Saturday Review of Literature* (19 July 1952): 20. The passage cited appears in a slightly different translation in AF, *The Diary of Anne Frank: The Critical Edition* (New York: Doubleday, 1989), 600.
36. BZ and ML to OF, 16 June 1952, Frank.
37. ML to OF, 16 June 1952, Levin.
38. ML to OF, 16 June 1952, Levin.
39. ML to Edmund Goulding, 16 June 1952, Levin.
40. ML, Deposition, ML v. OF and KB, 28 July 1957, 58, Levin.
41. ML to OF, 16 June 1952, Levin.
42. OF to Doubleday, 18 June 1952, Frank.
43. OF to ML, 19 June 1952, Frank.

44. BZ to OF, 17 June 1952, Frank.

45. BZ to FP, 17 June 1952, quoted in Graver, 24.

46. ML, Deposition, 65–66.

47. OF to BZ, 19 June 1952, Frank.

48. ML to OF, 19 June 1952, Levin.

49. TL to OF, 19 June 1952, Frank.

50. TL to OF, 23 June 1952, Frank.

51. BZ to OF, 23 June 1952, Frank.

52. ML to OF, 23 June 1952, Frank.

53. ML to OF, 23 June 1952, Frank.

54. ML, Deposition, 71–72.

55. ML to OF, 23 June 1952, Levin.

56. ML to OF, 24 June 1952, Levin.

57. OF to ML, 26 June 1952, Frank.

58. ML to OF, 8 July 1952 (cable and letter), Frank (a draft of this letter appears as ML to OF, 7 July 1952, Levin).

59. ML, Deposition, 71–72.

60. Reader's Report on ML, *Dupont Circle*, 23 August 1943, Salisbury.

61. ML to OF, 26 June 1952, Levin.

62. ML to OF, 27 June 1952, Levin.

63. TL to OF, 28 June 1952, Frank.

64. OF to ML, 28 June 1952, Frank.

65. OF to ML, 30 June 1952, Frank.

66. ML, "At Long Last We Have a Real Story of Jews Under Nazism," *Jewish National Post* (30 June 1952), clipping, Levin.

Chapter 3. A Particularly Powerful Force Against Bigotry

1. "Busy Bids on 'Frank,'" *Variety* (2 July 1952), clipping, Frank.

2. ML to OF, 2 July 1952, Levin.

3. OF to ML, 2 July 1952, Levin.

4. ML to OF, 3 July 1952, Levin; ML, Deposition, 77; CC to Marc Blitzstein, 25 June 1952, Crawford.

5. ML to OF, 8 July 1952, Levin.

6. CC, *One Naked Individual* (Indianapolis: Bobbs-Merrill, 1977), 203. For discussions of the portrayal of anti-Semitism and the Holocaust in American film, see Ilan Avisar, *Screening the Holocaust: Cinema's Images of the Unimaginable* (Bloomington: Indiana University Press, 1988); Lester D. Friedman, *Hollywood's Image of the Jew* (New York: Frederick Ungar, 1982); Annette Insdorf, *Indelible Shadows: Film and the Holocaust*, 2d ed. (New York: Cambridge University Press, 1990).

7. LH, "Statement," 14 April 1952; LH to John Wood, 19 May 1952; LH to Ruth Shipley, 5 February 1953, all in Joseph Rauh Papers, Library of Congress; Griffen Fariello, *Red Scare: Memories of the American Inquisition* (New York: W. W. Norton, 1995), 338–339.

8. Joan Mellen, *Hellman and Hammett: The Legendary Passion of Lillian Hellman and Dashiell Hammett* (New York: HarperCollins, 1996), 389, 427, 307.

9. LH, *Scoundrel Time* (Boston: Little, Brown, 1976), 133.

10. Norman Podhoretz, *Making It* (New York: Random House, 1967), 291.

11. Quoted in Sally Jacobs, "The Indomitable Diane Trilling," *Boston Globe* (20 September 1995): 55.

12. LH to BZ, 18 November 1980, Hellman.

13. CC, *One Naked Individual*, 69, 73–75, 76, 255. On Kazan's ambivalence over testifying, cf. Michel Ciment, *Kazan on Kazan* (New York: Viking, 1974), 83–85. Crawford was subpoenaed

by HUAC in 1957 but was spared when the committee unexpectedly ceased its inquisition (254–256).

14. ML, *New York Herald Tribune* (28 December 1948), clipping, Levin.

15. ML, "Writer Clarifies Controversy Over Jewish General," circular, [1950], Levin.

16. LH, *Conversations with Lillian Hellman*, Jackson Bryer, ed. (Jackson: University Press of Mississippi, 1986), 291.

17. For a detailed treatment of Stalin's anti-Semitism, based upon newly opened Soviet archives, see Gennadi Kostyrchenko, *Out of the Red Shadows: Anti-Semitism in Stalin's Russia* (Amherst, N.Y.: Prometheus, 1995).

18. Theodore Freedman, ed., *Antisemitism in the Soviet Union: Its Roots and Consequences* (New York: Anti-Defamation League, 1984), 518–522.

19. Ibid., 522–524.

20. Kostyrchenko, *Out of the Red Shadows*, 177.

21. Ibid., 193–194, 217.

22. Yakov Rapoport, *The Doctors' Plot of 1953* (Cambridge: Harvard University Press, 1991), 79.

23. Louis Rapoport, *Stalin's War Against the Jews* (New York: Free Press, 1990), 186–187.

24. LH to John Fistere, 23 January 1964, Hellman.

25. LH, "The Hand That Holds the Legend of Our Lives," *Ladies Home Journal* (April 1964): 57, 122–124.

26. Carl Rollyson, *Lillian Hellman: Her Legend and Her Legacy* (New York: St. Martin's, 1988), 485–488; Mellen, *Hellman and Hammett*, 142.

27. Mellen, *Hellman and Hammett*, 167, 170, 305, 317, 318, 421, 423.

28. Quoted in William Wright, *Lillian Hellman* (New York: Simon and Schuster, 1986), 488.

29. Frank E. Manuel, *A Requiem for Karl Marx* (Cambridge: Harvard University Press, 1995), quoted in *Chronicle of Higher Education* (22 September 1995): A15.

30. V. I. Lenin, *Lenin on the Jewish Question* (New York: International Publishers, 1974), 107–111.

31. Ralph Parker, "Moscow: No Hatred for Jews" (London) *Daily Worker* (15 January 1953): 1.

32. Louis Harap, "The Truth About the Prague Trial" (New York) *Daily Worker* (26 January 1953): 4.

33. A. B. Magil, "Wall Street, Zionism, and Anti-Semitism," *Masses and Mainstream* 6 (March 1953): 24.

34. Samuel Sillen, "Art as a Weapon" (New York) *Daily Worker* (13 February 1946): 6.

35. Janet Flanner, "Letters from Paris," *New Yorker* 27 (10 November 1950): 127–128.

36. "Preface for Today," *Masses and Mainstream* 1 (March 1948): 3.

37. Rollyson, *Lillian Hellman*, 352.

38. John Howard Lawson, "Chekhov's Drama: Challenge to Playwrights," *Masses and Mainstream* 7 (October 1954): 26.

39. "American Message," *Masses and Mainstream* 1 (May 1948): 4.

40. Samuel Sillen, "Stalin and Culture: The Fulfillment of Man," *Masses and Mainstream* 6 (April 1953): 2.

41. Howard Fast, *Being Red* (Garden City, N.Y.: Doubleday, 1990), 270–274.

42. ML, "Playwriting and Protest," unidentified article, [1931], Levin.

43. Ben Mark, "May Day in the Warsaw Ghetto," *Masses and Mainstream* 6 (May 1953): 42.

44. Naomi Replansky, "The Six Million," *Masses and Mainstream* 4 (November 1951): 23.

45. "Lillian Hellman Defies Un-Americans' Witchhunt" (New York) *Daily Worker* (22 May 1952): 3; "Banned, Branded, Burned," *Masses and Mainstream* 6 (August 1953): 12.

46. Wright, *Lillian Hellman*, 133. For Hellman's claim to apolitical status, see Rollyson, *Lillian Hellman*, 373.

47. LH, *Three* (Boston: Little, Brown, 1979), 2–3; Wright, *Lillian Hellman*, 319; Mellen, *Hellman and Hammett*, 113, 122, 126, 129, 432, 442.

48. Robert P. Newman, *The Cold War Romance of Lillian Hellman and John Melby* (Chapel Hill: University of North Carolina Press, 1989), 178.

49. LH, *The North Star* (New York: Viking, 1943), 118, 34, 23.

50. Mellen, *Hellman and Hammett*, 163; quotation from LH, *Conversations*, 7, 9.

51. Mellen, *Hellman and Hammett*, 103.

52. Rollyson, *Lillian Hellman*, 336.

53. LH, *Maybe* (Boston: Little, Brown, 1980), 50–51.

54. Quoted in Geoffrey Ward, "Making Up the Truth," *American Heritage* 38 (September–October 1987): 18.

55. Wright, *Lillian Hellman*, 109.

56. Michiko Kakutani, "Hellman-McCarthy Libel Suit Stirs Old Antagonisms," *New York Times* (19 March 1980).

57. Gore Vidal, "Book Sales, Prizes, Tenure, and Riotous Times at Bread Loaf," *At Random* (Fall 1995): 43.

58. LH, *Conversations*, 25, 57, 96; Mellen, *Hellman and Hammett*, 66–68.

59. LH, *Conversations*, 41, 87.

60. Murray Shumach, "Shaping a New Joan," *New York Times* (ca. 15 November 1955), clipping, Levin.

61. Mellen, *Hellman and Hammett*, 315.

62. LH, *Scoundrel Time*, 40–41; LH, ms. of *Scoundrel Time*, Hellman.

63. LH, *Conversations*, 196.

64. On Kazan and *Camino Real*, see Louis Calta, "Principals Get Set for 'Camino Real,'" *New York Times* (13 November 1952), clipping, Frank.

65. Victor Navasky, *Naming Names* (New York: Viking, 1980), 244.

66. William Phillips, *A Partisan View: Five Decades of the Literary Life* (New York: Stein and Day, 1983), 174.

67. Benjamin Gitlow, *I Confess: The Truth About American Communism* (New York: E. P. Dutton, 1940), 400.

68. ML to OF, 8 July 1952, Levin.

69. OF to ML, 8 July 1952, Frank.

70. CC to OF, 9 July 1952, Frank.

71. ML, "Another Way to Kill a Writer," [June 1955], Levin.

72. ML to OF, 11 July 1952, Levin.

73. ML to OF, 10 July 1952, Levin.

74. OF to TL, 12 July 1952, Levin.

75. OF to ML, 12 July 1952, Frank.

76. OF to CC, 16 July 1952, Frank.

77. OF to CC, 21 July 1952, Frank.

78. OF to ML, 18 July 1952, Levin.

79. ML to OF, 16 July 1952, Levin; OF to ML, 21 July 1952, Frank.

80. OF to BZ, 18 July 1952, Frank.

81. ML to OF, 22 July 1952, Levin.

82. ML to OF, 26 July 1952, Levin.

83. OF to ML, 31 July 1952, Levin.

84. OF to ML, 31 July 1952, Frank.

85. CC to OF, 30 July 1952, Frank; CC, *One Naked Individual*, 203.

86. LH's secretary to KB, 29 September 1948, Hellman.

87. Stefan Kanfer, *A Journal of the Plague Years* (New York: Athenaeum, 1973), 172–173.

88. Wright, *Lillian Hellman*, 257, 265.

89. "Kermit Bloomgarden . . . Dead," *New York Times* (21 September 1976), clipping, Frank.

90. KB to OF, 1 August 1952, Frank.

91. Carl Hess to Rosalie Davies, 1 August 1952, Bloomgarden.

92. Val Davies to OF, 5 August 1952, Bloomgarden.

93. OF to KB, 1 August 1952, Frank.

94. OF to ML, 1 August 1952, Frank.

95. Rosalie Davies to KB, 12 August 1952, Bloomgarden.

96. OF to KB, 1 August 1952, Frank.

97. ML to OF, 1 August 1952, Levin.

98. OF to ML, 4 August 1952, Frank.

99. ML to OF, ca. 5 August 1952 (misdated 28 August 1952), Levin.

100. ML, Deposition, [ca. 18 July 1956], 81–82, Levin.

101. OF to ML, 6 August 1952, Levin.

102. ML to OF, 8 August 1952, Levin.

103. Clipping, *New York Times* (8 August 1952), Frank; "Levin Writing Play," *New York Herald Tribune* (8 August 1952), clipping, Frank; "Cheryl Crawford Gets Anne Frank's 'Diary,'" *New York Compass* (8 August 1952), clipping, Frank; *New York Daily News* (8 August 1952), clipping, Frank.

104. ML to OF, 9 August 1952, Levin.

105. ML to OF, 9 August 1952, Levin; OF to ML, 11 August 1952, Levin.

106. OF to ML, 15 August 1952, Levin.

107. ML to OF, 16 August 1952, Levin.

108. Floria Lasky to ML, 19 August 1952, Levin.

109. OF to ML, 15 August 1952, Levin.

110. OF to ML, 20 August 1952, Frank.

111. ML to OF, 23 August 1952, Levin.

112. ML to OF, 23 August 1952, Levin.

113. OF to ML, 24 August 1952, Levin.

114. ML to OF, 28 August 1952, Levin.

115. OF, "Remarks," attached to ML to OF, 4 September 1952, Levin; ML to OF, 4 September 1952, Frank.

116. ML, "Anne Frank: The Diary of a Young Girl" (1st draft), 29–31, Frank.

117. ML to OF, 4 September 1952, Levin; OF to ML, 8 September 1952, Frank.

118. OF to ML, 18 September 1952, Frank.

119. ML, "Anne Frank: The Diary of a Young Girl" (broadcast script dated 14 December 1952), 17, Frank; ML to OF, 9 September 1952, Levin.

120. ML to OF, 10 September 1952, Levin.

121. Ibid.; OF to ML, 6 September 1952, Frank.

122. OF to CC, 6 September 1952, Frank.

123. CC to OF, 10 September 1952, Frank.

124. OF to ML, 18 September 1952, Frank. (Includes reference to ML to OF, 15 September 1952, the letter no longer extant.)

125. June Bundy, "Anne Frank: The Diary of a Young Girl," *Billboard* (27 September 1952), clipping with notations, Levin.

126. "Anne Frank: Diary of a Young Girl," *Variety* (24 September 1952), clipping, Frank.

127. ML, "Another Way to Kill a Writer," 8.

Chapter 4. Judgments About His Script

1. OF to FAH, 9 September 1955, Hackett.

2. OF, "Important Dates in Connection with the Levin-Case," attached to OF to Allan Ecker, 9 August 1957, Frank.

3. ML, "Another Way to Kill a Writer," [June 1955], 8, Levin; OF, "Important Dates."

4. OF, "Important Dates."

5. ML, "Another Way to Kill a Writer," 8; ML to Brooks Atkinson, 9 December 1952, Levin.

6. OF, "Important Dates"; William Zinneman, ML v. OF and KB, 27 December 1957, Levin.

7. ML, "Another Way to Kill a Writer," 8–9; CC to OF, 3 October 1952, Frank; OF, "Important Dates."

8. OF to TL, 7 November 1952, Levin.

9. Joan Mellen, *Hellman and Hammett: The Legendary Passion of Lillian Hellman and Dashiell Hammett* (New York: HarperCollins, 1996), 303.

10. Wolf Kaufman to ML, [1 October 1956], Levin; OF to MM, 26 July 1956, Frank.

11. Wolf Kaufman to ML, [1 October 1956], Levin.

12. OF to FAH, 21 January 1954, Hackett; OF to MM, 26 March 1956, Frank.

13. CC to ML, 7 October 1952, Levin.

14. OF to Allan Ecker, 12 August 1957, Frank.

15. OF, "Important Dates."

16. Ben Schankman to KB, 8 October 1947, Bloomgarden; Paul, Weiss to Dalton Trumbo, various dates, Dalton Trumbo Papers, Wisconsin State Historical Society.

17. Nathan Straus to ER, 19 April 1957, Frank.

18. OF, "Important Dates."

19. ML to Hanoch Bartov, [1973], Levin.

20. OF, "Important Dates."

21. Ibid.

22. ML to CC, 28 October 1952, Levin.

23. Ibid.

24. ML, "Another Way to Kill a Writer," 11.

25. ML to CC, 28 October 1952, Levin.

26. MM to Peter Capell, 29 October 1952, Levin.

27. MM to ML, 29 October 1952, Levin.

28. ML to OF, 30 October 1952, Levin.

29. ML to MM, 30 October 1952, Levin.

30. ML to Floria Lasky, 30 October 1952, Levin; Floria Lasky to ML, 3 November 1952, Levin.

31. ML to Floria Lasky, 5 November 1952, Levin.

32. OF to ML, 6 November 1952, Frank.

33. ML to OF, 6 November 1952, Levin.

34. OF, "Important Dates," entry misdated 6 November 1952; ML, "Producers List," 6 November 1952, Levin.

35. OF to TL, 7 November 1952, Levin.

36. OF to ML, 6 November 1952, Frank.

37. OF, "Important Dates."

38. Lawrence Graver, *An Obsession with Anne Frank* (Berkeley: University of California Press, 1995), 51.

39. Virginia Spencer Carr, *The Lonely Hunter: A Biography of Carson McCullers* (New York: Doubleday, 1975), 225–226, 305, 372–373.

40. Ibid., 412.

41. CC to CM, 13 November 1952, McCullers; Elia Kazan to ML, 8 December 1952, Levin.

42. OF, "Important Dates."

43. Ibid.; ML, "Another Way to Kill a Writer."

44. CM to CC, 17 November 1952, McCullers.

45. OF to ML, 19 January 1953, Frank.

46. BZ to OF, 18 November 1952, Frank.

47. ML, *The Obsession*, ms., 63, Levin.

48. OF to ML, 21 and 25 November 1952, Frank.

49. ML, "Another Way to Kill a Writer"; ML to OF, 12 January 1953, Levin; Miriam Howell, Deposition, ML v. OF and KB, 20 November 1957, Levin.

50. OF to ML, 21 and 25 November 1952, Frank.

51. ML to Maxwell Anderson, 2 December 1952, Levin.

52. OF to MM, 26 March 1956, Frank.

53. SF to Peter Capell, 18 November 1957, Levin; Peter Capell to SF, 22 November 1957, Levin.

54. BZ to MM, 23 November 1955, Frank; CC to Leon Kellman, 16 July 1953, Crawford.

55. OF to ML, 19 January 1953, Frank.

56. ML to OF, 21 January 1953, Frank.

57. CM to OF, 28 November 1952, Frank; OF to CM, 7 December 1952, McCullers.

58. CM to Mary Tucker, December 1952, cited in Carr, *Lonely Hunter*, 399.

59. CC to CM, 8 December 1952, McCullers.

60. ML to Elia Kazan, 9 December 1952, Levin.

61. ML to Brooks Atkinson, 9 December 1952, Levin.

62. Carr, *Lonely Hunter*, 399.

63. OF to ML, 16 December 1952, Frank.

64. Elia Kazan to ML, 18 December 1952, Levin.

65. Richard Myers to ML, 19 December 1952, Frank.

66. OF to Jewish Theological Seminary; Morton Wishigrad to OF, November 1952, Frank.

67. ML to OF, 22 December 1952, Levin; and CC, *One Naked Individual*, 203.

68. ML to OF, 23 December 1952, Frank.

69. MM to OF, ca. 25 December 1952, Frank.

70. ML to OF, 25 December 1952 (1), Levin.

71. ML to OF, 25 December 1952 (2), Levin.

72. ML to CM, ca. 25 December 1952, McCullers.

73. ML to OF, 31 December 1952, Levin.

74. OF to ML, 2 January 1953, Frank.

Chapter 5. The Most Suitable Producer

1. CC to CM, 3 January 1953, McCullers.

2. Lewis Funke, "News and Gossip Galore," *New York Times* (4 January 1953), clipping, Frank.

3. ML to OF, 6 January 1953, Levin.

4. ML to MM, 6 January 1953, Levin.

5. BZ to OF, 7 January 1953, Frank.

6. OF to ML, 8 January 1953, Frank.

7. CM to CC, 8 January 1953, McCullers.

8. Janet Flanner, *Darlingissima: Letters to a Friend* (New York: Random House, 1985), 184.

9. Telegram cited in OF to BZ, 9 January 1953, Frank; OF to CM, 8 January 1953, McCullers.

10. OF to BZ, 9 January 1953, Frank.

11. OF to ML, 8 January 1953, Frank.

12. ML to OF, 12 January 1953, Levin.

13. ML to Hobe Morrison, 12 January 1953, Levin.

14. ML to *Variety*, 12 January 1953, Levin.

15. MM to J. M. Japp, 13 January 1953, Frank.

16. MM to ML, 13 January 1953, Levin.

17. BZ to OF, 7 January 1953, Frank.

18. OF to ML, 14 January 1953, Frank.

19. ML to MM, 15 January 1953; Harold Taube to ML, [January 1953], Levin; Harold Clurman to ML, 16 January 1953, Levin.

20. ML to OF, 15 January 1953, Frank.

21. BZ to OF, 15 January 1953, Frank.

22. BZ to OF, 16 January 1953, Frank. Nearly twenty years later, Otto refused honorary membership in the Jewish Identity League, whose program of youth education included not only Jewish history and customs and Hebrew but also Yiddish, the language of East European Jewry. "I do not know a word of Jiddish and I do not believe in the possibility to preserve this language as a living one," he wrote as his reason (OF to Yaakov Riz, 25 August 1972, Frank).

23. OF to ML, 19 January 1953, Frank.

24. OF to ML, 20 January 1953, Frank.

25. OF to MM, 20 January 1953, Frank.

26. OF to CC, 20 January 1953, Frank; OF to CM, 20 January 1953, McCullers.

27. OF to BZ, 21 [misdated 20] January 1953, Frank.

28. CC to CM, [21 January 1953], McCullers.

29. CM to CC, [ca. 25 January 1953], McCullers.

30. ML to OF, 21 January 1953, Levin.

31. ML to OF, 23 January 1953, Levin.

32. OF to BZ, 26 January 1953, Frank.

33. ML to OF, 28 January 1953, Levin.

34. BZ to OF, 15 January 1953, Frank.

35. BZ to OF, 29 January 1953, Frank.

36. BZ to OF, 30 January 1953, Frank.

37. OF to ML, 2 February 1953, Frank (misdated 1 February 1953 in Levin).

38. OF to CC, 2 February 1953, Frank.

39. CC to OF, 6 February 1953, Frank.

40. BZ to OF, 9 February 1953, Frank.

41. ML to OF, 7 February 1953, Levin.

42. OF to BZ, 14 February 1953, Frank.

43. OF to BZ, 16 February 1953, Frank.

44. BZ to OF, 18 February 1953, Frank.

45. OF to CM, 18 February 1953, McCullers.

46. MM to OF, 28 February 1953, Frank; Harold Clurman to MM, 20 February 1953, Frank.

47. Eric Bentley, ed., *Thirty Years of Treason* (New York: Viking, 1971), 489.

48. BZ to OF, 6 March 1953, Frank.

49. BZ to OF, 31 March 1953, Frank.

50. MM to OF, 28 February 1953, Frank.

51. OF to MM, 5 April 1953, Frank.

52. MM to OF, 28 February 1953, Frank.

53. OF to MM, 5 April 1953, Frank.

54. BZ to OF, 3 September 1953, Frank.

55. "Memos," *New York Times* (19 April 1953), clipping, Frank.

56. CC to Frank, 22 April 1953, Frank; CC to CM, 22 April 1953, Crawford; CC to Samuel Silver, 22 April 1957, Crawford.

Chapter 6. Things You Should Never Tell Anybody

1. ML to OF, 26 April 1953, Levin.

2. OF to ML, 19 May 1953, Frank.

3. ML to OF, 31 May 1953, Levin.

4. CC to CM, 8 June 1953, McCullers.

5. Billy Rose to ML, 16 June 1953, Levin.

6. OF to ML, 30 July 1953, Levin.

7. ML to OF, 25 August 1953, Frank.

8. Terese Hayden to OF, 25 August 1953, Frank.

9. ML to MM, 28 August 1953, Levin.

10. ML to OF, 30 August 1953, Levin.

11. BZ to OF, 5 September 1953, Frank.

12. OF to ML, 5 September 1953, Frank.

13. OF to TL, 7 September 1953, Levin.

14. OF to BZ, 9 September 1953, Frank.

15. OF to MM, 9 September 1953, Frank; FAH to LS, 26 November 1955, Salisbury.

16. ML to OF, 9 September 1953, Levin.

17. OF to MM, 14 September 1953; MM to OF, 18 September 1953; OF to BZ, 9 September 1953, Frank.

18. ML to OF, 16 September 1953; ML to OF, 25 August 1953, Levin.

19. OF to ML, 21 September 1953, Frank; OF to ML, 21 July 1952, Levin.

20. OF to Terese Hayden, 26 September 1953, Frank.

21. "Agreement . . . Between Otto Frank and Kermit Bloomgarden," 1 October 1953, Levin.

22. *New York Times* (22 November 1953), clipping, Frank.

23. ML to OF, 2 October 1953, Frank.

24. ML to OF, 8 October 1953, Levin.

25. ML to KB, 19 October 1953, Levin.

26. ML to KB, 31 October 1953, Bloomgarden.

27. OF to ML, 23 October 1953, Frank.

28. ML to OF, 27 October 1953, Levin.

29. Joan Mellen, *Hellman and Hammett: The Legendary Passion of Lillian Hellman and Dashiell Hammett* (New York: HarperCollins, 1996), 315; LS to FAH, 19 November 1953, Hackett. The Hacketts would later misdate the letter as November 26 in their summary account, based on notes in a journal kept largely for tax purposes, of the process of writing the adaptation. That account was published in the *New York Times* (30 September 1956) as "The Diary of 'The Diary of Anne Frank'" (hereafter abbreviated as DOD).

30. Based upon FAH, "Biography," Hackett; "Albert Hackett," *New York Times* (18 March 1995). Subsequent materials on the Hacketts' careers are from these sources.

31. LH to Arthur Kober, 27 November 1942, Arthur Kober Papers, Wisconsin State Historical Society.

32. FAH to LS, 29 November 1953, Salisbury.

33. Mellen, *Hellman and Hammett*, 308, 310.

34. Ibid.: early acquaintance, 90, 94; Hellman and Party groups, 116–117, 128, 159, 165–169, 267; Hammett and the Party, 123; Hellman joins party, 107, 108. See also Benjamin Gitlow, *The Whole of Their Lives* (New York: Scribner's, 1948); Eugene Lyons, *The Red Decade: Stalinist Penetration of America* (Indianapolis: Bobbs-Merrill, 1941).

35. Mellen, *Hellman and Hammett*, 112–113, 115, 259.

36. FG to LS, n.d. [1936], Salisbury.

37. William Wright, *Lillian Hellman* (New York: Simon and Schuster, 1986), 116–118; Carl Rollyson, *Lillian Hellman: Her Legend and Her Legacy* (New York: St. Martin's, 1988), 79–80.

38. Mellen, *Hellman and Hammett*, 113.

39. AH, Oral History, Columbia University (1983), 117, 183, 184. For the file on the committee's charges, 1952–1953, Hackett.

40. LH to FAH, 6 January 1943, Hackett.

41. AH, Oral History, 161–163, 171.
42. Mellen, *Hellman and Hammett*, 315.
43. Harold Hobson, "Out of Step?" clipping, November 1956, Frank.
44. William Pepper, "Drama of 'Diary' is Nonsectarian," *New York World Telegram and Sun* (January 1956), clipping, Frank.
45. Brooks Atkinson, "Inspired Theatre," *New York Times* (16 October 1955), clipping, Frank.
46. FG to LS, 29 January 1962, Salisbury; FG to LS, 8 August 1966, Salisbury.
47. AH to LS, 23 January 1956, Salisbury.
48. FG, DOD, ms., 3 December 1953, Hackett; FAH to KB, 4 December 1953, Bloomgarden.
49. FG, DOD, ms., 8 December 1953.
50. FG to LS, 8 December 1953, Hackett.
51. FAH to LS, 11 December 1953, Hackett; LS to FAH, 10 December 1953, Hackett.
52. FAH to LS, 14 December 1953, Hackett; FG, DOD, ms., 12 and 13 December 1953.
53. FG to LS, n.d. [December 1953], Salisbury.
54. FG, DOD, 14 and 15 December 1953.
55. KB to FAH, 18 December 1953, Bloomgarden.

Chapter 7. Lilly's Suggestions Will Work Out

1. ML to FAH, 19 December 1953, Hackett; Louis Calta, "'Anne Frank' Is Set for Stage Version," *New York Times* (19 December 1953), clipping, Frank.
2. ML to OF, 20 December 1953, Levin.
3. OF to ML, 28 December 1953, Frank.
4. FG to KB, 26 December 1953, Bloomgarden.
5. FAH to OF, 27 December 1953, Hackett.
6. OF to FAH, 1 January 1954, Hackett.
7. FAH to KB, n.d. [ca. 29 December 1953], Bloomgarden.
8. FAH to ML, 27 December 1953, Hackett.
9. ML to FAH, 29 December 1953, Levin.
10. FG to KB, 5 January 1954, Bloomgarden.
11. FAH to LS, 7 January 1954, Hackett.
12. LS to FG, 20 August 1936, Salisbury.
13. LS to FG, 6 April 1938, Salisbury.
14. LS to OF, 2 February 1959, Salisbury.
15. ML to OF, 6 January 1954, Frank.
16. LS to FAH, 14 January 1954, Hackett.
17. FG to LS, 17 January 1954, Salisbury.
18. ML, "A Challenge to Kermit Bloomgarden," *New York Post* (13 January 1954), clipping, Levin.
19. KB to FAH, 18 January 1954, Hackett.
20. Copy of undated note from MM to OF, attached to ML to OF, 6 January 1954, Frank.
21. FP to OF, 19 January 1954, Frank.
22. OF to FG, 21 January 1954, Hackett.
23. FG to KB, 21 January 1954, Bloomgarden; FG to LS, [21 January 1954], Salisbury.
24. FG, "The Diary of 'The Diary of Anne Frank,'" *New York Times* (September 30, 1956), 21 January 1954 (hereafter abbreviated DOD).
25. FAH to OF, 26 January 1954, Hackett.
26. FG to KB, 30 January 1954, Bloomgarden.
27. KB to FAH, 11 February 1954, Bloomgarden.

28. OF to FAH, 6 February 1954, Hackett; OF, *Hervormd Nederland* (3 February 1979), quoted in Alex Grobman, *Anne Frank in Historical Perspective* (Los Angeles: Martyrs Memorial and Museum of the Holocaust, 1995), 19; AF, *The Diary of a Young Girl: The Definitive Edition* (New York: Doubleday, 1995), 59, 150, 324.

29. FG to OF, 17 February 1954, Hackett.

30. OF to FG, 22 February 1954, Hackett.

31. Ibid.

32. KB's secretary to KB, 19 February 1957, Bloomgarden.

33. ML to OF, 9 February 1954, Frank.

34. OF to ML, n.d.; ML, "A Challenge to Kermit Bloomgarden," clipping, Frank.

35. OF to ML, 10 March 1954, Frank.

36. OF to "Dear Madam/Dear Sir," 15 March 1954, Frank.

37. OF to "Madame Paz," 14 April 1954, Frank (author's translation).

38. ML to OF, 15 March 1954, Levin.

39. OF to ML, [19 March 1954], Frank. Letter not sent, according to a note in the "Chronology of Correspondence" later prepared as part of Otto's defense in the suit brought against him by Meyer.

40. MM to LS and Richard Killin, 8 February 1954, Bloomgarden; LS to FAH, 23 February 1954; LS to FAH, 8 March 1954, Hackett.

41. FG, DOD, 26 February 1954.

42. FAH to OF, 20 March 1954, Hackett.

43. FG to KB, 3 April 1954, Bloomgarden.

44. FG, DOD, 11 March 1954.

45. FG to KB, 3 April 1954, Bloomgarden.

46. OF to FAH, 7 April 1954, Hackett.

47. AH, DOD, 22 April 1954.

48. FG to OF, 24 April 1954, Hackett.

49. OF to TL, 13 April 1954, Levin.

50. ML to OF, 19 April 1954, Levin.

51. FG to LS, 24 April 1954, Salisbury.

52. FG, DOD, 14 May 1954.

53. FAH to KB, 20 May 1954, Bloomgarden. Typescript of the draft, "4th version," misdated 21 May 1954, Hackett.

54. FG to LS, 20 May 1954, Salisbury; FG, DOD, 21 May 1954.

55. FG to LS, 24 May 1954, Hackett.

56. LS to FAH, 21 May 1954, Hackett.

57. FAH to OF, 28 May 1954, Hackett.

58. OF to FAH, 7 June 1954, Hackett.

59. FG, DOD, 2 June 1954, 3 June 1954.

60. FAH to OF, 10 June 1954, Hackett.

61. KB to FAH, 1 June 1954, Hackett.

62. AF, *The Diary of Anne Frank: Critical Edition* (New York: Doubleday, 1989), 690–692.

63. AF, *Diary: Definitive Edition*, 244, 305.

64. KB to FAH, 1 June 1954, Hackett; AF, *Diary: Critical Edition*, 694.

65. AF, *Diary: Critical Edition*, 491–492.

66. Carl Rollyson, *Lillian Hellman: Her Legend and Her Legacy* (New York: St. Martin's, 1986), 353–359.

67. LH, *Conversations with Lillian Hellman*, Jackson Bryer, ed. (Jackson: University Press of Mississippi, 1986), 20–21.

68. Rollyson, *Lillian Hellman*, 353–359.

69. Murray Shumach, "Shaping a New Joan," *New York Times* (ca. 15 November 1955), clipping, Levin.

70. FAH, *Diary of a Young Girl*, 4th version, 20 May 1954 (misdated 21 May 1954), I-38, I-40–I-42, Hackett.

71. Nahum Glatzer, ed., *The Passover Haggadah* (New York: Schocken, 1969), 31.

72. FAH, *Diary*, 4th version, II-36–II-37.

73. ML, *The Diary of Anne Frank*, 110, 118.

74. FG to LS, 20 June 1954, Salisbury.

75. FG, DOD, 24 July 1954.

76. OF to FAH, 14 June 1954, Hackett; Alex Sagan, "Examining Optimism: Anne Frank's Place in Postwar Culture," in Grobman, *Anne Frank in Historical Perspective*, 57.

77. OF to MM, 14 March 1956, Salisbury.

78. MM to KB, 19 July 1954, Bloomgarden.

79. FAH to OF, 24 June 1954, Hackett.

80. FAH to KB, 15 July 1954, Hackett. Note the Hacketts' supplicant address of Bloomgarden in the third person.

81. KB, "2nd Draft Construction," August 1954, Bloomgarden.

82. ML to OF, 1 August [1954], Levin.

83. ML to OF, 18 August 1954 (postmarked 19 August 1954), Levin.

84. ML to FAH, 18 August 1954, Hackett.

85. FG, DOD, 19 August 1954.

86. FAH to Mary Jeanine, [ca. 20 December 1959], Hackett.

87. FAH, *Diary*, 5th version, 19 August 1954, I-6, I-40, Hackett.

88. Ibid., I-32–I-33.

89. Cf. FAH, *Diary*, 4th version, I-38.

90. FAH, *Diary*, 5th version, II-39.

91. FG, DOD, 23 August–5 September 1954.

92. KB to FAH, 9 September 1954, Bloomgarden.

93. FG, DOD, 11 September 1954.

Chapter 8. A Production That Isn't Faithful

1. FG, "The Diary of 'The Diary of Anne Frank,'" *New York Times* (September 30, 1956), 20 and 27 September, 8 October 1954 (hereafter abbreviated DOD); FAH, *Diary of a Young Girl*, 6th version, 8 October 1954, Hackett.

2. FG, DOD, ms., 9 October 1954.

3. GK, "Anne Frank at 50," *Newsweek* (25 June 1979): 15.

4. GK to Robert Sherwood, 12 October 1954, Kanin.

5. GK to Robert Sherwood, 10 April 1954, Kanin.

6. GK to Robert Sherwood, 4 August 1954, Kanin.

7. FG, DOD, 18 October 1954.

8. Jean Schick Grossman to FAH, [ca. 10 October 1954], Hackett.

9. OF to FAH, 25 October 1954, Hackett.

10. OF to FAH, 5 November 1954, Hackett.

11. FG, DOD, 29 October 1954; GK to FAH, 8 November 1954, Hackett.

12. KB to GK, [?] November 1954, Bloomgarden; FAH, *Diary*, 6th version, 1-2-35; 1-4-46, 58–59.

13. GK to FAH, 8 November 1954, Hackett; FG to LS, 21 November 1954, Salisbury.

14. FG, DOD, 12–22 November 1954; FAH to OF, 21 November 1954, Frank.

15. OF to FAH, 24 November 1954, Hackett.

16. FG to KB, 21 November 1954, Bloomgarden.

17. GK to KB, 27 November 1954, Bloomgarden.

18. GK to Robert Sherwood, 2 December 1954, Kanin.

19. KB to FAH, 5 December 1954, Hackett.

20. FG, DOD, 6–10 December 1954.
21. FAH to KB, 10 December 1954, Hackett.
22. FG, DOD, 11 December 1954.
23. OF to KB, 12 December 1954, Frank.
24. FAH, *Diary*, 7th version, 5 December 1954, title page, 2-5-38, Hackett.
25. Joseph Schildkraut to KB, 18 June 1955, Bloomgarden.
26. FAH, *Diary*, 6th version, 2-5-36; 8th version, 19 December 1954, Hackett.
27. FG, DOD, 20 December 1954; MM to OF, 5 January 1955, Frank.
28. ML to GK, 19 December 1954, Bloomgarden.
29. ML to Dorothy Schiff, 19 December 1954, Bloomgarden.
30. ML v. OF and CC, 30 December 1954, Levin.
31. MM to OF, 5 January 1955, Frank.
32. OF to MM, 10 January 1955; ML v. OF and CC, annotated by OF; OF to Joseph Schildkraut, 4 February 1955, Frank.
33. OF to MM, 23 January 1955, Frank.
34. GK to FAH, 10 January 1955, Hackett.
35. GK to FAH, 25 May 1955, Hackett.
36. LS to FAH, 12 January 1955, Hackett.
37. OF to FAH, 14 January 1955, Hackett.
38. FAH to OF, 29 January 1955, Hackett; OF to FAH, 21 February 1955, Hackett.
39. ML to GK, 16 January 1955, Levin.
40. GK to KB, 8 February 1955, Bloomgarden.
41. KB to GK, 14 February 1955, Bloomgarden; KB to S. Silver, 24 February 1955, Bloomgarden.
42. OF to Joseph Schildkraut, 4 February 1955, Frank.
43. Joseph Schildkraut to KB, 1 March 1955, Bloomgarden.
44. Joseph Schildkraut to KB, 30 April, 22 May 1955, Bloomgarden.
45. "Levin vs. Frank: Decision," 30 March 1955, Frank.
46. MM to OF, 29 April 1955, Frank.
47. ML to Sol Stern, 2 April 1955, Levin.
48. ML, "I Witnessed the Liberation," *Congress Weekly* 22 (18 April 1955): 3–4.
49. Ibid.; ML to Elia Kazan, 2 May 1955, Levin.
50. SF to MM, 2 May 1955, cited in MM to SF, 16 May 1955, Levin.
51. MM to SF, 16 May 1955, Levin.
52. SF to MM, 23 May 1955, cited in MM to SF, 31 May 1955, Levin.
53. MM to SF, 31 May 1955, Levin.
54. OF to ML, 25 November 1952, Frank.
55. ML, "Another Way to Kill a Writer" [June 1955], Levin, 8.
56. MM to OF, 2 June 1955; ML to OF, 25 April 1955, Frank.
57. ML to OF, 3 June 1955, Levin.
58. ML to OF, 12 June 1955, Levin.
59. MM to OF, 17 June 1955, Frank.
60. ML to OF, 1 July 1955, Levin.
61. ML to OF, 2 July 1955, 19 August 1955, Levin.
62. SF to MM, 7 July 1955, Frank; ML to OF, 1 August 1955, Levin.
63. TL to ML, 1 August 1955, Levin.
64. ML, notes on conversation with HS, 4 August 1955; ML to SF, 5 August 1955, Levin.
65. FG, DOD, 3 August 1955.
66. Lotte Stavisky to KB, 19 July 1955, Bloomgarden.
67. OF to FAH, 7 September 1955, Hackett.
68. "Who's Who in the Cast," *Playbill*, Bloomgarden.

69. ML, "Gusti Huber's Role in 'Anne Frank,'" unidentified clipping, [ca. 1955], Bloomgarden.

70. Herbert Luft to KB, 11 January 1957, to which is attached unidentified article, "Not a Jewish Mother," clipping, Bloomgarden.

71. OF to FAH, 31 August 1955, Hackett.

72. OF to FAH, 7 September 1955, Hackett.

73. OF to *Diary* cast and crew, 15 September 1955, Hackett.

74. GK to Robert Sherwood, 11 May 1955, Kanin.

75. FG, DOD, 22 August, 7 September 1955.

76. Ibid., 8–9 September 1955.

77. Bernard Kalb, "Diary Footnotes," *New York Times*, 2 October 1955, clipping used as Exhibit 13 of Bill of Particulars, ML v. OF and KB, 7 December 1956, Levin.

78. AH, Oral History, 171–172.

79. Lewis Funke, "Credit," *New York Times*, 27 May 1956, clipping; Bill of Particulars, Levin.

80. AH, Oral History, 5-171; FG, DOD, 19 September 1955.

81. AH, Oral History, 5-168–169.

82. See FAH, *Diary*, 15 September 1955, 1-3-40–41, Hackett; 24 September 1955, 1-3-41; 28–29 September 1955, 1-5-70; 1 October 1955, 2-1, 2-3, Kanin.

83. Ibid., 15 September 1955, 2-1-1, Hackett; 1 October 1955, 2-1, Kanin.

84. FAH, *Diary*, 27 September 1955, 1-4, Kanin; Yaffa Eliach, *Hassidic Tales of the Holocaust* (New York: Oxford University Press, 1982), 13–15.

85. FAH, *Diary*, 29 September 1955, 2-1-2, Kanin.

86. Ibid., 22 September 1955, 1-1-1, Kanin.

87. Ibid., 28 September 1955, 2-4-35, Kanin; 15 September 1955, 2-5-41, Hackett.

88. FG, DOD, 6 October 1955.

Chapter 9. Successfully Blocked

1. ML to OF, 24 September 1955, Levin.

2. Harry Raymond, "'Diary of Anne Frank,' Gripping Anti-Nazi Drama at the Cort" (New York) *Daily Worker* (10 October 1955): 6.

3. ML to OF, [?] October 1955, Levin.

4. Algene Ballif, "Anne Frank on Broadway," *Commentary* (November 1955): 465, 467.

5. Ies Spetter, "Onderduik Pret Broadway," *Vrij Nederland* (5 November 1955), translated clipping, Frank.

6. Herbert Luft, "Diary of Anne Frank," *B'nai B'rith Messenger* (3 February 1956): 27, clipping, Frank.

7. ML, "'Diary of Anne Frank' Stage Play Evades Book's Universal Theme," *National Jewish Post* (14 October 1955), clipping, Salisbury.

8. SF to MM, 11 October 1955, Frank.

9. MM to OF, 14 October 1955, Frank.

10. OF to MM, 18 October 1955, Frank.

11. ML to OF, 19 October 1955, Levin.

12. ML to OF, 23 October 1955, Levin.

13. Joan Mellen, *Hellman and Hammett: The Legendary Passion of Lillian Hellman and Dashiell Hammett* (New York: HarperCollins, 1996), 321.

14. OF to MM, 27 October 1955, Frank.

15. ML to OF, 10 November 1955, Levin.

16. GK to ML, 14 December 1955, Bloomgarden.

17. ML to OF, 17 December 1955, Levin.

18. OF to TL, 27 December 1955, Frank.

19. AH to LS, 23 January 1956, Salisbury.

20. LS to OF, 1 December 1955, Salisbury.

21. OF to LS, 13 December 1955, Salisbury.

22. FAH to LS, 15 December 1955, Salisbury.

23. AH to LS, 9 January 1956, Salisbury.

24. LS to AH, 12 January 1956, Salisbury.

25. LS to FAH, 26 January 1956, Salisbury.

26. LS to FAH, 2 February 1956, Salisbury.

27. LS to FAH, 12 January 1956, Salisbury.

28. LS to FAH, 9 November 1965, Salisbury.

29. SF to MM, 6 January 1956, Salisbury.

30. OF to MM, 15 January 1956, Frank.

31. ML to "Dear Rabbi," 4 February 1956, Levin.

32. ML to OF, 6 February 1956, Levin.

33. ML to OF, 7 February 1956, Levin.

34. ML to OF, 15 February 1956, Levin.

35. ML to FAH, 10 February 1956, Hackett.

36. ML to Philip Hockstein, 19 July 1980, Levin.

37. ML v. OF and KB, "Verified Complaint," 14 February 1956; KB, "Affidavit," ML and McCloskey v. The Diary Company, 3 December 1956, Levin.

38. ML v. OF and KB, 2, 7, 9, 12.

39. SF, "This structural comparison . . . ," Levin.

40. ML, Deposition, ML v. OF and KB, 24 February 1956, 3, 6–7, 8, 9–10, 11–12, Levin.

41. KB to Samuel Silver, 24 February 1956, Bloomgarden.

42. Ephraim London to ML, 27 February 1956, Levin.

43. ML to OF, 29 February 1956, Levin.

44. OF to MM, 7 March 1956, Frank; OF to TL, 27 December 1955, Frank.

45. OF to FAH, 8 March 1956, Hackett.

46. OF to FAH, 5 April 1956, Hackett.

47. OF to MM, 9 March 1956, Frank.

48. ML to Harry Nichols, 12 March 1956, Levin.

49. TL to OF, 13 March 1956, Frank.

50. OF to MM, 20 March 1956, Frank.

51. EC to OF, 12 March 1956, Frank.

52. EC to OF, 23 March 1956, Frank.

Chapter 10. Too Jewish

1. OF to MM, 26 March 1956, Frank.

2. OF to EC, 27 March 1956, Frank.

3. OF to MM, 14 April 1956, Frank.

4. FAH to MM, 11 April 1956, Hackett.

5. KB, "Answer" to ML v. OF and KB, 7 April 1956; CC to ML, 7 October 1952; OF, "Important Dates"; ML v. OF and KB, 14 February 1956, Levin.

6. ML, Deposition, ML v. OF and KB, 24 February 1956, Levin.

7. SF to EC, 13 April 1956, Frank.

8. OF, "Answer" to ML v. OF and KB, 22 May 1956, Frank.

9. MM to Ephraim London, 20 April 1956; OF to MM, 20 April 1956; MM to ML, 24 April 1956, Frank.

10. ML v. OF and CC, 23 April 1956, Levin; ML, "Levin Presents a Problem He Believes Is Jewish Community's," *National Jewish Post* (22 April 1956): 9; "Rabbis Urge New Version of

'Diary'" (Brookline, Mass.) *Jewish Times* (3 May 1956), clipping, Frank; ML, "Levin Bitter at Tactic of Anne Frank's Father," *National Jewish Post* (4 May 1956): 15.

11. "'Anne Frank' Gets Award of Critics," *New York Times* (18 April 1956), clipping, Frank; fragment of an article from H. A. Gomperts, *Het Parool* (28 April 1956), translated excerpts, Frank.

12. "Pulitzer Prize—1956 . . . Drama Award," Bloomgarden.

13. "The Pulitzer Awards," *New York Times* (8 May 1956), clipping, Frank.

14. John Chapman, "'Anne Frank' Wins Prize" (New York) *Sunday News* (13 May 1956), clipping, Frank.

15. "Good Hacks Find Out Two Pens Are Better Than One" (New York) *Sunday News* (27 May 1956), clipping, Frank.

16. William Schach, "Diary Into Drama," *Midstream* (June 1956): 2–4.

17. OF to LS, 3 May 1956, Salisbury.

18. ML to editors of the *Village Voice*, 7 May 1956, Levin.

19. Uri Cesari, "The Legacy of Anne Frank," *Haaretz* (15 June 1956), clipping, Levin.

20. OF to MM, 24 May 1956, Salisbury.

21. FAH to LS, 24 May 1956, Salisbury.

22. OF to W. W. Norton, 5 June 1956, Frank.

23. GK to James Proctor, 8 June 1956, Bloomgarden.

24. Robert Vaughan, *Only Victims: A Study of Show Business Blacklisting* (New York: G. P. Putnam, 1972), 231–232, 271.

25. GK to James Proctor, 8 June 1956, Bloomgarden.

26. James Proctor to GK, 18 June 1956, Bloomgarden.

27. FAH, "Who Was Anne Frank?" [October 1955], Bloomgarden.

28. "KB for the Creative Team," [October 1955], Bloomgarden.

29. "From the Office of Garson Kanin," [October 1955], Bloomgarden.

30. James Proctor to KB, [October 1955], Bloomgarden.

31. James Proctor, "About 'The Diary of Anne Frank,'" [June 1956]; James Proctor to Abe Glick, 16 June 1956, Bloomgarden.

32. "Production Daily Log," 8 December 1955 and various dates, Bloomgarden.

33. OF to LS, 26 June 1956, Hackett; GK to OF, 3 July 1956, Hackett.

34. GK to FAH, 2 July 1956, Hackett; LS to FAH, 26 June 1956, Hackett.

35. FAH to OF, 3 July 1956, Hackett.

36. LS to FAH, 26 June 1956, Hackett.

37. Allan Ecker, "Memos of Fact" re ML v. OF and KB, 1 August 1956, Frank; OF to MM, 18 August 1956, Frank.

38. ML to OF, 31 July 1956, Levin.

39. "Excerpts from Statements Made at a Conference at Columbia University," 13 August 1956, Levin.

40. MM to OF, 30 August 1956, Frank.

41. OF to MM, 3 September 1956, Frank.

42. MM to SF, 11 September 1956, Frank; ML to SF, 23 September 1956, Levin.

43. MM to OF, 11 September 1956, Frank.

44. ML to SF, 23 September 1956, Levin.

45. ML to "Dear Editor," 25 September 1956, Levin.

46. OF to LS, 1 October 1956, Salisbury.

47. FAH, "The Diary of 'The Diary of Anne Frank,'" *New York Times* (30 September 1956).

48. Allan Ecker to LS, 4 October 1956, Hackett.

49. Allan Ecker to FAH, 19 October 1956, Hackett.

50. ML to James Farrell, 9 October 1956, Levin.

51. Joan Mellen, *Hellman and Hammett: The Legendary Passion of Lillian Hellman and Dashiell Hammett* (New York: HarperCollins, 1996), 284.

52. ML to James Farrell, 9 October 1956, Levin; John Cagley, *Report on Blacklisting* (New York: Fund for the Republic, 1956), 32, 44; Harvey Klehr, *The American Communist Movement* (New York: Twayne, 1992), 178; Howard Fast, *Being Red* (Garden City, N.Y.: Doubleday, 1990), 352.

53. ML, "Background of Communist Connection with Diary of Anne Frank," [Fall 1956], Levin.

54. *Diary of Anne Frank*, financial records, 5 August 1955, Bloomgarden.

55. ML, "The exposure . . . " (untitled essay), [Fall 1956], Levin.

56. ML, "Background."

57. John and Marguerite Sanford to KB, 25 September 1956, Bloomgarden.

58. KB to John and Marguerite Sanford, 1 October 1956, Bloomgarden.

Chapter 11. Damn His Soul—That Levin

1. OF to FAH, 24, 25 October 1956, Salisbury.

2. Twentieth Century Fox to LS, 25 October 1956, Salisbury.

3. OF to LS, 25 October 1956, Salisbury.

4. FAH to LS, 9 November 1956, Salisbury.

5. "Amended Answer" and "Counterclaim" to ML v. OF and KB, dated [?] November 1956, submitted in mid-December according to Allan Ecker to OF, 4 December 1956, Frank.

6. Allan Ecker to OF, 4 December 1956, Frank.

7. "Bill of Particulars," ML v. OF and KB, 20–31, 7 December 1956, Frank.

8. OF, "Comments on answers of Meyer Levin to bill of particulars," [ca. 15 December 1956], Frank.

9. EC to OF, 11 January 1957, Frank.

10. Draft of Motion for Summary Judgment, attached to EC to OF, 11 January 1957, Frank.

11. OF to Doubleday, 18 June 1952, as "Exhibit I," ML, "Bill of Particulars," Levin.

12. Draft of Motion for Summary Judgment, attached to EC to OF, 11 January 1957, Frank; ML to Howard Phillips, 28 April 1952, Frank.

13. LS, memo to herself, 9 January 1957, Salisbury.

14. LS to FAH, 10 January 1957, Salisbury.

15. Draft of a Motion for Summary Judgment, attached to EC to OF, 11 January 1957, Frank; LS to FAH, 10 January 1957, Salisbury.

16. *Variety* (25 May 1949), untitled clipping, Salisbury.

17. FAH to Lloyd Almirall, 26 January 1957, Hackett.

18. OF to EC, 18 January 1957, Frank.

19. OF to Mrs. Silverman, 11 June 1970, Frank.

20. Howard Lindsay to ML, 30 November 1956, Levin.

21. ML to Brooks Atkinson, 9 December 1956, Levin.

22. ML to Ed Williams, 29 December 1956, Levin.

23. ML to Walter Winchell, 20 January 1957, Levin.

24. EC to OF, 22 January 1957, Frank.

25. ML to Walter Winchell, 20 January 1957, Levin.

26. ML, "Meyer Levin's Remarks on Mike Wallace Nightbeat Program," 7 February 1957, Frank.

27. ML, Barry Gray Show interview, 8 February 1957, Levin.

28. OF to FAH, 2 February 1957, Frank.

29. LS, notes on Gray interview, 8 February 1957, Salisbury.

30. ML, Gray interview.

31. ML, "Meyer Levin Talks of 'Anne Frank,'" 18 February 1957, Bloomgarden.

32. Allan Ecker to EC, 9 February 1957, Frank.

33. OF, "Comments on the Barry Gray Interview," [ca. 25 February 1957], Frank.

34. OF, "Comments on the Tex and Jinx McCrary Interview," [ca. 25 February 1957], Frank.

35. Allan Ecker to KB, 18 February 1957, Bloomgarden.

36. James Proctor to KB, 18 February 1957, Bloomgarden.

37. James Proctor, first draft of press release, March 1957, Bloomgarden; Bloomgarden, press release, 18 March 1957, Frank.

38. OF, notation on first draft of KB's press release, March 1957, Frank.

39. LH to Esther Kiss, 14 January 1954, Hellman.

40. LH, ms. of An Unfinished Woman, part 12 (originally 11), 4, dated 30 April [1967], Hellman.

41. LH to Literary Gazette, 26 March 1965, Hellman; Literary Gazette to LH, 24 February 1965, Hellman.

42. Paul, Weiss, press release, 26 April 1957, Bloomgarden; Frederick Woltman, "'Anne's Diary' Playing in Courtrooms Now," New York World Telegram and Sun (18 March 1957), clipping, Frank.

43. ER to OF, 2 April 1957, Frank.

44. OF to ER, 11 April 1957, Frank.

45. OF to FP, 10 April 1957, Frank.

46. OF to Nathan Straus, 14 April 1957, Frank.

47. Nathan Straus to OF, 22 April 1957, Frank.

48. Nathan Straus to ER, 19 April 1957, Frank.

49. ER to OF, 22 April 1957, Frank.

50. OF to Nathan Straus, 28 April 1957, Frank.

51. ER to TL, 5 June 1957, Levin; ER to FP, 10 July 1957, Frank.

52. TL to ER, 7 June 1957, Levin.

53. ML to ER, 7 June 1957, Levin.

54. ER to FP, 10 July 1957, Frank.

55. FP to ER, 3 July 1957, Frank.

56. Jacob Weinstein, "Betrayal of Anne Frank," Congress Weekly 24 (13 May 1957): 5–7.

57. Samuel Silverman to Jacob Weinstein, American Jewish Congress, and Congress Weekly (21 May 1957), clipping, Bloomgarden.

58. KB, "Meyer Levin and Anne Frank's Diary," Congress Weekly 24 (17 June 1957): 5–7.

59. Allan Ecker to KB, 5 June 1957, Bloomgarden; OF to president of B'nai B'rith, 16 April 1957, Bloomgarden.

60. ML, "On Anne Frank's Diary: A Reply by Meyer Levin," Congress Weekly 24 (22 July 1957): 19.

61. Charles Angoff to FAH, 27 April 1957, Hackett.

62. FAH to Charles Angoff, 7 May 1957, Hackett.

63. FAH to OF, 19 May 1957, Hackett.

64. Charles Angoff, "The Facts About Meyer Levin's Case Against 'The Diary of Anne Frank,'" National Jewish Monthly (June 1957): 10–11.

65. Herb Brin, "A Girl's Diary—And Meyer Levin's Battle . . . ," Heritage (15 August 1957), clipping, Frank.

66. Twentieth Century Fox, contract, 20 May 1957, Salisbury; FG to LS, 23 April 1957, Salisbury.

67. FAH, note found written in the German translation of The Diary of Anne Frank, Hackett.

68. FAH to Max Nussbaum, 8 August 1957, Hackett.

69. OF to Marguerite Sealtiel, 5 September 1957, Hackett.

70. OF to FAH, 22 April 1957, Hackett.

71. LS to Marguerite Sealtiel, 13 September 1957, Hackett; LS to Robert Sterling, 10 November 1957, Salisbury.

72. FAH to OF, 29 September 1957, Hackett.

73. John Stone to George Stevens, 23 December 1957, Hackett.

74. FAH, *The Diary of Anne Frank*, screenplay, "Final," 3 March 1958, bound with revisions, 25 April 1958, 65, Hackett.

75. OF to FAH, 22 April 1957, Hackett.

76. Charlotte Pfeffer to FAH, 8 April 1957, Hackett.

77. OF to FAH, 22 April 1957, Hackett.

78. LS to FAH, 16 April 1957, Hackett.

79. FAH to OF, 26 April 1957, Hackett.

80. OF to FAH, 11 May 1957, Hackett.

81. FAH, *Diary*, screenplay, 141.

82. ML, "Examination Before Trial," ML v. OF and KB, [ca. 18 July 1957], 99, Levin; OF to Allan Ecker, 9 August 1957, Frank; Transcript, ML v. OF and KB, 30 December 1957, Levin.

83. "Trial Brief for Defendant Cheryl Crawford," [Fall 1957], 7, 12, Levin.

84. ML, "Statement . . . for the National Conference on Jewish Writing and Jewish Writers," 15 November 1957, Levin.

85. ML, "The Voice from the Mass Grave," [1958], Levin.

86. Notes on Testimony, ML v. OF and KB, 30 December 1957, 83–86, Levin; "Diary of Anne Frank Script Rejected by Court," *New York Herald Tribune* (6 January 1958), clipping, Frank.

87. FG, transcript, ML v. OF and KB, Hackett.

88. FG to Lloyd Almirall, 4 January 1958, Hackett.

89. AH, Transcript, ML v. OF and KB, 31 December 1957, 121, Hackett.

90. FG, Transcript, ML v. OF and KB, 2 January 1958, 294–296, Hackett.

91. AH, Transcript, 96.

92. OF, undated remarks, ML v. OF and KB, Frank.

93. Notes on testimony, ML v. OF and KB, 3 January 1958, 108–110, Levin.

94. "Meyer Levin Wins $50,000 Over Play," *New York Times* (8 January 1958), clipping, Frank.

95. ML to Israel Goldstein, 12 January 1958, Levin.

96. LS to FAH, 9 January 1958, Hackett.

97. AH to GK, 11 January 1958, Hackett; FG to LS, 18 January 1958, Hackett.

98. FG to LS, 18 January 1958 [dated 20 January 1958 in Salisbury], Hackett.

99. FG to MM, 20 November 1957, Hackett.

100. FG to LS, 18 January 1958, Hackett; FG to LS, 15 January 1958, Salisbury.

101. FAH to LS, 2 July 1957, Salisbury. For Gilford's blacklisting, see Kate Mostel, *107 Years of Show Business* (New York: Random House, 1978).

102. AG to GK, 24 January 1957, Hackett.

103. AH to LS, 25 January 1957, Salisbury.

Chapter 12. The Struggle Is Not Over

1. "Motion to Dismiss Verdict," 27 January 1958, Frank.

2. Samuel Coleman, "Charge of the Court," 10 December 1957, Levin.

3. "$50,000 Award to Levin Set Aside in 'Anne Frank' Suit," *New York Herald Tribune* (1 March 1958), clipping, Frank; Lloyd Almirall to FAH, 30 April 1058, Hackett; Moshe Kohn, "Strange Case of Anne Frank," *Jerusalem Post* (6 June 1958), clipping, Frank.

4. Max Allentuck to KB, 9 January 1958, Bloomgarden.

5. FG to LS, 2 March 1958, Salisbury.

6. FG to LS, 6 March 1958, Salisbury.

7. SF to Twentieth Century Fox, 6 March 1958, Hackett.

8. "Notice of Motion," 29 May 1959, Levin.

9. Lloyd Almirall to FAH, 30 April 1958, Hackett; Samuel Coleman, "Levin v. Frank," 24 February 1959, clipping, Frank.

10. Samuel Silverman to KB, 23 May and 10 July 1958, Bloomgarden.

11. LS to Martin Ganz, 12 February 1958, Hackett; record of box office receipts, 2 January 1958, Bloomgarden; LS to FAH, 30 July 1958, Hackett.

12. "Anne Frank's Secret Annex Awaits the Wrecker's Ball," *Het Vrije Volk* (23 November 1955), quoted in Janrense Boonstra, *Anne Frank House: A Museum with a Story* (Amsterdam: Anne Frank Stichting, 1992), 78.

13. FG to LS, 27 July 1958, Salisbury.

14. LS to FAH, 30 July 1958, Salisbury.

15. Kohn, "Strange Case."

16. O. Ben Ami to Nathan Straus, 27 July 1958, Levin.

17. Interview with Otto Frank, *Maariv* (29 August 1958), translation, Frank.

18. ML, "An Open Letter to Otto Frank," *Maariv* (5 September 1958), translation, Frank.

19. ML to OF, 30 September 1958, Levin.

20. OF to ML, 5 October 1958, Levin.

21. FAH to OF, 7 February 1959, Hackett.

22. "Shouras: Anne Frank for All, Not Just Jews," 10 February 1959, clipping, Frank.

23. Jack Moffit, "'The Diary of Anne Frank' George Stevens' Masterpiece," *Hollywood Reporter* (18 March 1959): 3.

24. Sarah Gibson Blanding to [?] Strack, 4 August 1959, Hackett.

25. Samuel Coleman, "Levin v. Frank," 24 February 1959, clipping, Frank.

26. "Notice of Motion," 29 May 1959, Levin.

27. ML to OF, 30 September 1958, Levin.

28. ML, "Dear Rabbi," 15 March 1959, Frank.

29. ML, "Dear Rabbi," 11 November 1958, Frank.

30. Quoted in ML, "Dear Rabbi," 15 March 1959, Frank.

31. ML, "How to Kill a Writer," [1959], Levin.

32. "Levin Names a Committee for 'Diary' Fight," *New York Post* (24 April 1959).

33. ML, *The Story of Israel* (New York: Putnam, 1966), 12.

34. SF to ML, 10 July 1959, Levin.

35. ML to SF, 1 August 1959, Levin.

36. Abraham Katsh, Affidavit, 17 September 1977, Levin; EC to KB, 3 August 1959, Bloomgarden.

37. EC to KB, 8 July 1959, Bloomgarden; ML to William Maslow, 7 December 1966, Levin.

38. Lloyd Almirall to FG, 30 July 1959, Hackett; FG to Lloyd Almirall, 1 August 1959, Hackett; Lloyd Almirall to Samuel Silverman, 5 August 1959, Hackett; Lloyd Almirall to Weinstein and Fredman, 5 August 1959, Hackett; EC to KB, 3 August 1959, Bloomgarden; KB to EC, 5 August 1959, Bloomgarden.

39. EC to Joachim Prinz, 25 June 1959; EC to KB, 8 July, 3 August 1959; EC to OF, 11 August 1959; EC to OF, 21 August 1959, Bloomgarden.

40. EC to KB, 3 August 1959, Bloomgarden.

41. KB to EC, 5 August 1959, Bloomgarden.

42. Lloyd Almirall to EC, 5 August 1959, Hackett.

43. LS to FAH, 13 August 1959, Hackett.

44. FAH to OF, 22 September 1959, Hackett.

45. LS to FAH, 13 August 1959, Hackett.

46. EC to OF, 21 August 1959, Frank.

47. ML to SF, 16 August 1959, Levin.

48. SF to ML, 31 August 1959, Levin; SF to EC, 20 August 1959, Hackett.

49. EC to OF, 21 August 1959, Hackett.

50. SF to ML, 31 August 1959, Levin.

51. ML to OF and KB, 26 October 1959, Levin.

52. OF and KB to ML, 26 October 1959, Frank.

53. "Assignment of Copyright and Other Property Rights," 20 October 1959, Levin.

54. "Meyer Levin v. Otto Frank and Kermit Bloomgarden," Stipulation, attached to Ernest Rubenstein to KB, 22 December 1959, Bloomgarden.

55. EC to OF, 13 January 1960, Frank.

56. Ernest Rubenstein to KB, 22 December 1959, Bloomgarden.

57. Lloyd Almirall to FAH, 11 December 1959, Hackett.

58. Max Grossman to OF, 11 January 1960, Frank.

59. Fritzi Frank to Max Grossman, 17 January 1960, Frank.

60. Sidney Gruson, "Bonn Parliament Decries Outrages," New York Times (21 January 1960); "German Teacher Apologizes," New York Times (18 October 1961). For a detailed account of the Stielau claim and subsequent trial, see David Barnouw, "Attacks on the Authenticity of the Diary," in AF, The Diary of Anne Frank: The Critical Edition (New York: Doubleday, 1989), 84–90.

61. MM to OF, 14 January 1960; OF to MM, 21 January 1960, Frank.

62. Lloyd Almirall to FAH, 14 January 1960, Hackett.

63. LS to FAH, 15 January 1960, Hackett.

64. FAH to Lloyd Almirall, 16 January 1960, Hackett.

65. Lloyd Almirall to FAH, 26 January 1960, Hackett.

66. ML to OF, 21 January 1960, Levin.

67. SF to ML, 5 February 1960, Levin.

68. ML to OF, 14 February 1960, Levin.

69. OF, fund-raising pamphlet for the International Youth Center of the Anne Frank Foundation, attached to OF to FAH, 7 March 1960, Hackett.

70. "Anne Frank House Opens," New York Times (4 May 1960).

71. ML, "An Open Letter to Otto Frank," Jerusalem Post (25 March 1960), clipping, Frank.

72. "Otto Frank Denies M. Levin's Charges," Jerusalem Post (28 March 1960), clipping, Frank.

73. Edwin Eytan to OF, 18 April 1960, Frank.

74. OF to Edwin Eytan, 23 April 1960, Frank.

75. Martin Dworkin, "The Vanishing Diary of Anne Frank," Jewish Frontier (April 1960): 7–10.

76. ML, "What Happened to Anne Frank," A.J.A. [Anglo-Jewish Association] Quarterly 6 (October 1960): 1–10.

77. ML, Eva: A Novel of the Holocaust (New York: Simon and Schuster, 1959), 1.

78. ML, untitled, "I wrote Eva . . . ," [1959], Levin.

79. ML, Eva, 300; Robert Shapiro, "'The Holocaust': Canonization of Historical Term," Martyrdom and Resistance 22 (May–June 1966): 13.

80. ML, Eva, 301–302.

81. Ibid., quotations from, respectively, 305, 309, 303, 311.

Chapter 13. An Unrepentant Stalinist

1. "Anti-Cosmopolitanism," Time (24 November 1961), clipping, Frank.

2. ML, "Dear Reader," [ca. 25 November 1961], Frank.

3. Harry Golden to ML, 30 April 1961, Levin.

4. ML to Abel Green, 24 June 1961, Levin.

5. ML to Harry Golden, 9 May 1961, Levin.

6. ML to Arnold Forster, 9 May 1961, Levin.

7. ML to Harry Golden, 7 June 1961, Levin.

8. ML, "Dear Reader."

9. ML to Abel Green, 24 June 1961, Levin.

10. ML, "Dear Reader."

11. ML, "Another Kind of Blacklist," Congress Weekly 28 (30 October 1961): 5–7.

12. ML, "Dear Reader."

13. EC to OF, 15 November 1961, Frank.

14. EC to Samuel Caplan, 27 November 1961, Frank.

15. EC to Samuel Caplan, 18 December 1961, Bloomgarden.

16. Joachim Prinz to EC, 27 December 1961, Bloomgarden.

17. EC to KB, 12 February 1962, Bloomgarden.

18. ML, "Why?" [ca. February 1962], Bloomgarden.

19. EC to Samuel Caplan, 13 February 1962, Bloomgarden.

20. EC, "Refutes Meyer Levin's Assertion," Congress Weekly 29 (5 March 1962): 14.

21. Ernest Rubenstein to LH, 2 March 1962, Bloomgarden.

22. FG to LS, 26 April 1962, Salisbury.

23. ML, The Fanatic (New York: Simon and Schuster, 1964), 353.

24. ML to Harry Golden, 7 June 1961, Levin; ML, "The Lesson Yet to Be Learned," Congress Weekly 29 (8 January 1962): 5–7.

25. ML, untitled, "I have tried . . . ," [1962], Levin.

26. Robert Gottlieb to ML, 9 January 1963, Levin.

27. ML, The Fanatic, 106.

28. Ephraim London to ML, 6 June 1963, Levin.

29. ML to Ephraim London, 10 June 1963, Levin.

30. ML to Robert Gottlieb, 10, 14, 15 June 1963, Levin.

31. ML, The Obsession (New York: Simon and Schuster, 1973), 217–218.

32. ML, The Fanatic, 9; David Boroff, review, New York Times Book Review (26 January 1964): 5.

33. ML, The Fanatic, 353.

34. The editors, "To The Reader," New York Review of Books, Special Issue (February 1963): 2.

35. Stanley Kauffman, "Season in Hell," New York Review of Books 2 (20 February 1964): 5–6.

36. ML, The Fanatic, 84.

37. ML, "What Has Been Learned," Jerusalem Post (16 April 1965), clipping, Levin.

38. ML, The Stronghold (New York: Simon and Schuster, 1965), 34.

39. ML, "What Has Been Learned."

40. ML, The Stronghold, 318.

41. Peter Frye to ML, 2 May 1966, Levin.

42. "What Is Between Anna and Yohanna," Maariv (13 October 1966), translation, Levin.

43. Quoted in ML, The Obsession, 270–272.

44. "Anne Frank Play Staged in Israel," New York Times (27 November 1966).

45. "Father Protests Anne Frank Play," New York Times (12 December 1966).

46. H. J. Brodie to Paul, Weiss, 9 December 1966, Levin.

47. Quoted in ML, The Obsession, 272–278; Samuel Freeman to Chief Education Officer of the Israel Defense Forces, 29 November 1966, Levin.

48. H. J. Brodie to Paul, Weiss, 16 December 1966, Levin.

49. ML to Joachim Prinz, 19 January 1967, Levin.

50. "Anne Frank Play Halted in Israel," *New York Times* (10 January 1967).

51. Yehiel Dinur to ML, 18 January 1967, Levin.

52. "Holocaust Writers Condemn Ban on Anne Frank Drama," *Jerusalem Post* (22 January 1967), clipping, Levin; Robert Gary, "Death Camp Authors Support Levin's 'Anne Frank,'" [1967], press release, Levin.

53. "White-Gloved Killers," *Newsweek* (30 January 1967): 48.

54. "Levin Prints Forbidden Play," [1967], press release, Levin; "Holocaust Writers . . . ."

55. ML, "This play has been suppressed . . . ," (untitled), n.d., 1, 5, 12, [13], Levin.

56. EC to OF, 20 January 1967, Frank; OF to EC, 15 March 1967, Frank.

57. EC to OF, 20 January 1967, Frank.

58. ML to Robert Gottlieb, 10 June 1963, Levin; Abraham Katsh to ML, 16 March 1967, Levin.

59. ML to Abraham Katsh, 18 March 1967, Levin.

60. OF, "The Living Legacy of Anne Frank," *Ladies Home Journal* 84 (September 1967): 87, 154.

61. OF, *Haagse Post* (1 August 1969), quoted in Alex Grobman, *Anne Frank in Historical Perspective* (Los Angeles: Martyrs Memorial and Museum of the Holocaust, 1995), 22; OF, "Dedication," in Anne Steenmeijer, ed., *A Tribute to Anne Frank* (Garden City, N.Y.: Doubleday, 1971), 7.

62. Editor's Note to OF, "Living Legacy," 87.

63. OF to Cara Wilson, 19 June 1968, in Cara Wilson, *Love, Otto: The Legacy of Anne Frank* (Kansas City, Mo.: Andrews and McMeel, 1995), 50.

64. ML to John Wharton, 9 May 1968, Levin.

65. ML to Morris Abram, 8 November 1968, Levin.

66. ML to Martha Gellhorn, 17 November 1968, Levin.

67. Martha Gellhorn to ML, 23 November [1968], Levin.

68. Gideon Hausner to ML, 16 March 1970, Levin.

69. World Federation of Bergen Belsen Associations, "This is the twenty-fifth anniversary . . . ," [April 1970], Levin.

70. Charles Flood to ML, 20 August 1969 and 24 July 1970, Levin; Thomas Fleming to ML, 22 June 1971; Geoffrey Ripo to ML, 1 October 1980, Levin.

71. Tifereth Israel (Malden, Mass.), "Dramatic Reading of Meyer Levin's Play 'Anne Frank,'" 26 February 1971, Levin.

72. Shoshana Pakziarz, "A Jewish Anne Frank," *genesis* 2 (20 April 1972), clipping, Levin.

73. *Meyer Levin: Fifty Years in Writing* (New York: Simon and Schuster, 1973), 8.

74. ML, *The Obsession*, 7; Joseph Stein to ML, [1973], Levin.

75. *Meyer Levin*, 8, 6.

76. ML, *The Obsession*, ms., 15–16, Levin.

77. ML, *The Obsession*, 201–202.

78. EC to Leon Shimkin, 17 January 1974, Bloomgarden.

79. LH to Joseph Rauh, 22 January 1974, Joseph Rauh Papers, Library of Congress.

80. ML, *The Obsession*, 76.

81. Joan Mellen, *Hellman and Hammett: The Legendary Passion of Lillian Hellman and Dashiell Hammett* (New York: HarperCollins, 1996), 314, 523.

82. ML, *The Obsession*, 30, 32, 316.

83. LH, "A Scene from an Unfinished Play," *New Republic* 171 (30 November 1974): 39.

84. LH, "For Truth, Justice and the American Way," *New York Times* (4 June 1975). "Spitball malice" from LH, "The Time of the 'Foxes,'" *New York Times* (22 October 1967).

85. Mellen, 138, 170, 308, 433.

86. Ibid., 371; LH, *Scoundrel Time*, ms., 7, Hellman.

87. *Show Magazine* (6 May 1964), clipping, Hellman.

88. "The Films Now Know Miss Hellman" *(New York) Herald Tribune* (1 July 1935).

89. Mellen, *Hellman and Hammett*, 263–264.

90. Ibid., 382; Phyllis Jacobean, "A Trio of Assorted Scoundrels," *New Politics* 11 (Fall 1976): 14–24.

91. Arthur Schlesinger, Jr., to LH, 20 October 1976, Hellman; Arthur Schlesinger, Jr., to Joseph Rauh, 22 October 1976, Hellman.

92. Irving Howe, "Lillian Hellman and the McCarthy Years," *Dissent* (Fall 1976): 378–382.

93. ML, *The Obsession*, 310.

94. Henry T. Moore, "Ah, Paranoia!" *New Republic* 170 (2 February 1974): 21.

95. Dorothy Rabinowitz, "Books in Brief," *Saturday Review of Literature* (23 February 1974): 28.

96. Victor Navasky, "The Ordeal of Meyer Levin," *New York Times Book Review* (3 February 1974): 5–6.

97. ML and KB, "Letters to the Editor," *New York Times Book Review* (3 March 1974): 34–35.

98. OF to Cyrus Hand, 6 June 1974, Frank.

99. ML to Joachim Prinz, 21 May 1974, Levin.

100. Joachim Prinz to ML, 20 June 1974, Levin.

101. EC to Edward Katz, 10 May 1974, Levin.

102. Charles Angoff to ML, 20 October 1974, Levin.

103. Abraham Katsh to ML, 18 October 1974, Levin.

104. Abraham Katsh, Affidavit, 17 September 1977, Levin.

105. ML to Hanoch Bartov, [1973], Levin.

106. ML to Hanno [Hanoch Bartov], [1974], Levin.

107. Benno Weiser Varon, "The Haunting of Meyer Levin," *Midstream* 22 (August–September 1976): 19–23. Varon made brief reference to this affair two years later in "Meyer Levin Completes His Work as a Novelist," *American Zionist* (May 1978): 21.

108. Saul Shapiro, Archie Lieberman, Peggy Mann, Harry Zohn, James Michener, and Myron Kaufmann, "Letters," *Midstream* 23 (January 1977): 85–86, 95.

109. Benno Weiser Varon, "Letters," *Midstream* 23 (January 1977): 87–96.

110. Quoted ibid.

111. Ibid.

Chapter 14. A Jewish Work of Universal Importance

1. ML to Irving Greenberg, 4 December 1976, Levin.

2. ML to Esther Malament, 17 April 1977, Levin.

3. ML, "Bitch Time," *Jerusalem Post*, International Book Fair Supplement (26 April 1977): 14–15.

4. LH, notes for *Watch on the Rhine, Unfinished Woman*, and 1944 trip to Russia, Hellman.

5. ML, "Bitch Time"; Simon Rifkind to ML, 29 November 1976, Levin.

6. Simon Rifkind, *One Man's World*, 2 vols. (New York: Paul, Weiss, Rifkind, Wharton, and Garrison, 1986), 1: 29, 227.

7. Ibid., 1: 402, 406–407, 381.

8. Pearl Bell, "Meyer Levin's Obsessions," *Commentary* (June 1978): 67.

9. ML to Howard Squadron, 15 June 1978, Levin.

10. FG to OF, 24 November 1978, Frank.

11. OF to FAH, 30 November 1978, Frank.

12. GK, "Anne Frank at 50," *Newsweek* (25 June 1979): 14–15.

13. ML, "A Writer's Appeal," [1974]; list of signers to earlier writers' petitions, Levin; Lawrence Ferlinghetti to ML, 18 April 1979, Levin.

14. Norman Mailer to ML, 20 April 1979, Levin.

15. Elie Wiesel, "Pilgrimage to the Country of Night," *New York Times* (4 November 1979).

16. Arnold Forster to ML, 10 March 1977, Levin.

17. Edward Alexander, untitled clipping, *Seattle Times*, 4 November 1979, sent to the author by Levin.

18. Enclosure, Isaac Imber to RM, 5 February 1980, Melnick.

19. FAH to OF and Fritzi Frank, 25 April 1980, Frank.

20. Rund van der Rol, *Anne Frank: Beyond the Diary* (New York: Viking, 1993), 104–105.

21. Alvin Rosenfeld, *A Double Dying: Reflections on Holocaust Literature* (Bloomington: Indiana University Press, 1980), 160.

22. Fritzi Frank to FAH, 20 May 1980, Frank.

23. Alvin Rosenfeld to ML, 28 May 1980, Levin.

24. FAH to Fritzi Frank, 29 May 1980, Frank.

25. Shale Stiller to ML, 21 May 1980, Levin.

26. Shale Stiller to ML, 19 August 1980, Levin; "Otto Frank, Father of Anne, Dead at 91," *New York Times* (21 August 1980), clipping, Levin.

27. "Anne Frank's Father, Otto, Is Dead at 91," *Jewish Week* (31 August 1980): 23.

28. ML, "The Suppressed Anne Frank," *Jewish Week* (31 August 1980): 22–23; Harold Ribalow, "Levin at 75: Most Committed Jewish Writer in English," *Jewish Week* (31 August 1980): 24.

29. Philip Hockstein, "De-Judaizing Holocaust Is Major Issue," *Jewish Week* (31 August 1980): 21.

30. ML to RM, [1981], Melnick.

31. [ML?], "Meyer Levin's Summation at Seventy-Five," Levin.

32. ML, "Fania Fenelon Can't Understand Why She's 'Alone' in Stand on Vanessa," *Jewish Week* (28 September 1980): 15.

33. David Gross, "De-Judaizing of Anne Frank Forerunner of Universalized Holocaust, Says Levin," *Jewish Week* (14 October 1980), clipping, Levin.

34. TL to ML, [September 1980], Levin.

35. FAH to Fritzi Frank, 18 November 1980, Frank.

36. Fritzi Frank to FAH, [ca. 1 April 1981], Frank.

37. ML to TL, [September 1980], Levin.

38. ML to Simon Wiesenthal, 22 December 1980, Levin.

39. Estelle Gilson, "An Authentic Jewish Writer," *Present Tense* (Fall 1981): 36.

40. ML, "The Suppressed Anne Frank," [1979], Melnick.

41. ML, "My Ethical Will As to Authorship," 27 May 1981, Levin.

42. ML, "Levin's Own Story: How Anne Frank's Vow Was Distorted?" *Jewish Week* (26 July 1981): 5; Herbert Mitgang, "Meyer Levin, Writer, 75, Dies," *New York Times* (11 July 1981).

43. Aharon Megged, "Meyer Levin's Dybbuk," *Jerusalem Post* (31 July 1981).

44. ML, untitled essay, [1949], Levin.

45. Megged, "Meyer Levin's Dybbuk," 12–13.

46. Myron Kaufmann to TL, 10 July 1981, Levin.

47. Stephen Fife, "Meyer Levin's Obsession," *New Republic* 187 (2 August 1982): 26–30.

48. ML to Richard Baker, 15 April 1981; Richard Baker to ML, 28 April 1981, Levin.

49. Anthony Tommasini, "Serious, Skillful Telling of 'The Diary of Anne Frank,'" *Boston Globe* (30 January 1991).

50. Jane Pratt, "The Anne Frank We Remember," *McCall's* 113 (January 1986): 72.

51. Mel Gussow, "Albert Hackett, 95, Half of Prolific Drama Team," *New York Times* (18 March 1995).

52. Edward Rothstein, "Anne Frank: The Girl and the Icon," *New York Times* (25 February 1996).

53. Lawrence Graver, *An Obsession with Anne Frank* (Berkeley: University of California Press, 1995), 234–235.

54. Frank Rich, "Betrayed by Broadway," *New York Times Book Review* (17 September 1995): 9–11; Robert Alter, "The View from the Attic," *New Republic* (4 December 1995): 38–42. For a moderately critical account of the lack of historical context in Graver's work, see Rebecca Steinitz, "In Search of the Real Anne," *Women's Review of Books* 13 (January 1996): 12–13.

55. Elia Kazan, *A Life* (New York: Alfred Knopf, 1983), 262, 136.

56. Rothstein, "Anne Frank," 24.

57. Patricia Hampl, "The Whole Anne Frank," *New York Times Book Review* (5 March 1995): 21.

58. ML, *The Obsession* (New York: Simon and Schuster, 1973), 316.

59. ML, "The Suppressed Anne Frank."

Index